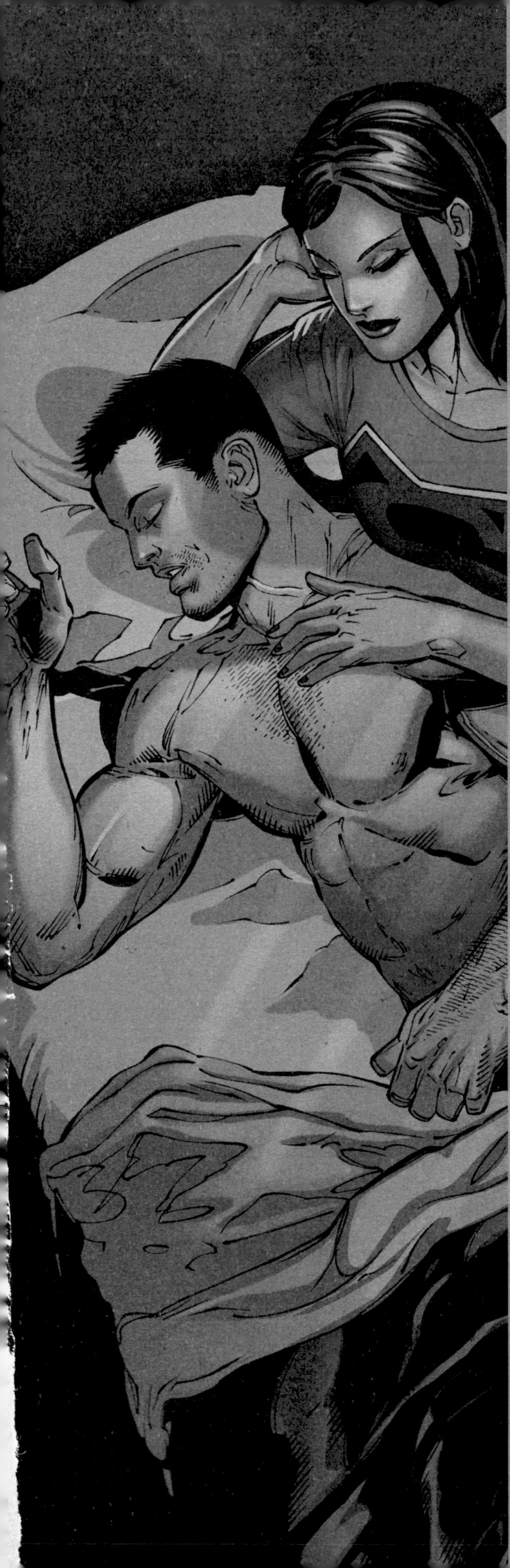

SUPERMAN/WONDER WOMAN

VOLUME 4
DARK TRUTH

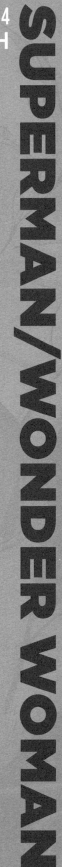

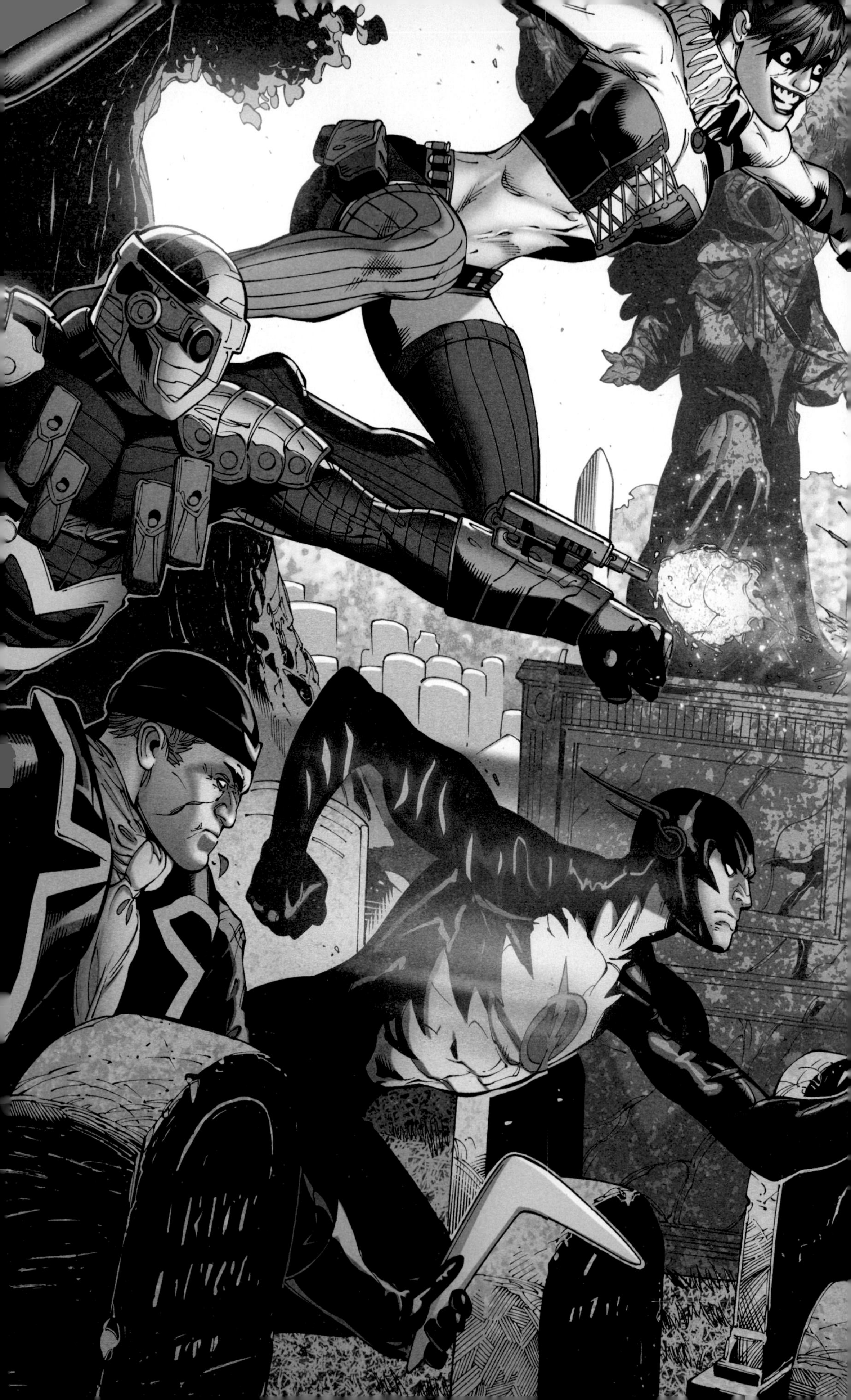

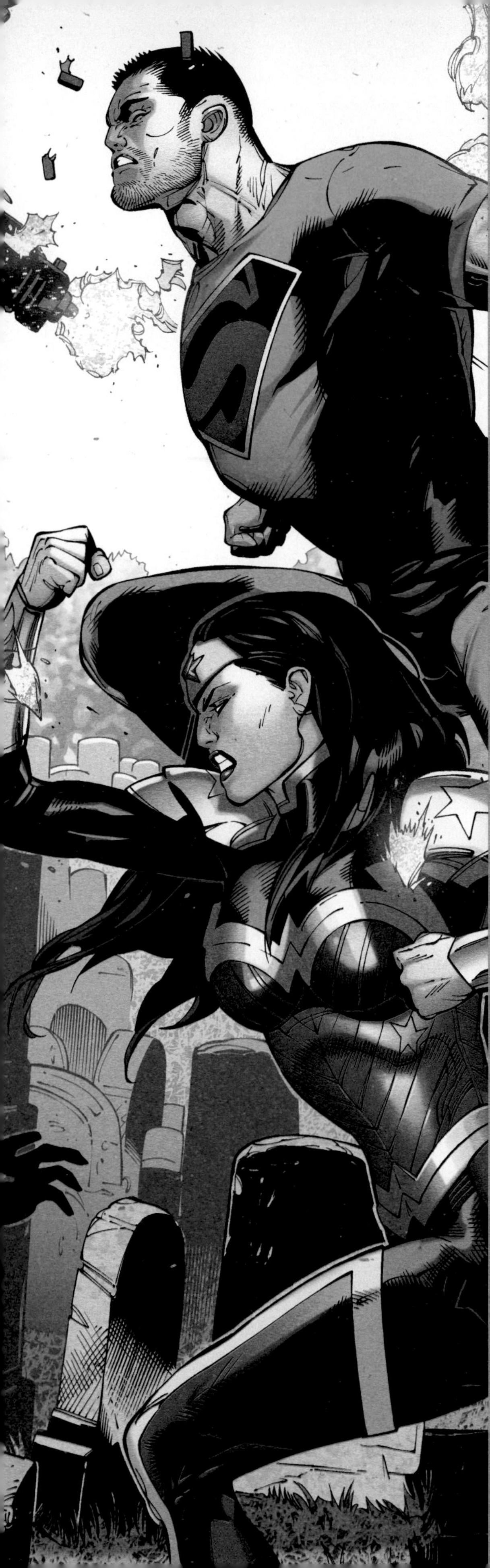

SUPERMAN/WONDER WOMAN

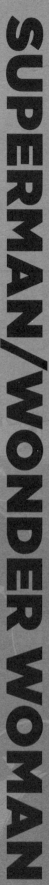

VOLUME 4
DARK TRUTH

WRITTEN BY
PETER J. TOMASI

PENCILS BY
DOUG MAHNKE
ARDIAN SYAF
TOM DERENICK

INKS BY
JAIME MENDOZA
RAY McCARTHY
JONATHAN GLAPION
MARC DEERING
SEAN PARSONS
MARK IRWIN
SCOTT HANNA
JOHNNY DESJARDINS
KEITH CHAMPAGNE
TOM DERENICK
JORDI TARRAGONA

COLOR BY
WIL QUINTANA
ULISES ARREOLA
TOMEU MOREY

LETTERS BY
ROB LEIGH
TRAVIS LANHAM
TOM NAPOLITANO

COLLECTION COVER ART BY
CARY NORD

SUPERMAN CREATED BY
JERRY SIEGEL &
JOE SHUSTER
BY SPECIAL ARRANGEMENT
WITH THE JERRY SIEGEL FAMILY

WONDER WOMAN CREATED BY
WILLIAM MOULTON MARSTON

EDDIE BERGANZA Editor – Original Series
ANDREW MARINO JEREMY BENT Assistant Editors – Original Series
JEB WOODARD Group Editor – Collected Editions
SUZANNAH ROWNTREE Editor – Collected Edition
STEVE COOK Design Director – Books
DAMIAN RYLAND Publication Design

BOB HARRAS Senior VP – Editor-in-Chief, DC Comics

DIANE NELSON President
DAN DIDIO and JIM LEE Co-Publishers
GEOFF JOHNS Chief Creative Officer
AMIT DESAI Senior VP – Marketing & Global Franchise Management
NAIRI GARDINER Senior VP – Finance
SAM ADES VP – Digital Marketing
BOBBIE CHASE VP – Talent Development
MARK CHIARELLO Senior VP – Art, Design & Collected Editions
JOHN CUNNINGHAM VP – Content Strategy
ANNE DEPIES VP – Strategy Planning & Reporting
DON FALLETTI VP – Manufacturing Operations
LAWRENCE GANEM VP – Editorial Administration & Talent Relations
ALISON GILL Senior VP – Manufacturing & Operations
HANK KANALZ Senior VP – Editorial Strategy & Administration
JAY KOGAN VP – Legal Affairs
DEREK MADDALENA Senior VP – Sales & Business Development
JACK MAHAN VP – Business Affairs
DAN MIRON VP – Sales Planning & Trade Development
NICK NAPOLITANO VP – Manufacturing Administration
CAROL ROEDER VP – Marketing
EDDIE SCANNELL VP – Mass Account & Digital Sales
COURTNEY SIMMONS Senior VP – Publicity & Communications
JIM (SKI) SOKOLOWSKI VP – Comic Book Specialty & Newsstand Sales
SANDY YI Senior VP – Global Franchise Management

SUPERMAN/WONDER WOMAN VOLUME 4: DARK TRUTH

DC Comics, 2900 West Alameda Ave., Burbank, CA 91505
Printed by RR Donnelley, Salem, VA, USA. 5/6/16. First Printing.
ISBN: 978-1-4012-6322-5

Library of Congress Cataloging-in-Publication Data

Names: Tomasi, Peter, author. | Mahnke, Doug, illustrator.
Title: Superman/Wonder Woman. Volume 4, Dark truth / Peter J. Tomasi, writer
; Doug Mahnke, artist.
Other titles: Dark truth
Description: Burbank, CA : DC Comics, [2016]
Identifiers: LCCN 2016006922 | ISBN 9781401263225 (hardback)
Subjects: LCSH: Graphic novels. | Superhero comic books, strips, etc. |
BISAC: COMICS & GRAPHIC NOVELS / Superheroes.
Classification: LCC PN6728.S9 T67 2016 | DDC 741.5/973–dc23
LC record available at http://lccn.loc.gov/2016006922

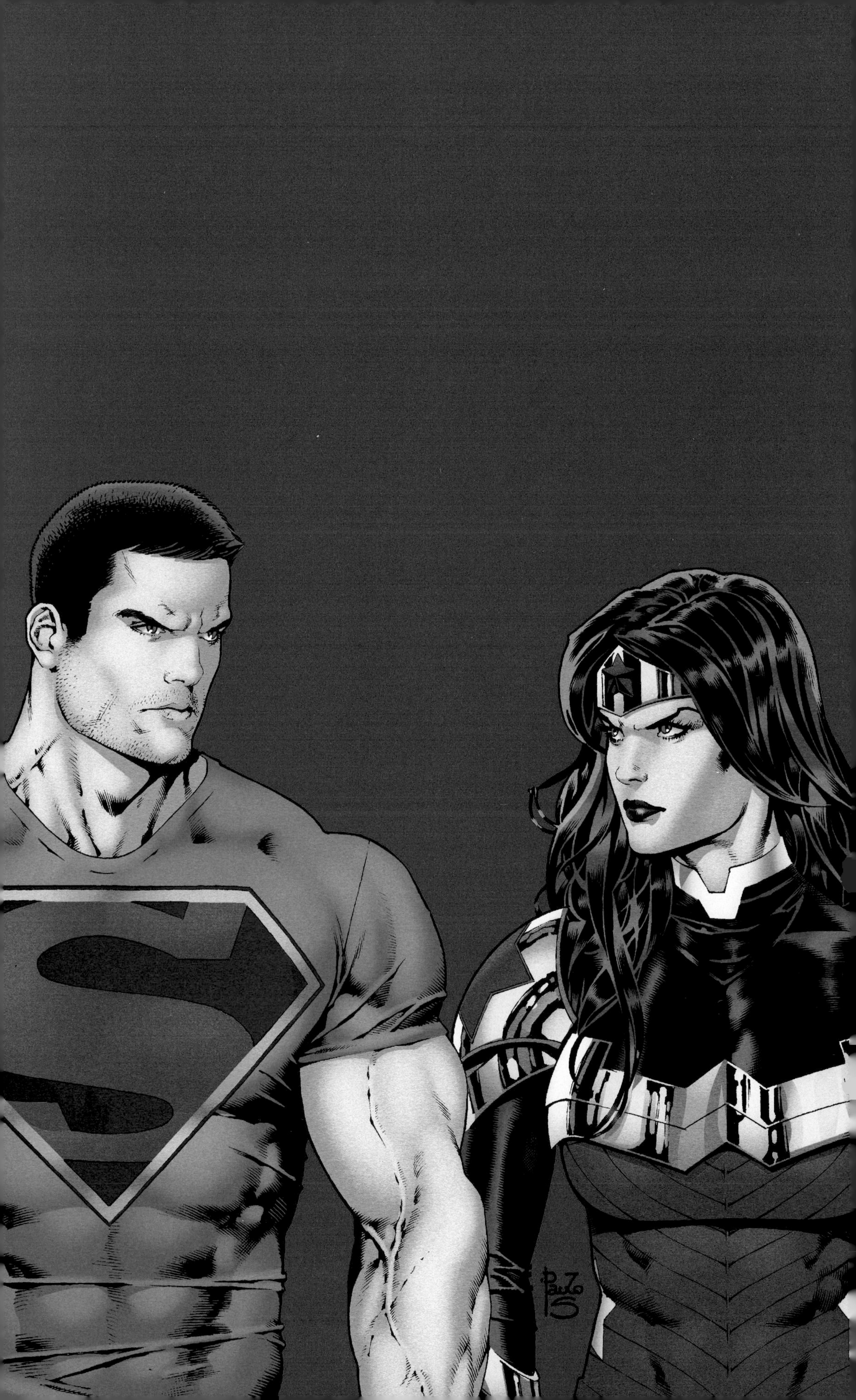

DARK TRUTH PART ONE

PETER J. TOMASI writer **DOUG MAHNKE** penciller **JAIME MENDOZA RAY MCCARTHY JONATHAN GLAPION MARC DEERING** inkers **WIL QUINTANA** colorist
ROB LEIGH letterer cover by **PAULO SIQUEIRA & HI-FI**

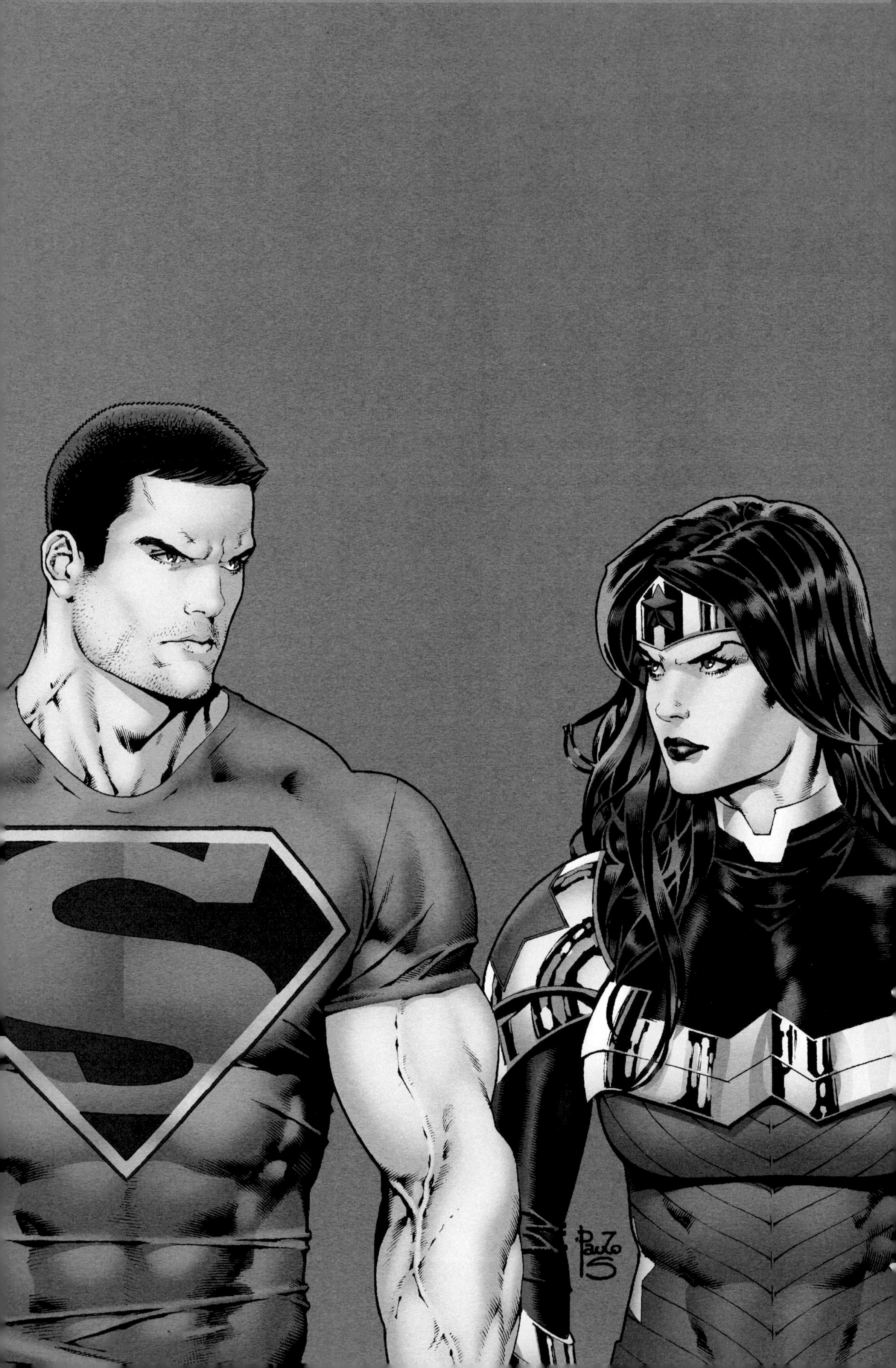

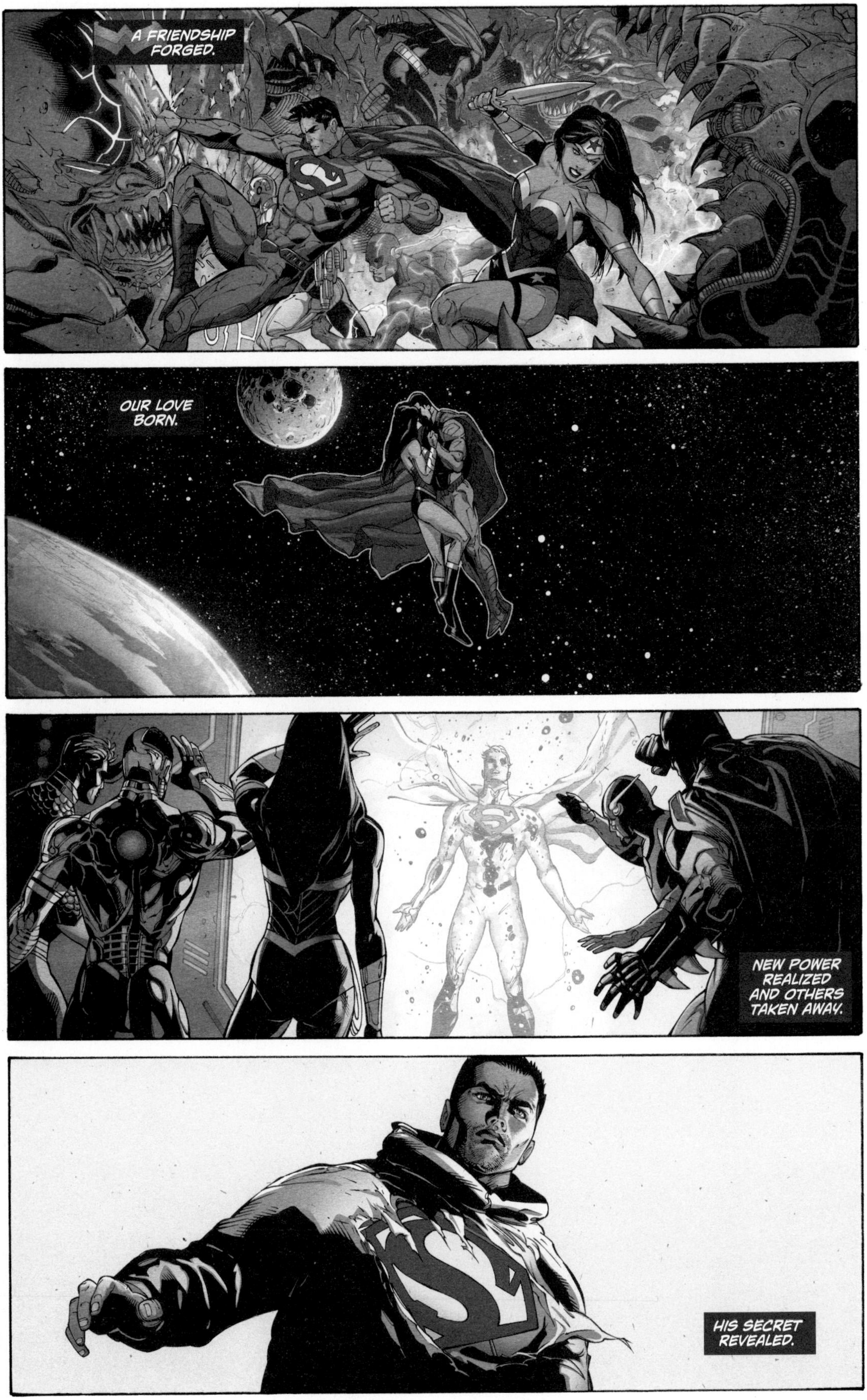
A FRIENDSHIP FORGED.
OUR LOVE BORN.
NEW POWER REALIZED AND OTHERS TAKEN AWAY.
HIS SECRET REVEALED.

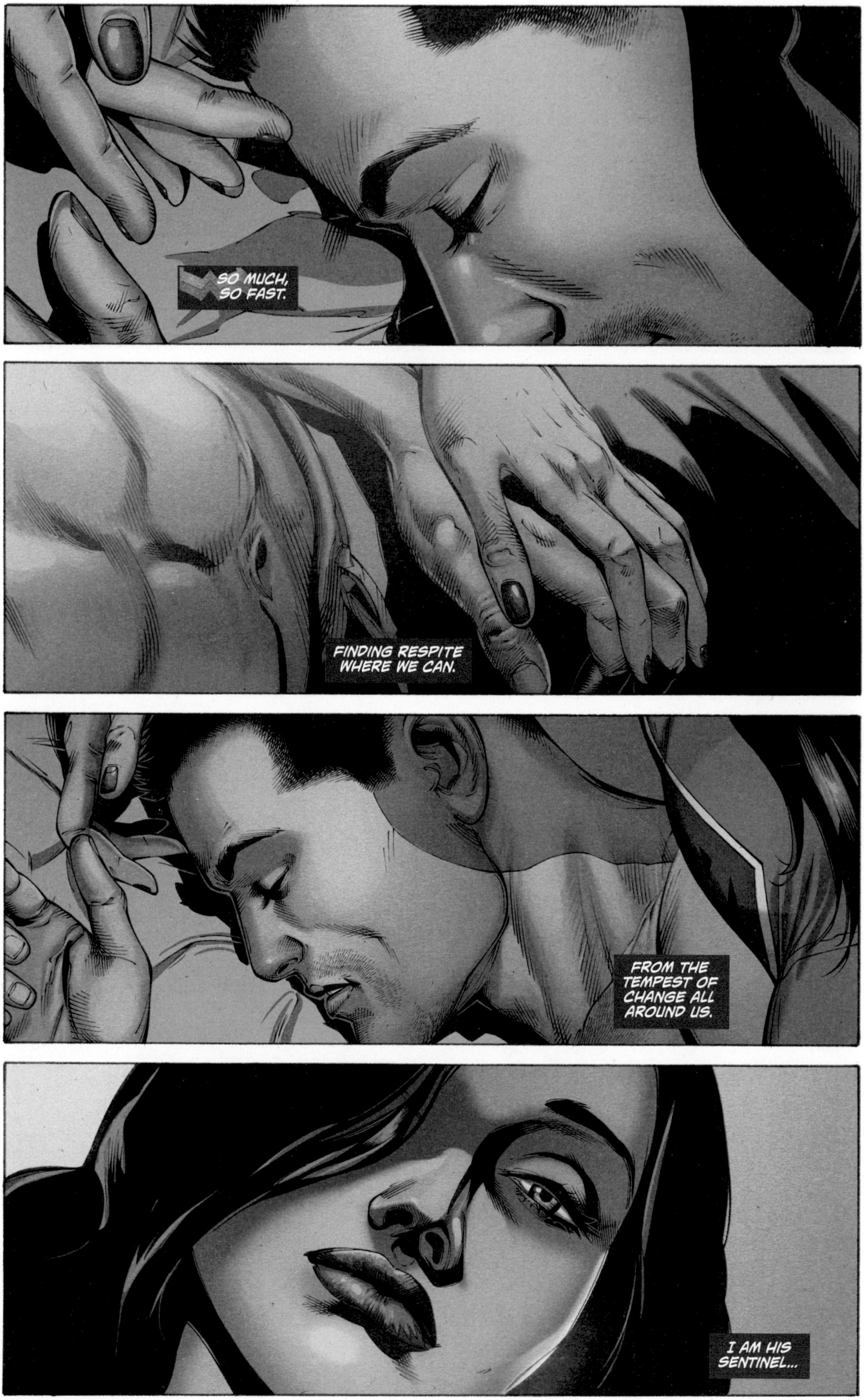
SO MUCH, SO FAST.
FINDING RESPITE WHERE WE CAN.
FROM THE TEMPEST OF CHANGE ALL AROUND US.
I AM HIS SENTINEL...

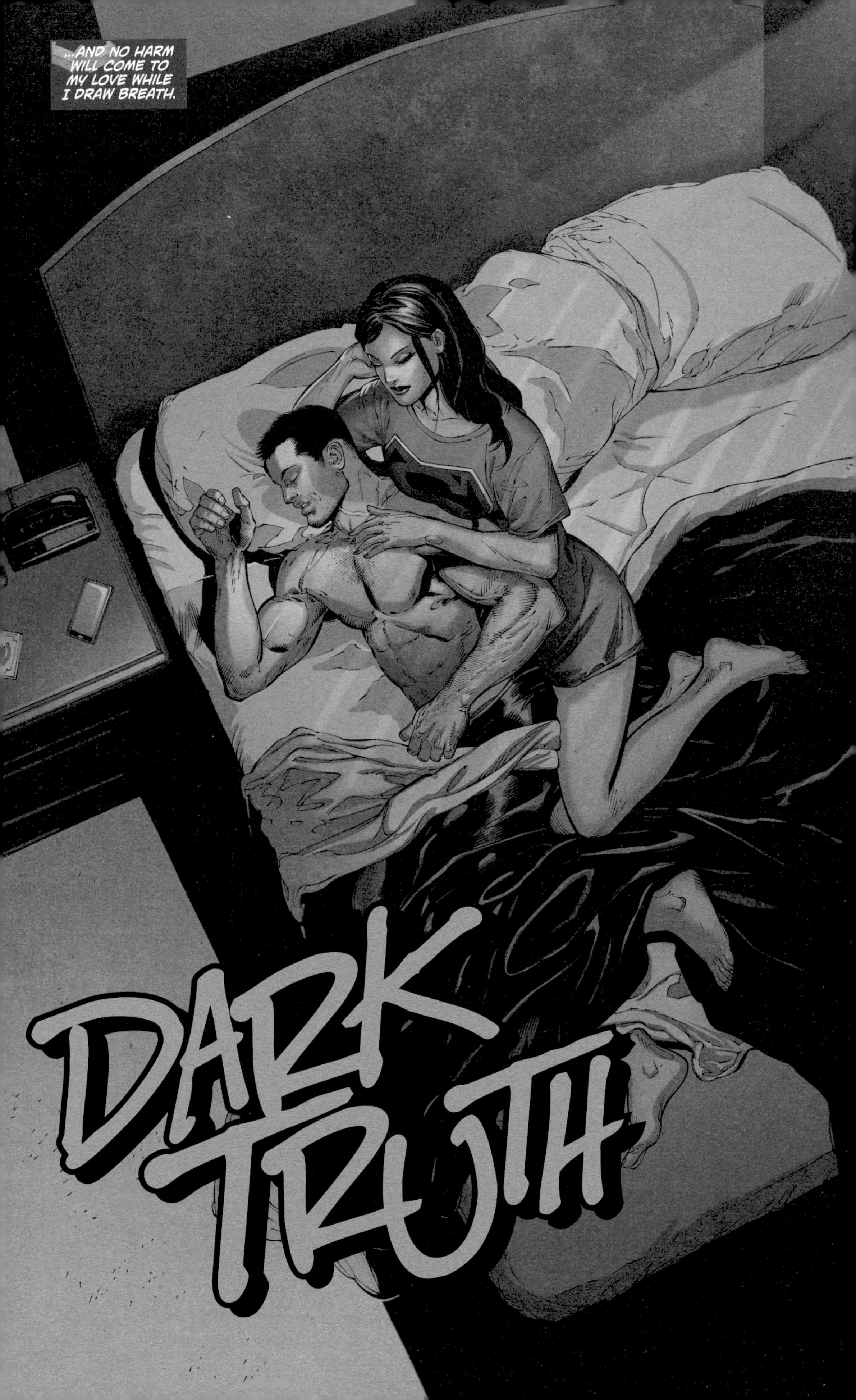
...AND NO HARM WILL COME TO MY LOVE WHILE I DRAW BREATH.
DARK TRUTH

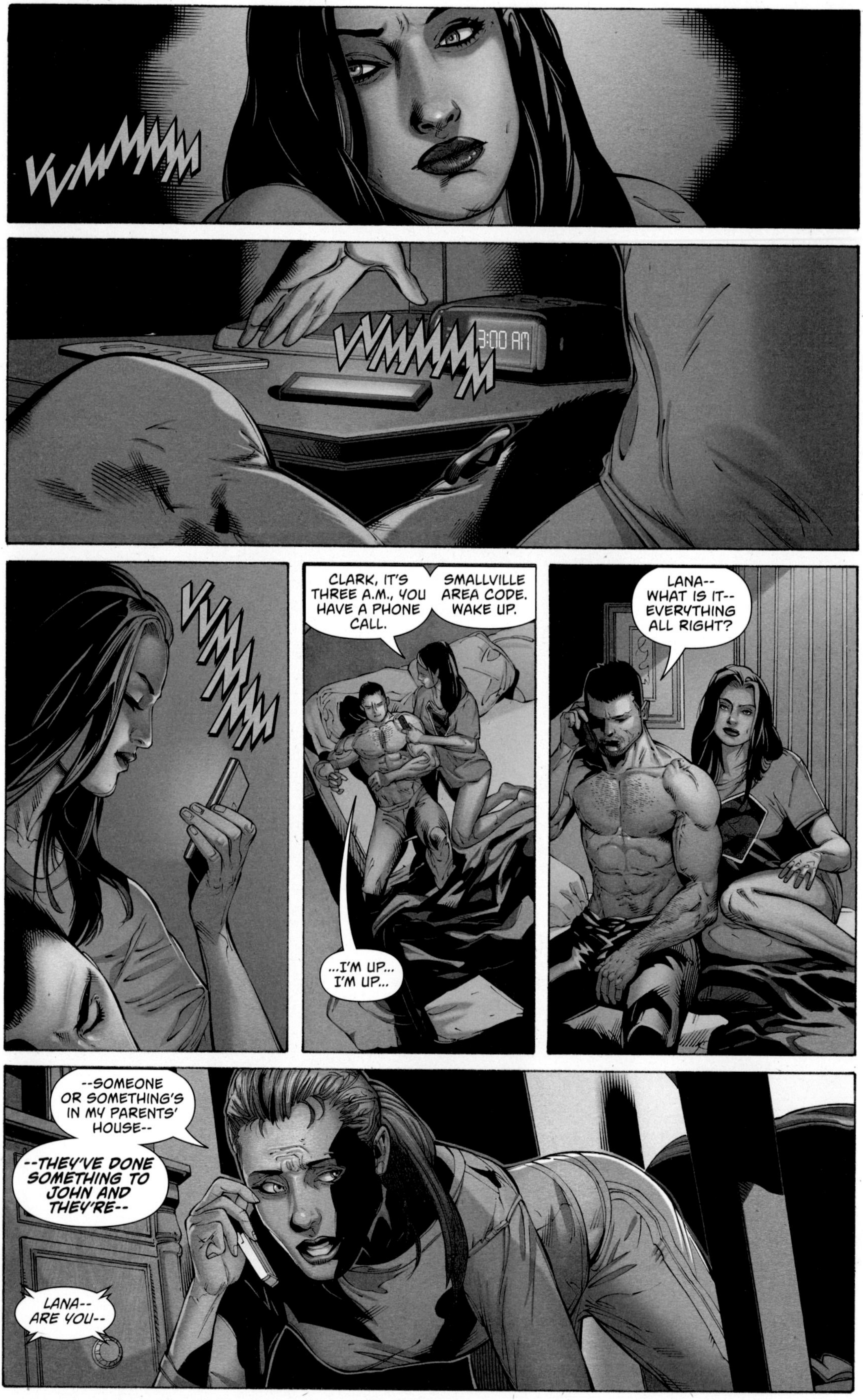
VVMMMM
VVMMMM
3:00 AM
VVMMMM
CLARK, IT'S THREE A.M., YOU HAVE A PHONE CALL.
SMALLVILLE AREA CODE. WAKE UP.
...I'M UP... I'M UP...
LANA-- WHAT IS IT-- EVERYTHING ALL RIGHT?
--SOMEONE OR SOMETHING'S IN MY PARENTS' HOUSE--
--THEY'VE DONE SOMETHING TO JOHN AND THEY'RE--
LANA-- ARE YOU--

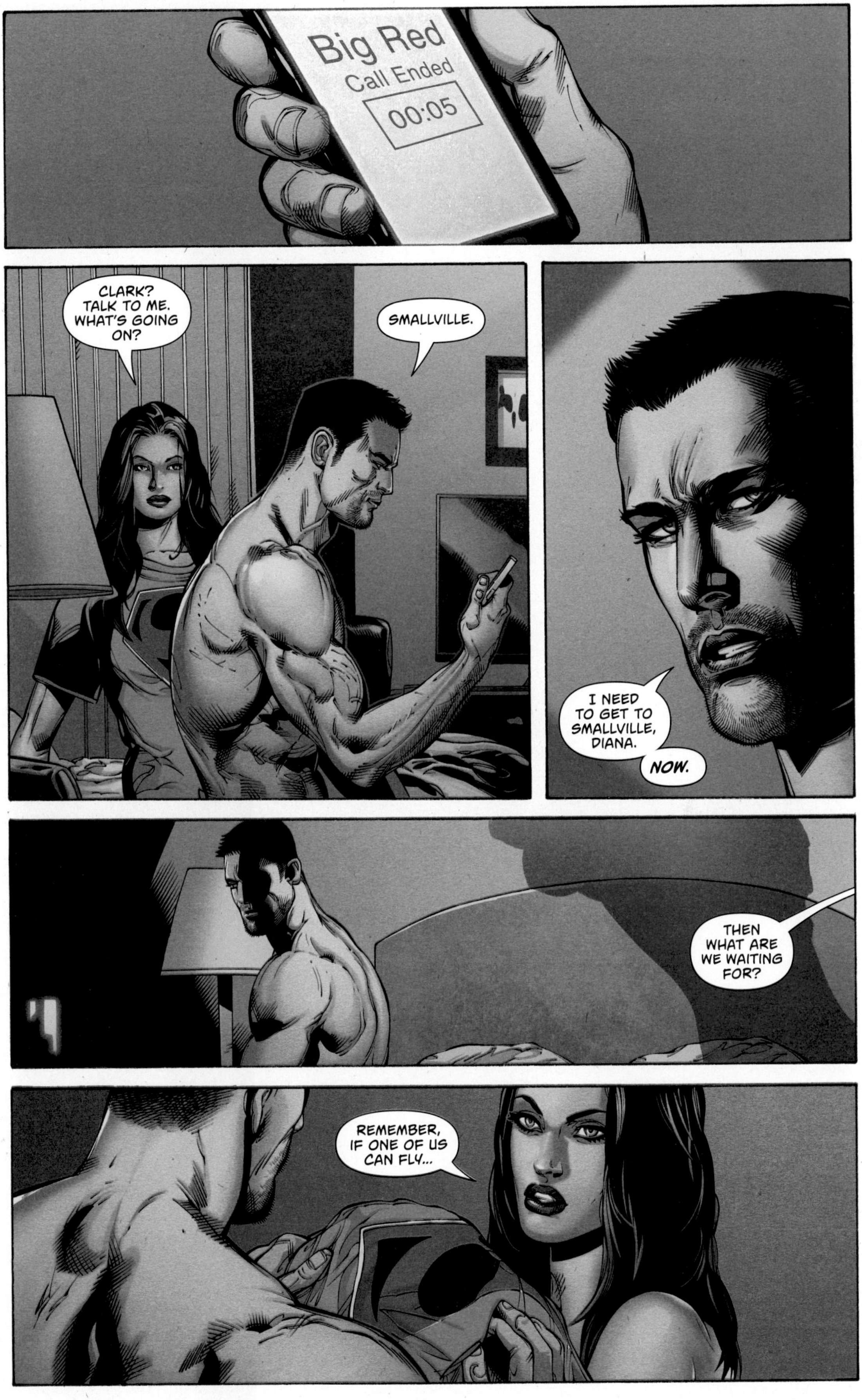
Big Red
Call Ended
00:05
CLARK? TALK TO ME. WHAT'S GOING ON?
SMALLVILLE.
I NEED TO GET TO SMALLVILLE, DIANA.
NOW.
THEN WHAT ARE WE WAITING FOR?
REMEMBER, IF ONE OF US CAN FLY...

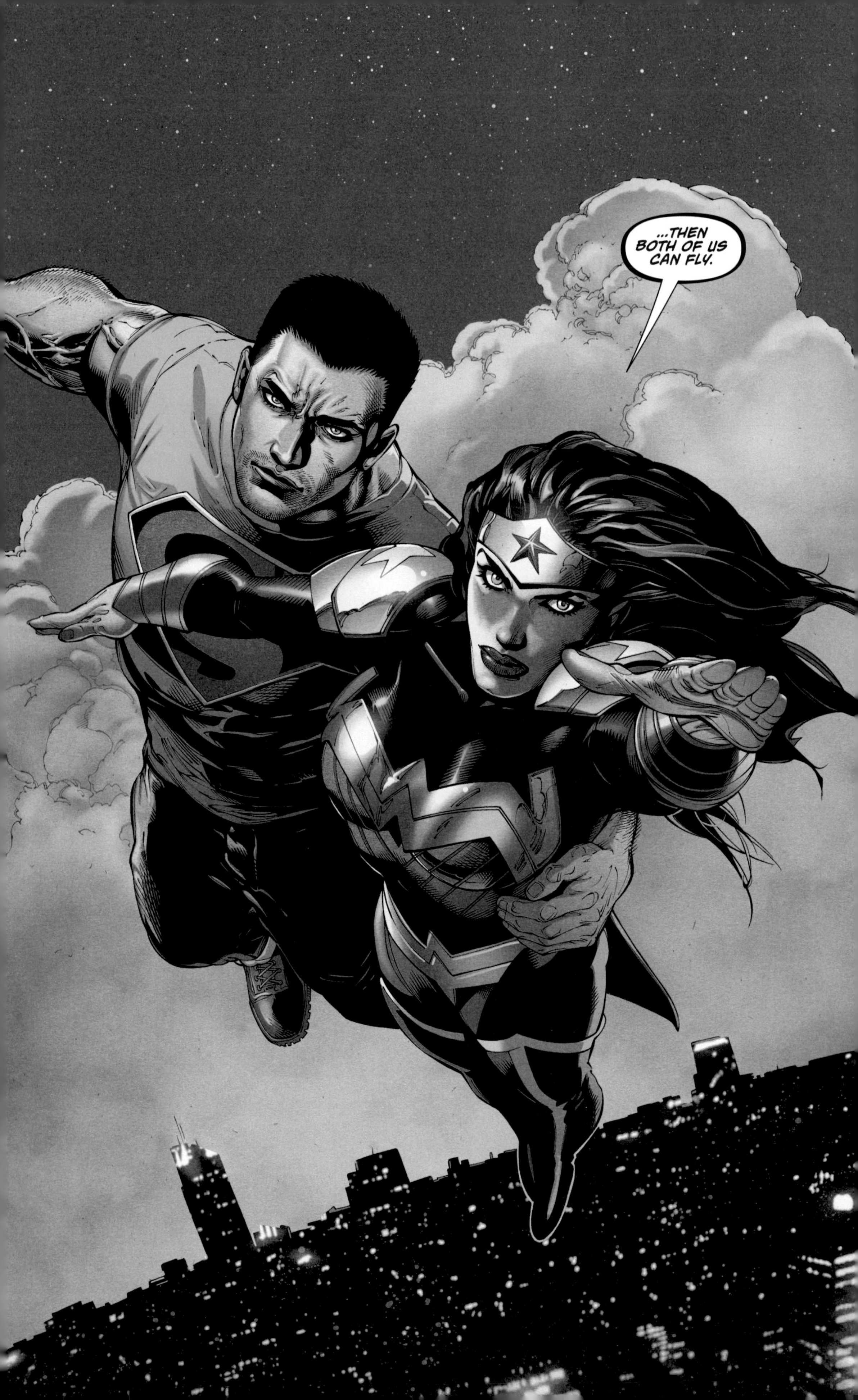
...THEN BOTH OF US CAN FLY.

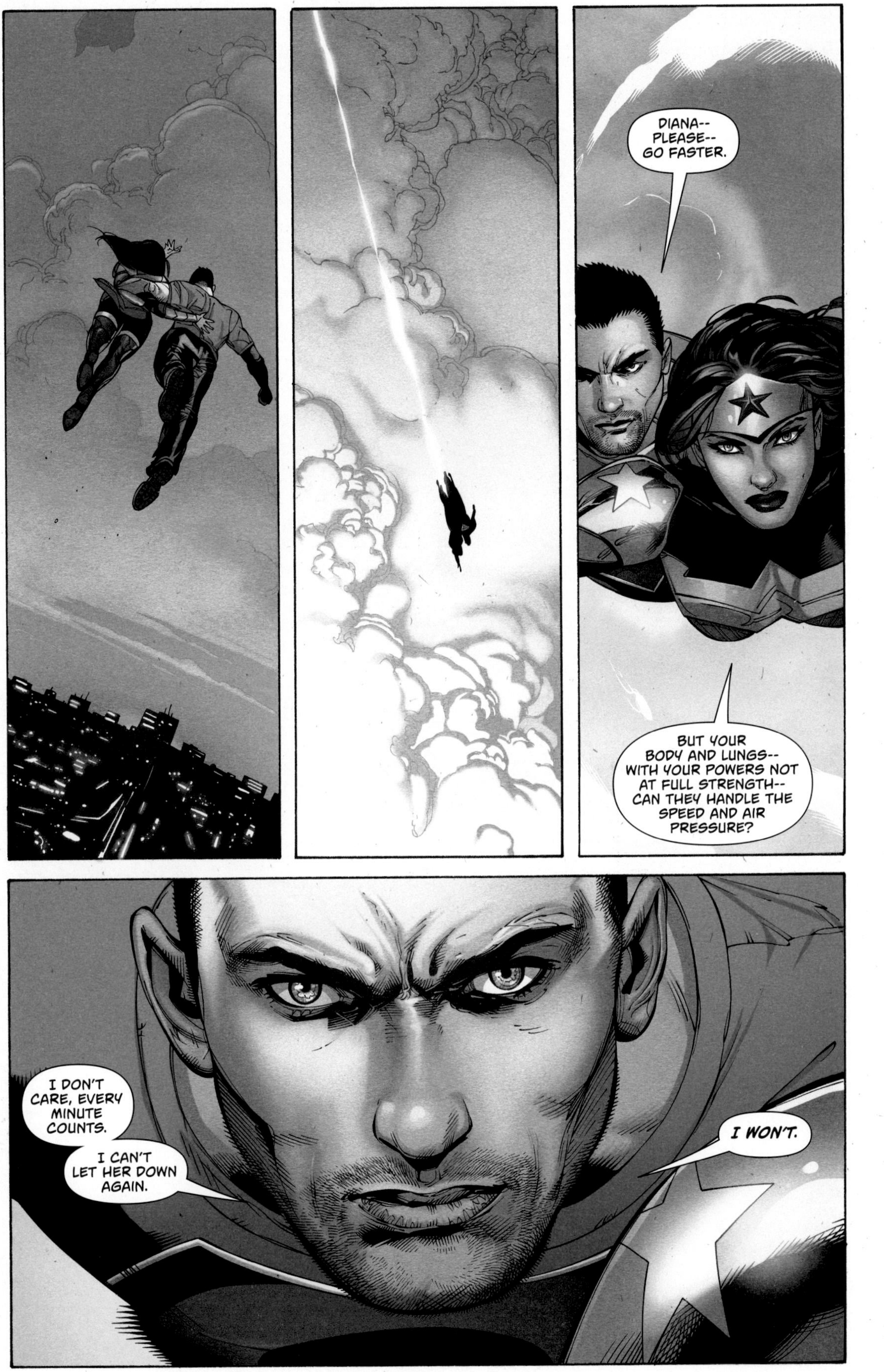
DIANA--
PLEASE--
GO FASTER.
BUT YOUR
BODY AND LUNGS--
WITH YOUR POWERS NOT
AT FULL STRENGTH--
CAN THEY HANDLE THE
SPEED AND AIR
PRESSURE?
I DON'T
CARE, EVERY
MINUTE
COUNTS.
I CAN'T
LET HER DOWN
AGAIN.
I WON'T.

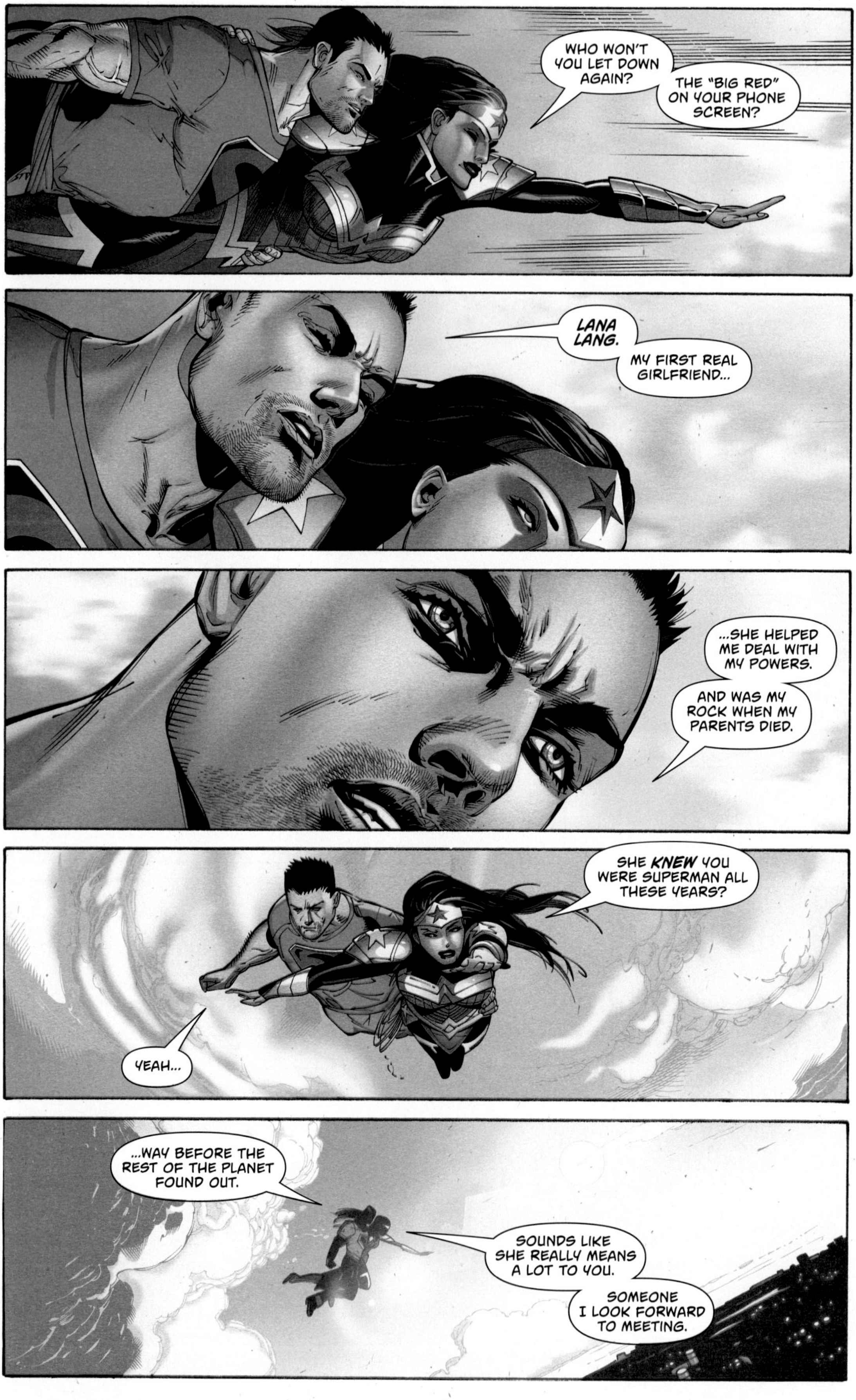
WHO WON'T YOU LET DOWN AGAIN?
THE "BIG RED" ON YOUR PHONE SCREEN?
LANA LANG.
MY FIRST REAL GIRLFRIEND...
...SHE HELPED ME DEAL WITH MY POWERS.
AND WAS MY ROCK WHEN MY PARENTS DIED.
SHE KNEW YOU WERE SUPERMAN ALL THESE YEARS?
YEAH...
...WAY BEFORE THE REST OF THE PLANET FOUND OUT.
SOUNDS LIKE SHE REALLY MEANS A LOT TO YOU.
SOMEONE I LOOK FORWARD TO MEETING.

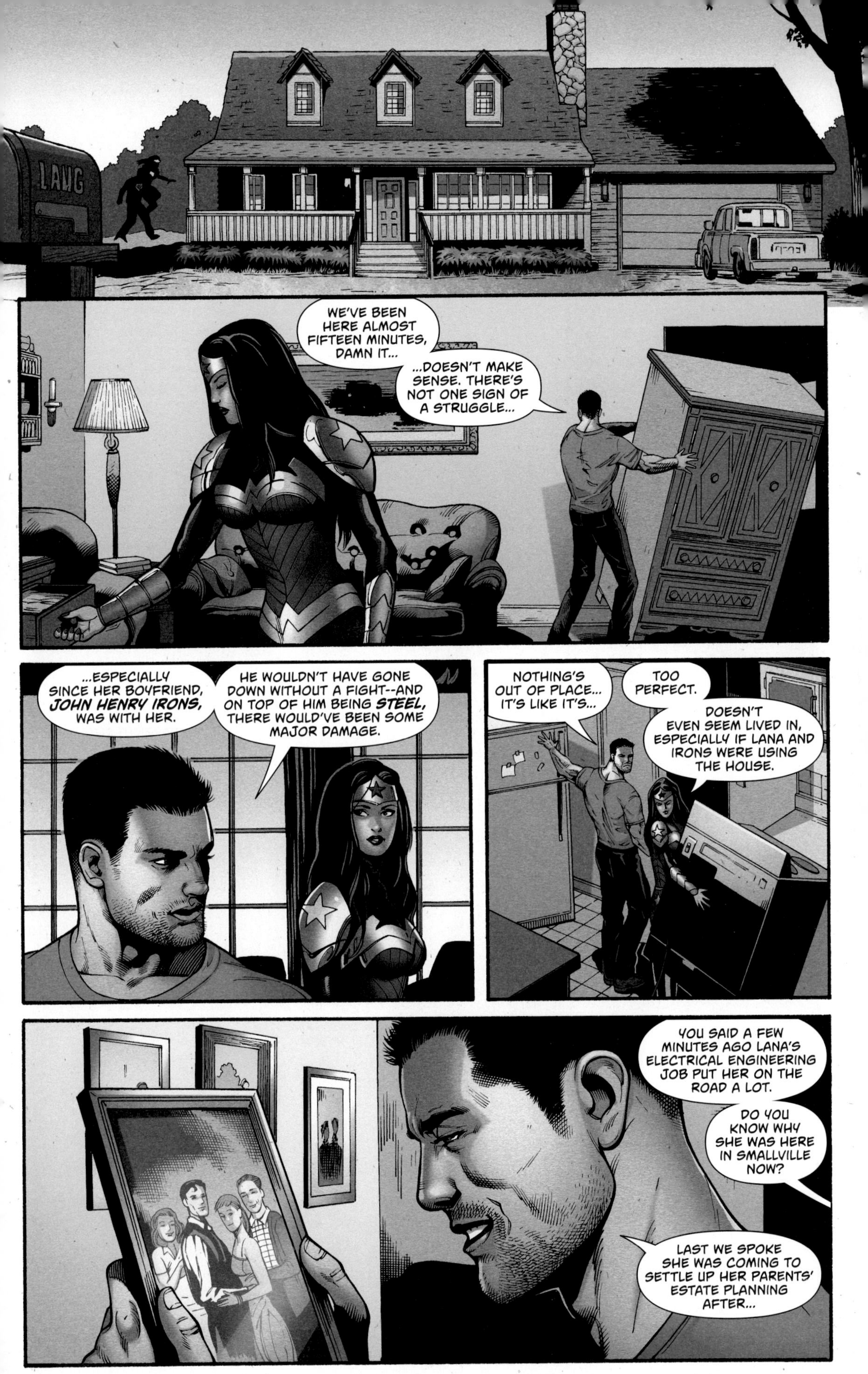
LANG
WE'VE BEEN HERE ALMOST FIFTEEN MINUTES, DAMN IT...
...DOESN'T MAKE SENSE. THERE'S NOT ONE SIGN OF A STRUGGLE...
...ESPECIALLY SINCE HER BOYFRIEND, JOHN HENRY IRONS, WAS WITH HER.
HE WOULDN'T HAVE GONE DOWN WITHOUT A FIGHT--AND ON TOP OF HIM BEING STEEL, THERE WOULD'VE BEEN SOME MAJOR DAMAGE.
NOTHING'S OUT OF PLACE... IT'S LIKE IT'S...
TOO PERFECT.
DOESN'T EVEN SEEM LIVED IN, ESPECIALLY IF LANA AND IRONS WERE USING THE HOUSE.
YOU SAID A FEW MINUTES AGO LANA'S ELECTRICAL ENGINEERING JOB PUT HER ON THE ROAD A LOT.
DO YOU KNOW WHY SHE WAS HERE IN SMALLVILLE NOW?
LAST WE SPOKE SHE WAS COMING TO SETTLE UP HER PARENTS' ESTATE PLANNING AFTER...

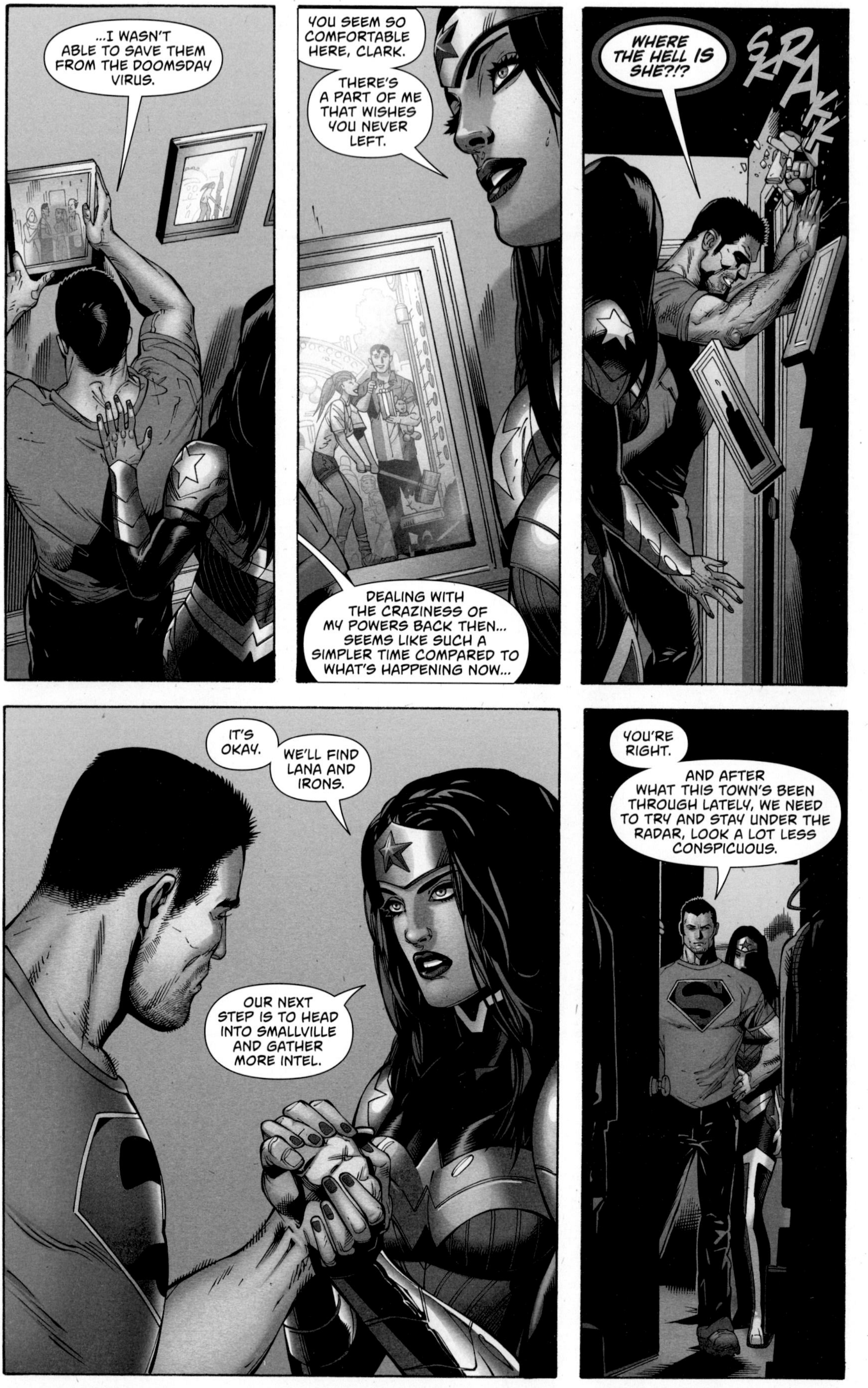
...I WASN'T ABLE TO SAVE THEM FROM THE DOOMSDAY VIRUS.
YOU SEEM SO COMFORTABLE HERE, CLARK.
THERE'S A PART OF ME THAT WISHES YOU NEVER LEFT.
DEALING WITH THE CRAZINESS OF MY POWERS BACK THEN... SEEMS LIKE SUCH A SIMPLER TIME COMPARED TO WHAT'S HAPPENING NOW...
WHERE THE HELL IS SHE?!?
SKRAKK
IT'S OKAY.
WE'LL FIND LANA AND IRONS.
OUR NEXT STEP IS TO HEAD INTO SMALLVILLE AND GATHER MORE INTEL.
YOU'RE RIGHT.
AND AFTER WHAT THIS TOWN'S BEEN THROUGH LATELY, WE NEED TO TRY AND STAY UNDER THE RADAR, LOOK A LOT LESS CONSPICUOUS.

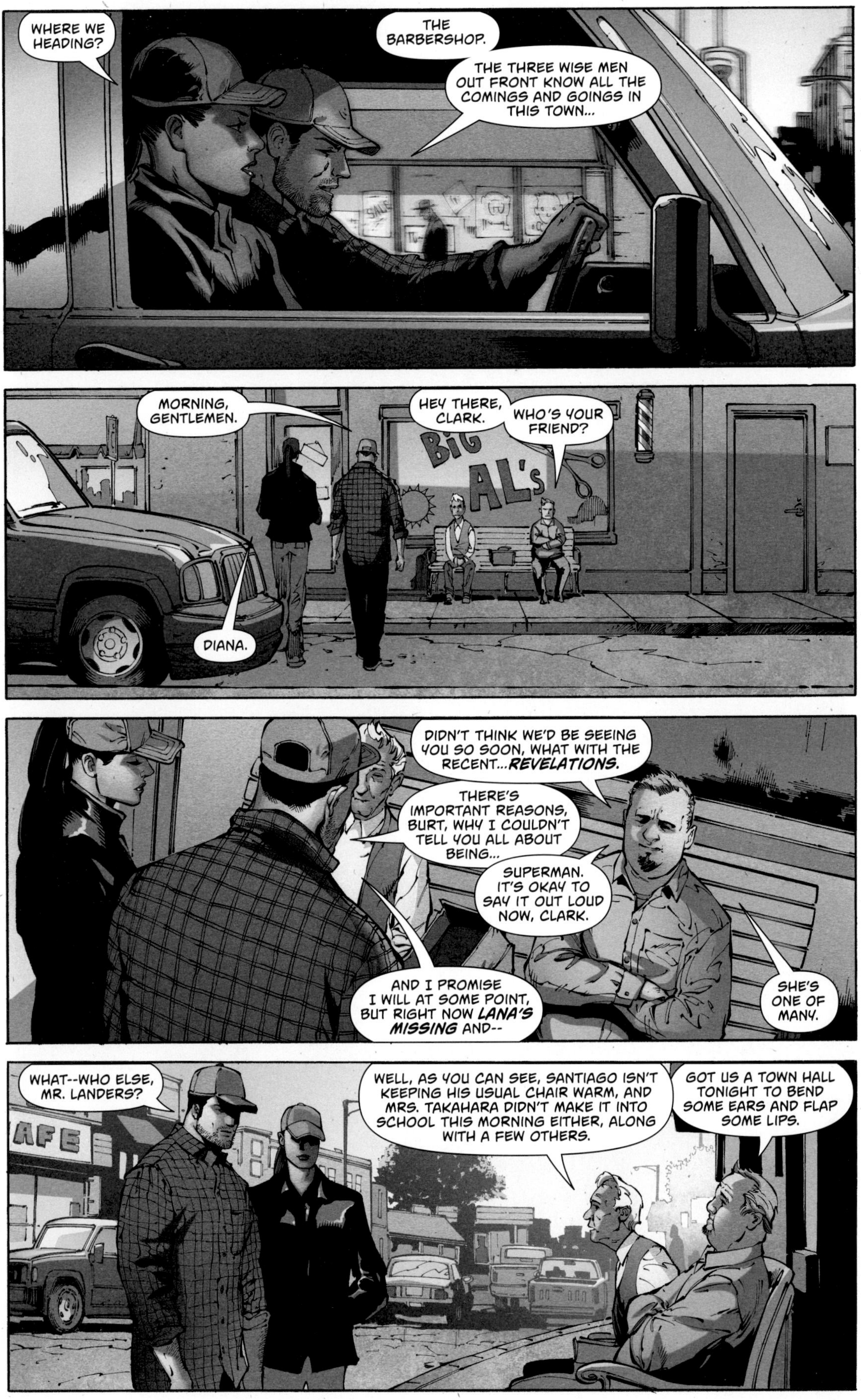
WHERE WE HEADING?
THE BARBERSHOP.
THE THREE WISE MEN OUT FRONT KNOW ALL THE COMINGS AND GOINGS IN THIS TOWN...
MORNING, GENTLEMEN.
HEY THERE, CLARK.
WHO'S YOUR FRIEND?
BIG AL's
DIANA.
DIDN'T THINK WE'D BE SEEING YOU SO SOON, WHAT WITH THE RECENT...*REVELATIONS*.
THERE'S IMPORTANT REASONS, BURT, WHY I COULDN'T TELL YOU ALL ABOUT BEING...
SUPERMAN. IT'S OKAY TO SAY IT OUT LOUD NOW, CLARK.
AND I PROMISE I WILL AT SOME POINT, BUT RIGHT NOW *LANA'S MISSING* AND--
SHE'S ONE OF MANY.
WHAT--WHO ELSE, MR. LANDERS?
WELL, AS YOU CAN SEE, SANTIAGO ISN'T KEEPING HIS USUAL CHAIR WARM, AND MRS. TAKAHARA DIDN'T MAKE IT INTO SCHOOL THIS MORNING EITHER, ALONG WITH A FEW OTHERS.
GOT US A TOWN HALL TONIGHT TO BEND SOME EARS AND FLAP SOME LIPS.

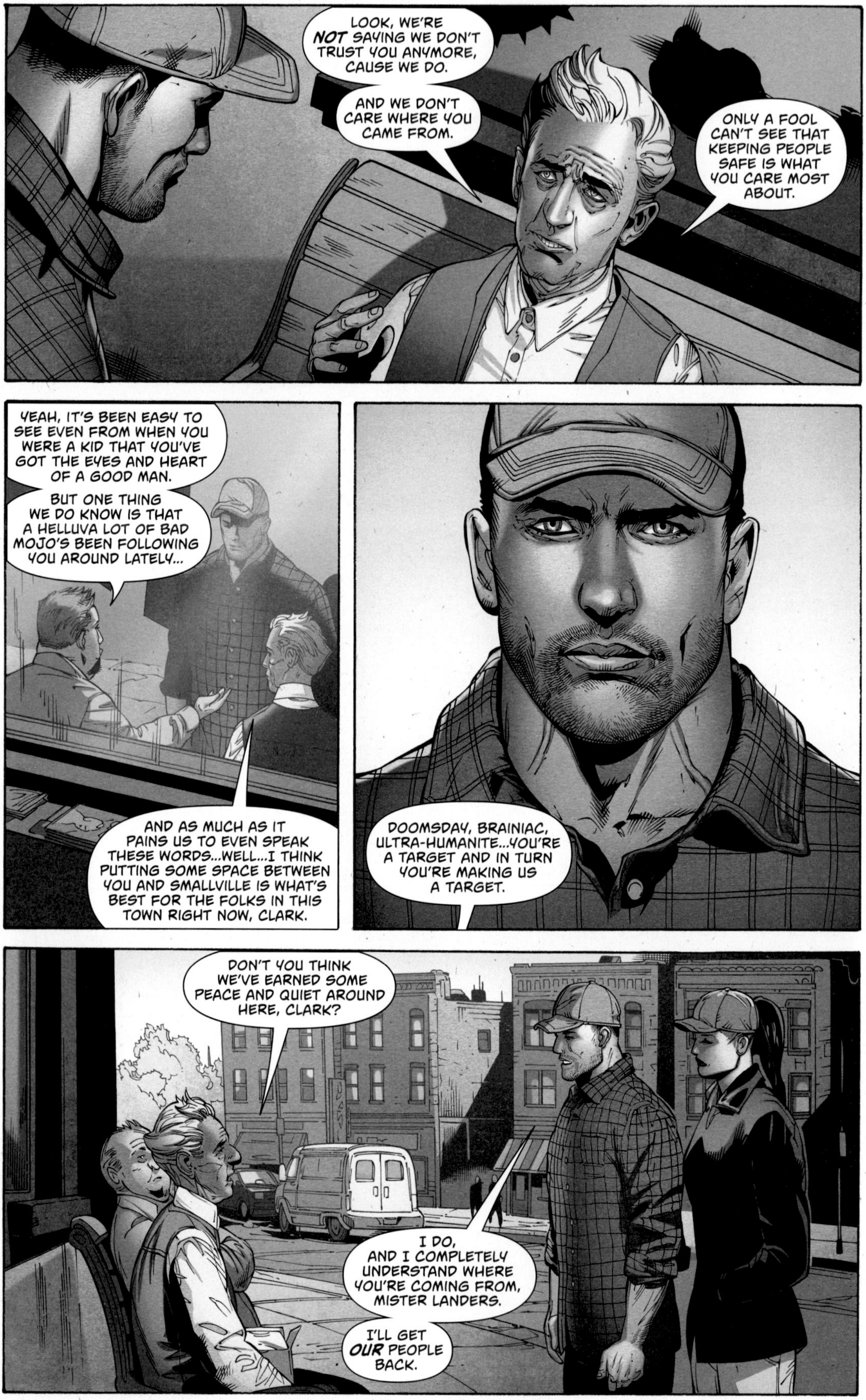
LOOK, WE'RE *NOT* SAYING WE DON'T TRUST YOU ANYMORE, CAUSE WE DO.
AND WE DON'T CARE WHERE YOU CAME FROM.
ONLY A FOOL CAN'T SEE THAT KEEPING PEOPLE SAFE IS WHAT YOU CARE MOST ABOUT.
YEAH, IT'S BEEN EASY TO SEE EVEN FROM WHEN YOU WERE A KID THAT YOU'VE GOT THE EYES AND HEART OF A GOOD MAN.
BUT ONE THING WE DO KNOW IS THAT A HELLUVA LOT OF BAD MOJO'S BEEN FOLLOWING YOU AROUND LATELY...
AND AS MUCH AS IT PAINS US TO EVEN SPEAK THESE WORDS...WELL...I THINK PUTTING SOME SPACE BETWEEN YOU AND SMALLVILLE IS WHAT'S BEST FOR THE FOLKS IN THIS TOWN RIGHT NOW, CLARK.
DOOMSDAY, BRAINIAC, ULTRA-HUMANITE...YOU'RE A TARGET AND IN TURN YOU'RE MAKING US A TARGET.
DON'T YOU THINK WE'VE EARNED SOME PEACE AND QUIET AROUND HERE, CLARK?
I DO, AND I COMPLETELY UNDERSTAND WHERE YOU'RE COMING FROM, MISTER LANDERS.
I'LL GET *OUR* PEOPLE BACK.

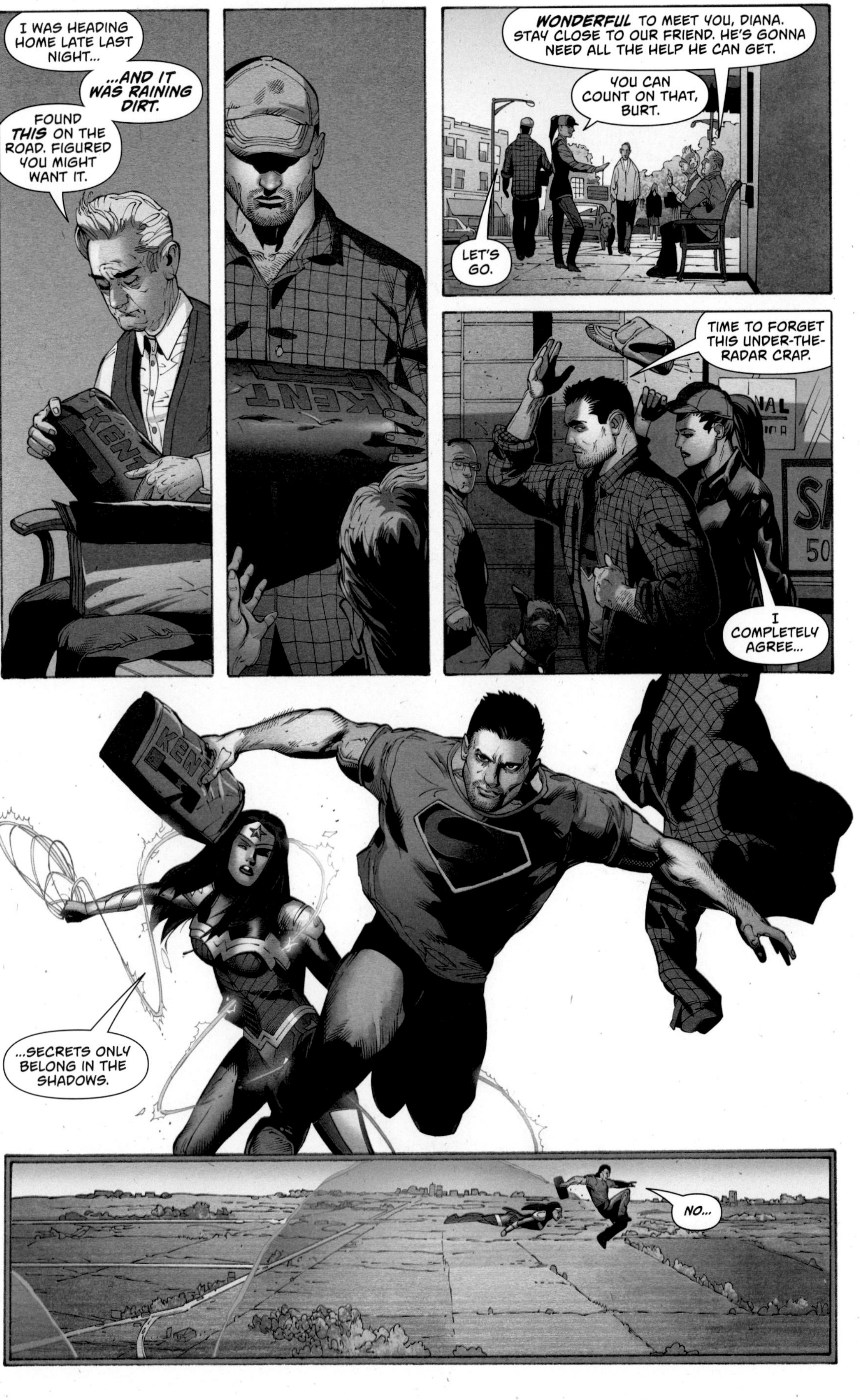
I WAS HEADING HOME LATE LAST NIGHT...
...AND IT WAS RAINING DIRT.
FOUND THIS ON THE ROAD. FIGURED YOU MIGHT WANT IT.
KENT
KENT
WONDERFUL TO MEET YOU, DIANA. STAY CLOSE TO OUR FRIEND. HE'S GONNA NEED ALL THE HELP HE CAN GET.
YOU CAN COUNT ON THAT, BURT.
LET'S GO.
TIME TO FORGET THIS UNDER-THE-RADAR CRAP.
I COMPLETELY AGREE...
KENT
...SECRETS ONLY BELONG IN THE SHADOWS.
NO...

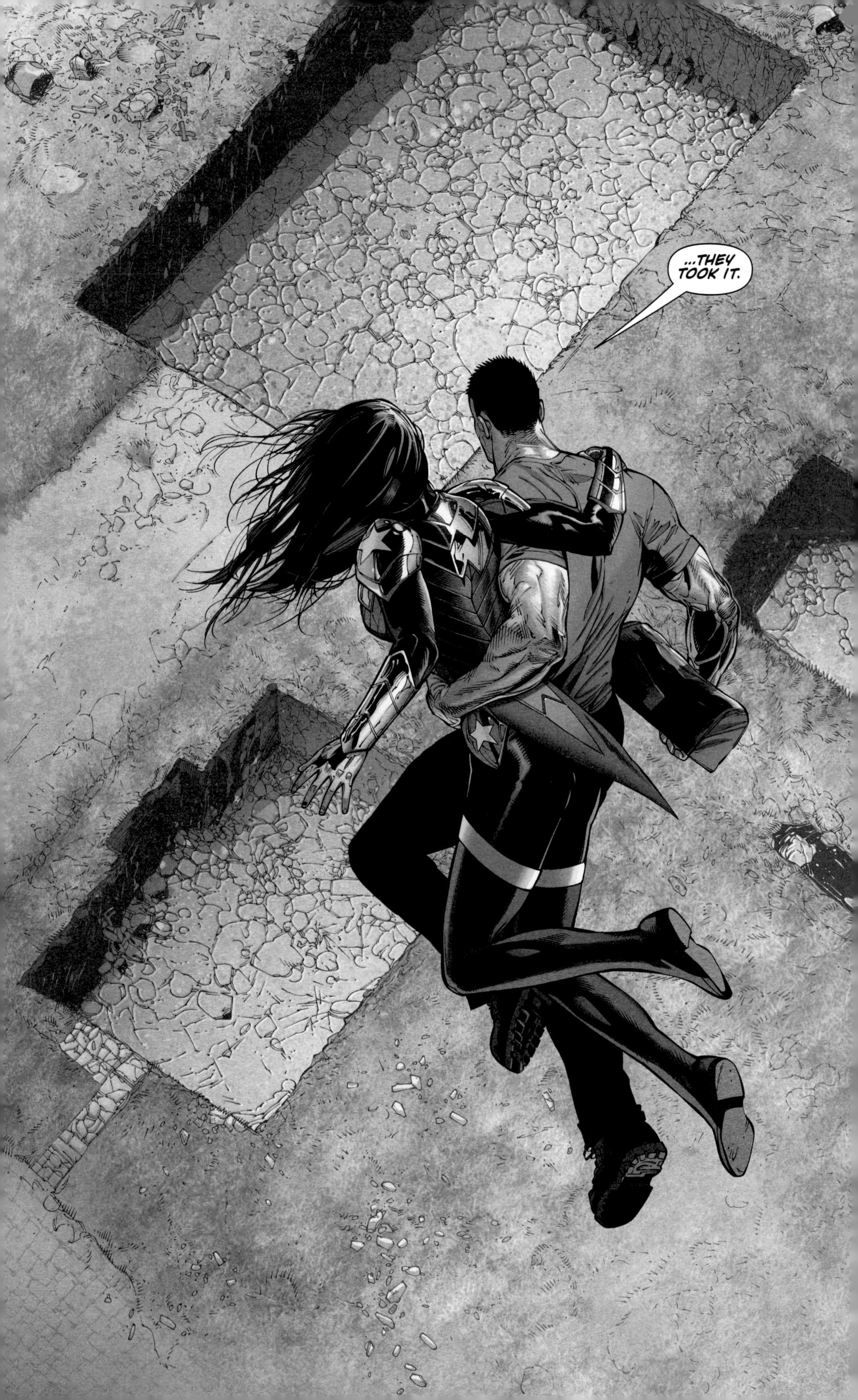
...THEY TOOK IT.

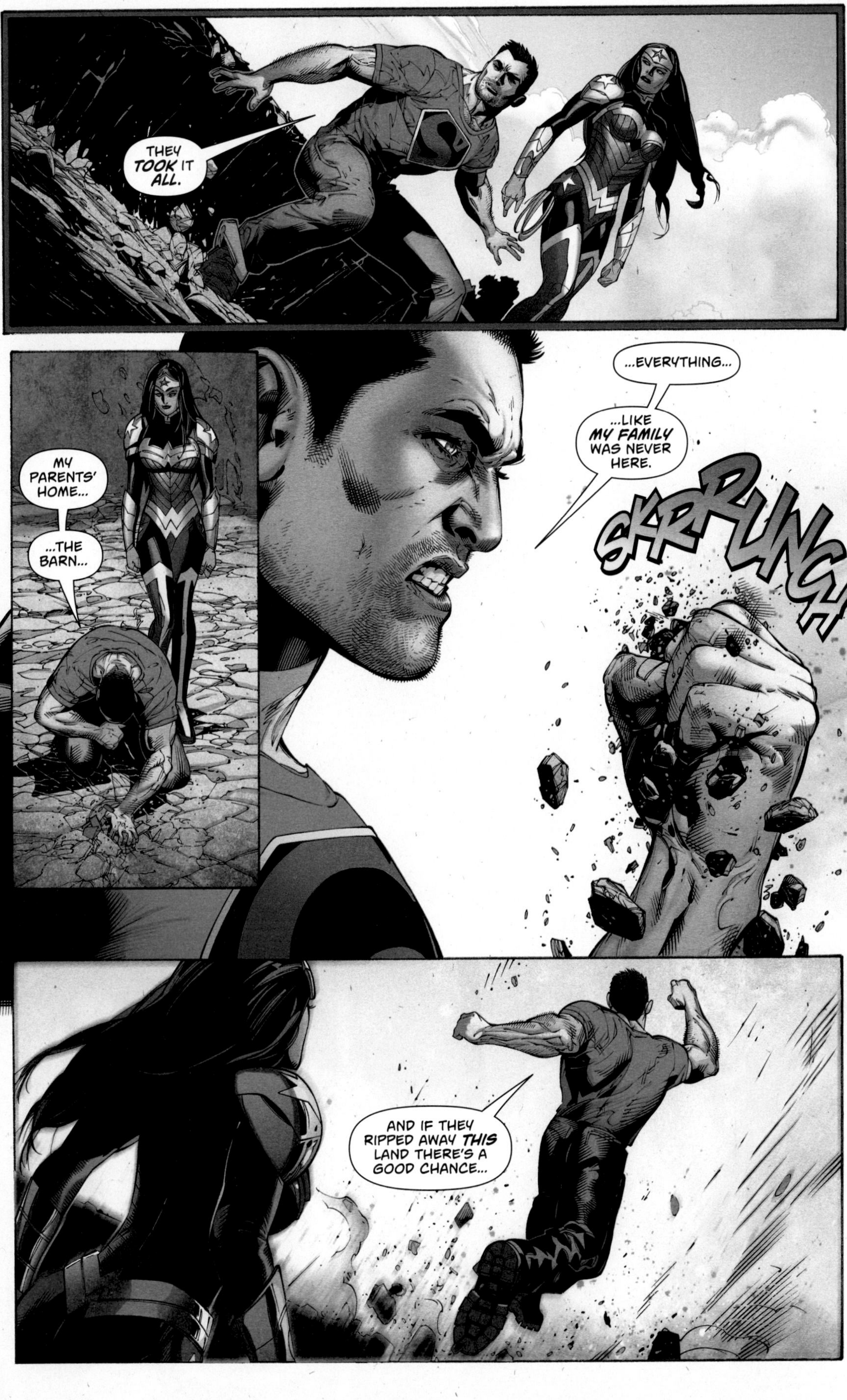
THEY TOOK IT ALL.
MY PARENTS' HOME...
...THE BARN...
...EVERYTHING...
...LIKE MY FAMILY WAS NEVER HERE.
SKRRUNCH
AND IF THEY RIPPED AWAY THIS LAND THERE'S A GOOD CHANCE...

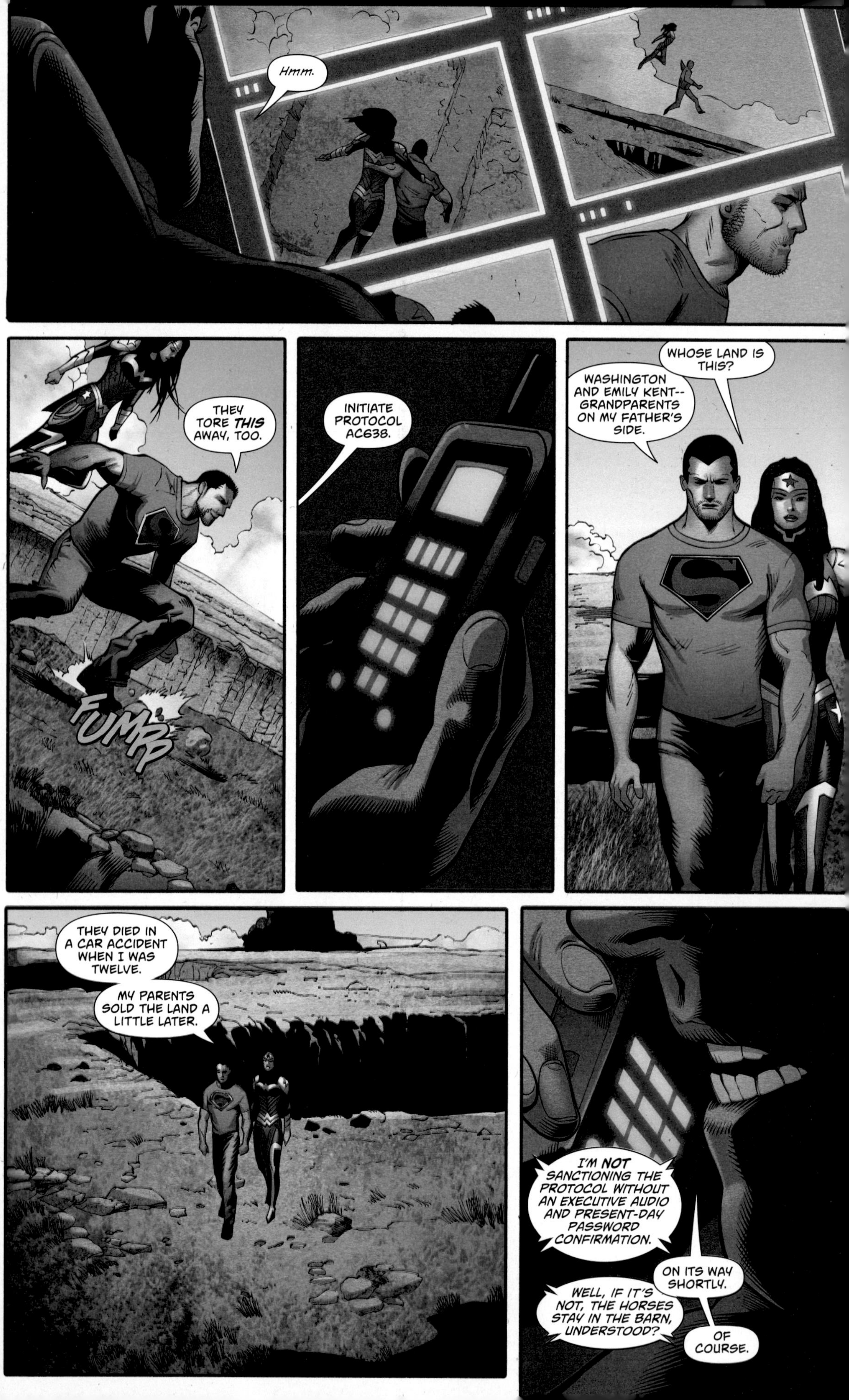
Hmm.
THEY TORE THIS AWAY, TOO.
FUMP
INITIATE PROTOCOL AC638.
WHOSE LAND IS THIS?
WASHINGTON AND EMILY KENT--GRANDPARENTS ON MY FATHER'S SIDE.
THEY DIED IN A CAR ACCIDENT WHEN I WAS TWELVE.
MY PARENTS SOLD THE LAND A LITTLE LATER.
I'M NOT SANCTIONING THE PROTOCOL WITHOUT AN EXECUTIVE AUDIO AND PRESENT-DAY PASSWORD CONFIRMATION.
ON ITS WAY SHORTLY.
WELL, IF IT'S NOT, THE HORSES STAY IN THE BARN, UNDERSTOOD?
OF COURSE.

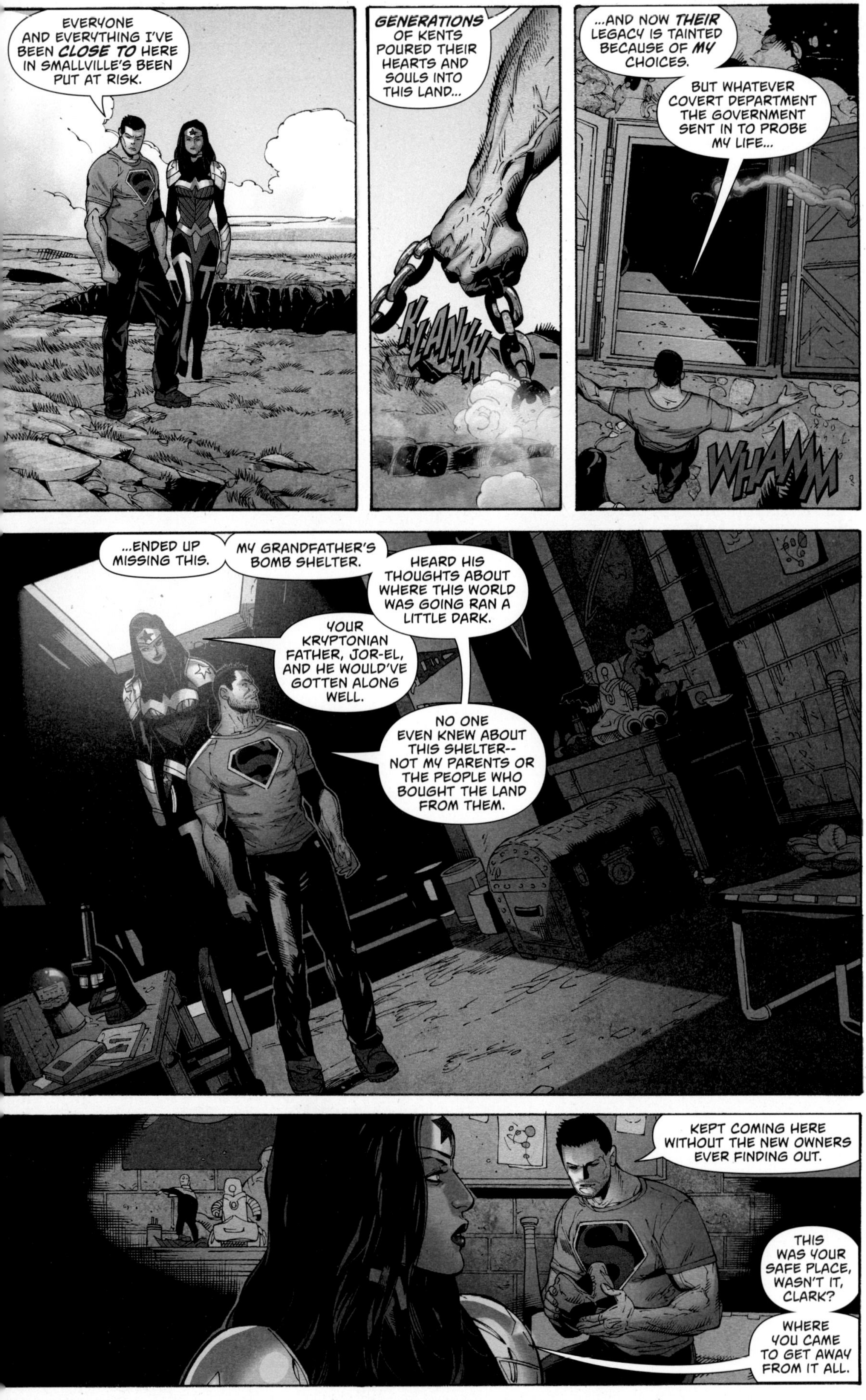
EVERYONE AND EVERYTHING I'VE BEEN CLOSE TO HERE IN SMALLVILLE'S BEEN PUT AT RISK.
GENERATIONS OF KENTS POURED THEIR HEARTS AND SOULS INTO THIS LAND...
KLANKK
...AND NOW THEIR LEGACY IS TAINTED BECAUSE OF MY CHOICES.
BUT WHATEVER COVERT DEPARTMENT THE GOVERNMENT SENT IN TO PROBE MY LIFE...
WHAMM
...ENDED UP MISSING THIS.
MY GRANDFATHER'S BOMB SHELTER.
HEARD HIS THOUGHTS ABOUT WHERE THIS WORLD WAS GOING RAN A LITTLE DARK.
YOUR KRYPTONIAN FATHER, JOR-EL, AND HE WOULD'VE GOTTEN ALONG WELL.
NO ONE EVEN KNEW ABOUT THIS SHELTER-- NOT MY PARENTS OR THE PEOPLE WHO BOUGHT THE LAND FROM THEM.
KEPT COMING HERE WITHOUT THE NEW OWNERS EVER FINDING OUT.
THIS WAS YOUR SAFE PLACE, WASN'T IT, CLARK?
WHERE YOU CAME TO GET AWAY FROM IT ALL.

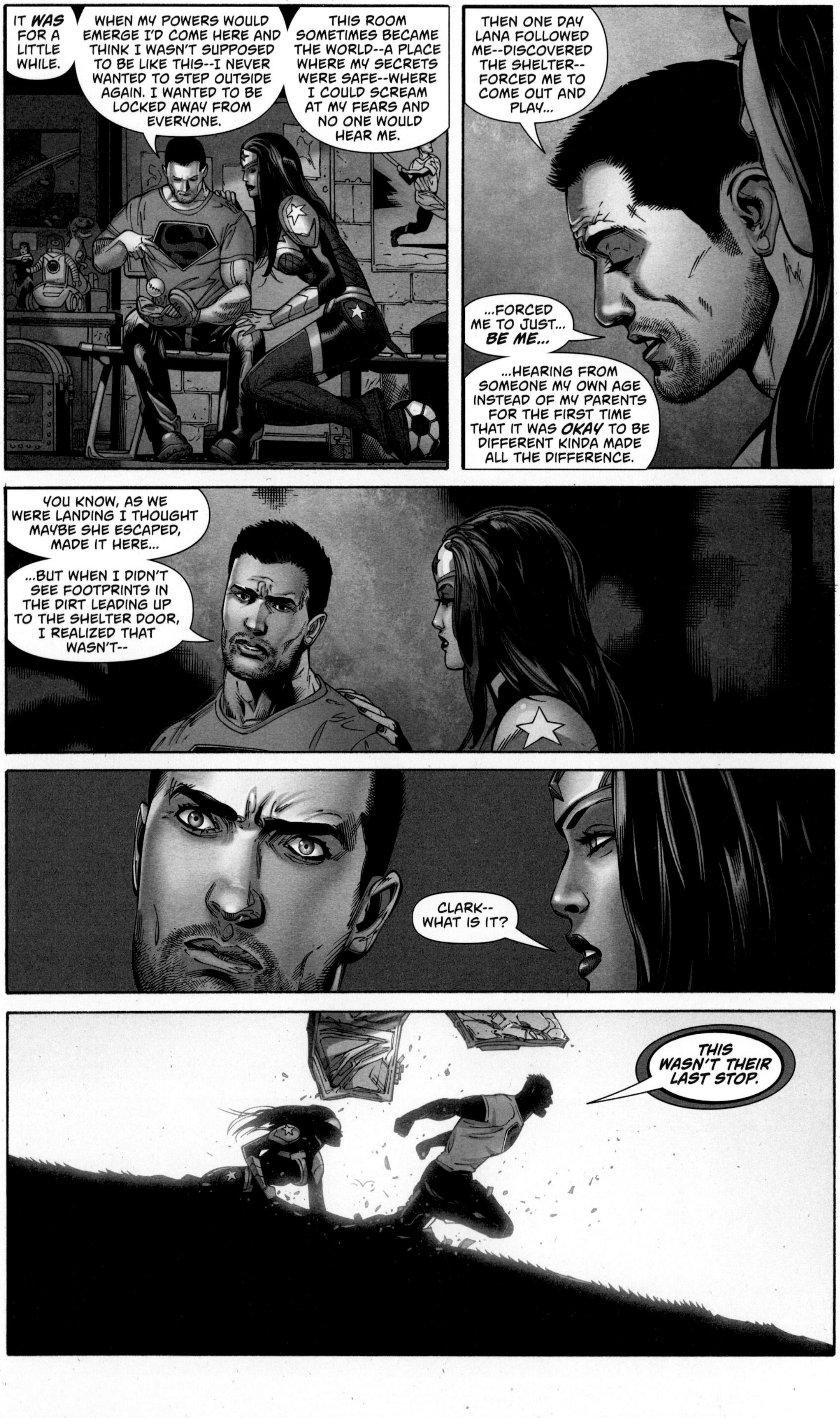
IT WAS FOR A LITTLE WHILE.
WHEN MY POWERS WOULD EMERGE I'D COME HERE AND THINK I WASN'T SUPPOSED TO BE LIKE THIS--I NEVER WANTED TO STEP OUTSIDE AGAIN. I WANTED TO BE LOCKED AWAY FROM EVERYONE.
THIS ROOM SOMETIMES BECAME THE WORLD--A PLACE WHERE MY SECRETS WERE SAFE--WHERE I COULD SCREAM AT MY FEARS AND NO ONE WOULD HEAR ME.
THEN ONE DAY LANA FOLLOWED ME--DISCOVERED THE SHELTER--FORCED ME TO COME OUT AND PLAY...
...FORCED ME TO JUST... BE ME...
...HEARING FROM SOMEONE MY OWN AGE INSTEAD OF MY PARENTS FOR THE FIRST TIME THAT IT WAS OKAY TO BE DIFFERENT KINDA MADE ALL THE DIFFERENCE.
YOU KNOW, AS WE WERE LANDING I THOUGHT MAYBE SHE ESCAPED, MADE IT HERE...
...BUT WHEN I DIDN'T SEE FOOTPRINTS IN THE DIRT LEADING UP TO THE SHELTER DOOR, I REALIZED THAT WASN'T--
CLARK-- WHAT IS IT?
THIS WASN'T THEIR LAST STOP.

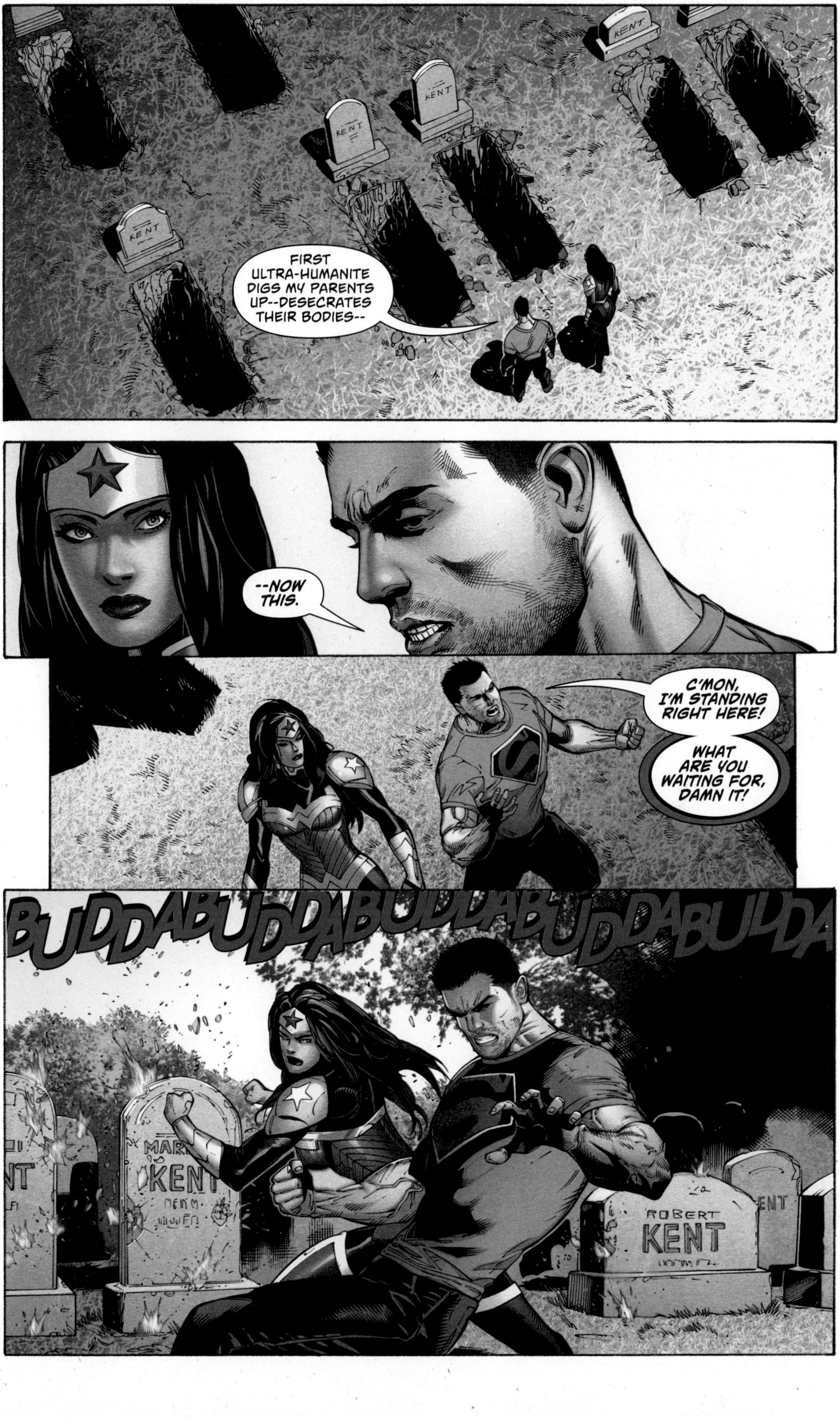
KENT
KENT
KENT
KENT
FIRST ULTRA-HUMANITE DIGS MY PARENTS UP--DESECRATES THEIR BODIES--
--NOW THIS.
C'MON, I'M STANDING RIGHT HERE!
WHAT ARE YOU WAITING FOR, DAMN IT!
BUDDABUDDABUDDABUDDABUDDA
KENT
ROBERT KENT

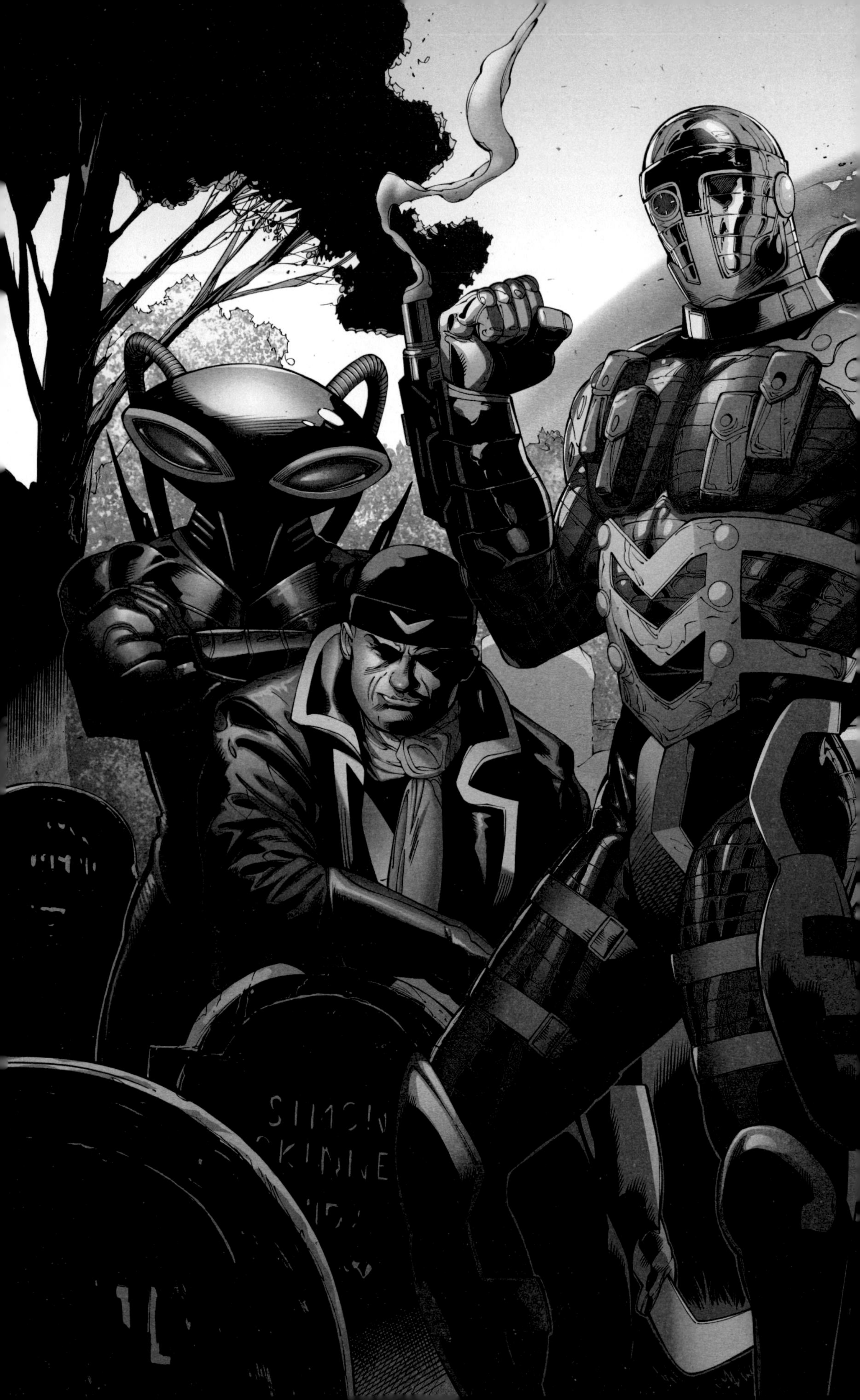

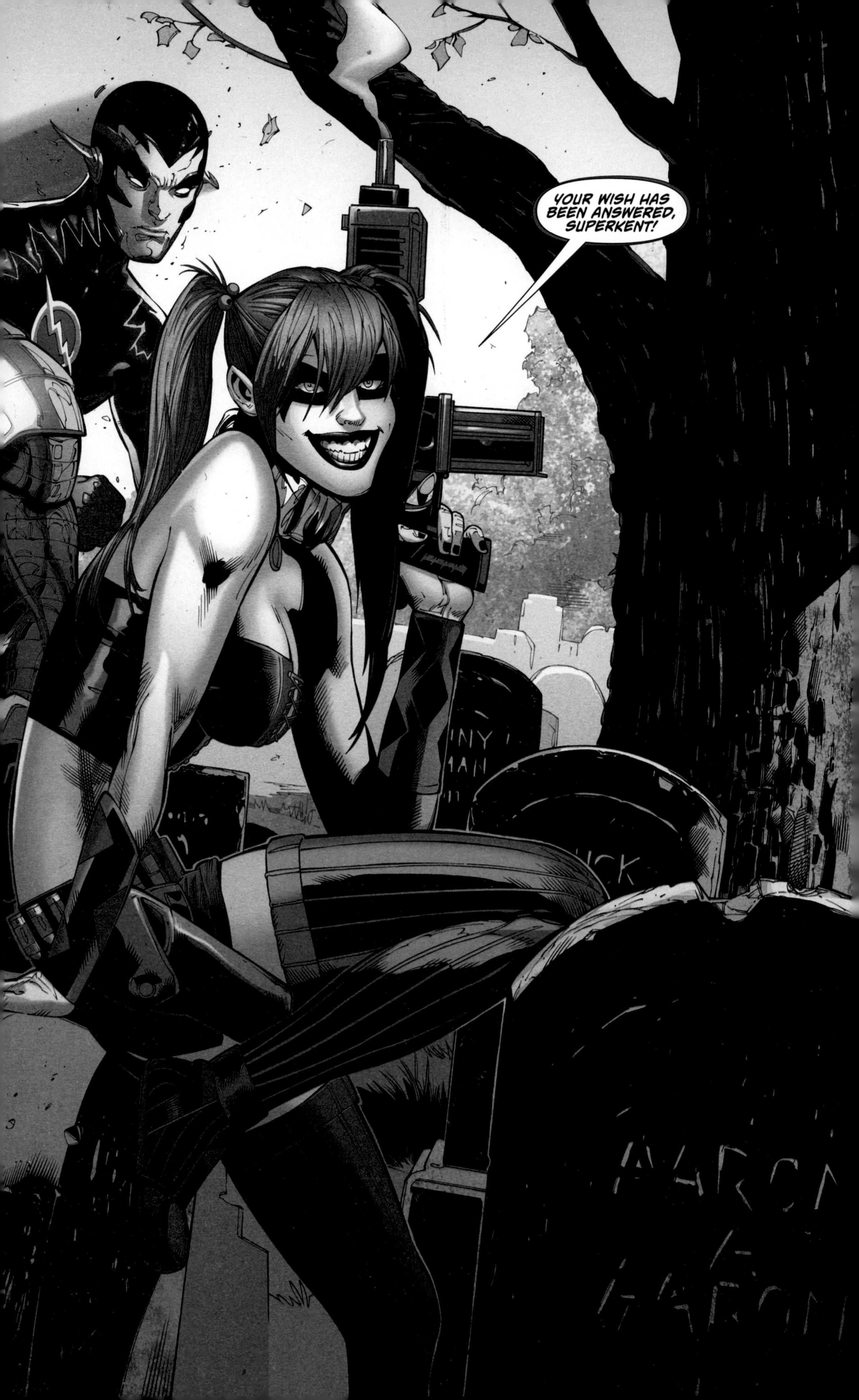
YOUR WISH HAS BEEN ANSWERED, SUPERKENT!

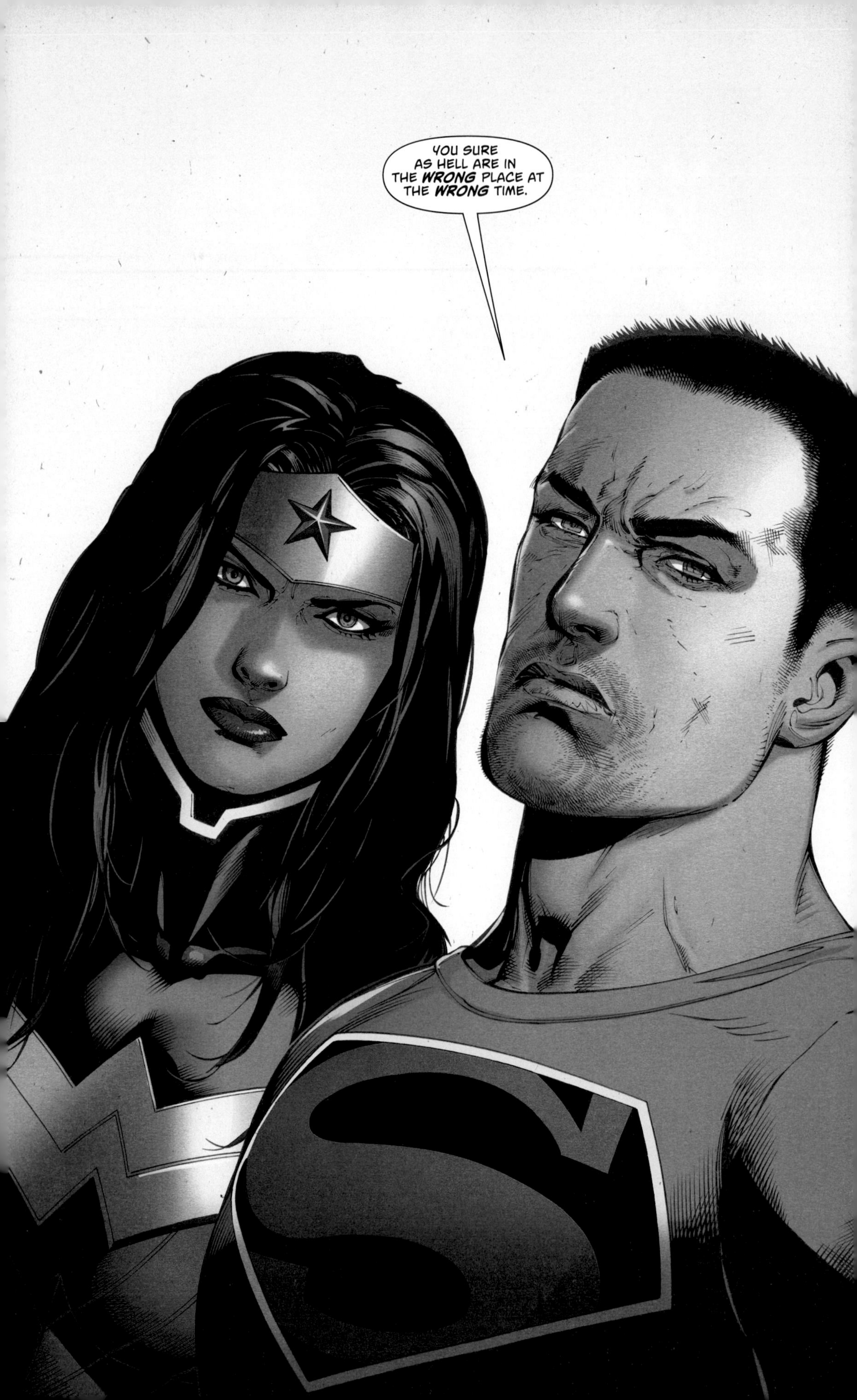
YOU SURE AS HELL ARE IN THE WRONG PLACE AT THE WRONG TIME.

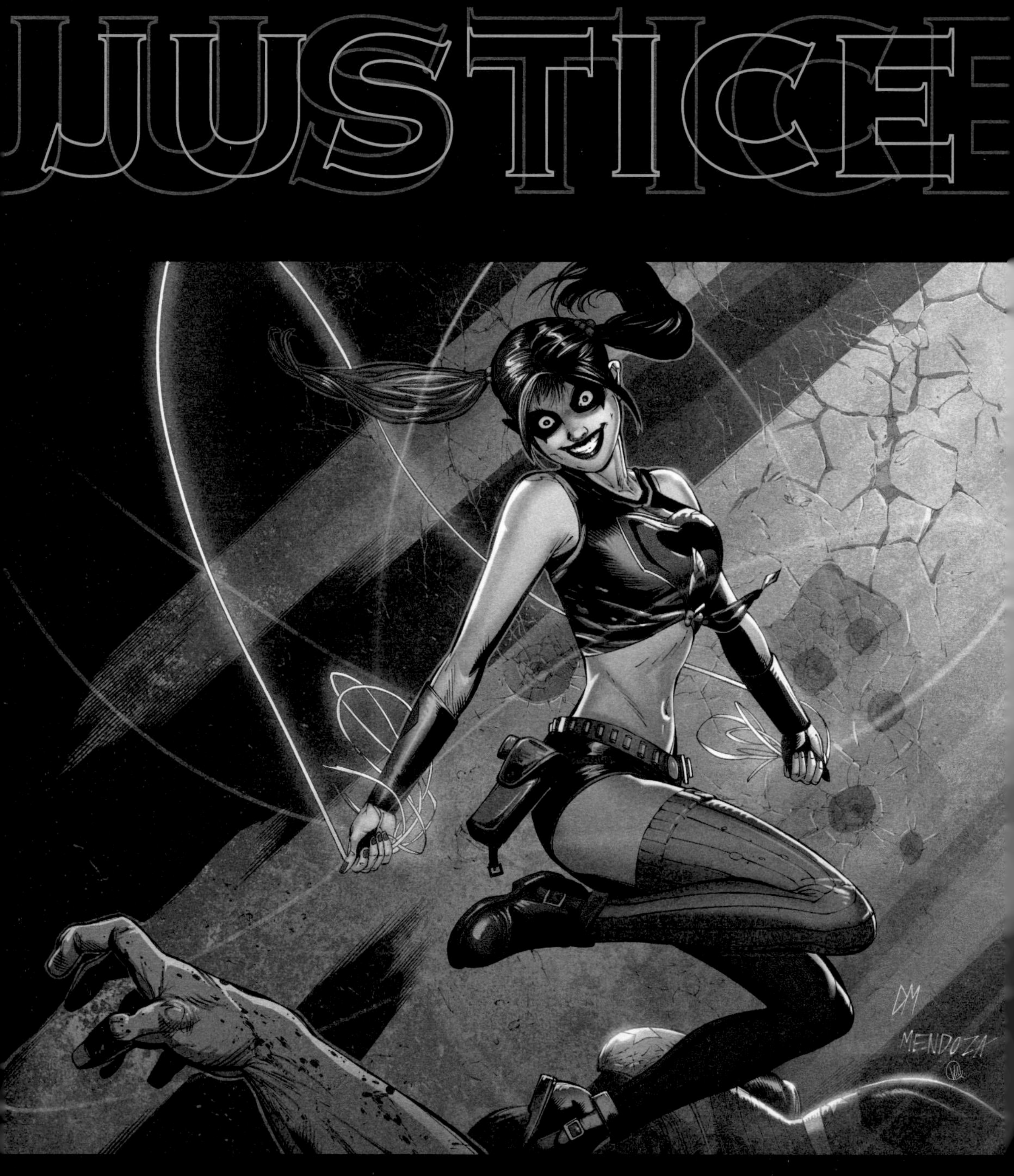
JUSTICE
MENDOZA

DARK TRUTH PART TWO

PETER J. TOMASI writer **DOUG MAHNKE** penciller **JAIME MENDOZA** inker **WIL QUINTANA** colorist **ROB LEIGH** letterer
cover by **DOUG MAHNKE, JAIME MENDOZA & WIL QUINTANA**

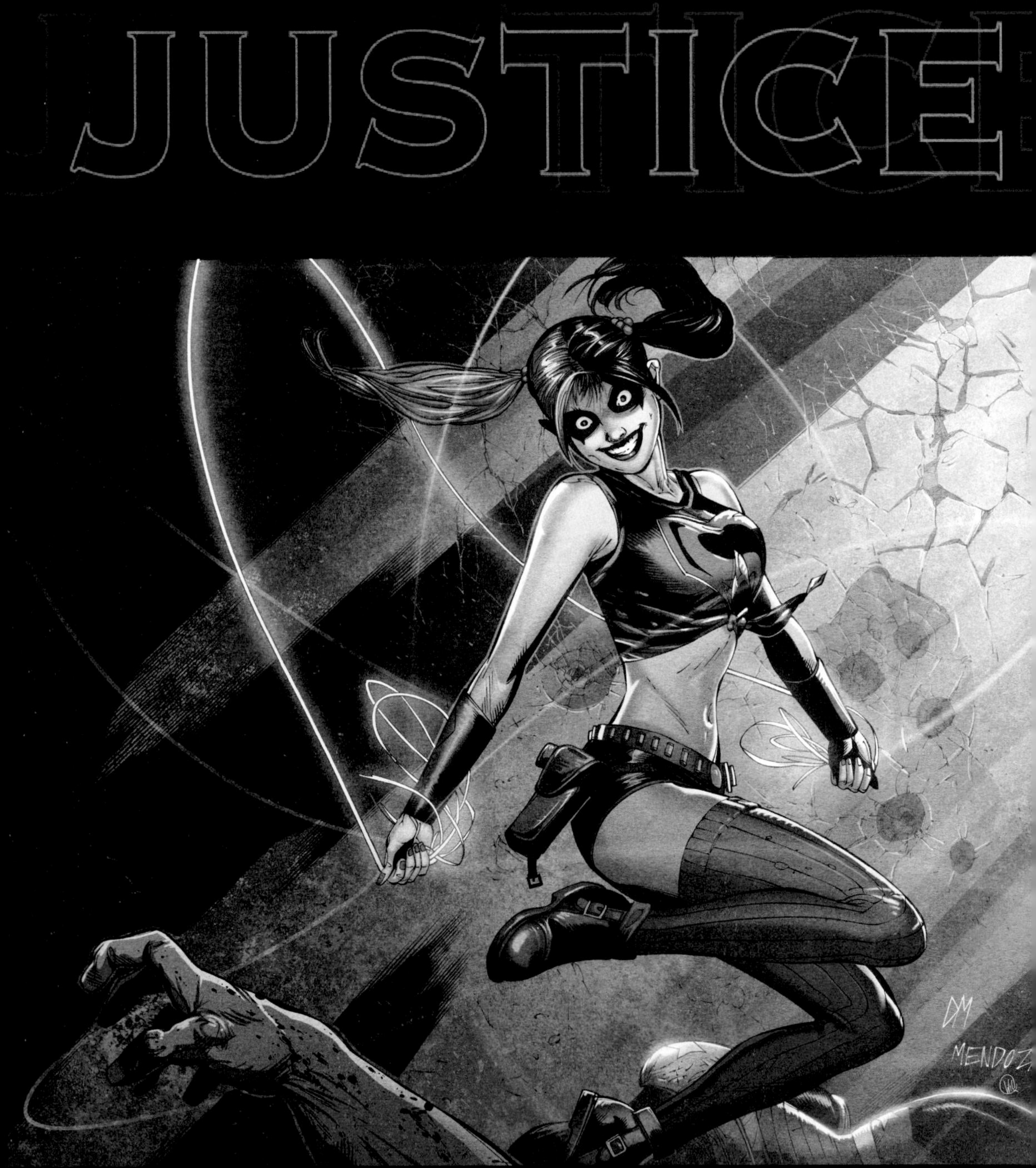
JUSTICE

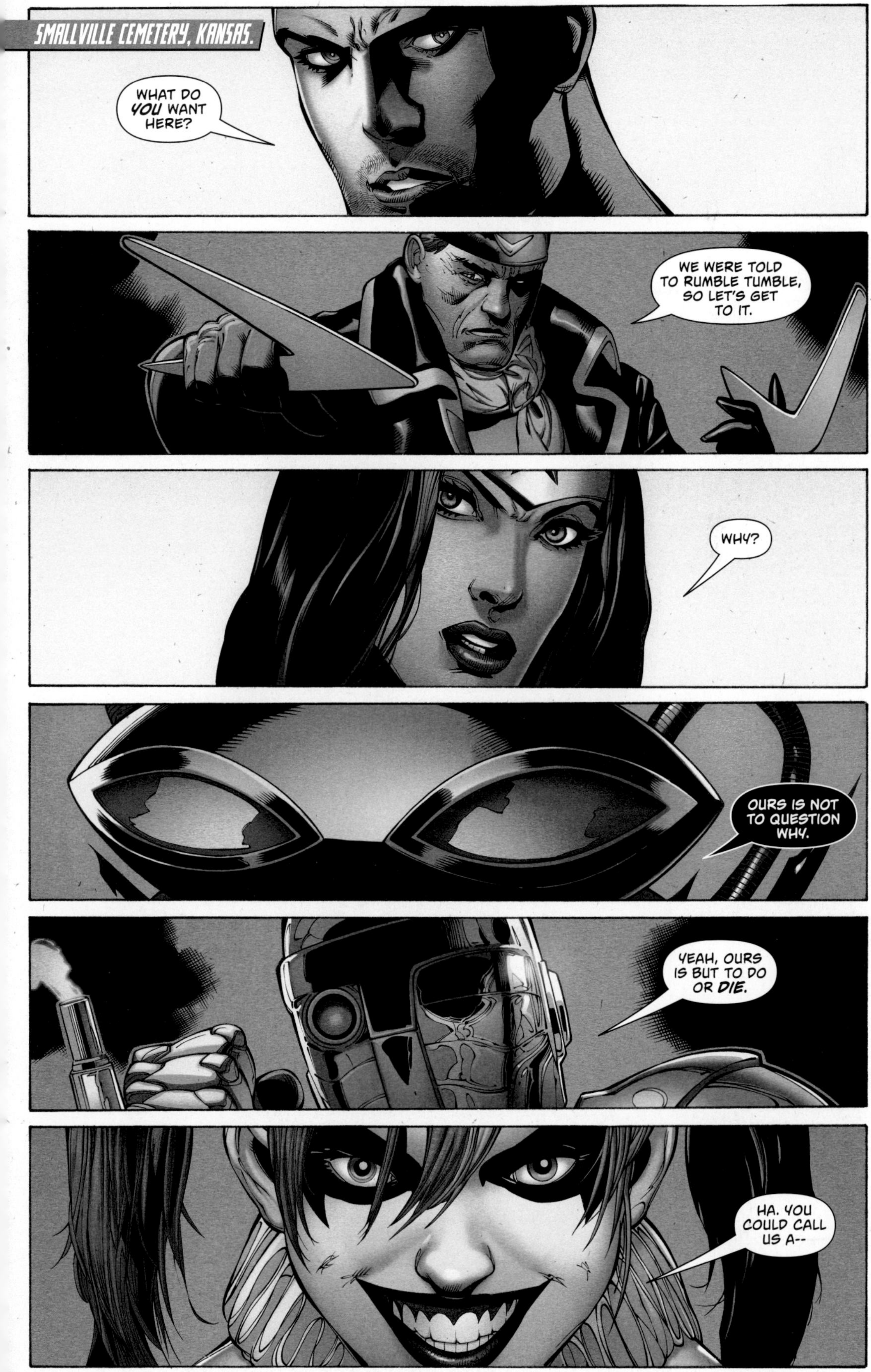
SMALLVILLE CEMETERY, KANSAS.
WHAT DO YOU WANT HERE?
WE WERE TOLD TO RUMBLE TUMBLE, SO LET'S GET TO IT.
WHY?
OURS IS NOT TO QUESTION WHY.
YEAH, OURS IS BUT TO DO OR DIE.
HA. YOU COULD CALL US A--

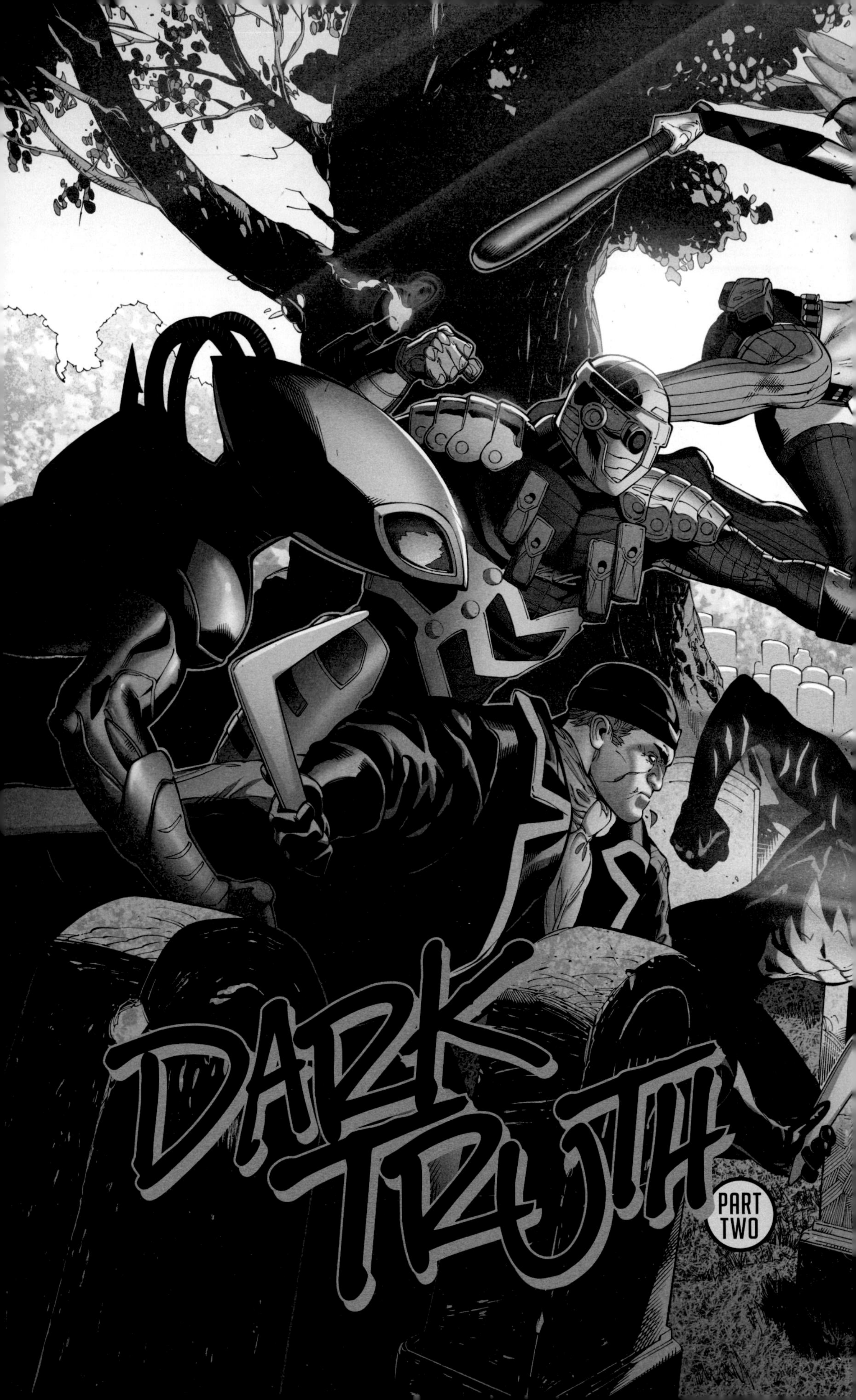
DARK TRUTH...
PART TWO

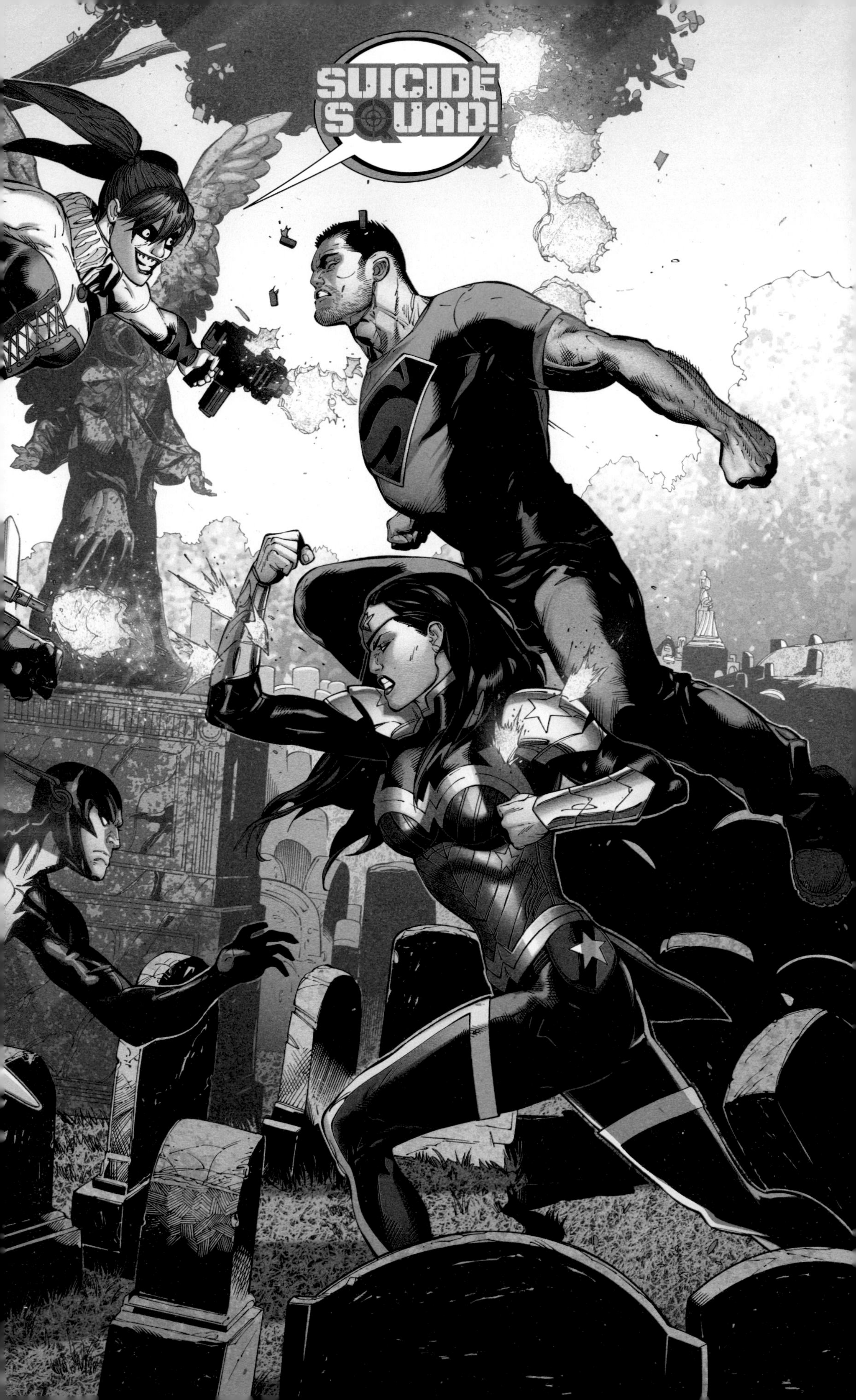
SUICIDE SQUAD!

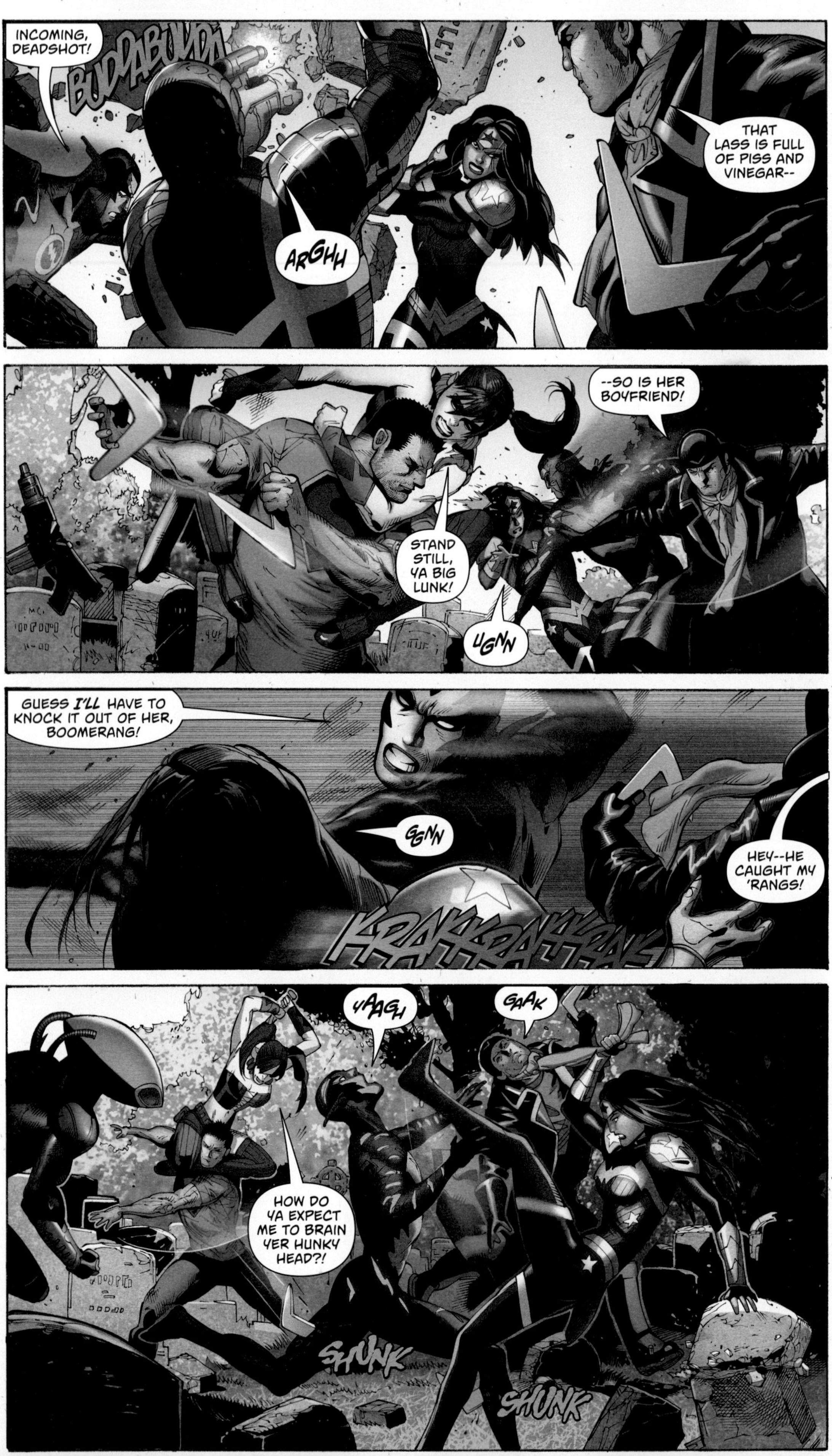
INCOMING, DEADSHOT!
BUDDABUDDA
ARGHH
THAT LASS IS FULL OF PISS AND VINEGAR--
--SO IS HER BOYFRIEND!
STAND STILL, YA BIG LUNK!
UGNN
GUESS I'LL HAVE TO KNOCK IT OUT OF HER, BOOMERANG!
GGNN
HEY--HE CAUGHT MY 'RANGS!
KRAKKRAKKRAKKRAK
YAAAGH
GAAK
HOW DO YA EXPECT ME TO BRAIN YER HUNKY HEAD?!
SHUNK
SHUNK

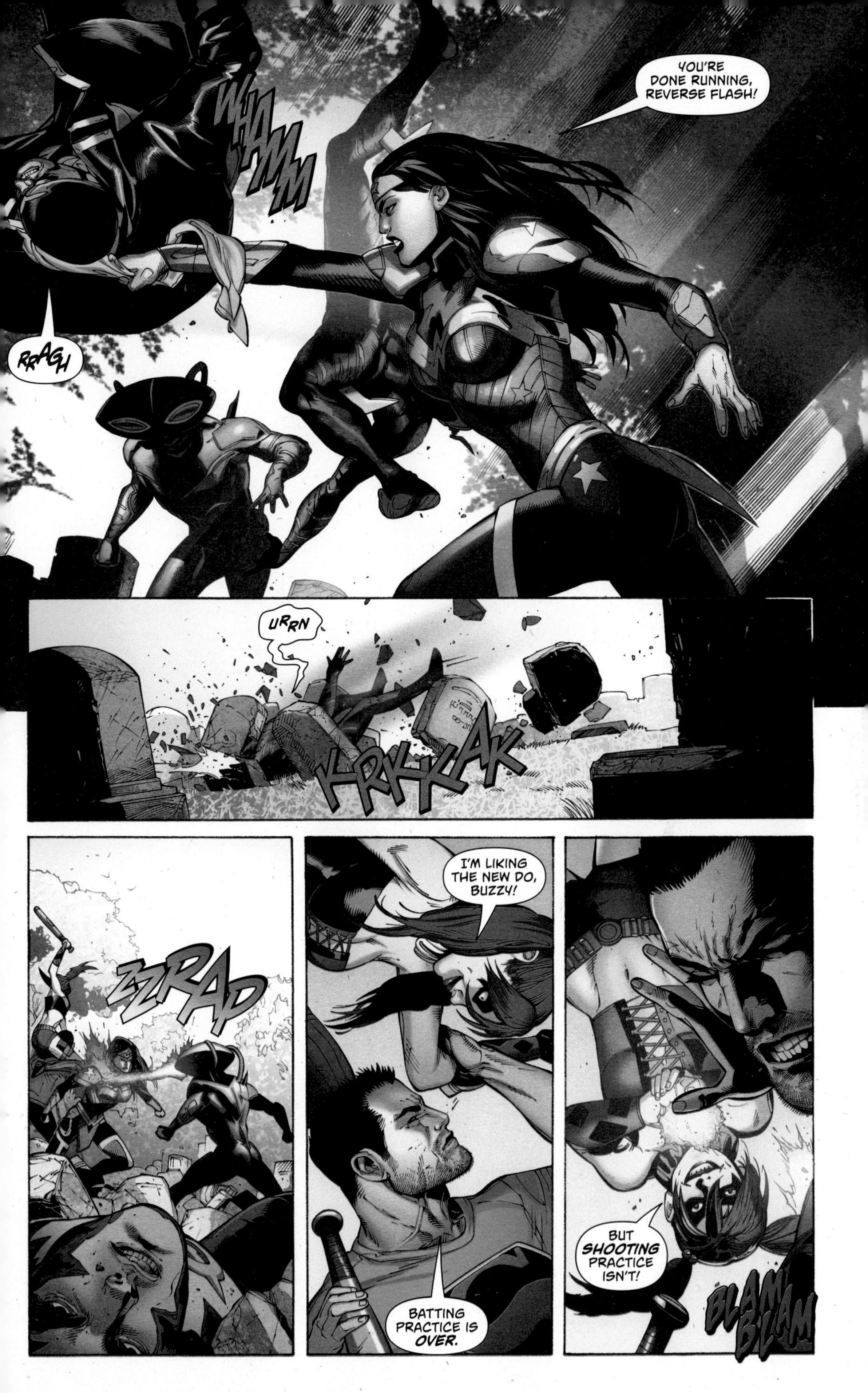

YOU'RE DONE RUNNING, REVERSE FLASH!
WHAMM
RRAGH
URRN
KRKKKAK
ZZRAP
I'M LIKING THE NEW DO, BUZZY!
BATTING PRACTICE IS OVER.
BUT SHOOTING PRACTICE ISN'T!
BLAM BLAM

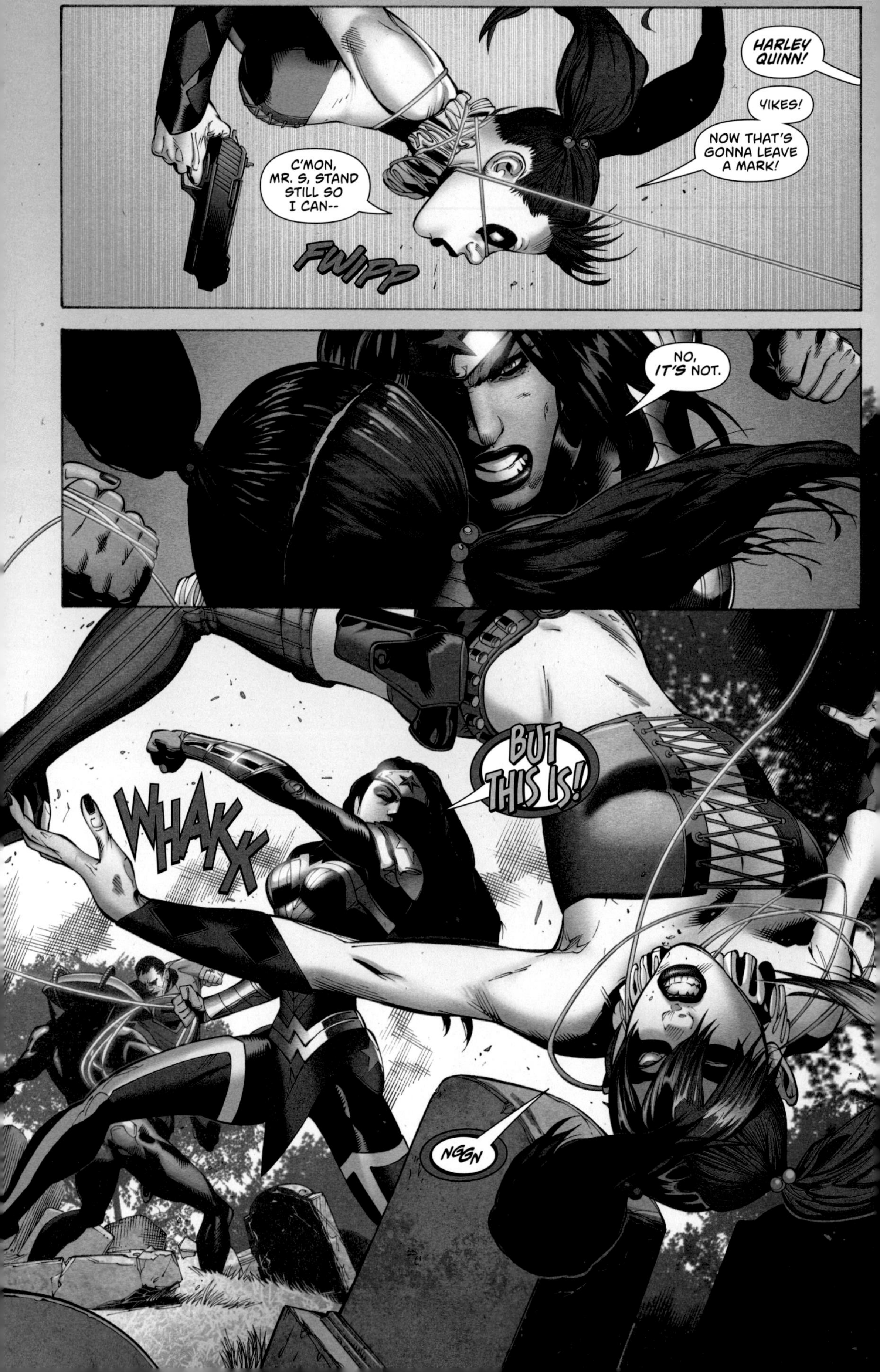
HARLEY QUINN!
YIKES!
NOW THAT'S GONNA LEAVE A MARK!
C'MON, MR. S, STAND STILL SO I CAN--
FWIPP
NO, IT'S NOT.
BUT THIS IS!
WHAKK
NGGN

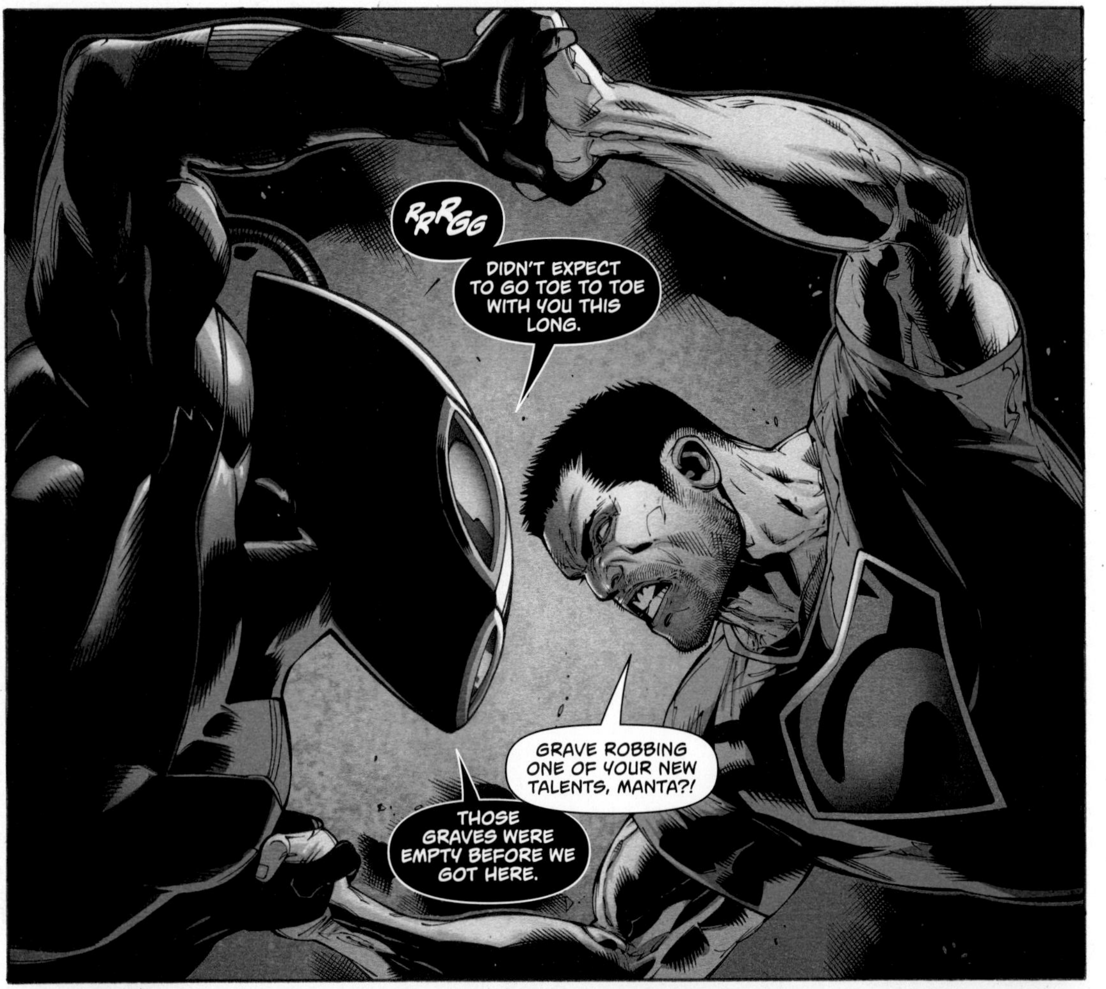
RRRGG
DIDN'T EXPECT TO GO TOE TO TOE WITH YOU THIS LONG.
GRAVE ROBBING ONE OF YOUR NEW TALENTS, MANTA?!
THOSE GRAVES WERE EMPTY BEFORE WE GOT HERE.

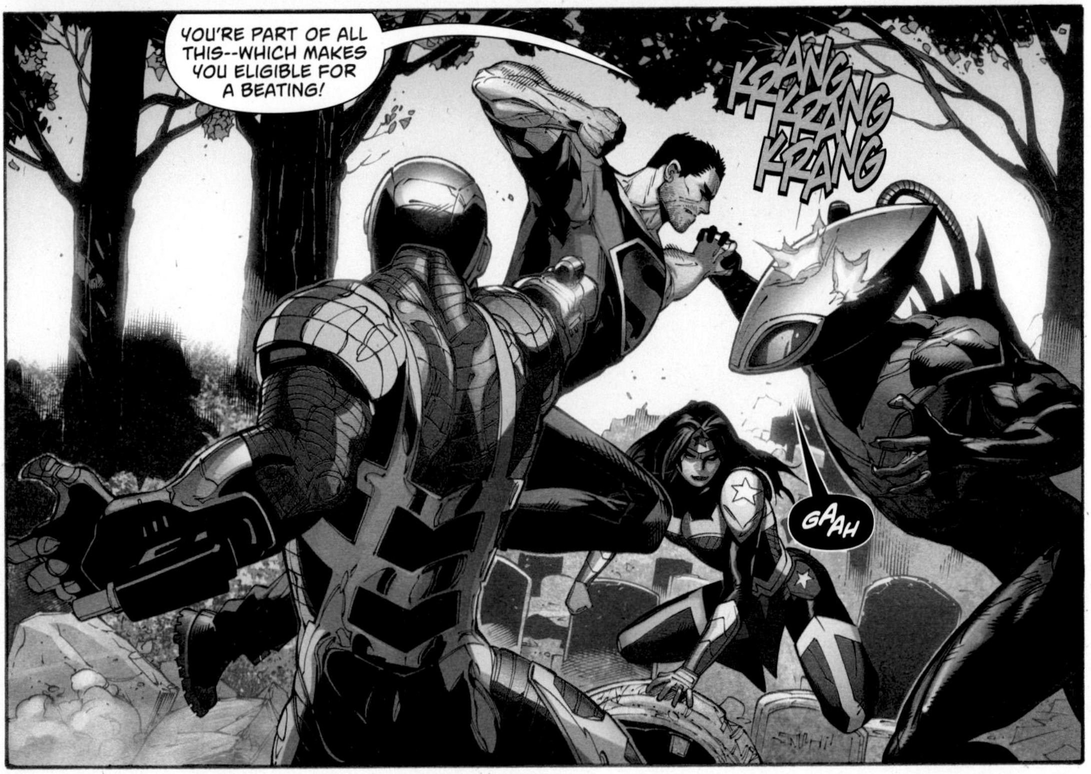
YOU'RE PART OF ALL THIS--WHICH MAKES YOU ELIGIBLE FOR A BEATING!
KRANG KRANG KRANG
GAAH

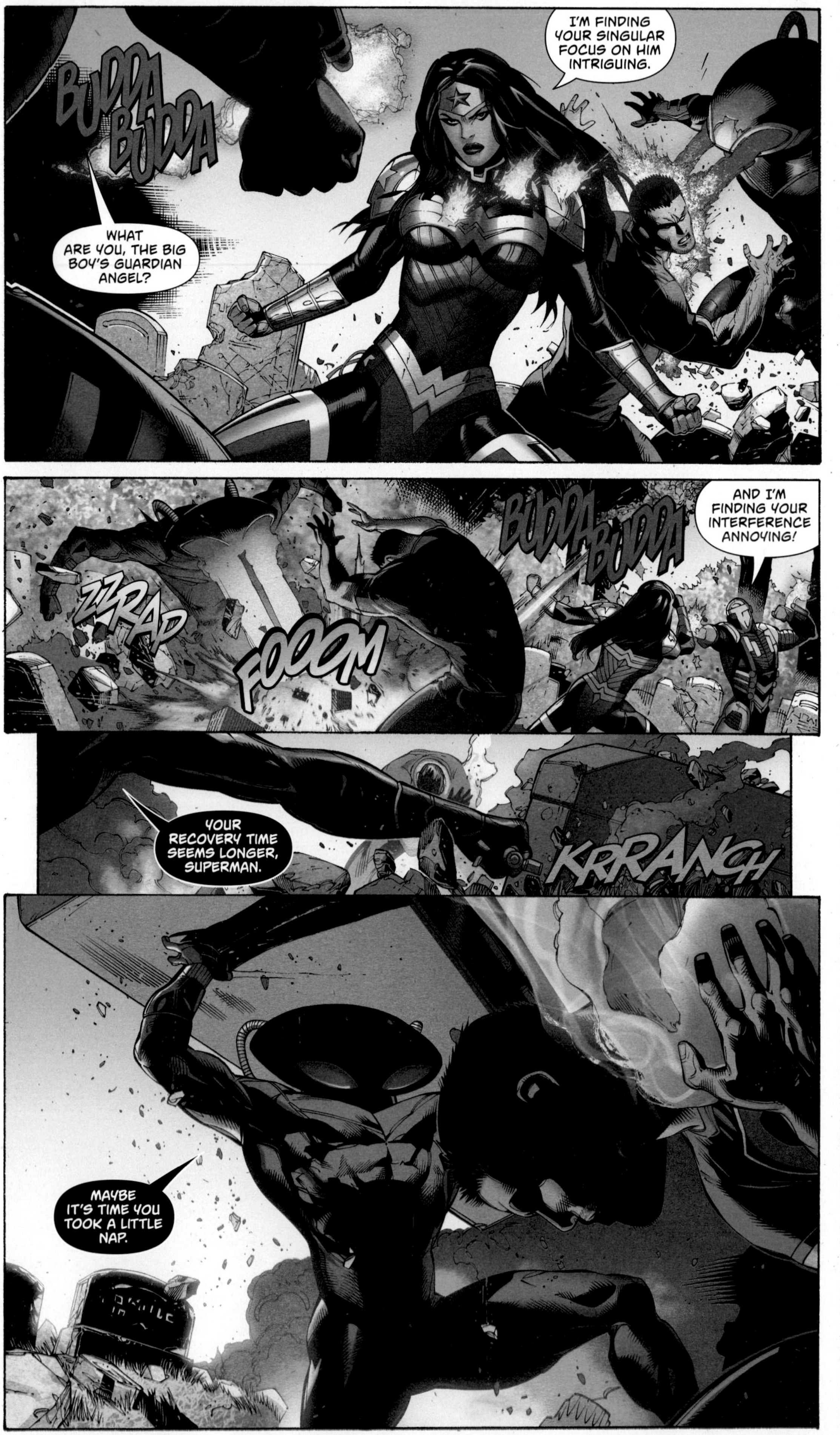
BUDDA BUDDA
I'M FINDING YOUR SINGULAR FOCUS ON HIM INTRIGUING.
WHAT ARE YOU, THE BIG BOY'S GUARDIAN ANGEL?
ZZZRAP
FOOOM
BUDDA BUDDA
AND I'M FINDING YOUR INTERFERENCE ANNOYING!
YOUR RECOVERY TIME SEEMS LONGER, SUPERMAN.
KRRANCH
MAYBE IT'S TIME YOU TOOK A LITTLE NAP.

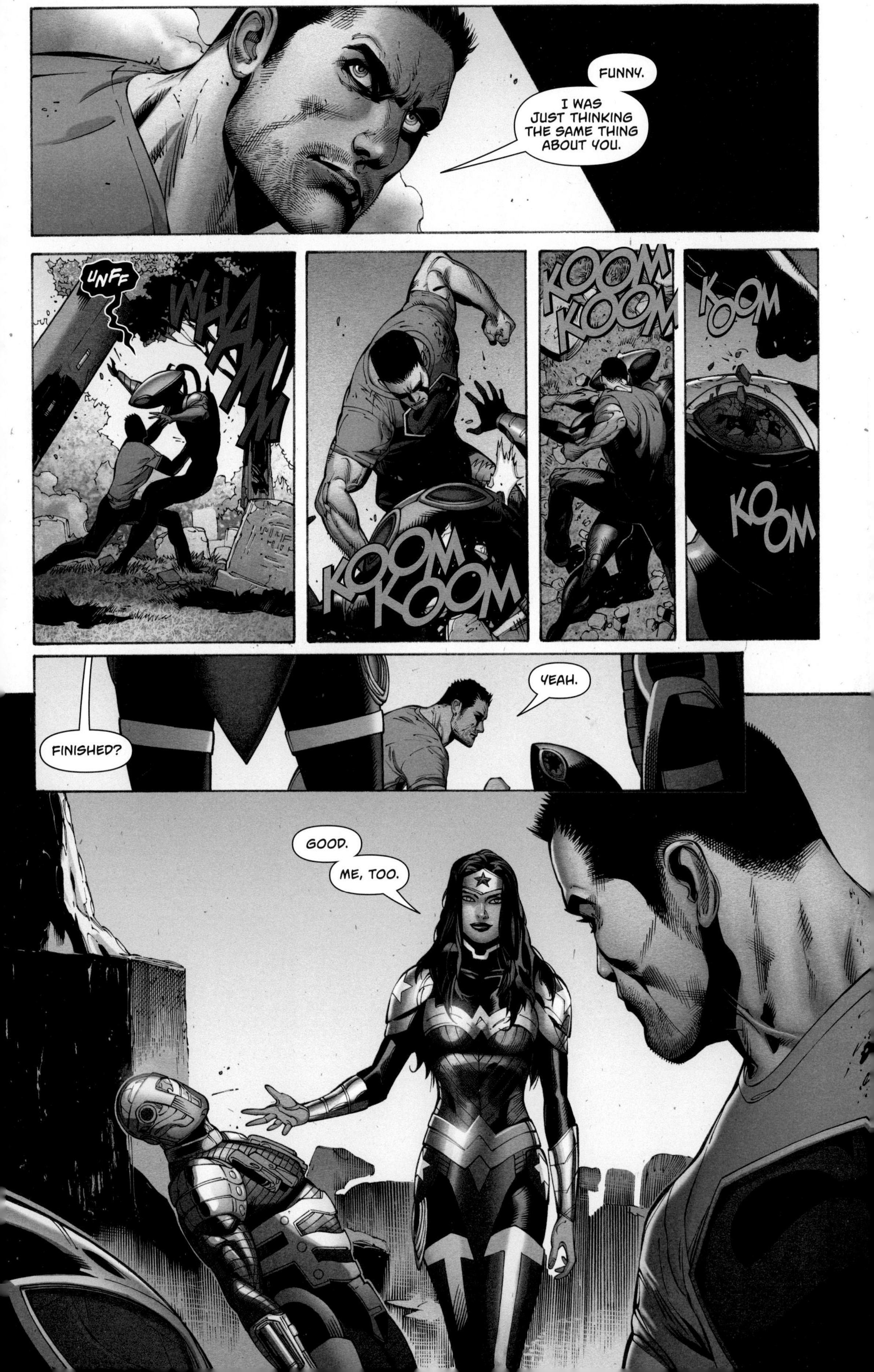
FUNNY.
I WAS JUST THINKING THE SAME THING ABOUT YOU.
UNFF
WHAM
KOOM KOOM
KOOM KOOM
KOOM
KOOM
FINISHED?
YEAH.
GOOD.
ME, TOO.

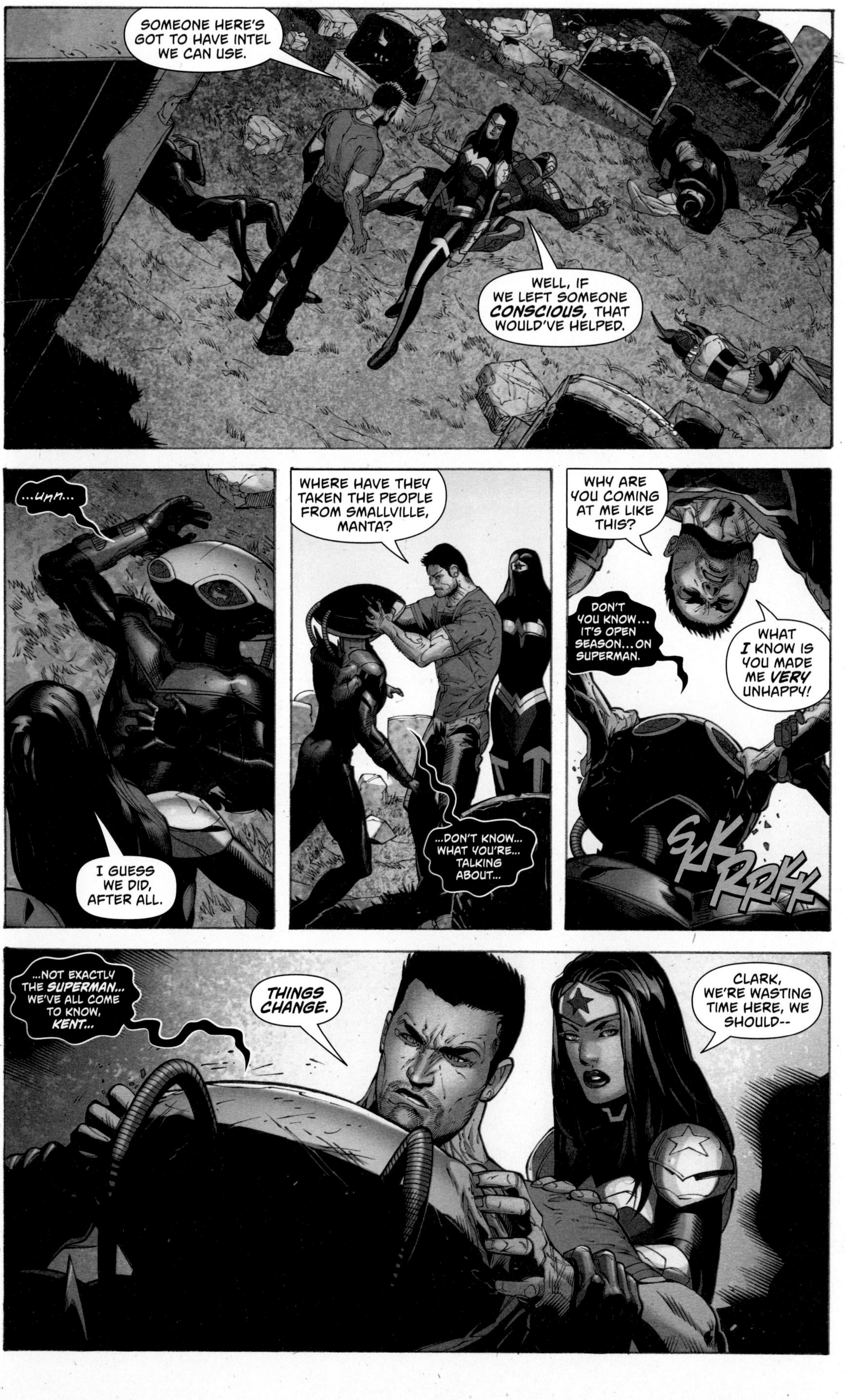
SOMEONE HERE'S GOT TO HAVE INTEL WE CAN USE.
WELL, IF WE LEFT SOMEONE CONSCIOUS, THAT WOULD'VE HELPED.
...unn...
I GUESS WE DID, AFTER ALL.
WHERE HAVE THEY TAKEN THE PEOPLE FROM SMALLVILLE, MANTA?
...DON'T KNOW... WHAT YOU'RE... TALKING ABOUT...
WHY ARE YOU COMING AT ME LIKE THIS?
DON'T YOU KNOW... IT'S OPEN SEASON... ON SUPERMAN.
WHAT I KNOW IS YOU MADE ME VERY UNHAPPY!
SKKRRKK
...NOT EXACTLY THE SUPERMAN... WE'VE ALL COME TO KNOW, KENT...
THINGS CHANGE.
CLARK, WE'RE WASTING TIME HERE, WE SHOULD--

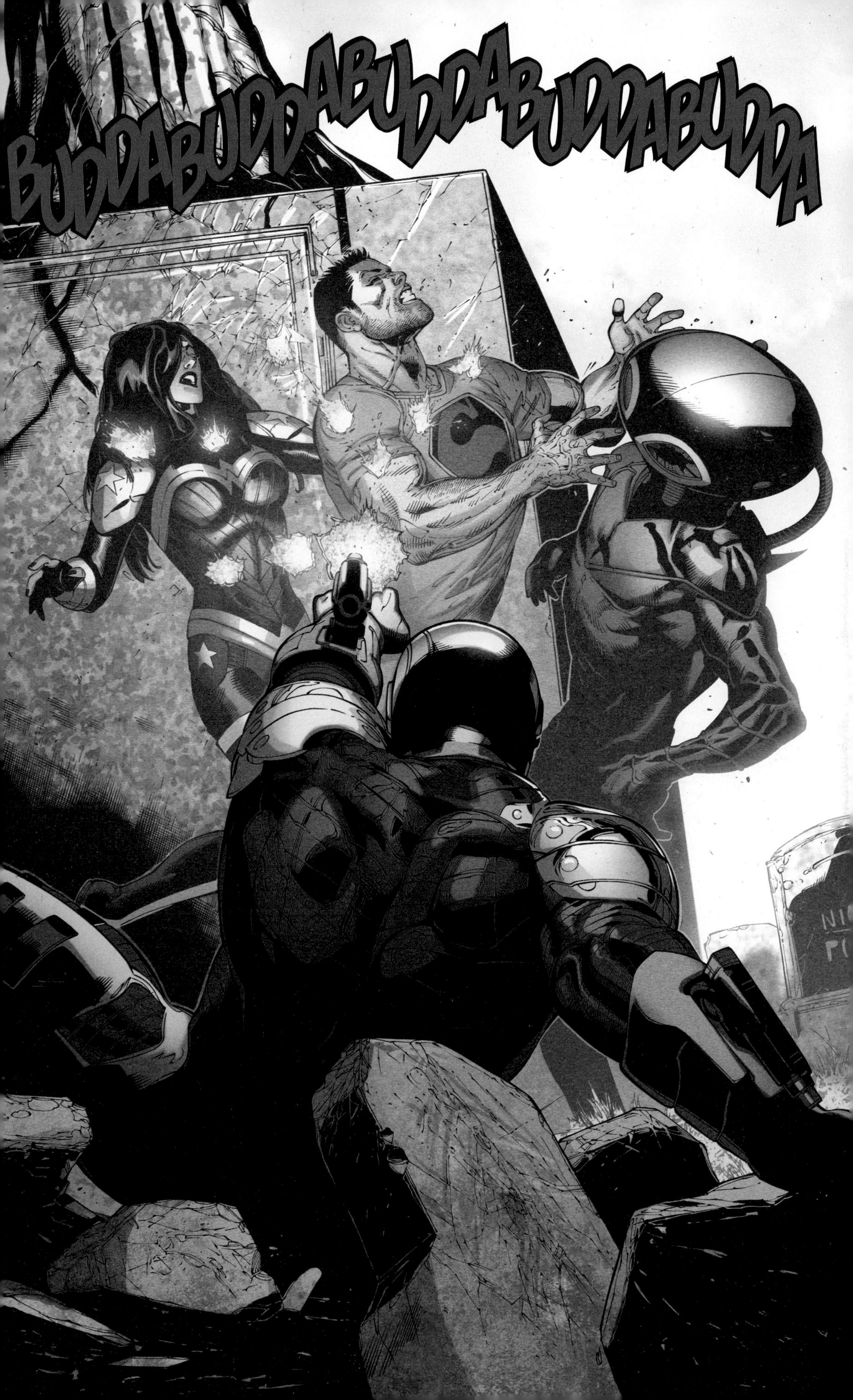
BUDDABUDDABUDDABUDDABUDDA

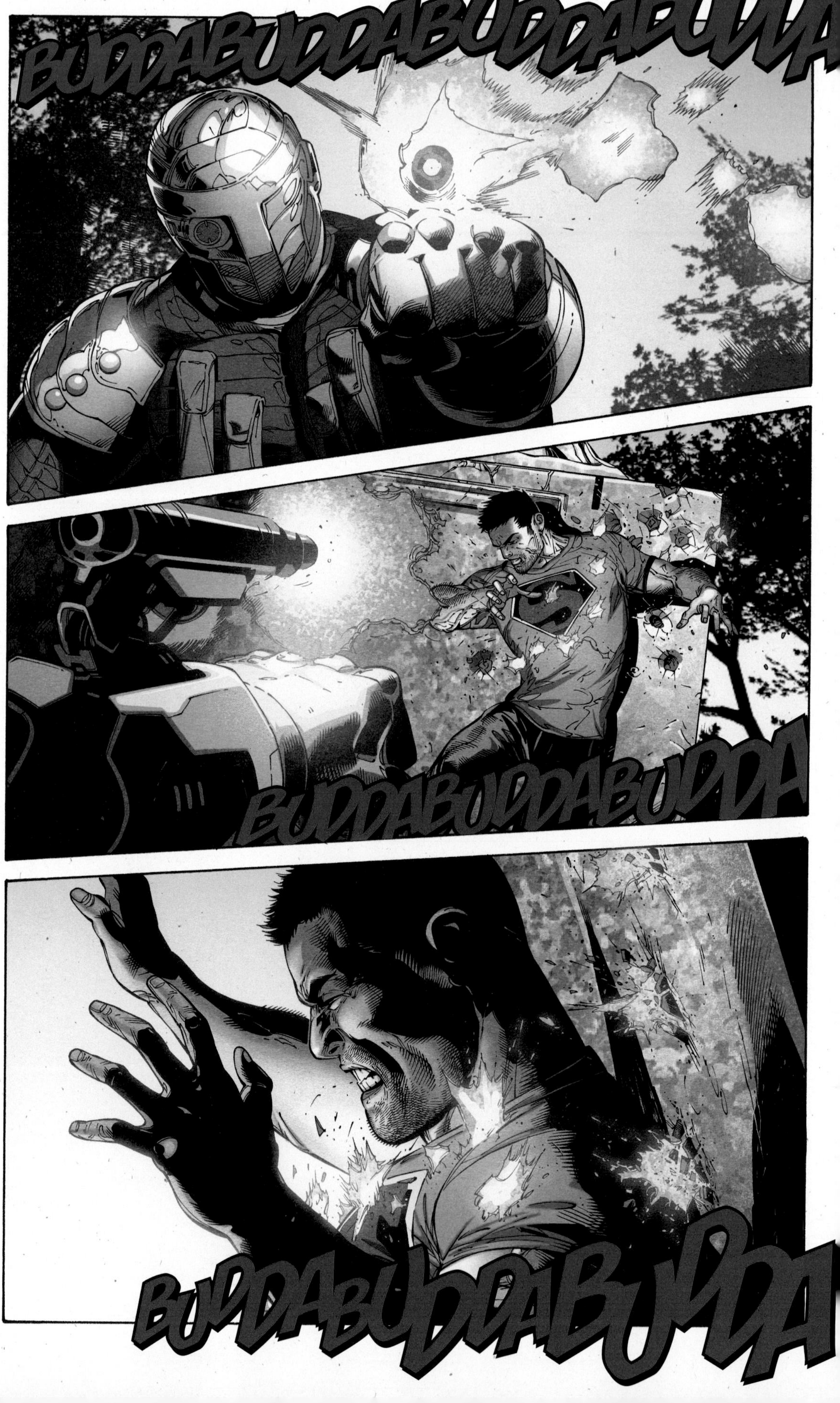
BUDDABUDDABUDDABUDDA
BUDDABUDDABUDDA
BUDDABUDDABUDDA

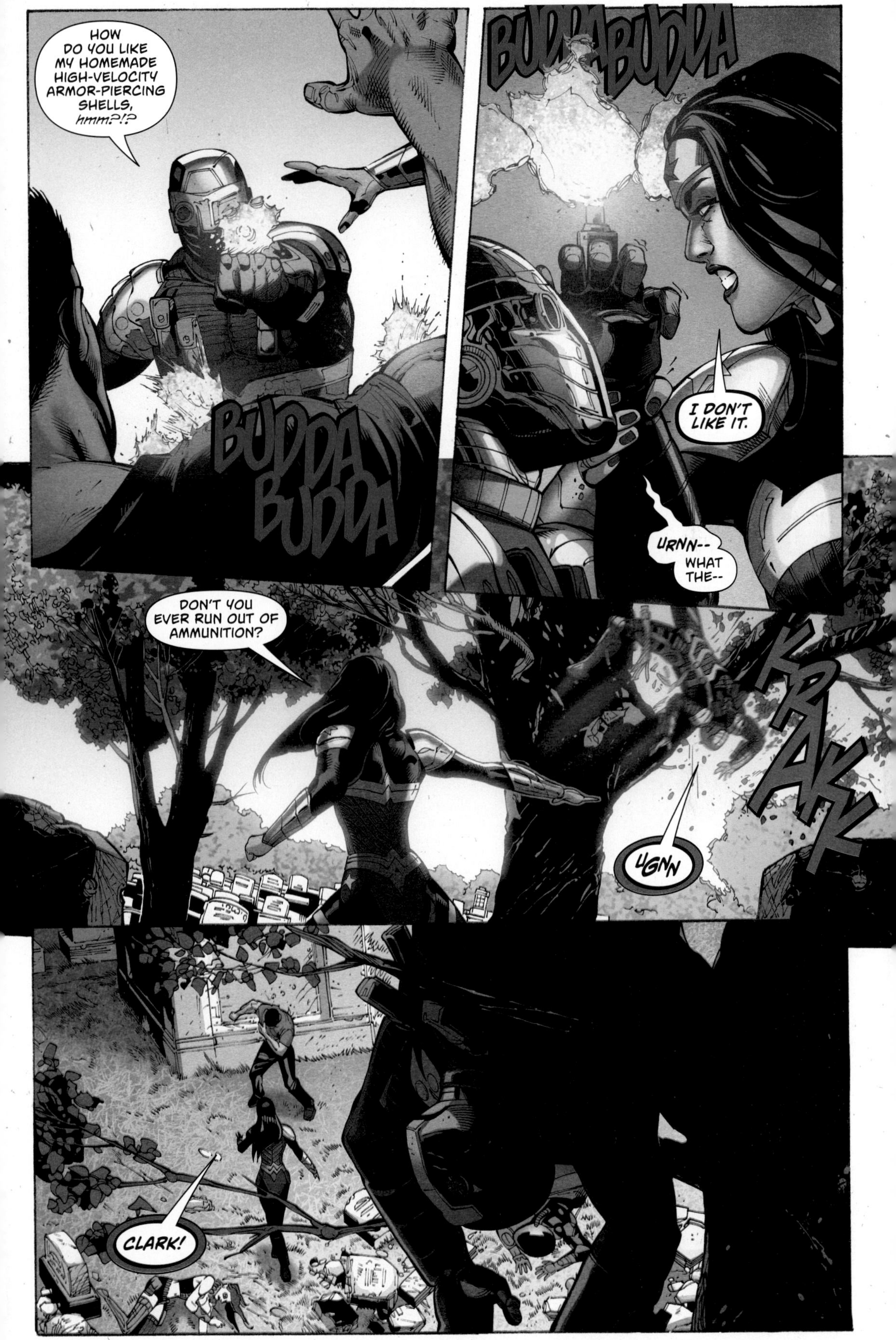
HOW DO YOU LIKE MY HOMEMADE HIGH-VELOCITY ARMOR-PIERCING SHELLS, *hmm?!?*
BUDDA BUDDA
BUDDABUDDA
I DON'T LIKE IT.
URNN-- WHAT THE--
DON'T YOU EVER RUN OUT OF AMMUNITION?
KRAKK
UGNN
CLARK!

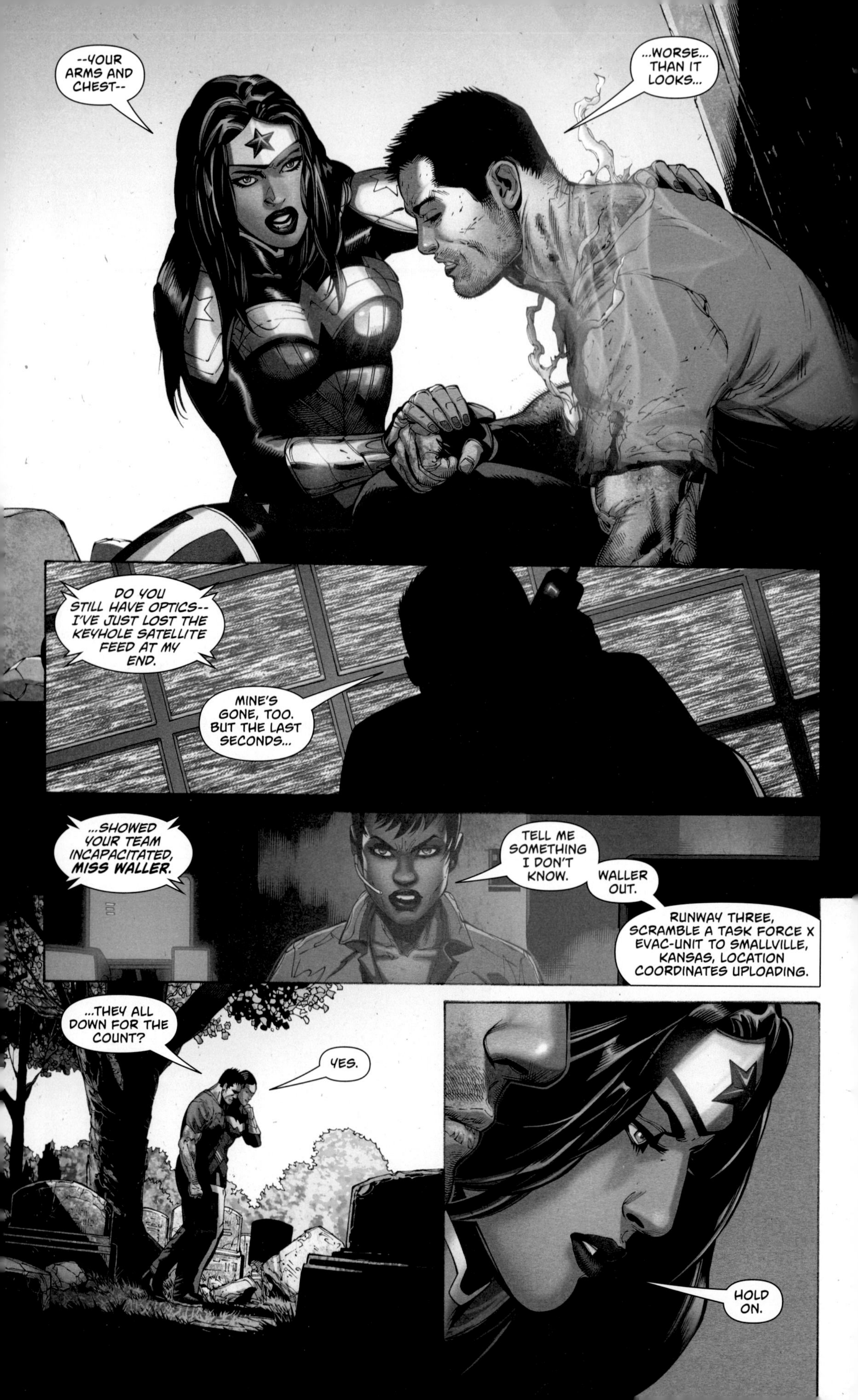
--YOUR ARMS AND CHEST--
...WORSE... THAN IT LOOKS...
DO YOU STILL HAVE OPTICS-- I'VE JUST LOST THE KEYHOLE SATELLITE FEED AT MY END.
MINE'S GONE, TOO. BUT THE LAST SECONDS...
...SHOWED YOUR TEAM INCAPACITATED, **MISS WALLER**.
TELL ME SOMETHING I DON'T KNOW.
WALLER OUT.
RUNWAY THREE, SCRAMBLE A TASK FORCE X EVAC-UNIT TO SMALLVILLE, KANSAS, LOCATION COORDINATES UPLOADING.
...THEY ALL DOWN FOR THE COUNT?
YES.
HOLD ON.

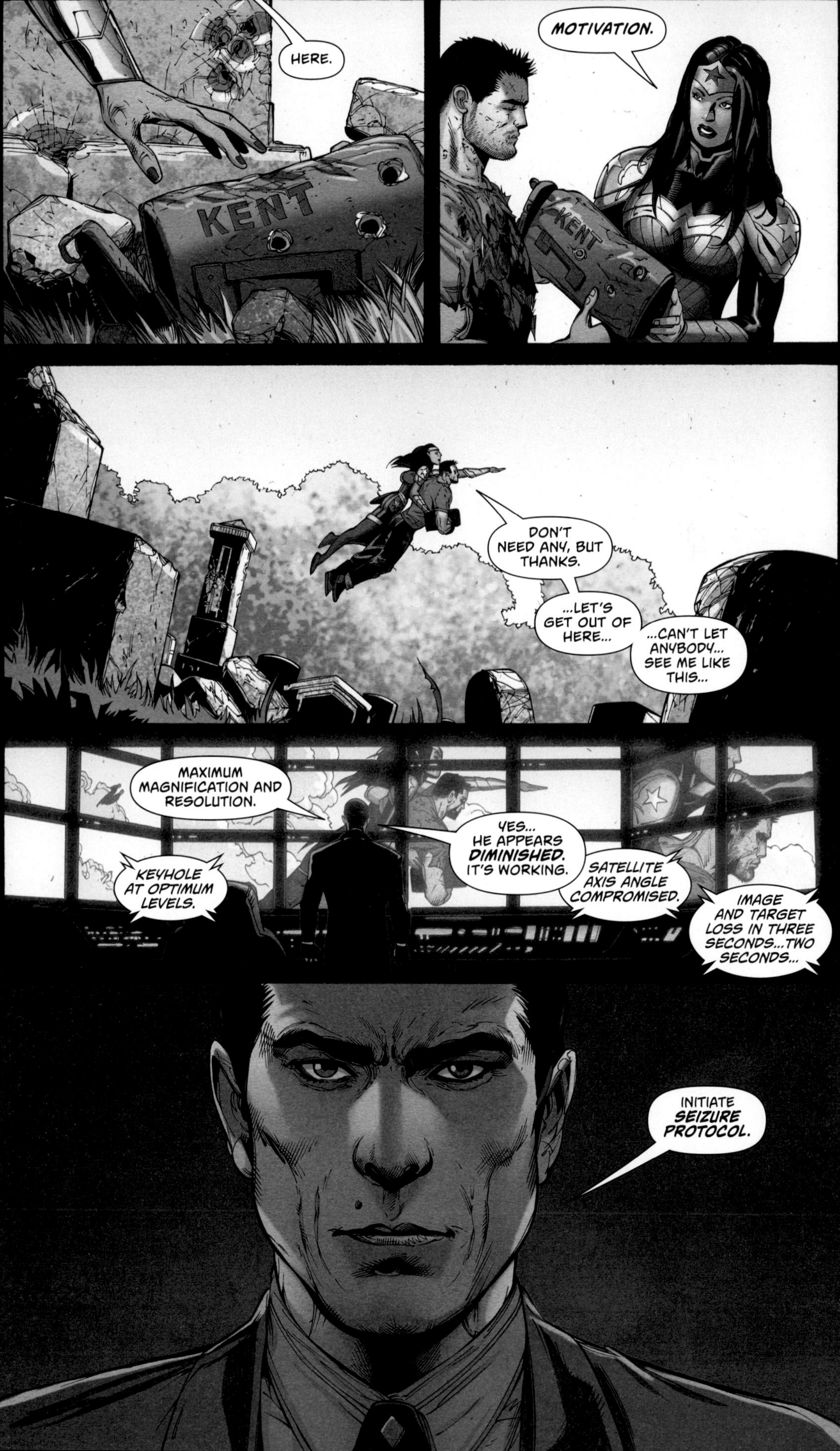
HERE.
MOTIVATION.
DON'T NEED ANY, BUT THANKS.
...LET'S GET OUT OF HERE...
...CAN'T LET ANYBODY... SEE ME LIKE THIS...
MAXIMUM MAGNIFICATION AND RESOLUTION.
YES... HE APPEARS DIMINISHED. IT'S WORKING.
KEYHOLE AT OPTIMUM LEVELS.
SATELLITE AXIS ANGLE COMPROMISED.
IMAGE AND TARGET LOSS IN THREE SECONDS...TWO SECONDS...
INITIATE SEIZURE PROTOCOL.

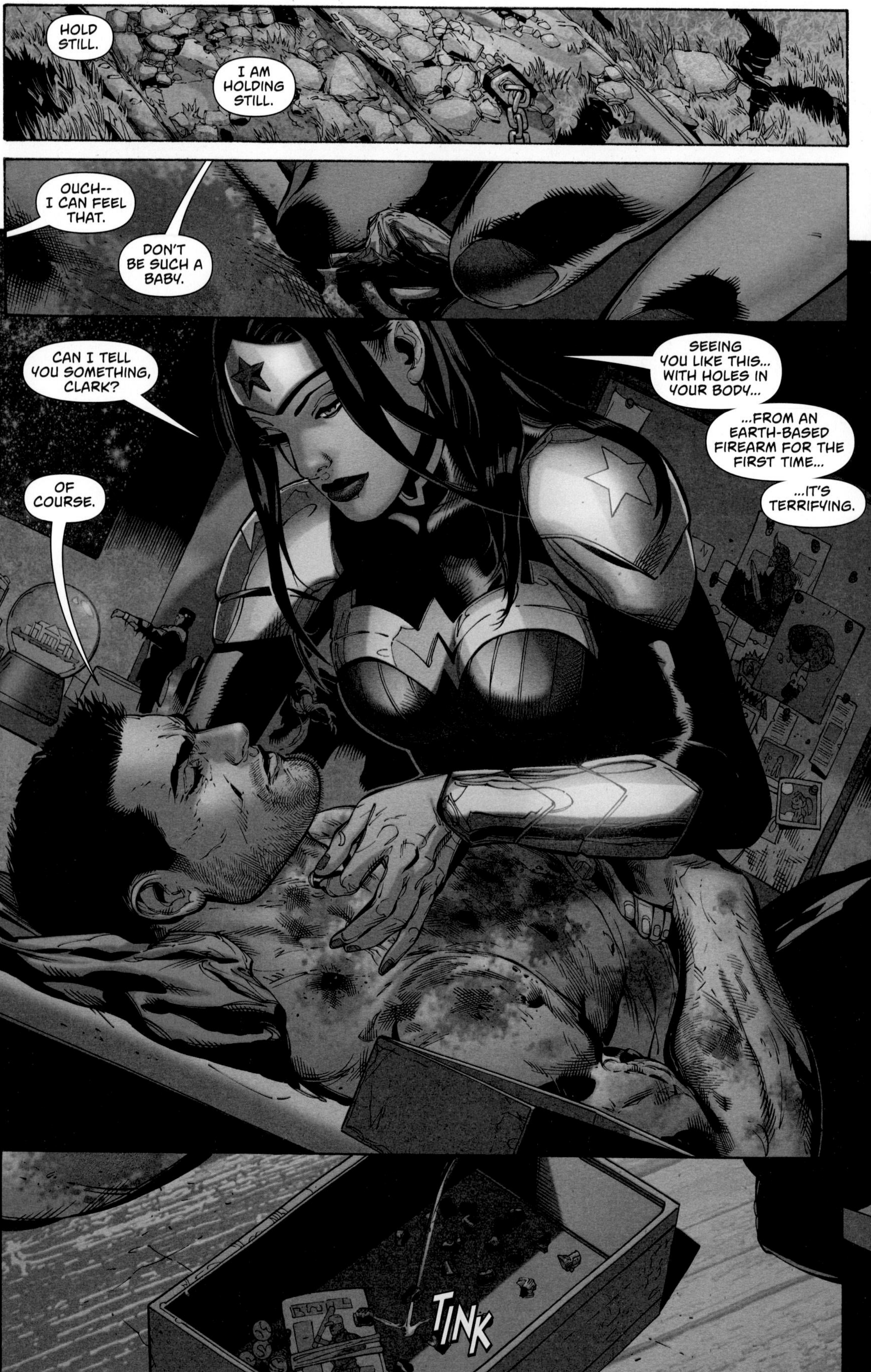
HOLD STILL.
I AM HOLDING STILL.
OUCH-- I CAN FEEL THAT.
DON'T BE SUCH A BABY.
CAN I TELL YOU SOMETHING, CLARK?
OF COURSE.
SEEING YOU LIKE THIS... WITH HOLES IN YOUR BODY...
...FROM AN EARTH-BASED FIREARM FOR THE FIRST TIME...
...IT'S TERRIFYING.
TINK

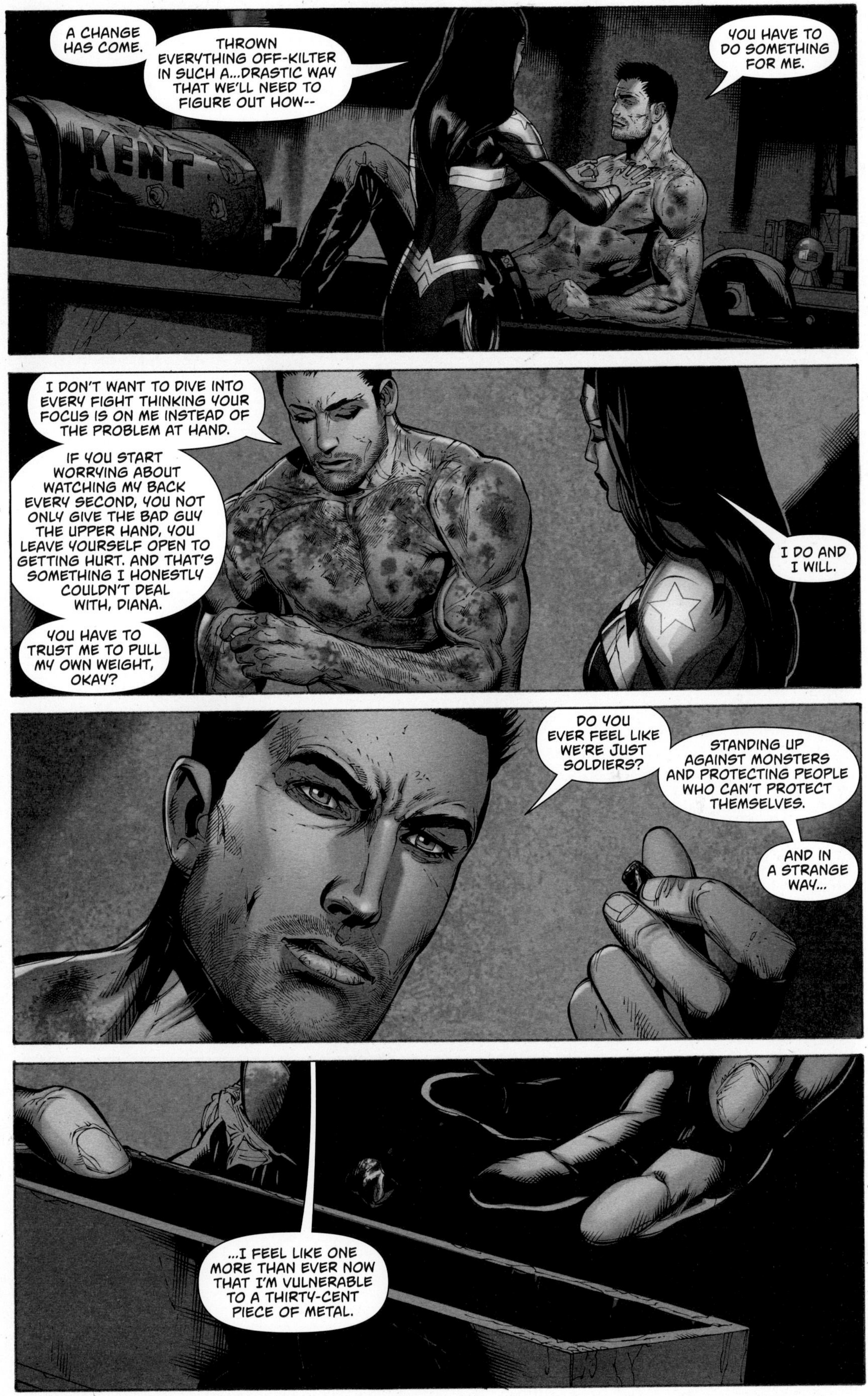
A CHANGE HAS COME.
THROWN EVERYTHING OFF-KILTER IN SUCH A...DRASTIC WAY THAT WE'LL NEED TO FIGURE OUT HOW--
YOU HAVE TO DO SOMETHING FOR ME.
KENT
I DON'T WANT TO DIVE INTO EVERY FIGHT THINKING YOUR FOCUS IS ON ME INSTEAD OF THE PROBLEM AT HAND.
IF YOU START WORRYING ABOUT WATCHING MY BACK EVERY SECOND, YOU NOT ONLY GIVE THE BAD GUY THE UPPER HAND, YOU LEAVE YOURSELF OPEN TO GETTING HURT. AND THAT'S SOMETHING I HONESTLY COULDN'T DEAL WITH, DIANA.
YOU HAVE TO TRUST ME TO PULL MY OWN WEIGHT, OKAY?
I DO AND I WILL.
DO YOU EVER FEEL LIKE WE'RE JUST SOLDIERS?
STANDING UP AGAINST MONSTERS AND PROTECTING PEOPLE WHO CAN'T PROTECT THEMSELVES.
AND IN A STRANGE WAY...
...I FEEL LIKE ONE MORE THAN EVER NOW THAT I'M VULNERABLE TO A THIRTY-CENT PIECE OF METAL.

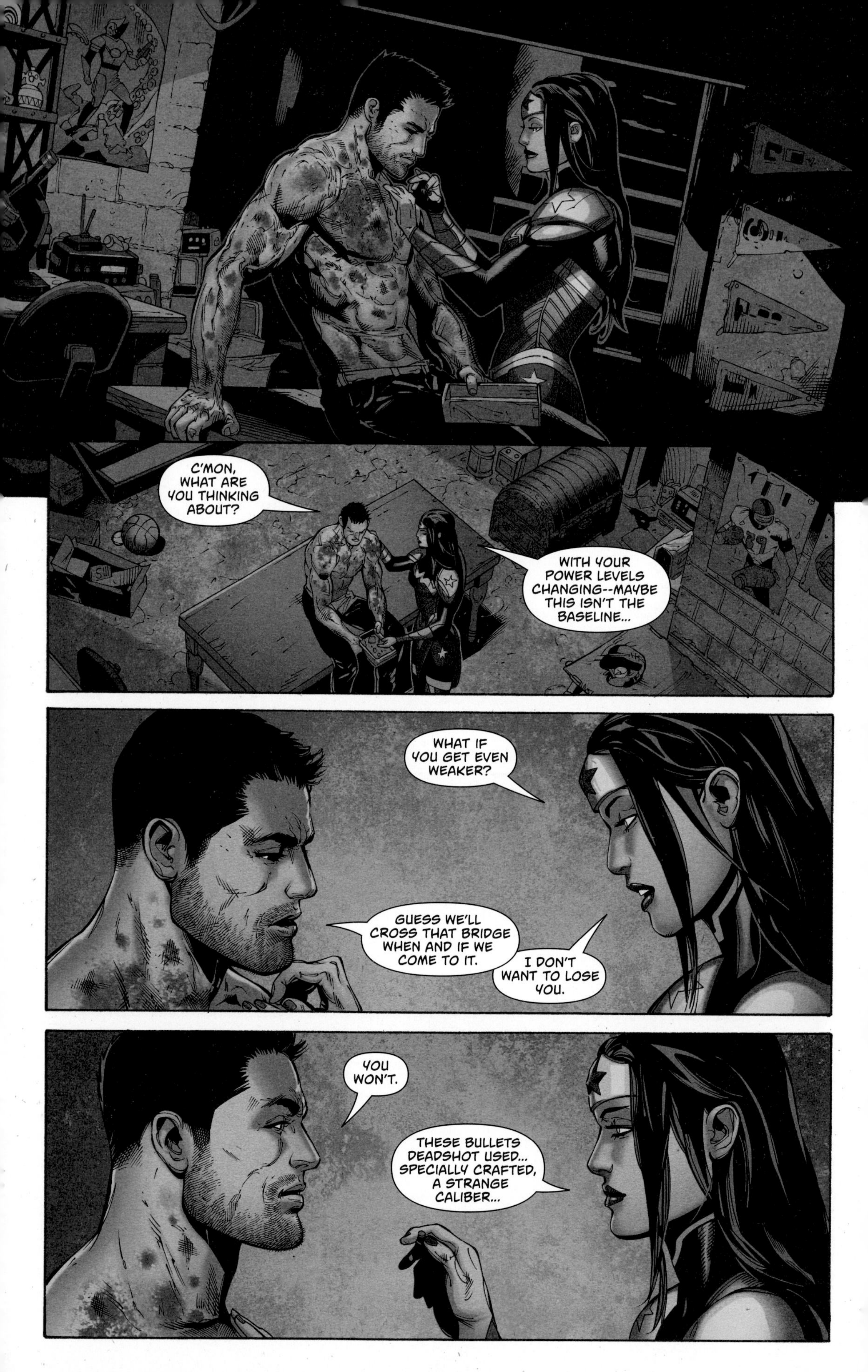

C'MON, WHAT ARE YOU THINKING ABOUT?
WITH YOUR POWER LEVELS CHANGING--MAYBE THIS ISN'T THE BASELINE...
WHAT IF YOU GET EVEN WEAKER?
GUESS WE'LL CROSS THAT BRIDGE WHEN AND IF WE COME TO IT.
I DON'T WANT TO LOSE YOU.
YOU WON'T.
THESE BULLETS DEADSHOT USED... SPECIALLY CRAFTED, A STRANGE CALIBER...

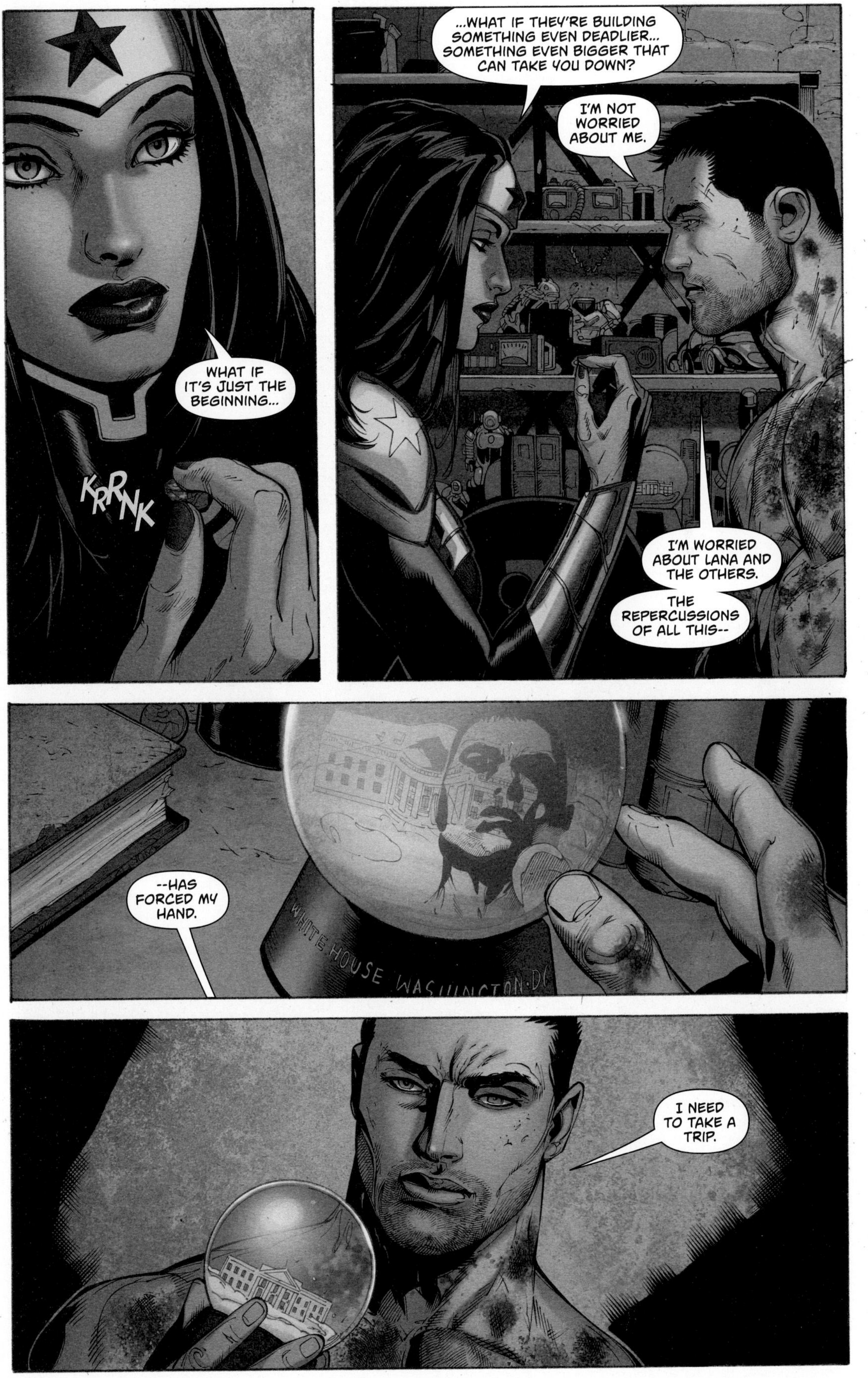
WHAT IF IT'S JUST THE BEGINNING...
KRRNK
...WHAT IF THEY'RE BUILDING SOMETHING EVEN DEADLIER... SOMETHING EVEN BIGGER THAT CAN TAKE YOU DOWN?
I'M NOT WORRIED ABOUT ME.
I'M WORRIED ABOUT LANA AND THE OTHERS.
THE REPERCUSSIONS OF ALL THIS--
--HAS FORCED MY HAND.
WHITE HOUSE WASHINGTON·DC
I NEED TO TAKE A TRIP.

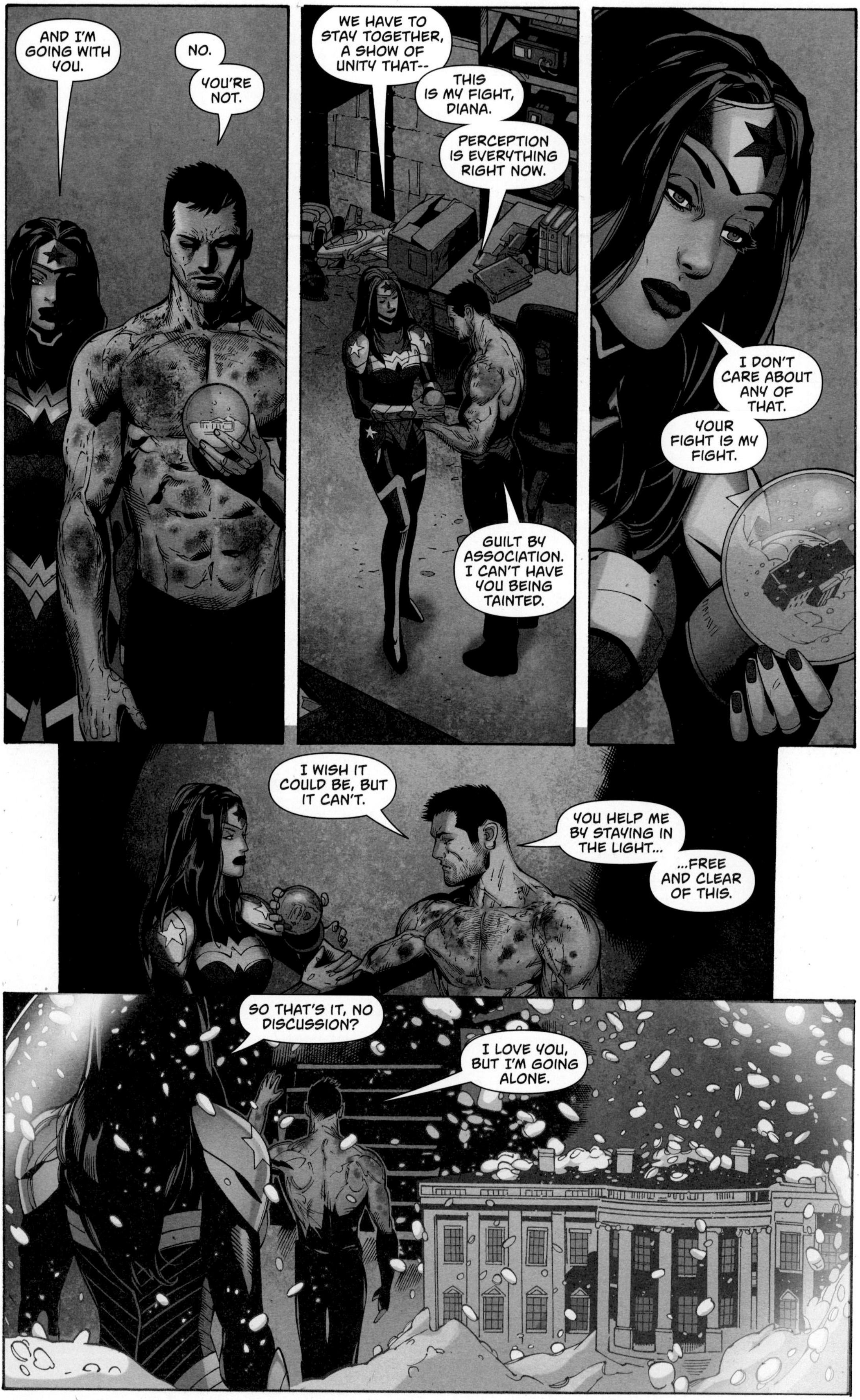
AND I'M GOING WITH YOU.
NO.
YOU'RE NOT.
WE HAVE TO STAY TOGETHER, A SHOW OF UNITY THAT--
THIS IS MY FIGHT, DIANA.
PERCEPTION IS EVERYTHING RIGHT NOW.
GUILT BY ASSOCIATION. I CAN'T HAVE YOU BEING TAINTED.
I DON'T CARE ABOUT ANY OF THAT.
YOUR FIGHT IS MY FIGHT.
I WISH IT COULD BE, BUT IT CAN'T.
YOU HELP ME BY STAYING IN THE LIGHT...
...FREE AND CLEAR OF THIS.
SO THAT'S IT, NO DISCUSSION?
I LOVE YOU, BUT I'M GOING ALONE.

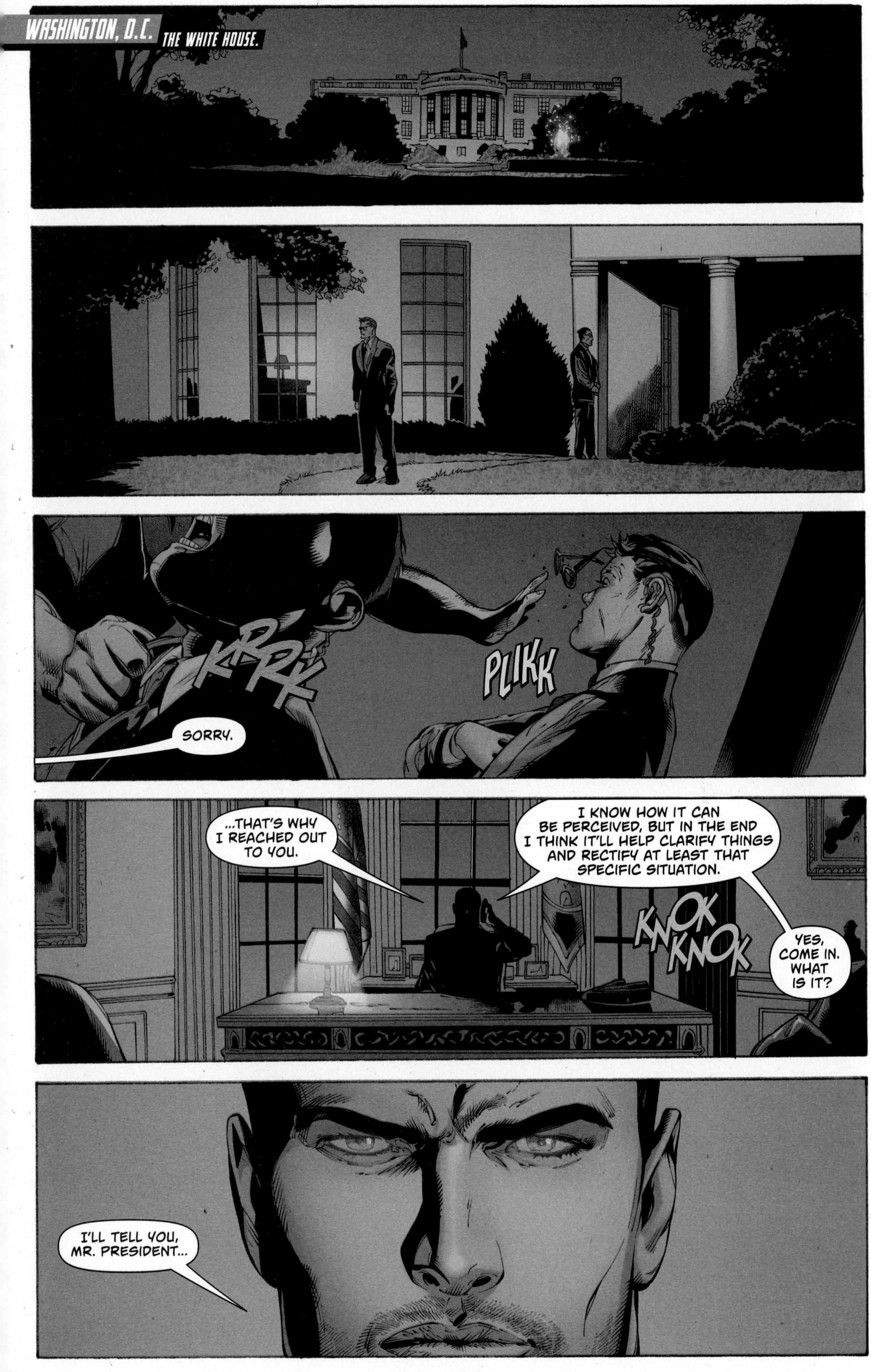

WASHINGTON, D.C.
THE WHITE HOUSE.
KRRK
PLIKK
SORRY.
...THAT'S WHY I REACHED OUT TO YOU.
I KNOW HOW IT CAN BE PERCEIVED, BUT IN THE END I THINK IT'LL HELP CLARIFY THINGS AND RECTIFY AT LEAST THAT SPECIFIC SITUATION.
KNOK KNOK
YES, COME IN. WHAT IS IT?
I'LL TELL YOU, MR. PRESIDENT...

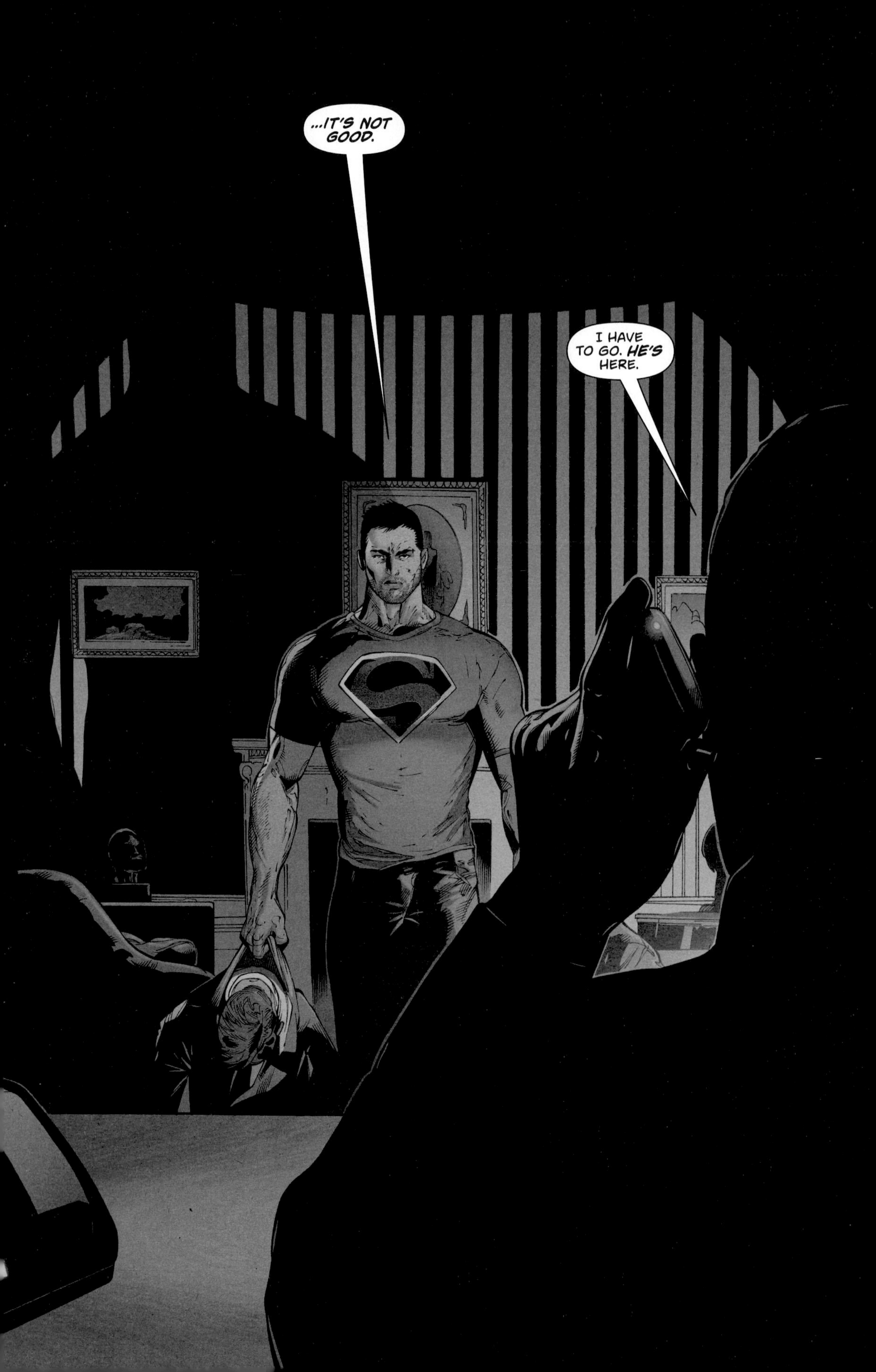
...IT'S NOT GOOD.
I HAVE TO GO. HE'S HERE.

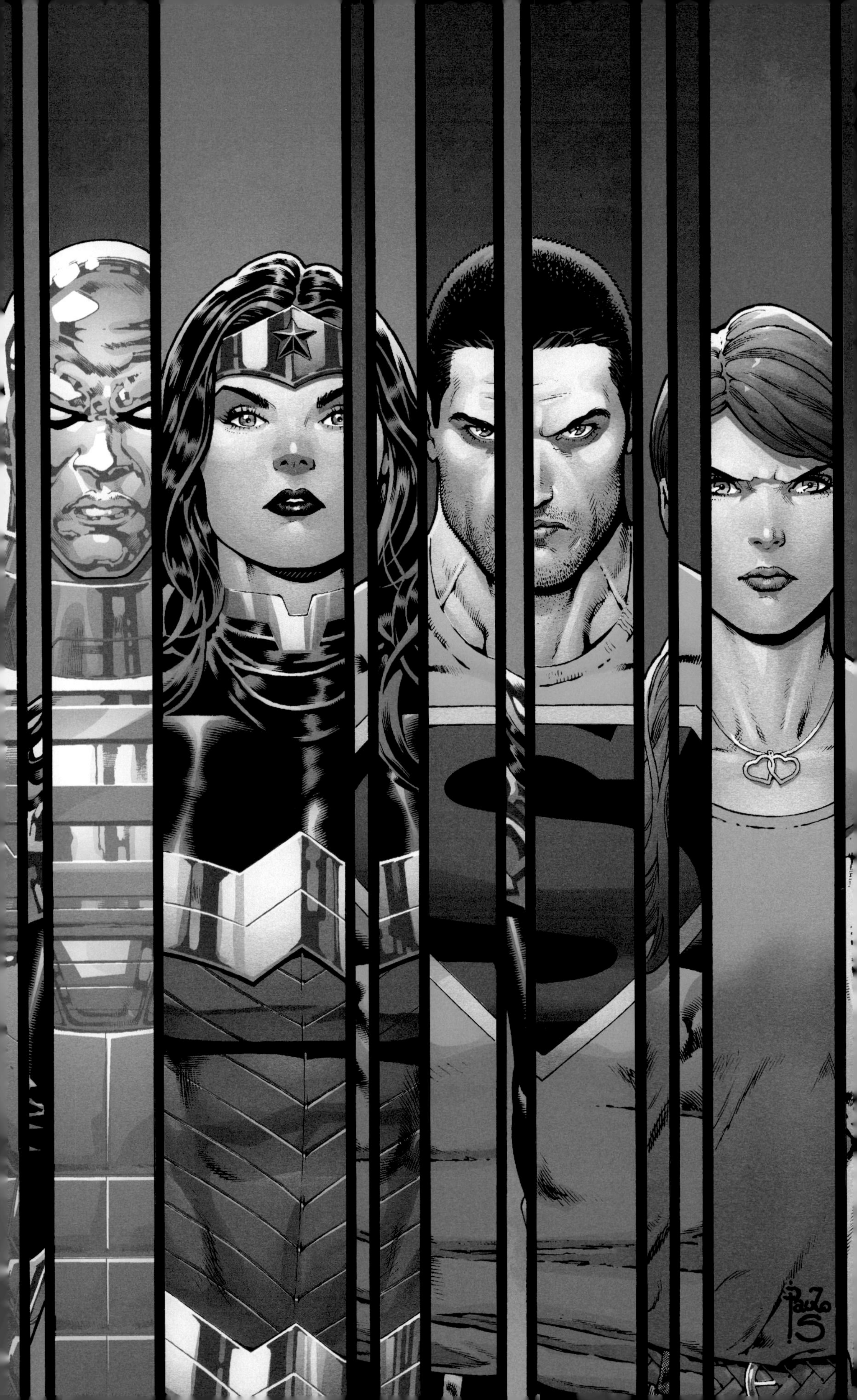

DARK TRUTH PART THREE

PETER J. TOMASI writer DOUG MAHNKE penciller JAIME MENDOZA SEAN PARSONS inkers WIL QUINTANA colorist
ROB LEIGH letterer cover by PAULO SIQUEIRA & HI-FI

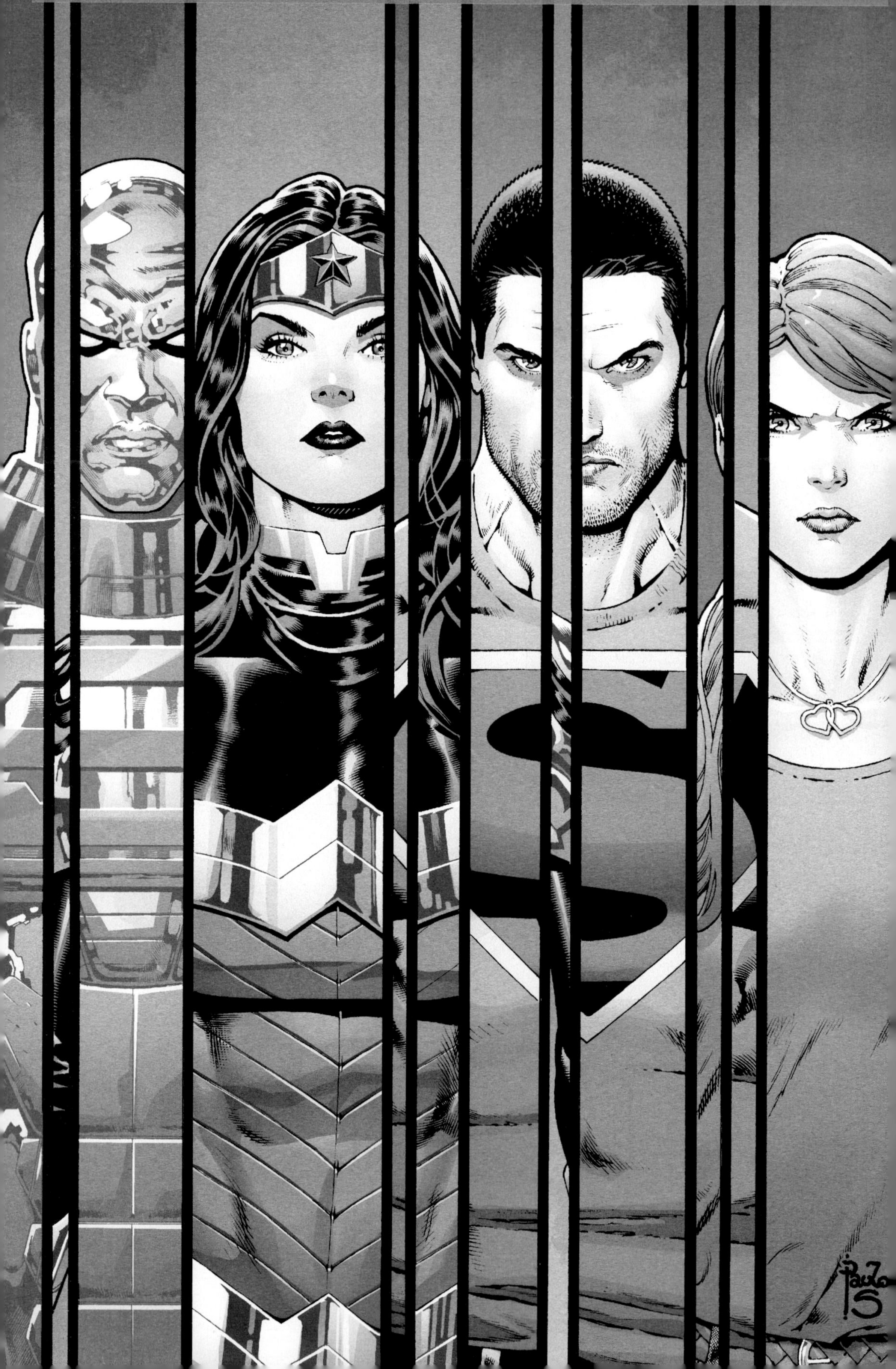

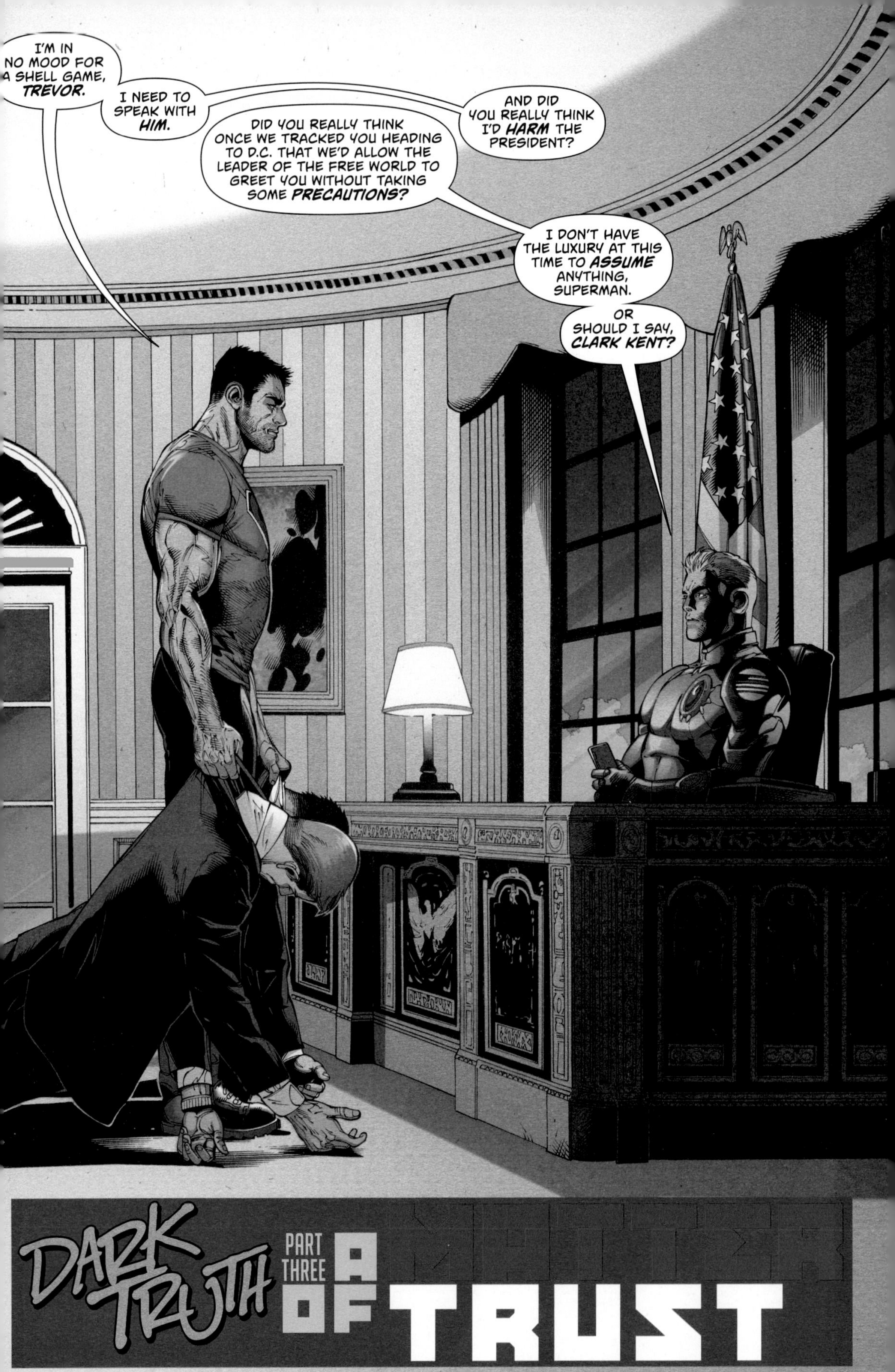
I'M IN NO MOOD FOR A SHELL GAME, TREVOR.
I NEED TO SPEAK WITH HIM.
DID YOU REALLY THINK ONCE WE TRACKED YOU HEADING TO D.C. THAT WE'D ALLOW THE LEADER OF THE FREE WORLD TO GREET YOU WITHOUT TAKING SOME PRECAUTIONS?
AND DID YOU REALLY THINK I'D HARM THE PRESIDENT?
I DON'T HAVE THE LUXURY AT THIS TIME TO ASSUME ANYTHING, SUPERMAN.
OR SHOULD I SAY, CLARK KENT?
DARK TRUTH
PART THREE
A
OF TRUST

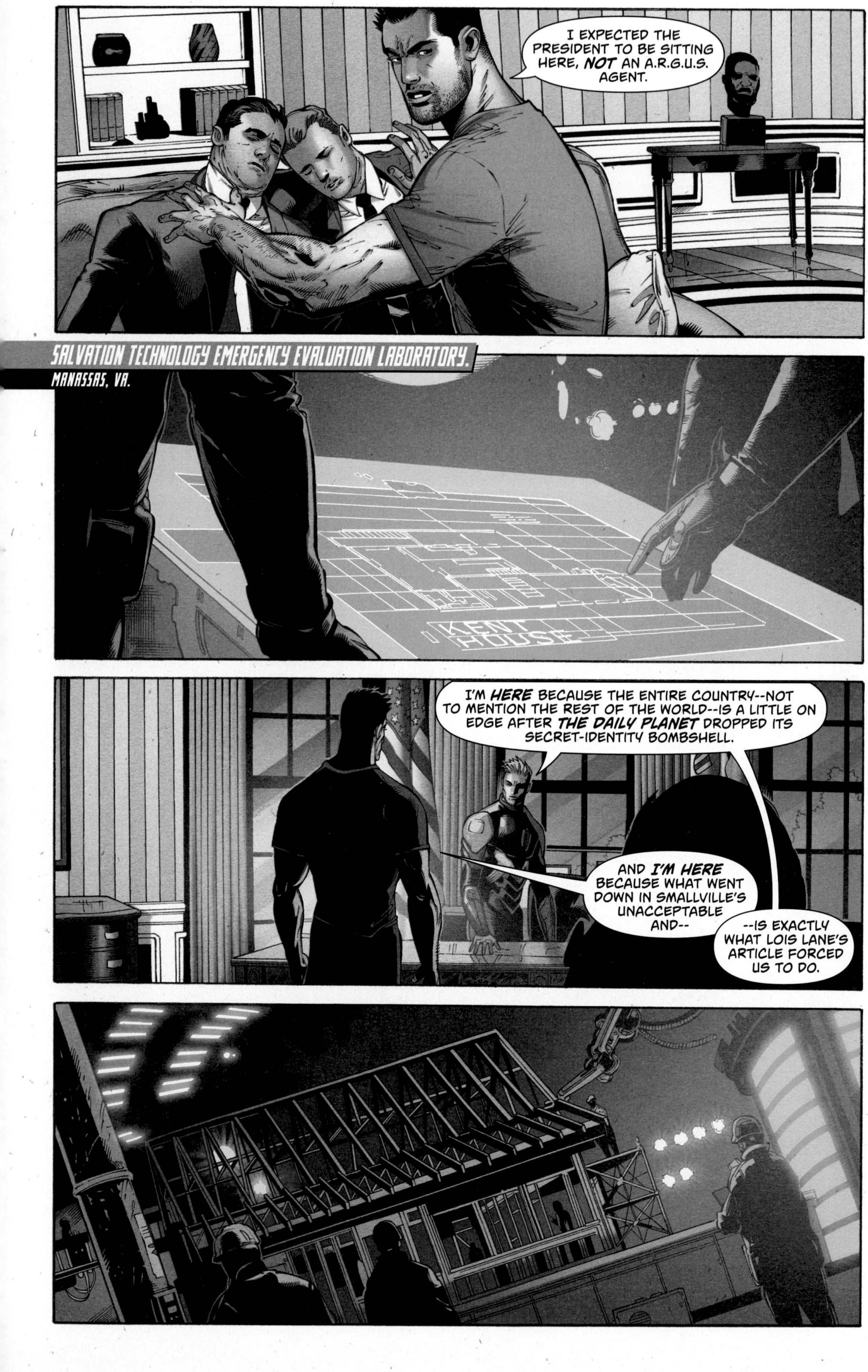

I EXPECTED THE PRESIDENT TO BE SITTING HERE, NOT AN A.R.G.U.S. AGENT.
SALVATION TECHNOLOGY EMERGENCY EVALUATION LABORATORY.
MANASSAS, VA.
KENT HOUSE
I'M HERE BECAUSE THE ENTIRE COUNTRY--NOT TO MENTION THE REST OF THE WORLD--IS A LITTLE ON EDGE AFTER THE DAILY PLANET DROPPED ITS SECRET-IDENTITY BOMBSHELL.
AND I'M HERE BECAUSE WHAT WENT DOWN IN SMALLVILLE'S UNACCEPTABLE AND--
--IS EXACTLY WHAT LOIS LANE'S ARTICLE FORCED US TO DO.

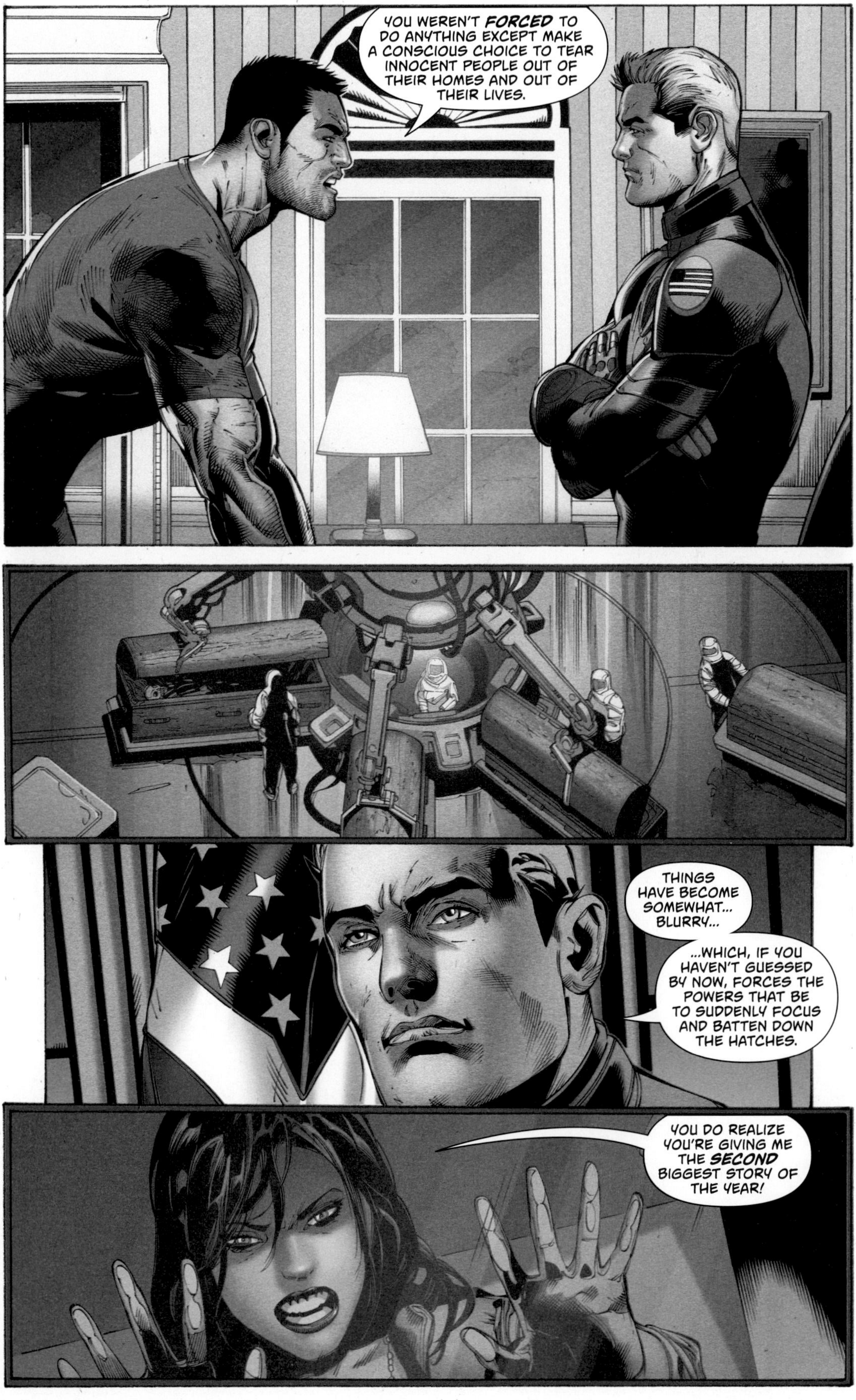
YOU WEREN'T FORCED TO DO ANYTHING EXCEPT MAKE A CONSCIOUS CHOICE TO TEAR INNOCENT PEOPLE OUT OF THEIR HOMES AND OUT OF THEIR LIVES.
THINGS HAVE BECOME SOMEWHAT... BLURRY...
...WHICH, IF YOU HAVEN'T GUESSED BY NOW, FORCES THE POWERS THAT BE TO SUDDENLY FOCUS AND BATTEN DOWN THE HATCHES.
YOU DO REALIZE YOU'RE GIVING ME THE SECOND BIGGEST STORY OF THE YEAR!

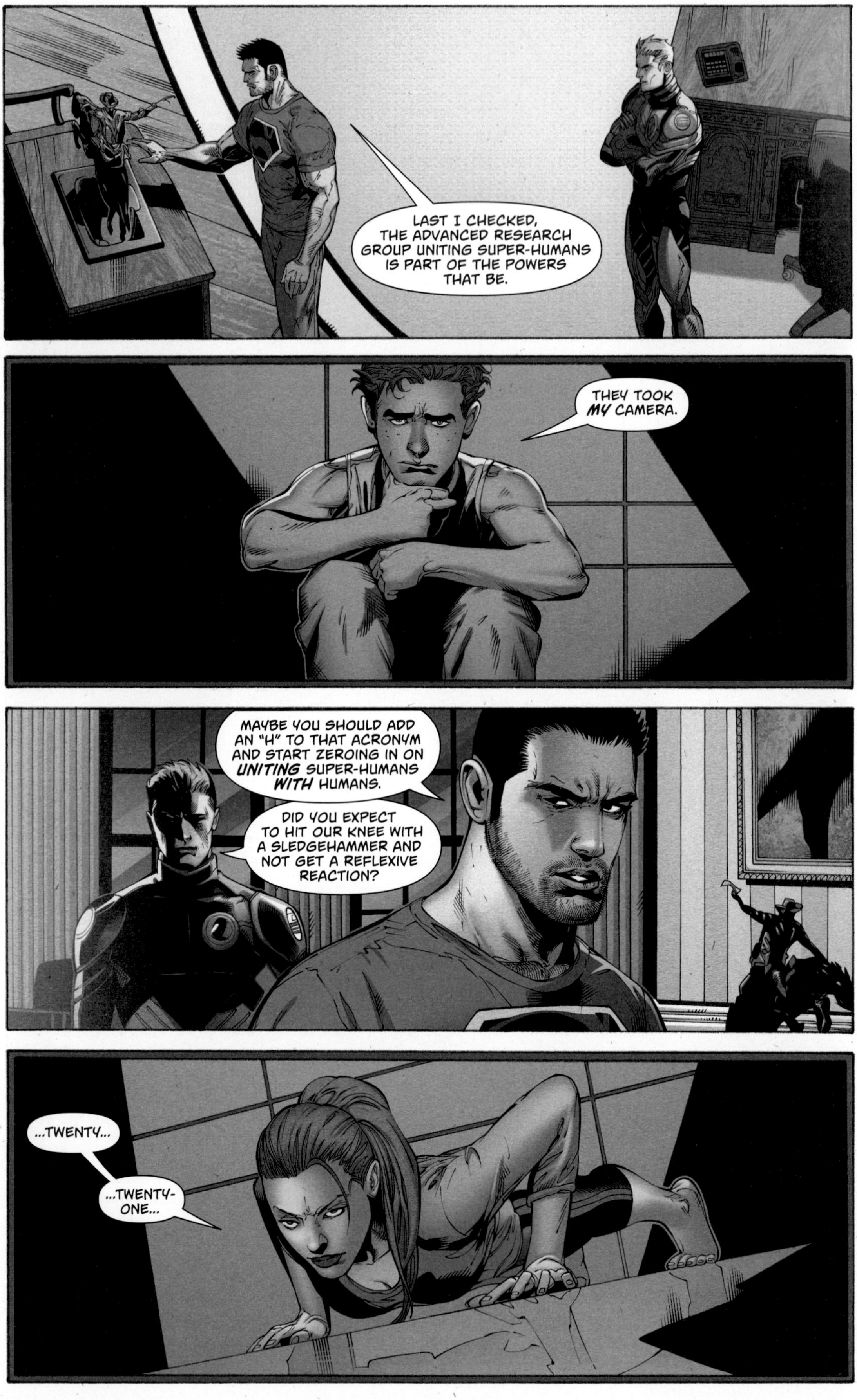
LAST I CHECKED, THE ADVANCED RESEARCH GROUP UNITING SUPER-HUMANS IS PART OF THE POWERS THAT BE.
THEY TOOK *MY* CAMERA.
MAYBE YOU SHOULD ADD AN "H" TO THAT ACRONYM AND START ZEROING IN ON *UNITING* SUPER-HUMANS *WITH* HUMANS.
DID YOU EXPECT TO HIT OUR KNEE WITH A SLEDGEHAMMER AND NOT GET A REFLEXIVE REACTION?
...TWENTY...
...TWENTY-ONE...

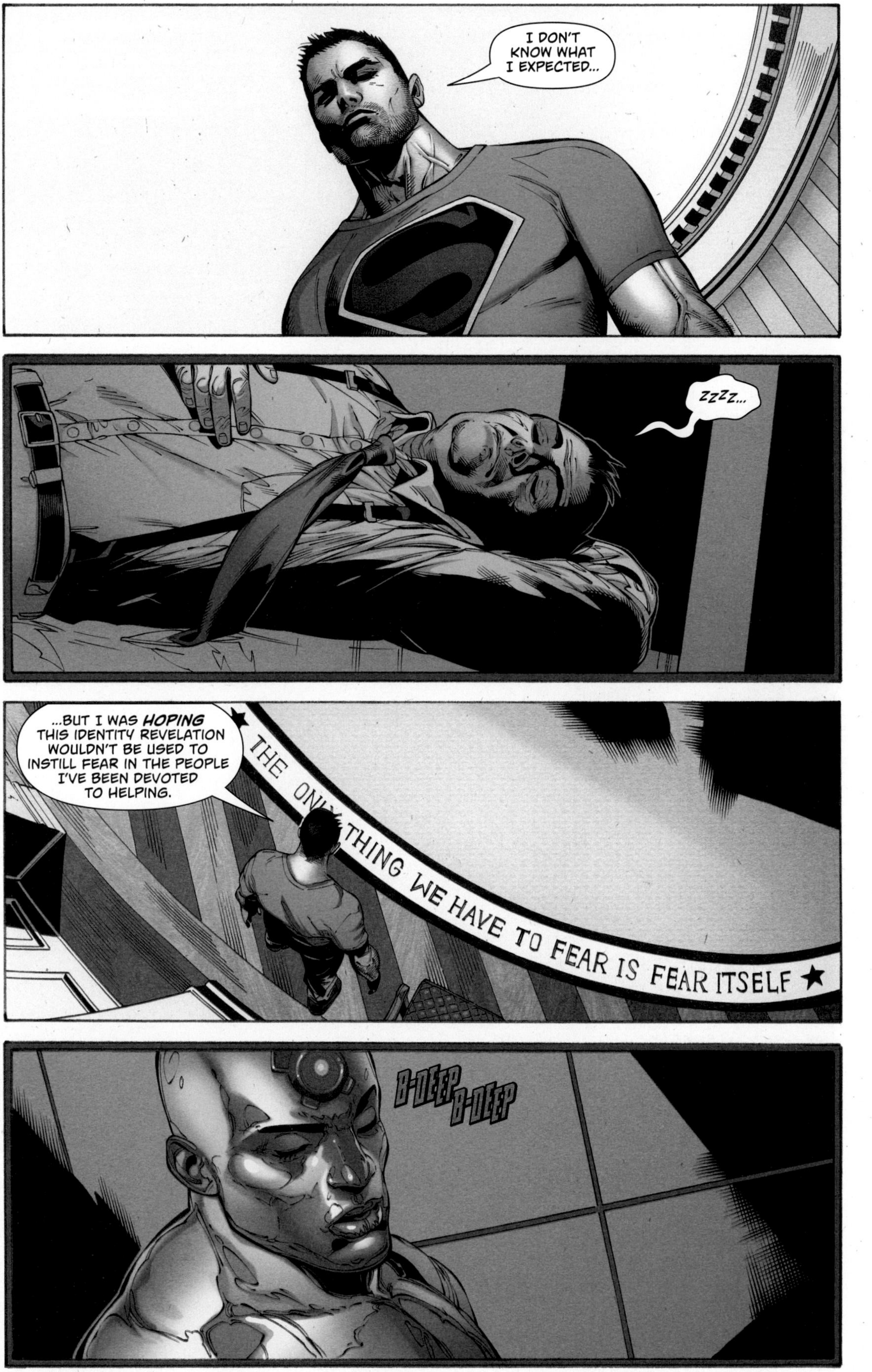
I DON'T KNOW WHAT I EXPECTED...
ZZZZ...
...BUT I WAS HOPING THIS IDENTITY REVELATION WOULDN'T BE USED TO INSTILL FEAR IN THE PEOPLE I'VE BEEN DEVOTED TO HELPING.
THE ONLY THING WE HAVE TO FEAR IS FEAR ITSELF
B-DEEP B-DEEP

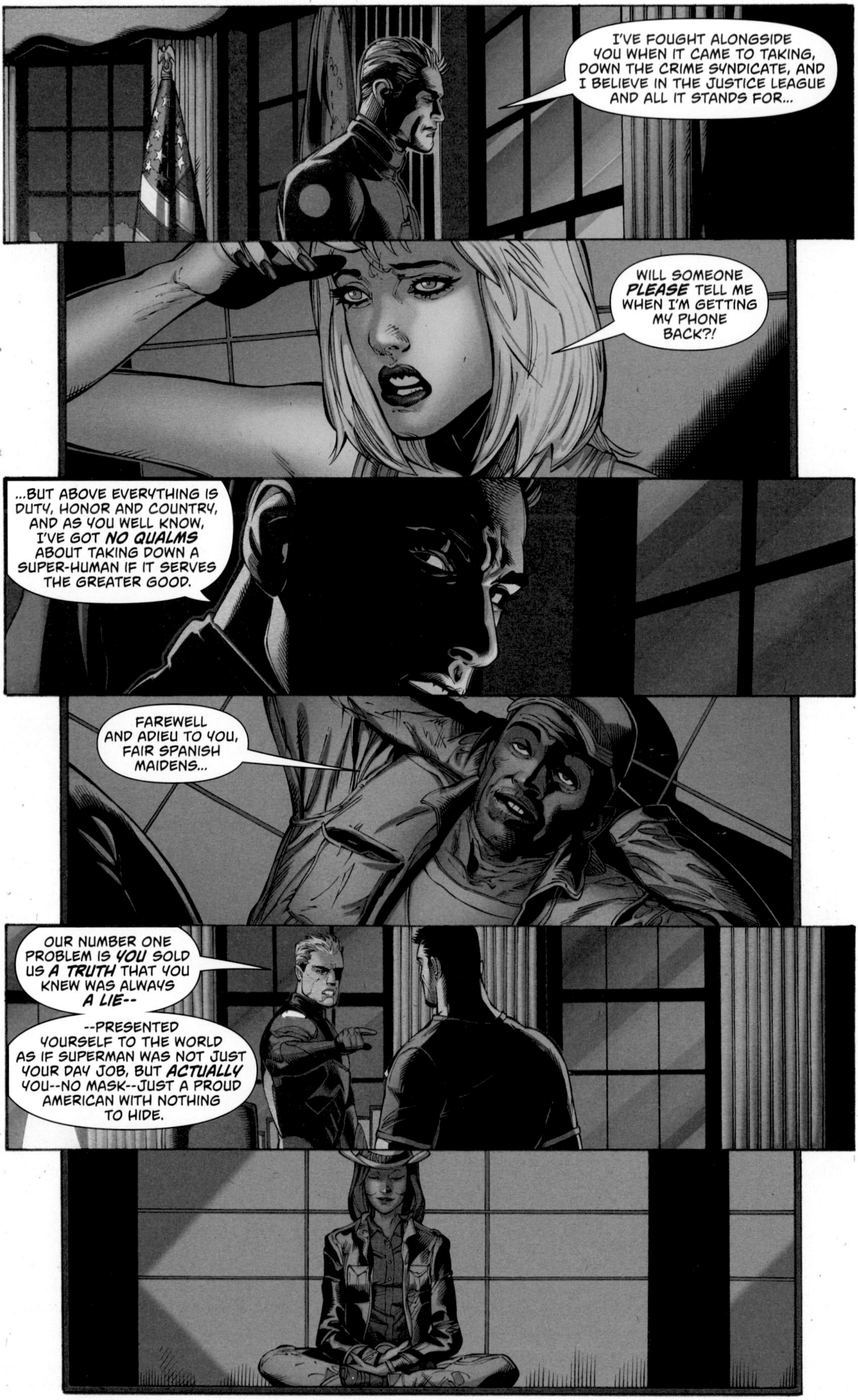
I'VE FOUGHT ALONGSIDE YOU WHEN IT CAME TO TAKING, DOWN THE CRIME SYNDICATE, AND I BELIEVE IN THE JUSTICE LEAGUE AND ALL IT STANDS FOR...
WILL SOMEONE PLEASE TELL ME WHEN I'M GETTING MY PHONE BACK?!
...BUT ABOVE EVERYTHING IS DUTY, HONOR AND COUNTRY, AND AS YOU WELL KNOW, I'VE GOT NO QUALMS ABOUT TAKING DOWN A SUPER-HUMAN IF IT SERVES THE GREATER GOOD.
FAREWELL AND ADIEU TO YOU, FAIR SPANISH MAIDENS...
OUR NUMBER ONE PROBLEM IS YOU SOLD US A TRUTH THAT YOU KNEW WAS ALWAYS A LIE--
--PRESENTED YOURSELF TO THE WORLD AS IF SUPERMAN WAS NOT JUST YOUR DAY JOB, BUT ACTUALLY YOU--NO MASK--JUST A PROUD AMERICAN WITH NOTHING TO HIDE.

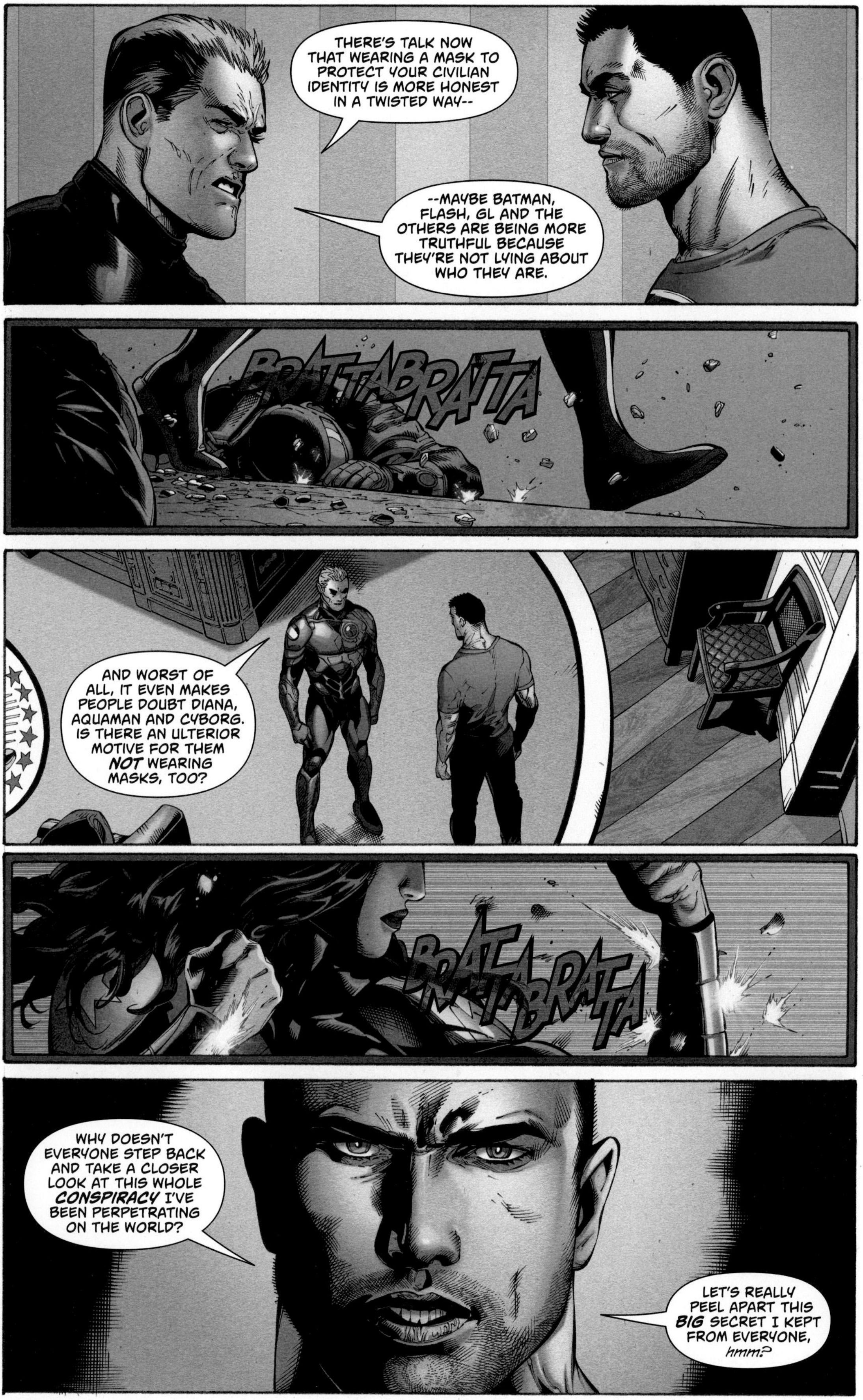
THERE'S TALK NOW THAT WEARING A MASK TO PROTECT YOUR CIVILIAN IDENTITY IS MORE HONEST IN A TWISTED WAY--
--MAYBE BATMAN, FLASH, GL AND THE OTHERS ARE BEING MORE TRUTHFUL BECAUSE THEY'RE NOT LYING ABOUT WHO THEY ARE.
BRATTABRATTA
AND WORST OF ALL, IT EVEN MAKES PEOPLE DOUBT DIANA, AQUAMAN AND CYBORG. IS THERE AN ULTERIOR MOTIVE FOR THEM *NOT* WEARING MASKS, TOO?
BRATTABRATTA
WHY DOESN'T EVERYONE STEP BACK AND TAKE A CLOSER LOOK AT THIS WHOLE *CONSPIRACY* I'VE BEEN PERPETRATING ON THE WORLD?
LET'S REALLY PEEL APART THIS *BIG* SECRET I KEPT FROM EVERYONE, *hmm?*

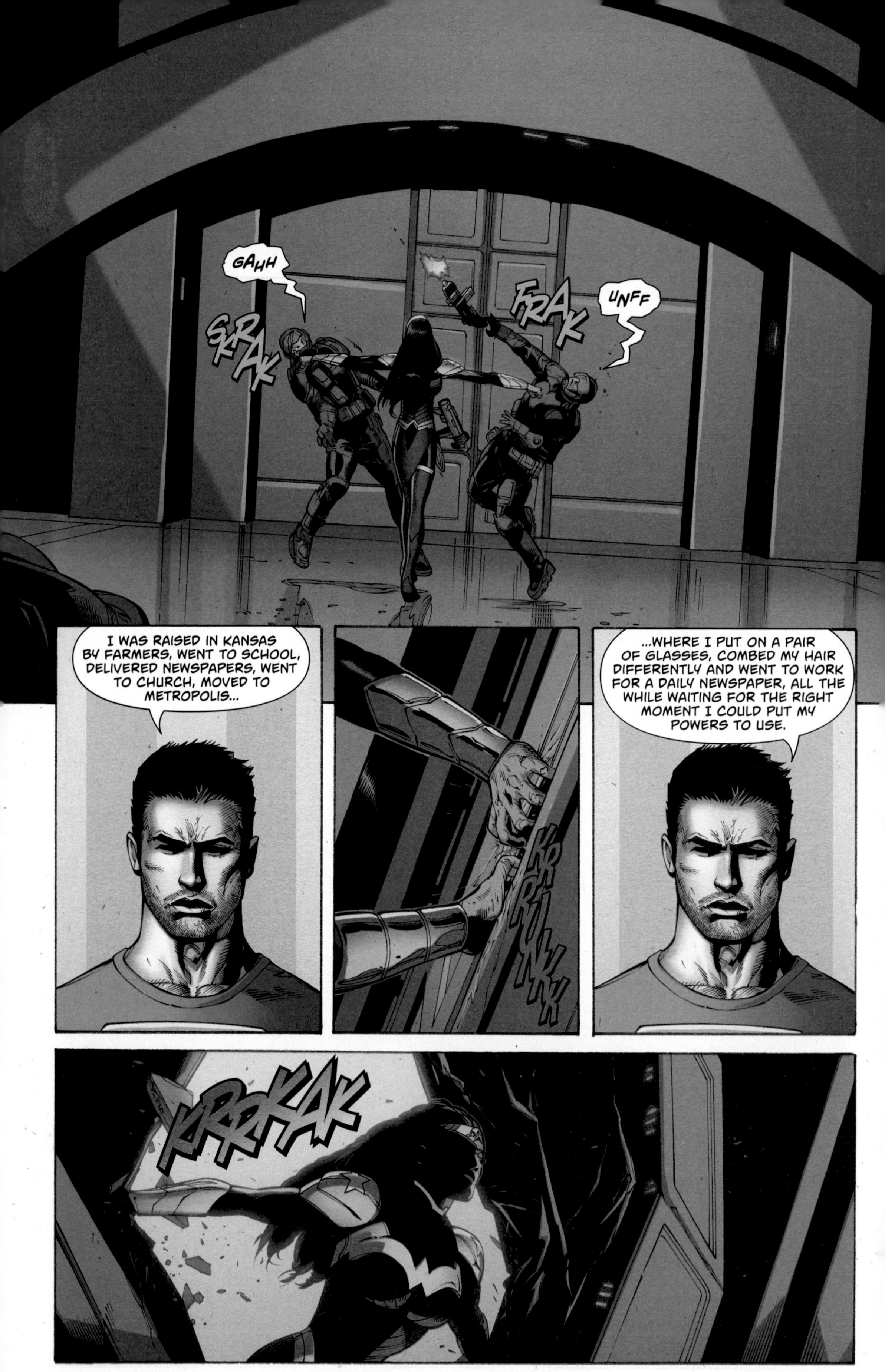

GAHH
SKRAK
FRAK
UNFF
I WAS RAISED IN KANSAS BY FARMERS, WENT TO SCHOOL, DELIVERED NEWSPAPERS, WENT TO CHURCH, MOVED TO METROPOLIS...
KRRUNKK
...WHERE I PUT ON A PAIR OF GLASSES, COMBED MY HAIR DIFFERENTLY AND WENT TO WORK FOR A DAILY NEWSPAPER, ALL THE WHILE WAITING FOR THE RIGHT MOMENT I COULD PUT MY POWERS TO USE.
KRRKAK

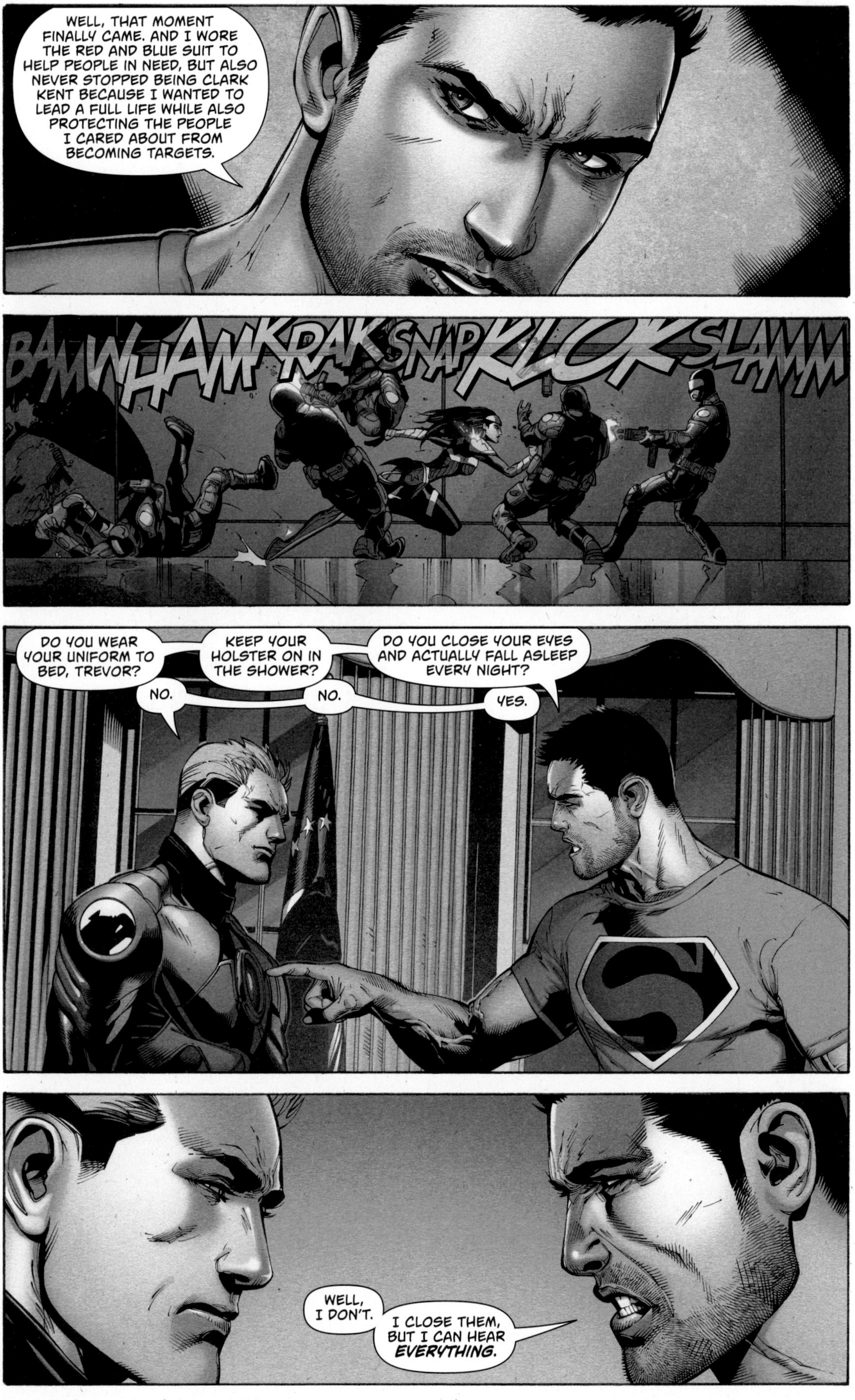
WELL, THAT MOMENT FINALLY CAME. AND I WORE THE RED AND BLUE SUIT TO HELP PEOPLE IN NEED, BUT ALSO NEVER STOPPED BEING CLARK KENT BECAUSE I WANTED TO LEAD A FULL LIFE WHILE ALSO PROTECTING THE PEOPLE I CARED ABOUT FROM BECOMING TARGETS.
BAM
WHAM
KRAK
SNAP
KLOK
SLAMM
DO YOU WEAR YOUR UNIFORM TO BED, TREVOR?
NO.
KEEP YOUR HOLSTER ON IN THE SHOWER?
NO.
DO YOU CLOSE YOUR EYES AND ACTUALLY FALL ASLEEP EVERY NIGHT?
YES.
WELL, I DON'T.
I CLOSE THEM, BUT I CAN HEAR *EVERYTHING*.

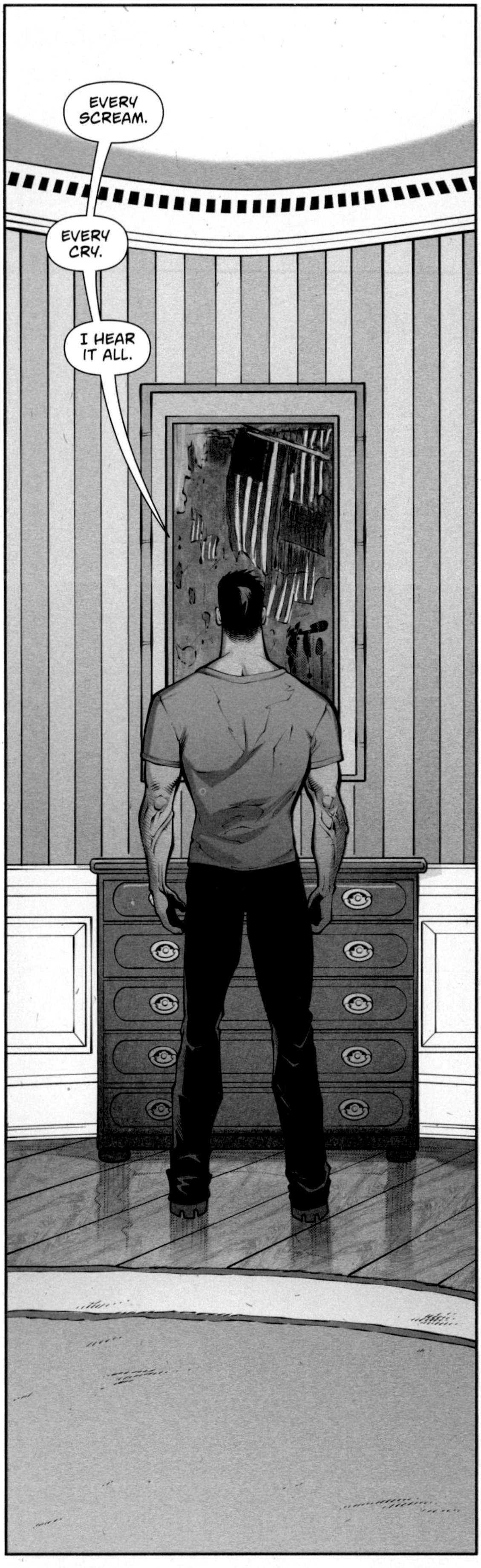
EVERY SCREAM.
EVERY CRY.
I HEAR IT ALL.

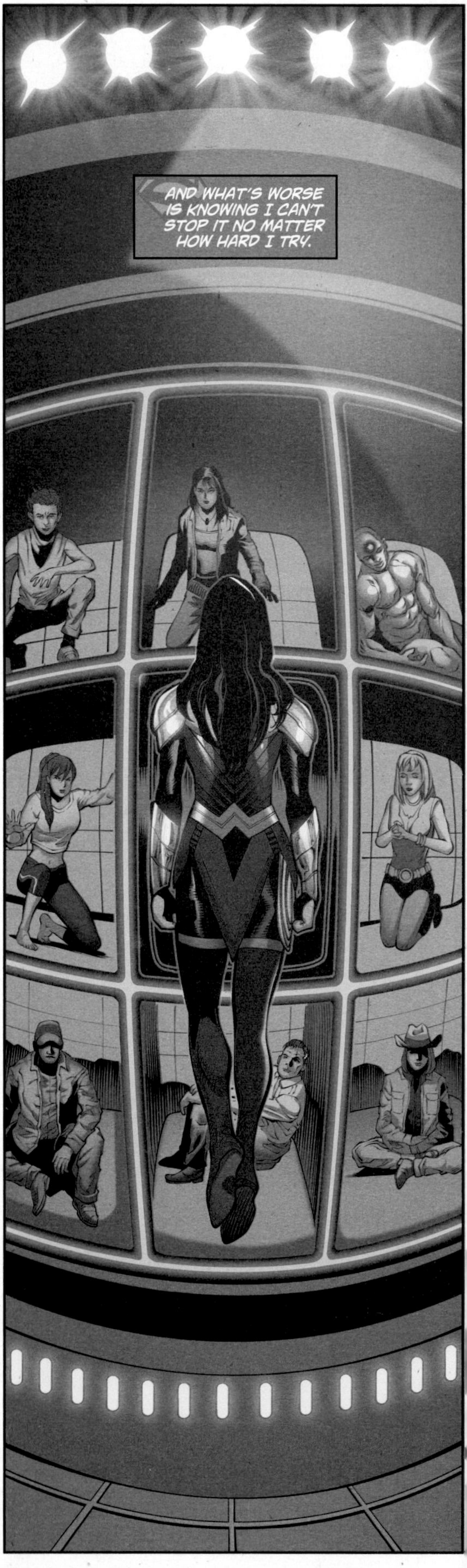
AND WHAT'S WORSE IS KNOWING I CAN'T STOP IT NO MATTER HOW HARD I TRY.

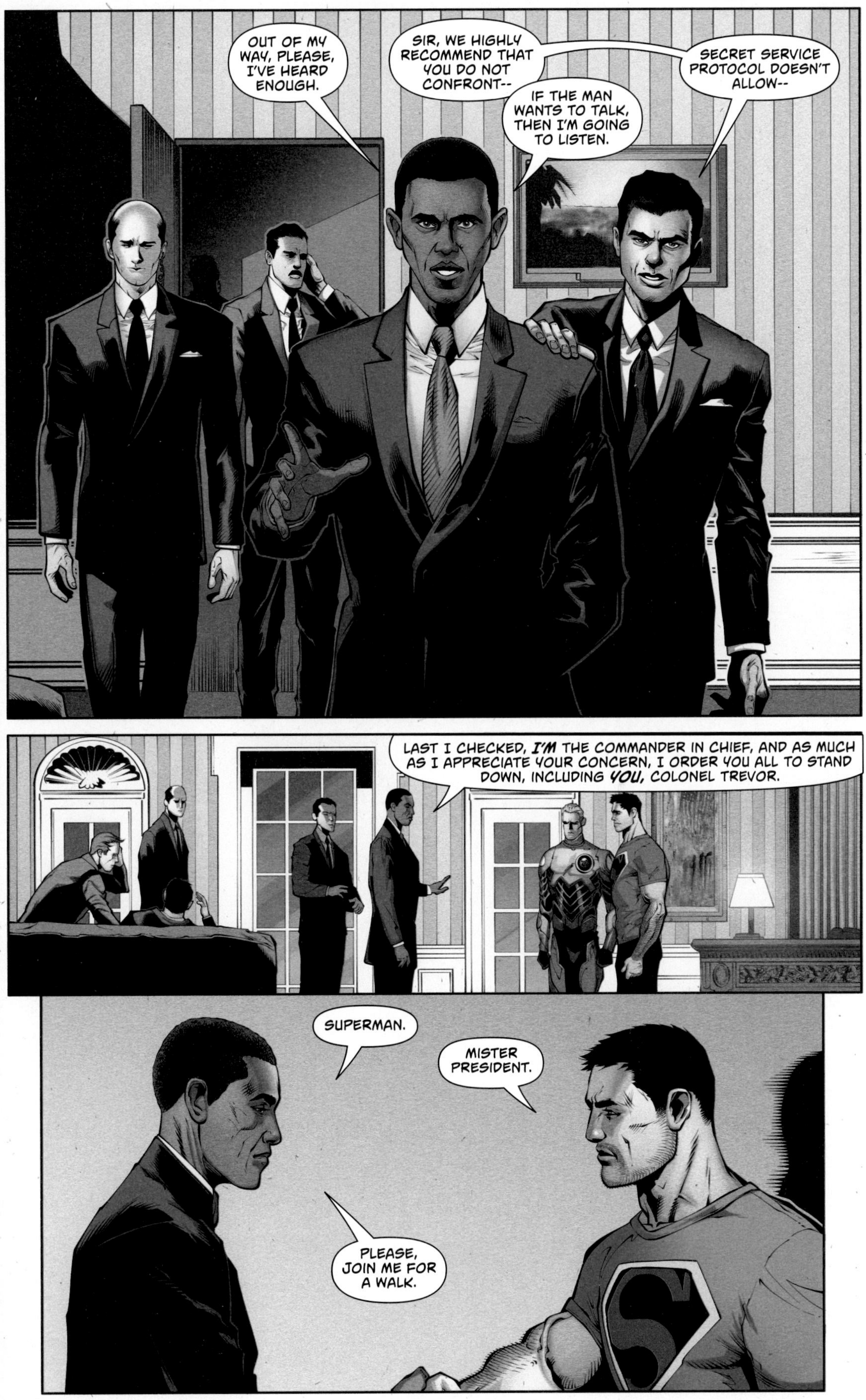
OUT OF MY WAY, PLEASE, I'VE HEARD ENOUGH.
SIR, WE HIGHLY RECOMMEND THAT YOU DO NOT CONFRONT--
SECRET SERVICE PROTOCOL DOESN'T ALLOW--
IF THE MAN WANTS TO TALK, THEN I'M GOING TO LISTEN.
LAST I CHECKED, *I'M* THE COMMANDER IN CHIEF, AND AS MUCH AS I APPRECIATE YOUR CONCERN, I ORDER YOU ALL TO STAND DOWN, INCLUDING *YOU*, COLONEL TREVOR.
SUPERMAN.
MISTER PRESIDENT.
PLEASE, JOIN ME FOR A WALK.

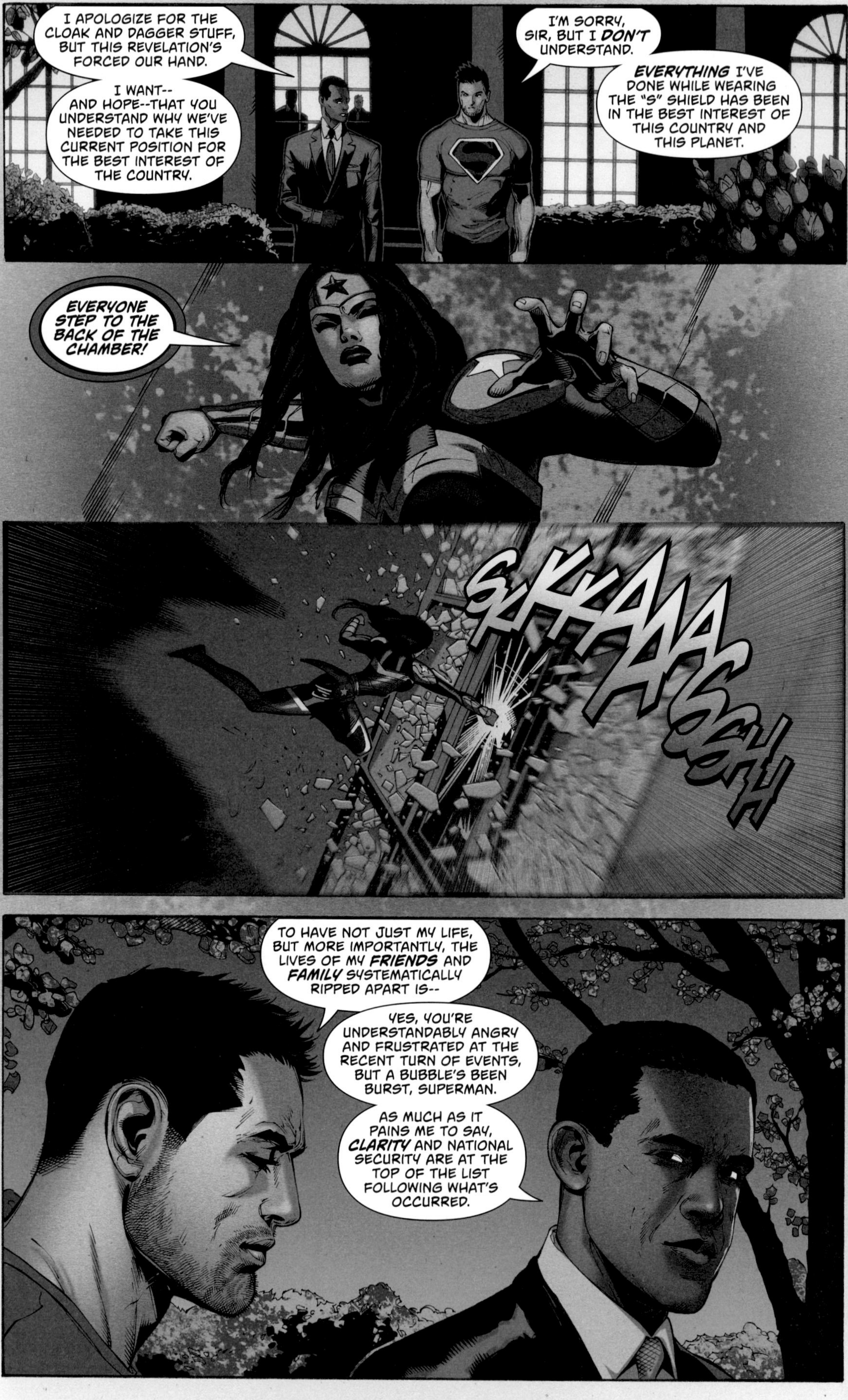
I APOLOGIZE FOR THE CLOAK AND DAGGER STUFF, BUT THIS REVELATION'S FORCED OUR HAND.
I WANT-- AND HOPE--THAT YOU UNDERSTAND WHY WE'VE NEEDED TO TAKE THIS CURRENT POSITION FOR THE BEST INTEREST OF THE COUNTRY.
I'M SORRY, SIR, BUT I DON'T UNDERSTAND.
EVERYTHING I'VE DONE WHILE WEARING THE "S" SHIELD HAS BEEN IN THE BEST INTEREST OF THIS COUNTRY AND THIS PLANET.
EVERYONE STEP TO THE BACK OF THE CHAMBER!
SKKAAAASCHH
TO HAVE NOT JUST MY LIFE, BUT MORE IMPORTANTLY, THE LIVES OF MY FRIENDS AND FAMILY SYSTEMATICALLY RIPPED APART IS--
YES, YOU'RE UNDERSTANDABLY ANGRY AND FRUSTRATED AT THE RECENT TURN OF EVENTS, BUT A BUBBLE'S BEEN BURST, SUPERMAN.
AS MUCH AS IT PAINS ME TO SAY, CLARITY AND NATIONAL SECURITY ARE AT THE TOP OF THE LIST FOLLOWING WHAT'S OCCURRED.

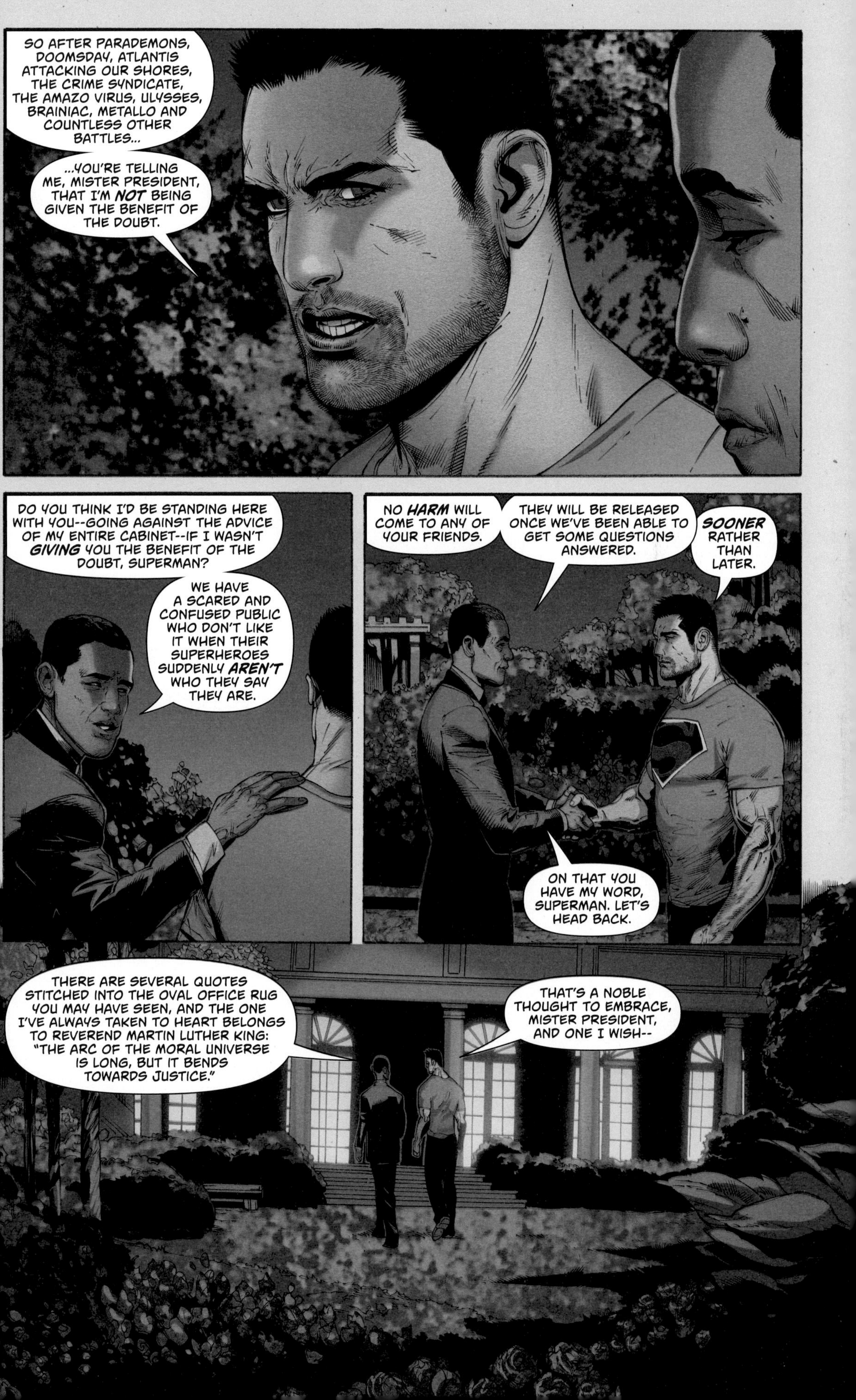

SO AFTER PARADEMONS, DOOMSDAY, ATLANTIS ATTACKING OUR SHORES, THE CRIME SYNDICATE, THE AMAZO VIRUS, ULYSSES, BRAINIAC, METALLO AND COUNTLESS OTHER BATTLES...
...YOU'RE TELLING ME, MISTER PRESIDENT, THAT I'M NOT BEING GIVEN THE BENEFIT OF THE DOUBT.
DO YOU THINK I'D BE STANDING HERE WITH YOU--GOING AGAINST THE ADVICE OF MY ENTIRE CABINET--IF I WASN'T GIVING YOU THE BENEFIT OF THE DOUBT, SUPERMAN?
WE HAVE A SCARED AND CONFUSED PUBLIC WHO DON'T LIKE IT WHEN THEIR SUPERHEROES SUDDENLY AREN'T WHO THEY SAY THEY ARE.
NO HARM WILL COME TO ANY OF YOUR FRIENDS.
THEY WILL BE RELEASED ONCE WE'VE BEEN ABLE TO GET SOME QUESTIONS ANSWERED.
SOONER RATHER THAN LATER.
ON THAT YOU HAVE MY WORD, SUPERMAN. LET'S HEAD BACK.
THERE ARE SEVERAL QUOTES STITCHED INTO THE OVAL OFFICE RUG YOU MAY HAVE SEEN, AND THE ONE I'VE ALWAYS TAKEN TO HEART BELONGS TO REVEREND MARTIN LUTHER KING: "THE ARC OF THE MORAL UNIVERSE IS LONG, BUT IT BENDS TOWARDS JUSTICE."
THAT'S A NOBLE THOUGHT TO EMBRACE, MISTER PRESIDENT, AND ONE I WISH--

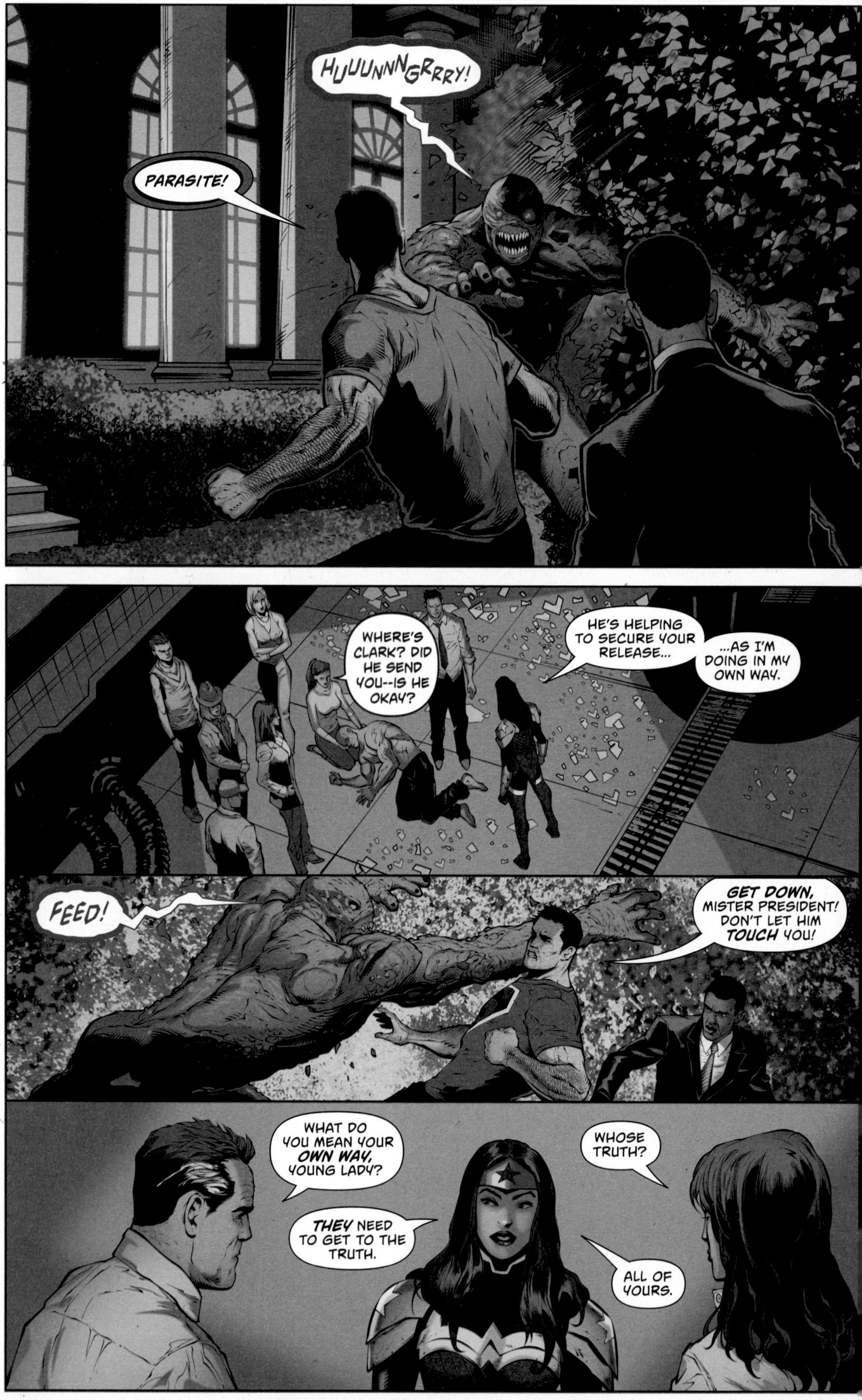
HUUUNNNGRRRY!
PARASITE!
WHERE'S CLARK? DID HE SEND YOU--IS HE OKAY?
HE'S HELPING TO SECURE YOUR RELEASE...
...AS I'M DOING IN MY OWN WAY.
FEED!
GET DOWN, MISTER PRESIDENT! DON'T LET HIM TOUCH YOU!
WHAT DO YOU MEAN YOUR OWN WAY, YOUNG LADY?
THEY NEED TO GET TO THE TRUTH.
WHOSE TRUTH?
ALL OF YOURS.

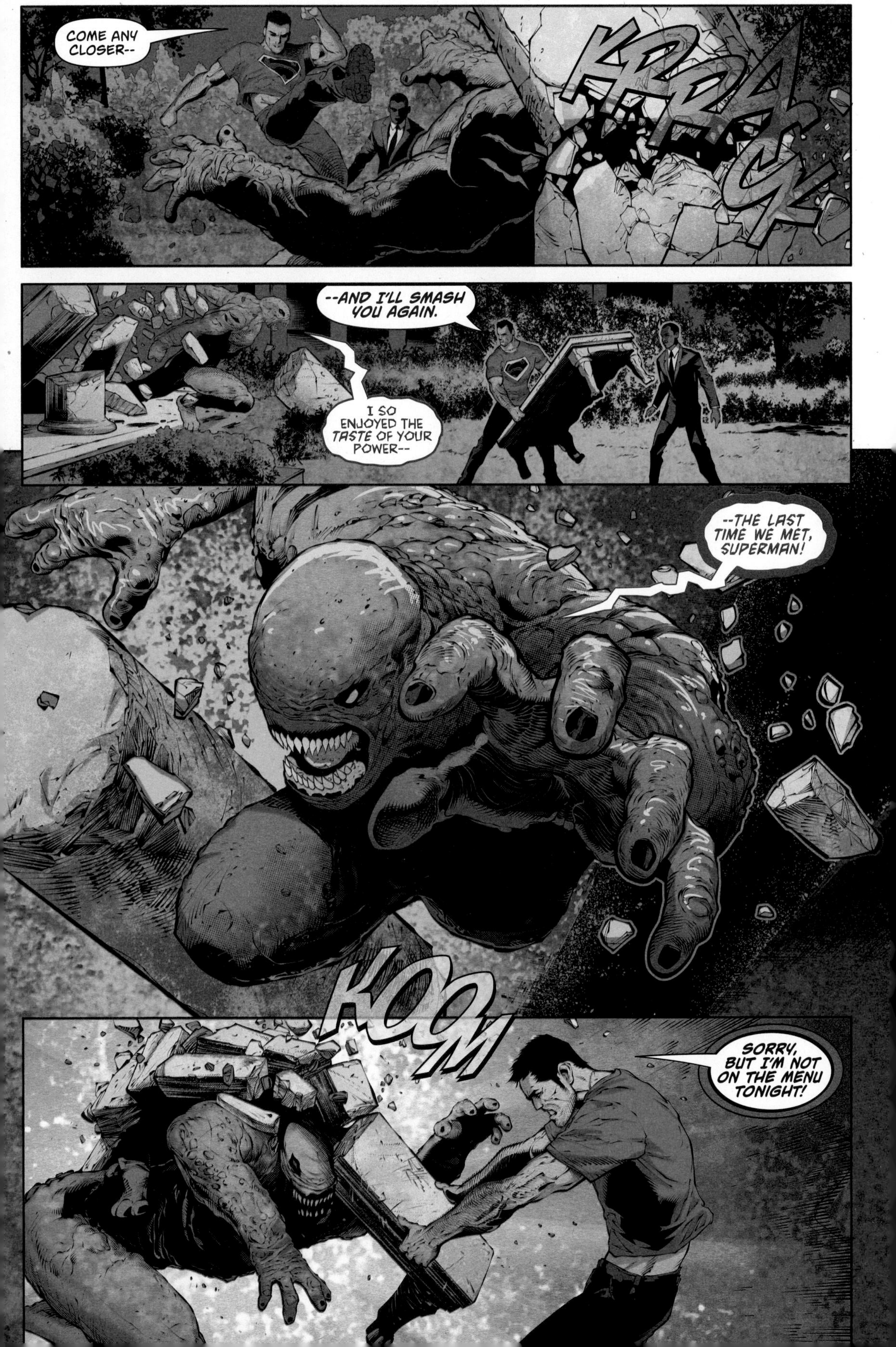
COME ANY CLOSER--
KRAKASH
--AND I'LL SMASH YOU AGAIN.
I SO ENJOYED THE TASTE OF YOUR POWER--
--THE LAST TIME WE MET, SUPERMAN!
KOOM
SORRY, BUT I'M NOT ON THE MENU TONIGHT!

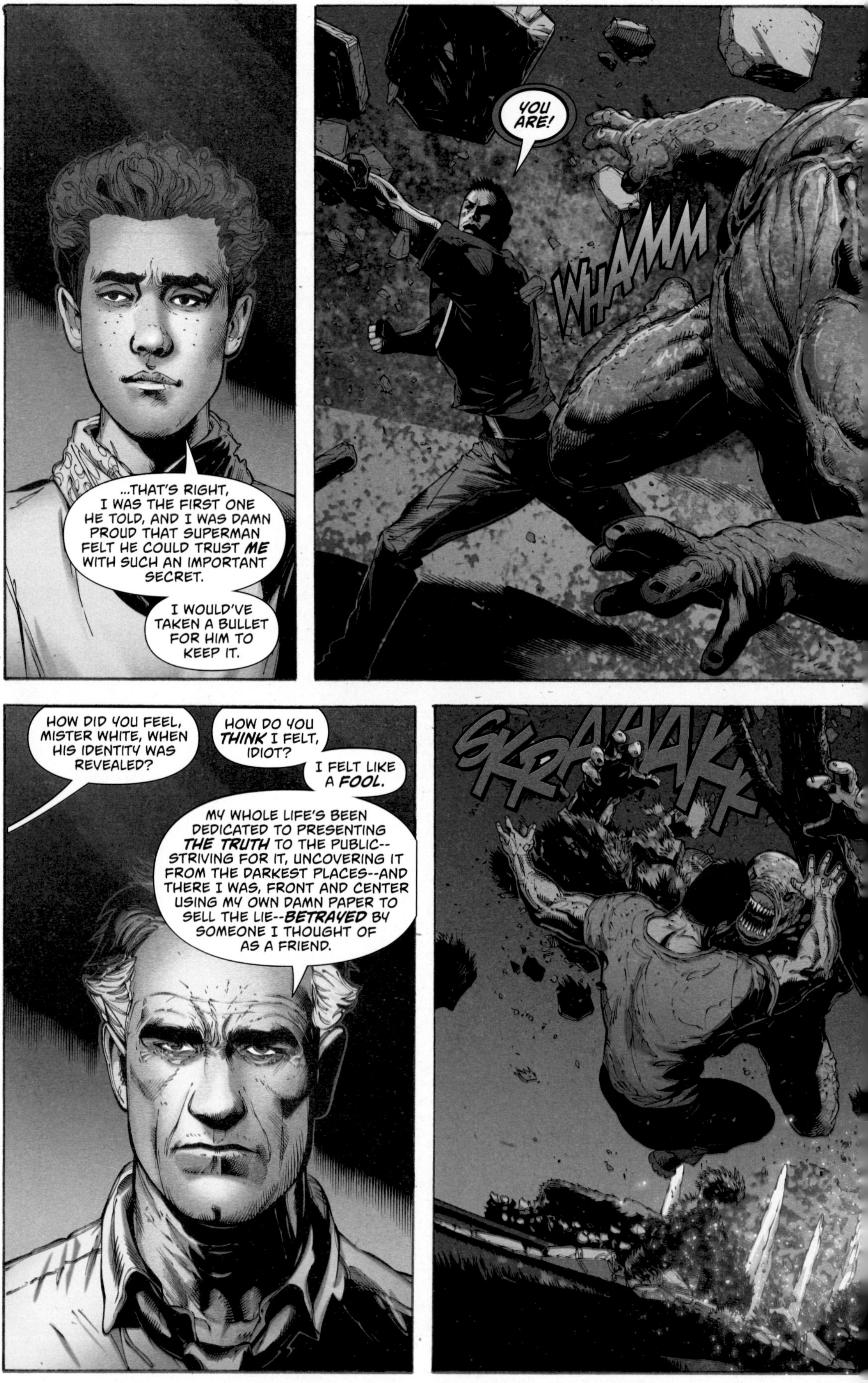

...THAT'S RIGHT, I WAS THE FIRST ONE HE TOLD, AND I WAS DAMN PROUD THAT SUPERMAN FELT HE COULD TRUST *ME* WITH SUCH AN IMPORTANT SECRET.
I WOULD'VE TAKEN A BULLET FOR HIM TO KEEP IT.
YOU ARE!
WHAMM
HOW DID YOU FEEL, MISTER WHITE, WHEN HIS IDENTITY WAS REVEALED?
HOW DO YOU *THINK* I FELT, IDIOT?
I FELT LIKE A *FOOL*.
MY WHOLE LIFE'S BEEN DEDICATED TO PRESENTING *THE TRUTH* TO THE PUBLIC--STRIVING FOR IT, UNCOVERING IT FROM THE DARKEST PLACES--AND THERE I WAS, FRONT AND CENTER USING MY OWN DAMN PAPER TO SELL THE LIE--*BETRAYED* BY SOMEONE I THOUGHT OF AS A FRIEND.
SKRAAAKK

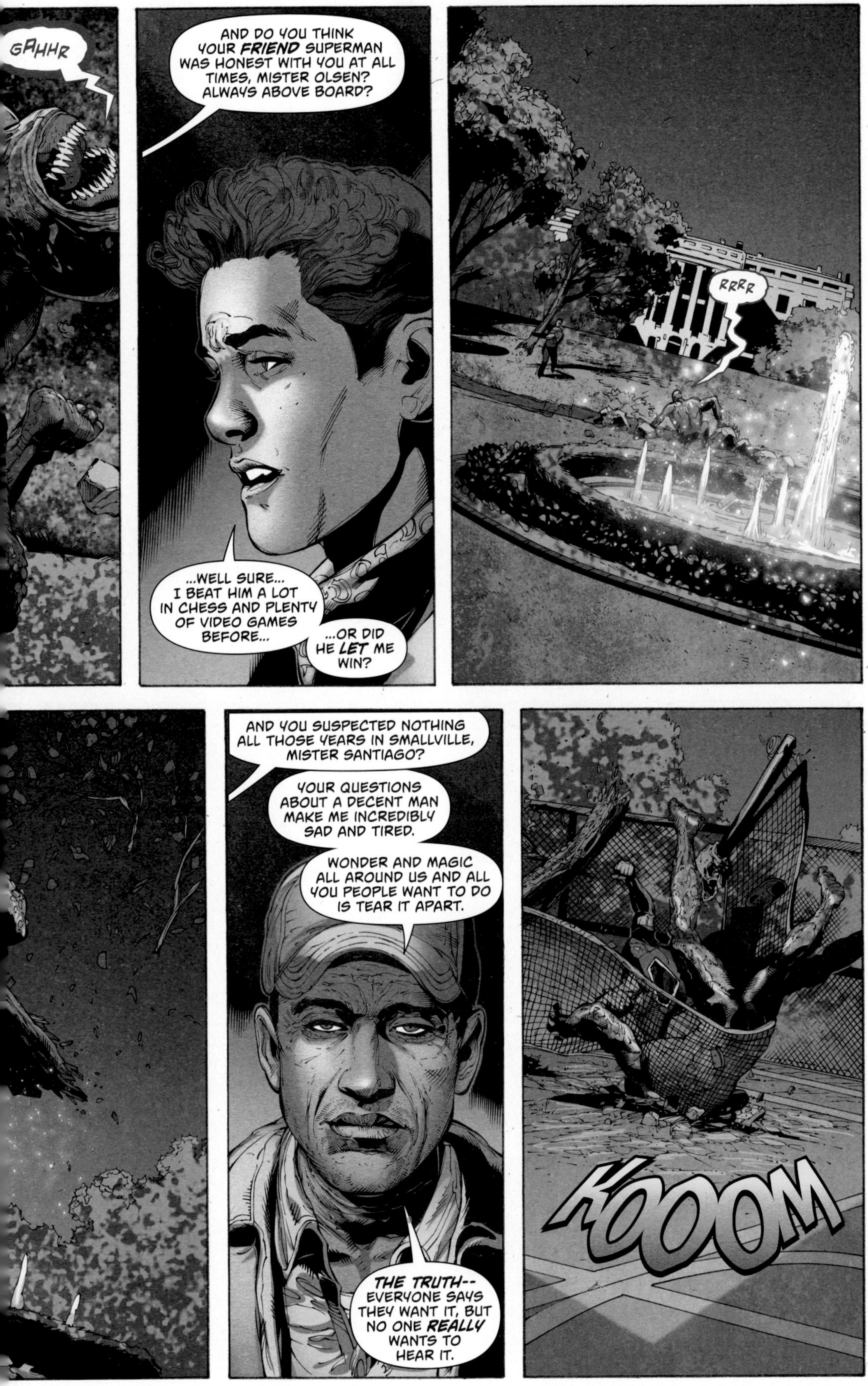
GAHHR
AND DO YOU THINK YOUR FRIEND SUPERMAN WAS HONEST WITH YOU AT ALL TIMES, MISTER OLSEN? ALWAYS ABOVE BOARD?
...WELL SURE... I BEAT HIM A LOT IN CHESS AND PLENTY OF VIDEO GAMES BEFORE...
...OR DID HE LET ME WIN?
RRRR
AND YOU SUSPECTED NOTHING ALL THOSE YEARS IN SMALLVILLE, MISTER SANTIAGO?
YOUR QUESTIONS ABOUT A DECENT MAN MAKE ME INCREDIBLY SAD AND TIRED.
WONDER AND MAGIC ALL AROUND US AND ALL YOU PEOPLE WANT TO DO IS TEAR IT APART.
THE TRUTH-- EVERYONE SAYS THEY WANT IT, BUT NO ONE REALLY WANTS TO HEAR IT.
KOOOM

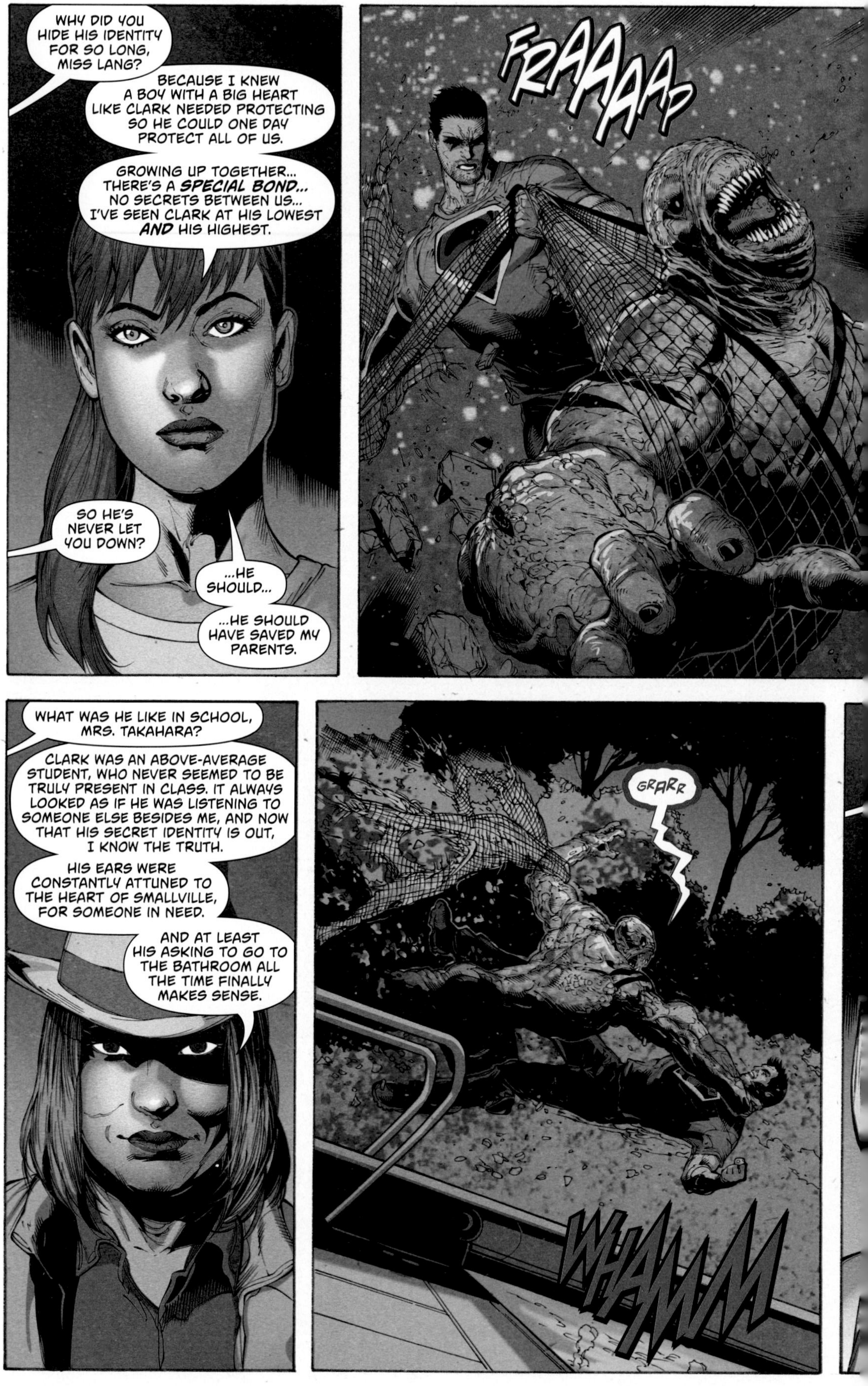
WHY DID YOU HIDE HIS IDENTITY FOR SO LONG, MISS LANG?
BECAUSE I KNEW A BOY WITH A BIG HEART LIKE CLARK NEEDED PROTECTING SO HE COULD ONE DAY PROTECT ALL OF US.
GROWING UP TOGETHER... THERE'S A SPECIAL BOND... NO SECRETS BETWEEN US... I'VE SEEN CLARK AT HIS LOWEST AND HIS HIGHEST.
SO HE'S NEVER LET YOU DOWN?
...HE SHOULD...
...HE SHOULD HAVE SAVED MY PARENTS.
FRAAAAAP
WHAT WAS HE LIKE IN SCHOOL, MRS. TAKAHARA?
CLARK WAS AN ABOVE-AVERAGE STUDENT, WHO NEVER SEEMED TO BE TRULY PRESENT IN CLASS. IT ALWAYS LOOKED AS IF HE WAS LISTENING TO SOMEONE ELSE BESIDES ME, AND NOW THAT HIS SECRET IDENTITY IS OUT, I KNOW THE TRUTH.
HIS EARS WERE CONSTANTLY ATTUNED TO THE HEART OF SMALLVILLE, FOR SOMEONE IN NEED.
AND AT LEAST HIS ASKING TO GO TO THE BATHROOM ALL THE TIME FINALLY MAKES SENSE.
GRARR
WHAMM

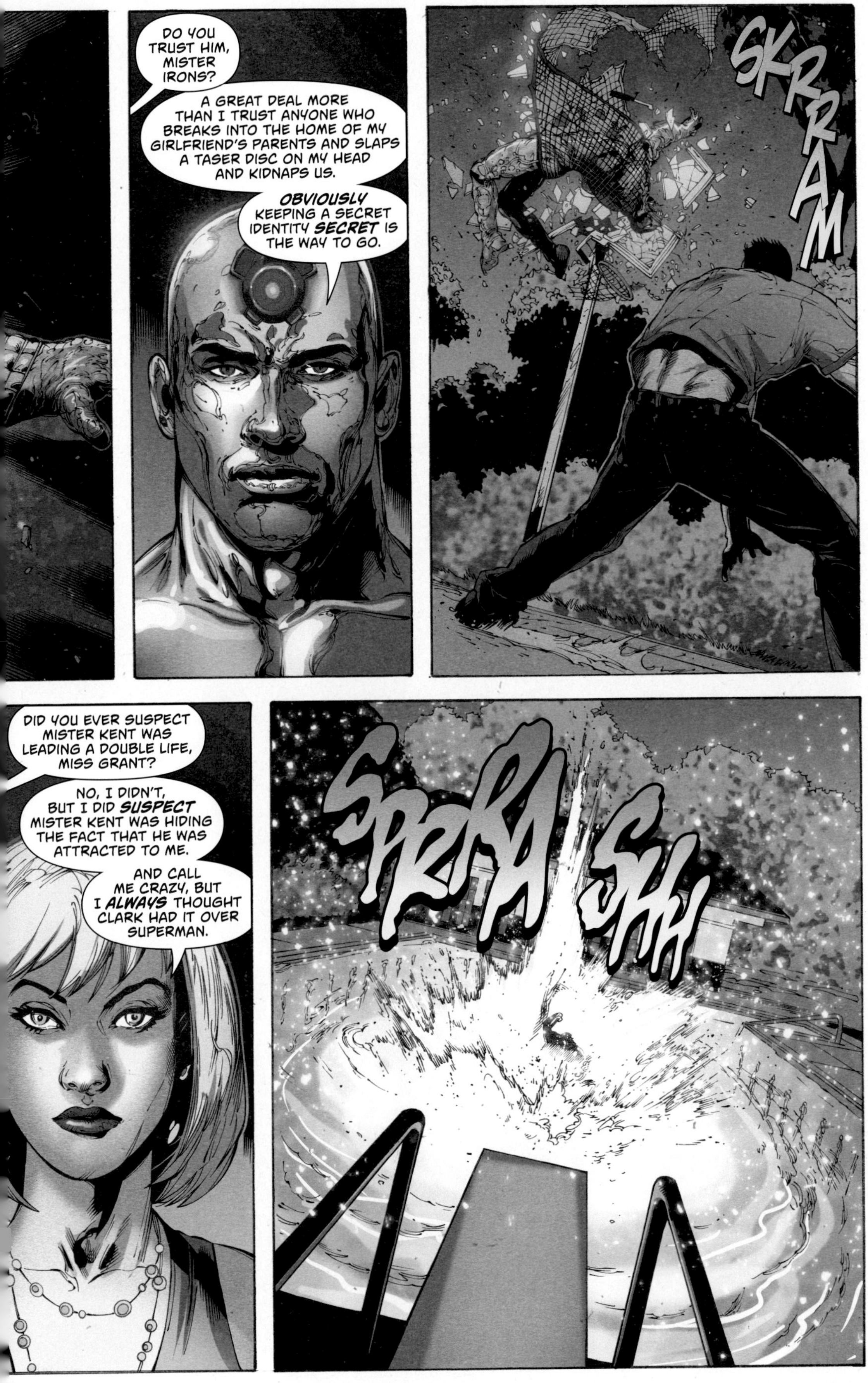
DO YOU TRUST HIM, MISTER IRONS?
A GREAT DEAL MORE THAN I TRUST ANYONE WHO BREAKS INTO THE HOME OF MY GIRLFRIEND'S PARENTS AND SLAPS A TASER DISC ON MY HEAD AND KIDNAPS US.
OBVIOUSLY KEEPING A SECRET IDENTITY SECRET IS THE WAY TO GO.
SKRRRAM
DID YOU EVER SUSPECT MISTER KENT WAS LEADING A DOUBLE LIFE, MISS GRANT?
NO, I DIDN'T, BUT I DID SUSPECT MISTER KENT WAS HIDING THE FACT THAT HE WAS ATTRACTED TO ME.
AND CALL ME CRAZY, BUT I ALWAYS THOUGHT CLARK HAD IT OVER SUPERMAN.
SPRRASHH

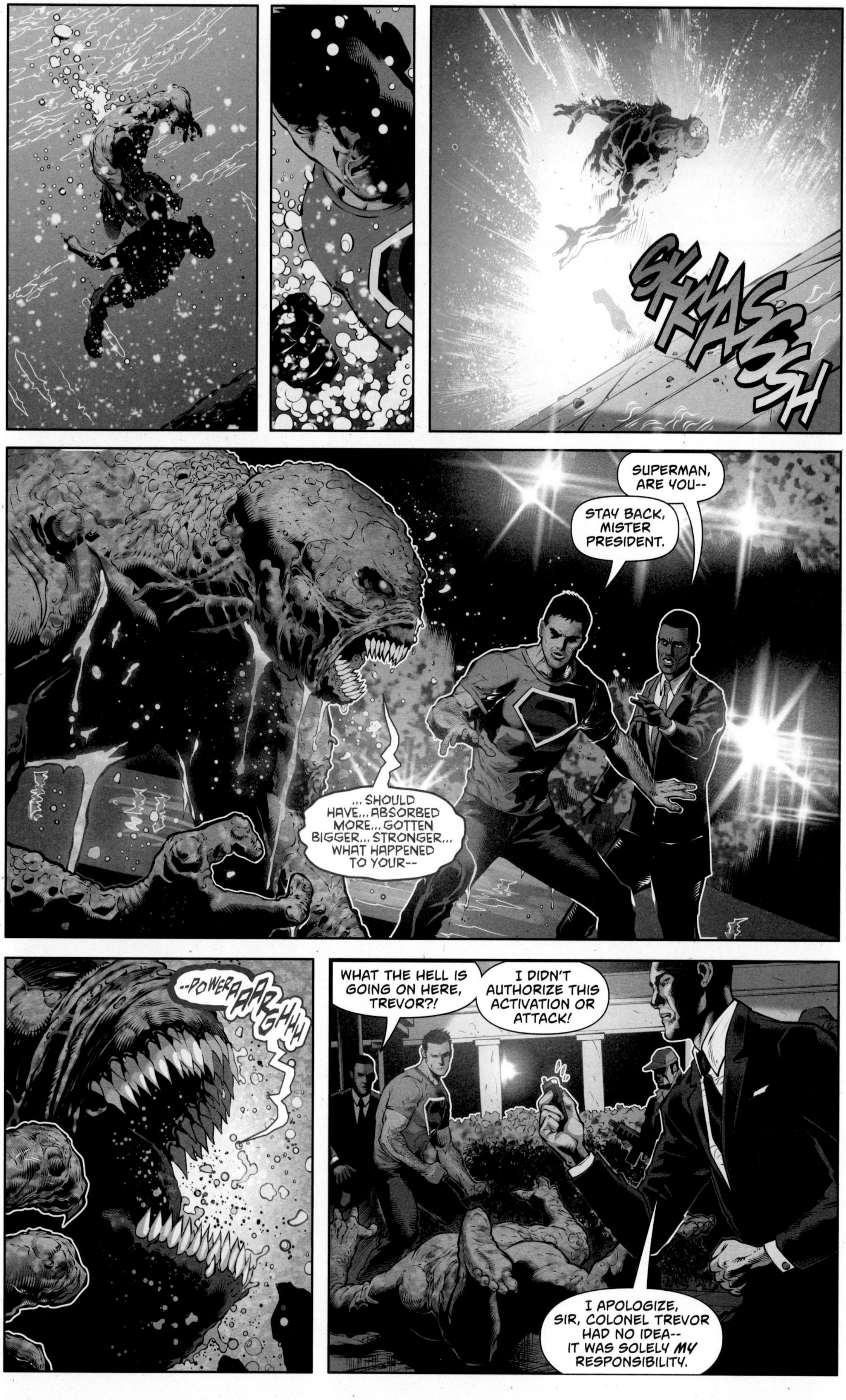
SKKASSH
SUPERMAN, ARE YOU--
STAY BACK, MISTER PRESIDENT.
...SHOULD HAVE...ABSORBED MORE...GOTTEN BIGGER...STRONGER... WHAT HAPPENED TO YOUR--
--POWERAAARGHHH
WHAT THE HELL IS GOING ON HERE, TREVOR?!
I DIDN'T AUTHORIZE THIS ACTIVATION OR ATTACK!
I APOLOGIZE, SIR, COLONEL TREVOR HAD NO IDEA-- IT WAS SOLELY MY RESPONSIBILITY.

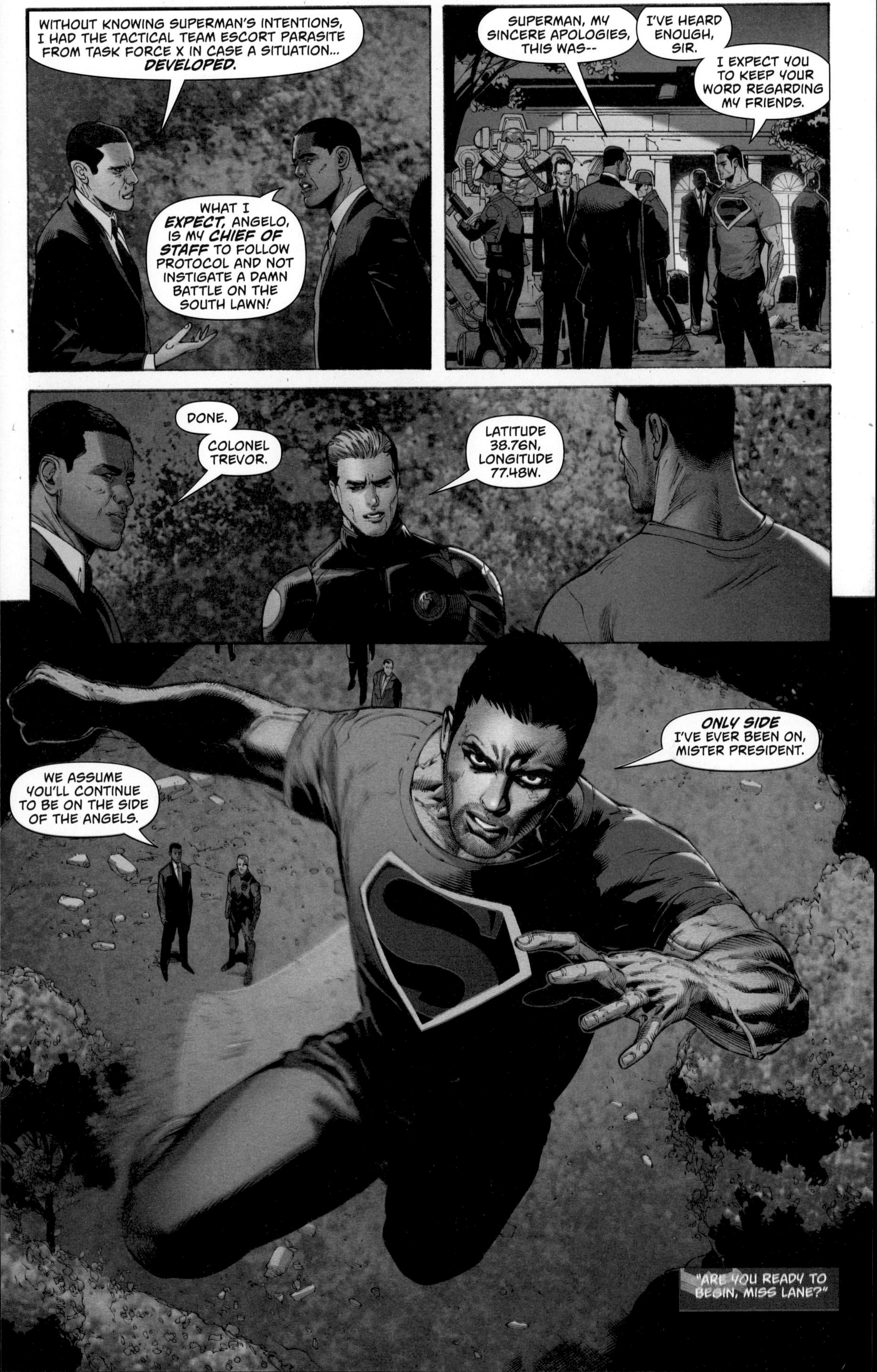
WITHOUT KNOWING SUPERMAN'S INTENTIONS, I HAD THE TACTICAL TEAM ESCORT PARASITE FROM TASK FORCE X IN CASE A SITUATION... DEVELOPED.
WHAT I EXPECT, ANGELO, IS MY CHIEF OF STAFF TO FOLLOW PROTOCOL AND NOT INSTIGATE A DAMN BATTLE ON THE SOUTH LAWN!
SUPERMAN, MY SINCERE APOLOGIES, THIS WAS--
I'VE HEARD ENOUGH, SIR.
I EXPECT YOU TO KEEP YOUR WORD REGARDING MY FRIENDS.
DONE.
COLONEL TREVOR.
LATITUDE 38.76N, LONGITUDE 77.48W.
WE ASSUME YOU'LL CONTINUE TO BE ON THE SIDE OF THE ANGELS.
ONLY SIDE I'VE EVER BEEN ON, MISTER PRESIDENT.
"ARE YOU READY TO BEGIN, MISS LANE?"

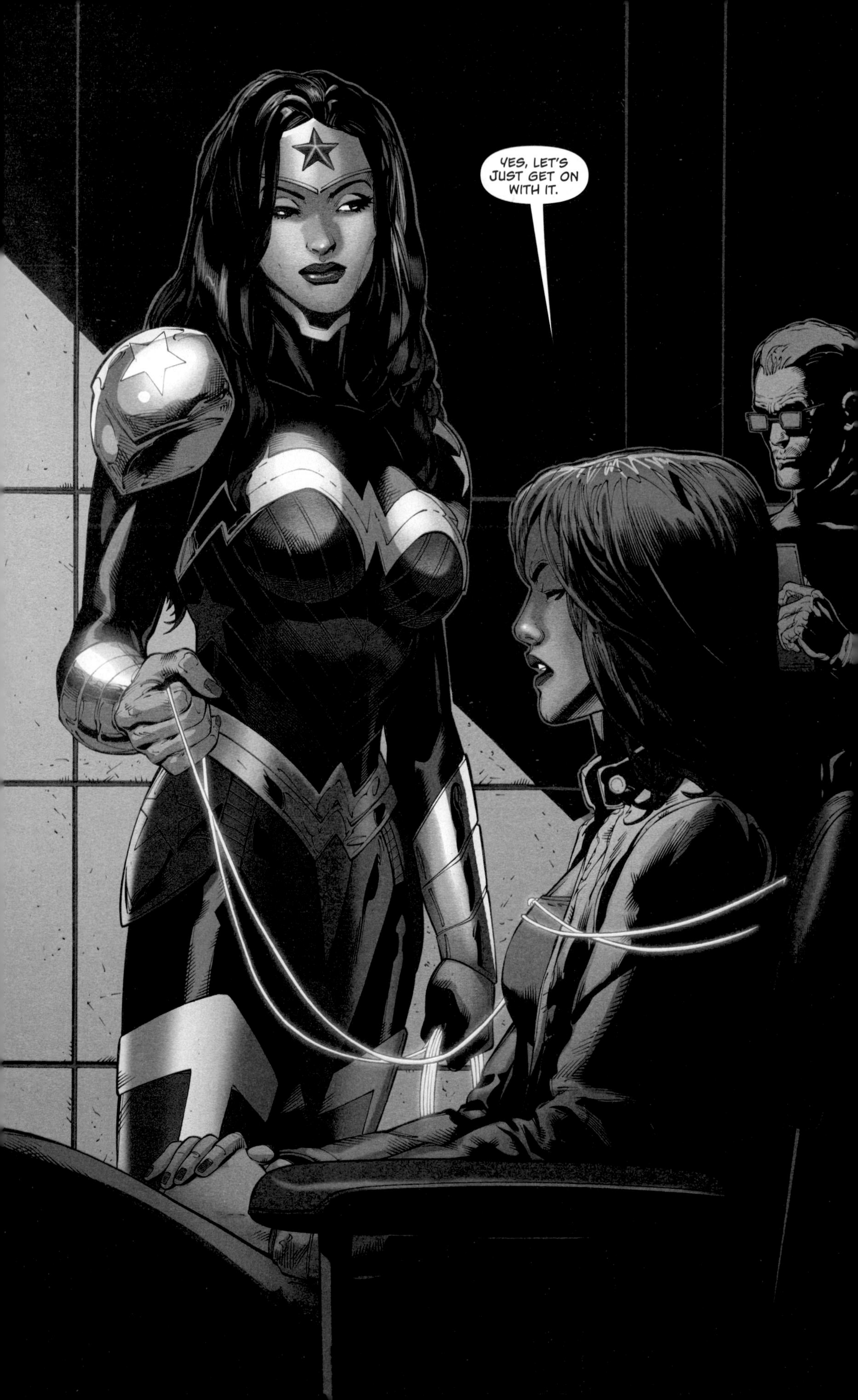
YES, LET'S JUST GET ON WITH IT.

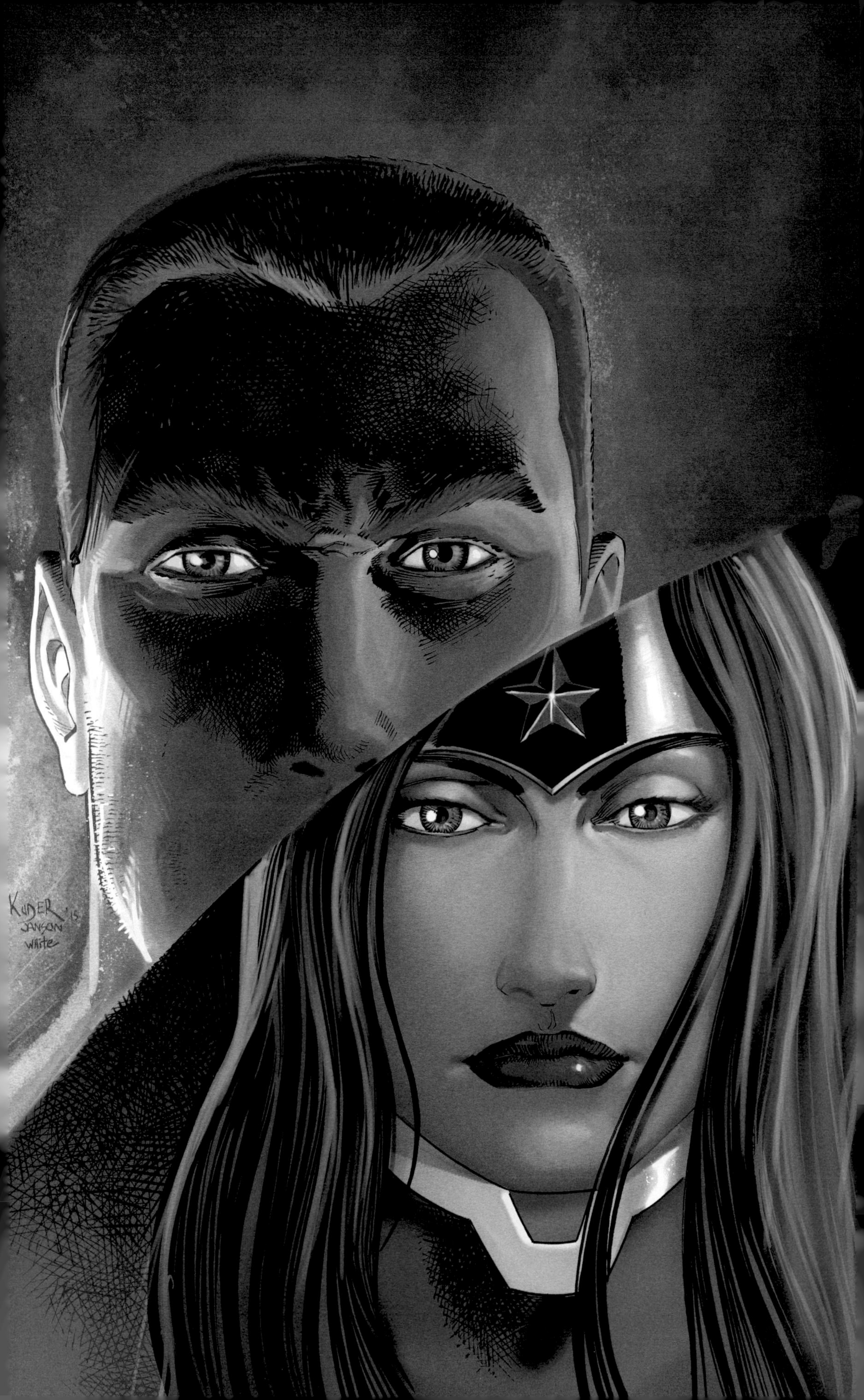
KUDER '15
JANSON
white

DARK TRUTH PART FOUR

PETER J. TOMASI writer DOUG MAHNKE penciller JAIME MENDOZA MARK IRWIN SEAN PARSONS SCOTT HANNA inkers WIL QUINTANA ULISES ARREOLA TOMEU MOREY colorists ROB LEIGH letterer cover by DOUG MAHNKE AARON KUDER KLAUS JANSON & DEAN WHITE

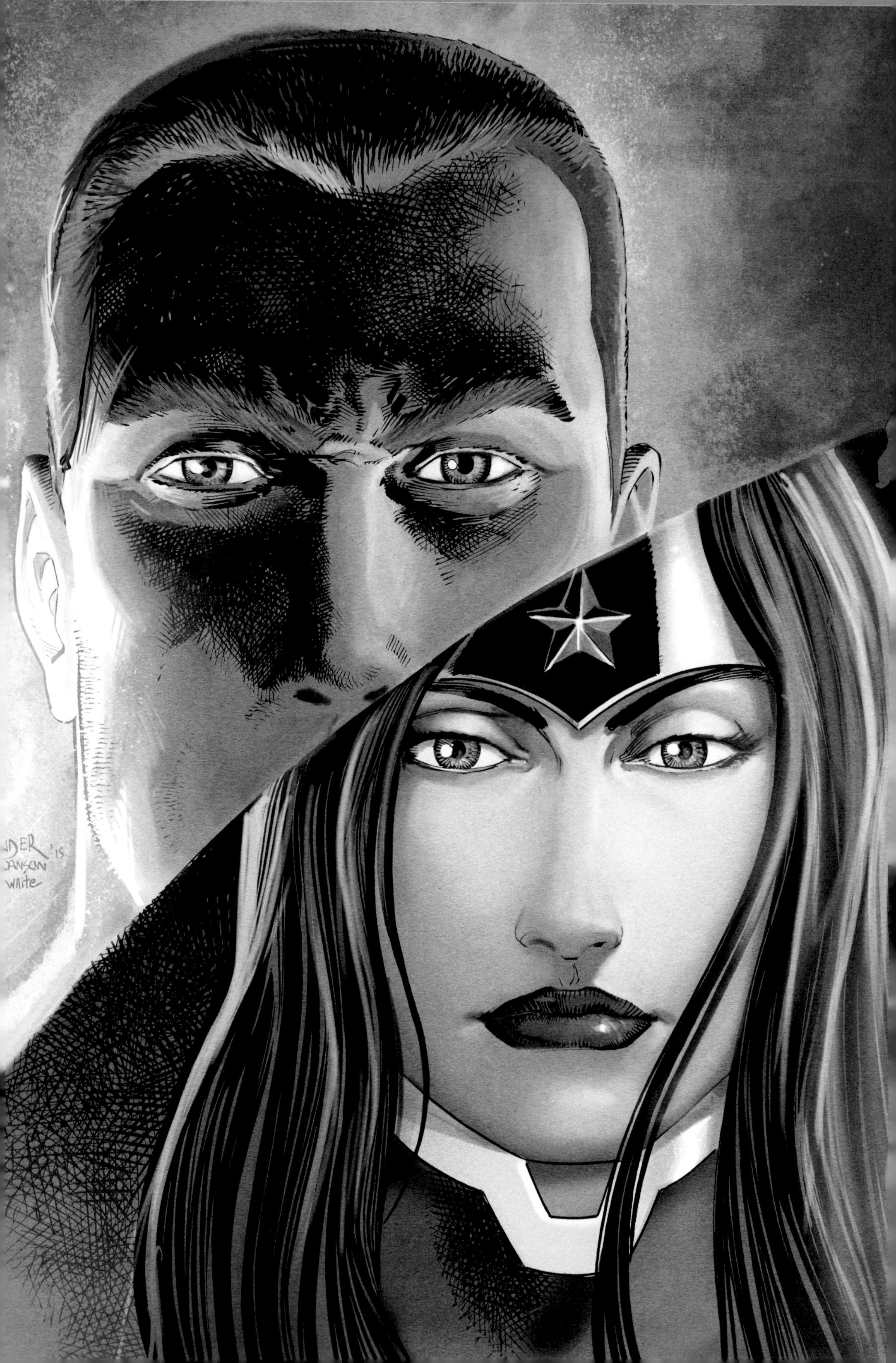

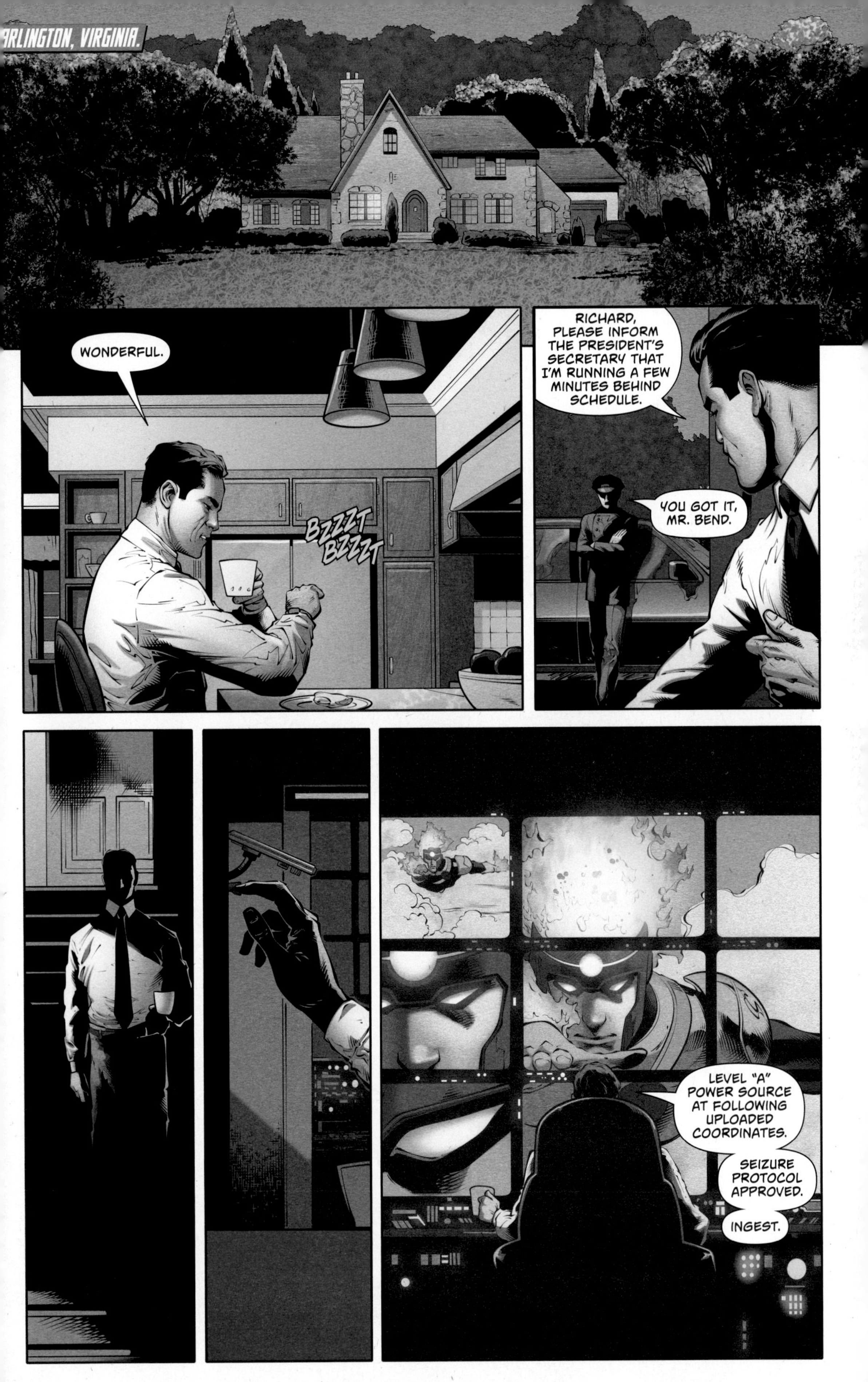
ARLINGTON, VIRGINIA.
WONDERFUL.
BZZZT BZZZT
RICHARD, PLEASE INFORM THE PRESIDENT'S SECRETARY THAT I'M RUNNING A FEW MINUTES BEHIND SCHEDULE.
YOU GOT IT, MR. BEND.
LEVEL "A" POWER SOURCE AT FOLLOWING UPLOADED COORDINATES.
SEIZURE PROTOCOL APPROVED.
INGEST.

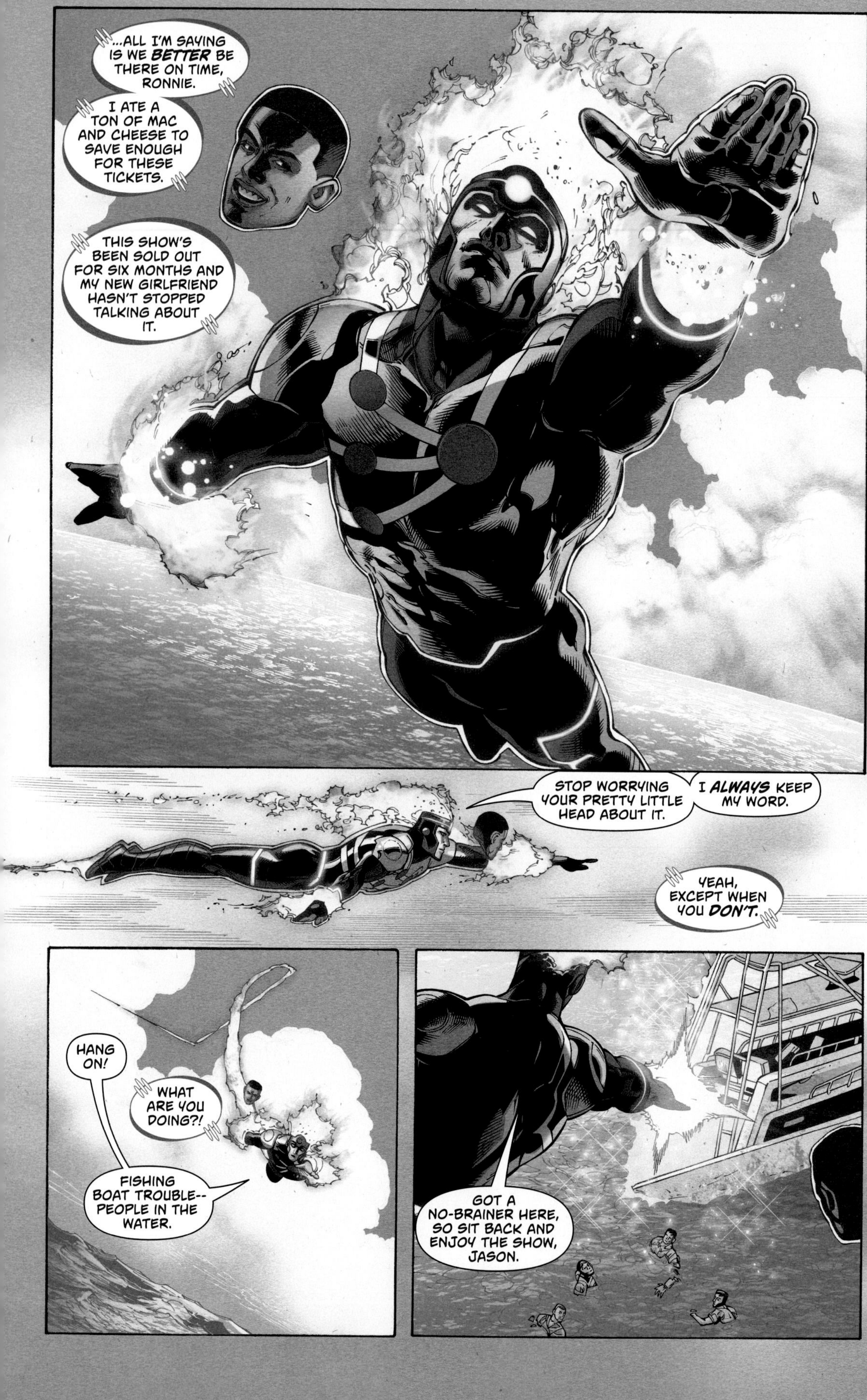
...ALL I'M SAYING IS WE BETTER BE THERE ON TIME, RONNIE.
I ATE A TON OF MAC AND CHEESE TO SAVE ENOUGH FOR THESE TICKETS.
THIS SHOW'S BEEN SOLD OUT FOR SIX MONTHS AND MY NEW GIRLFRIEND HASN'T STOPPED TALKING ABOUT IT.
STOP WORRYING YOUR PRETTY LITTLE HEAD ABOUT IT.
I ALWAYS KEEP MY WORD.
YEAH, EXCEPT WHEN YOU DON'T.
HANG ON!
WHAT ARE YOU DOING?!
FISHING BOAT TROUBLE--PEOPLE IN THE WATER.
GOT A NO-BRAINER HERE, SO SIT BACK AND ENJOY THE SHOW, JASON.

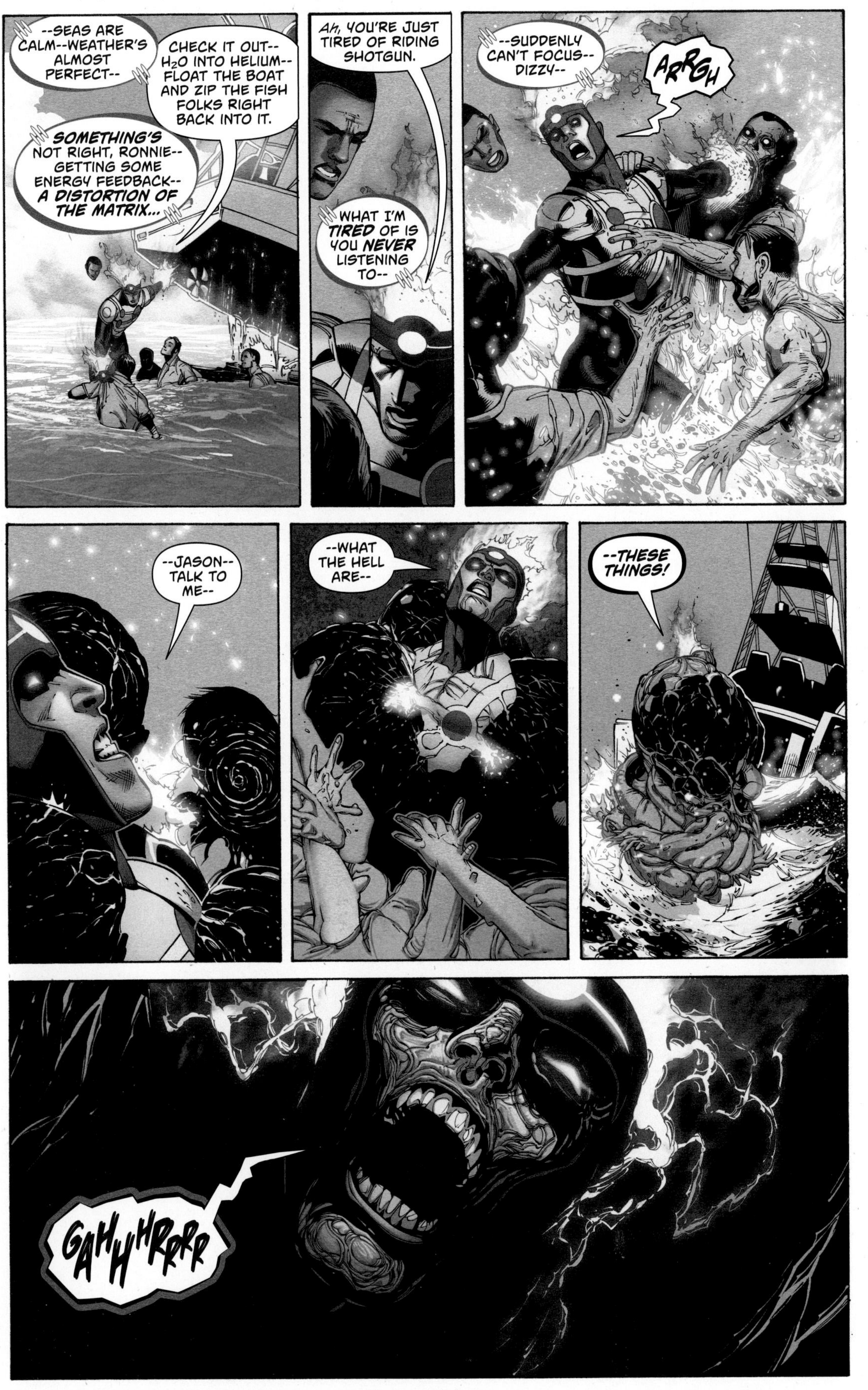
--SEAS ARE CALM--WEATHER'S ALMOST PERFECT--
CHECK IT OUT-- H_2O INTO HELIUM--FLOAT THE BOAT AND ZIP THE FISH FOLKS RIGHT BACK INTO IT.
SOMETHING'S NOT RIGHT, RONNIE--GETTING SOME ENERGY FEEDBACK--A DISTORTION OF THE MATRIX...
AH, YOU'RE JUST TIRED OF RIDING SHOTGUN.
WHAT I'M TIRED OF IS YOU NEVER LISTENING TO--
--SUDDENLY CAN'T FOCUS--DIZZY--
ARRRGH
--JASON--TALK TO ME--
--WHAT THE HELL ARE--
--THESE THINGS!
GAHHHRRRR

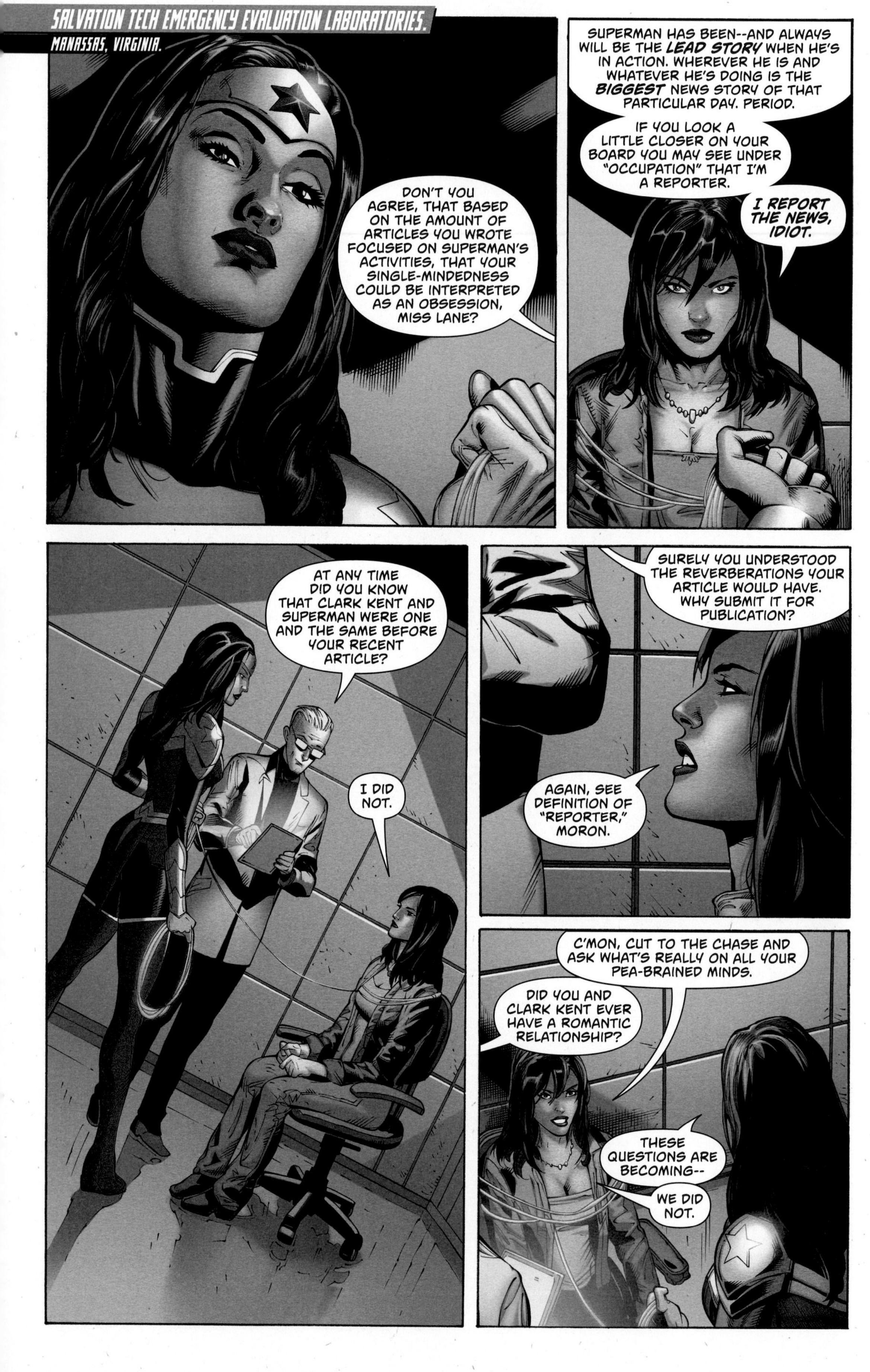
SALVATION TECH EMERGENCY EVALUATION LABORATORIES.
MANASSAS, VIRGINIA.
DON'T YOU AGREE, THAT BASED ON THE AMOUNT OF ARTICLES YOU WROTE FOCUSED ON SUPERMAN'S ACTIVITIES, THAT YOUR SINGLE-MINDEDNESS COULD BE INTERPRETED AS AN OBSESSION, MISS LANE?
SUPERMAN HAS BEEN--AND ALWAYS WILL BE THE LEAD STORY WHEN HE'S IN ACTION. WHEREVER HE IS AND WHATEVER HE'S DOING IS THE BIGGEST NEWS STORY OF THAT PARTICULAR DAY. PERIOD.
IF YOU LOOK A LITTLE CLOSER ON YOUR BOARD YOU MAY SEE UNDER "OCCUPATION" THAT I'M A REPORTER.
I REPORT THE NEWS, IDIOT.
AT ANY TIME DID YOU KNOW THAT CLARK KENT AND SUPERMAN WERE ONE AND THE SAME BEFORE YOUR RECENT ARTICLE?
I DID NOT.
SURELY YOU UNDERSTOOD THE REVERBERATIONS YOUR ARTICLE WOULD HAVE. WHY SUBMIT IT FOR PUBLICATION?
AGAIN, SEE DEFINITION OF "REPORTER," MORON.
C'MON, CUT TO THE CHASE AND ASK WHAT'S REALLY ON ALL YOUR PEA-BRAINED MINDS.
DID YOU AND CLARK KENT EVER HAVE A ROMANTIC RELATIONSHIP?
THESE QUESTIONS ARE BECOMING--
WE DID NOT.

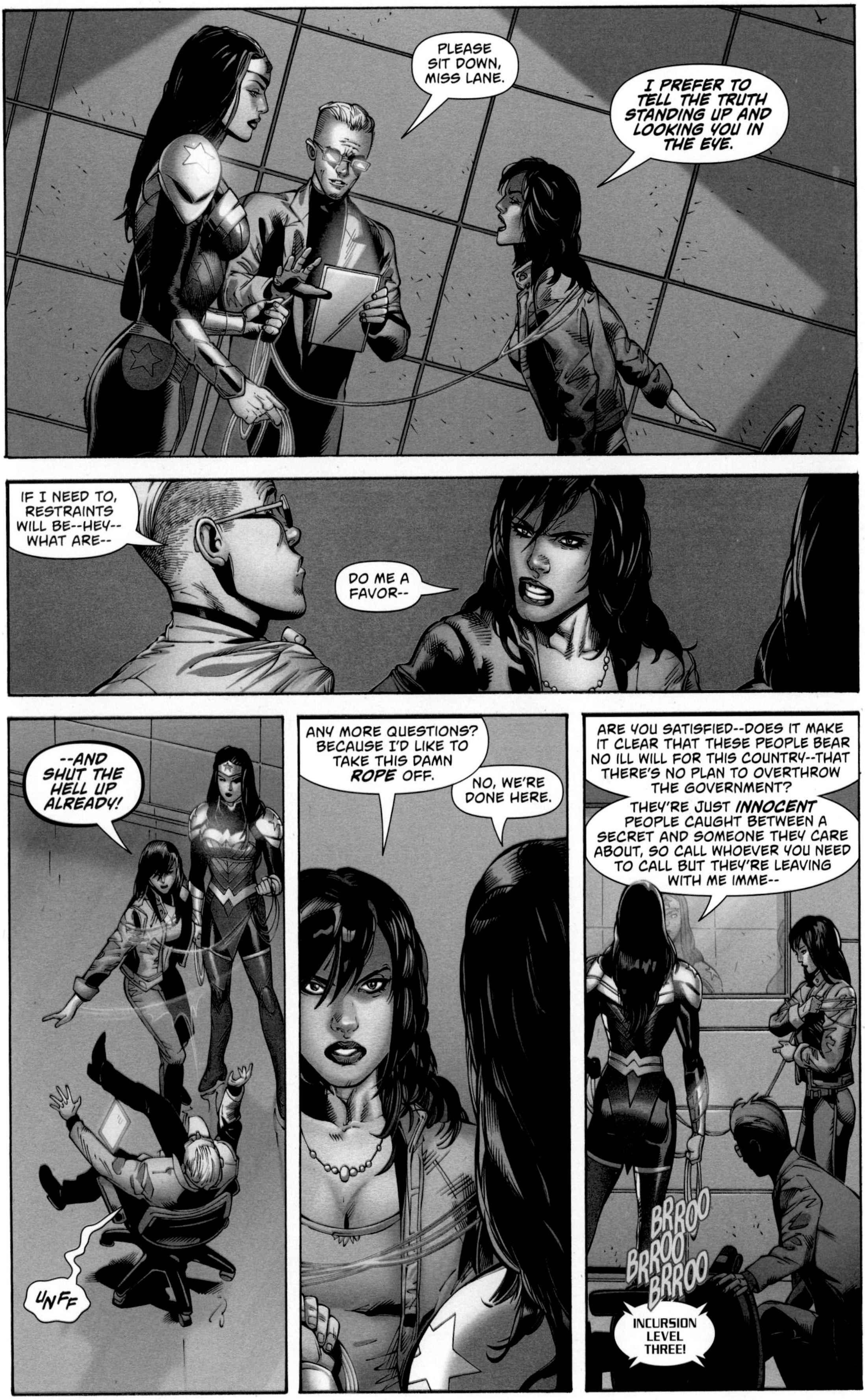
PLEASE SIT DOWN, MISS LANE.
I PREFER TO TELL THE TRUTH STANDING UP AND LOOKING YOU IN THE EYE.
IF I NEED TO, RESTRAINTS WILL BE--HEY--WHAT ARE--
DO ME A FAVOR--
--AND SHUT THE HELL UP ALREADY!
UNFF
ANY MORE QUESTIONS? BECAUSE I'D LIKE TO TAKE THIS DAMN ROPE OFF.
NO, WE'RE DONE HERE.
ARE YOU SATISFIED--DOES IT MAKE IT CLEAR THAT THESE PEOPLE BEAR NO ILL WILL FOR THIS COUNTRY--THAT THERE'S NO PLAN TO OVERTHROW THE GOVERNMENT?
THEY'RE JUST INNOCENT PEOPLE CAUGHT BETWEEN A SECRET AND SOMEONE THEY CARE ABOUT, SO CALL WHOEVER YOU NEED TO CALL BUT THEY'RE LEAVING WITH ME IMME--
BRROO BRROO BRROO
INCURSION LEVEL THREE!

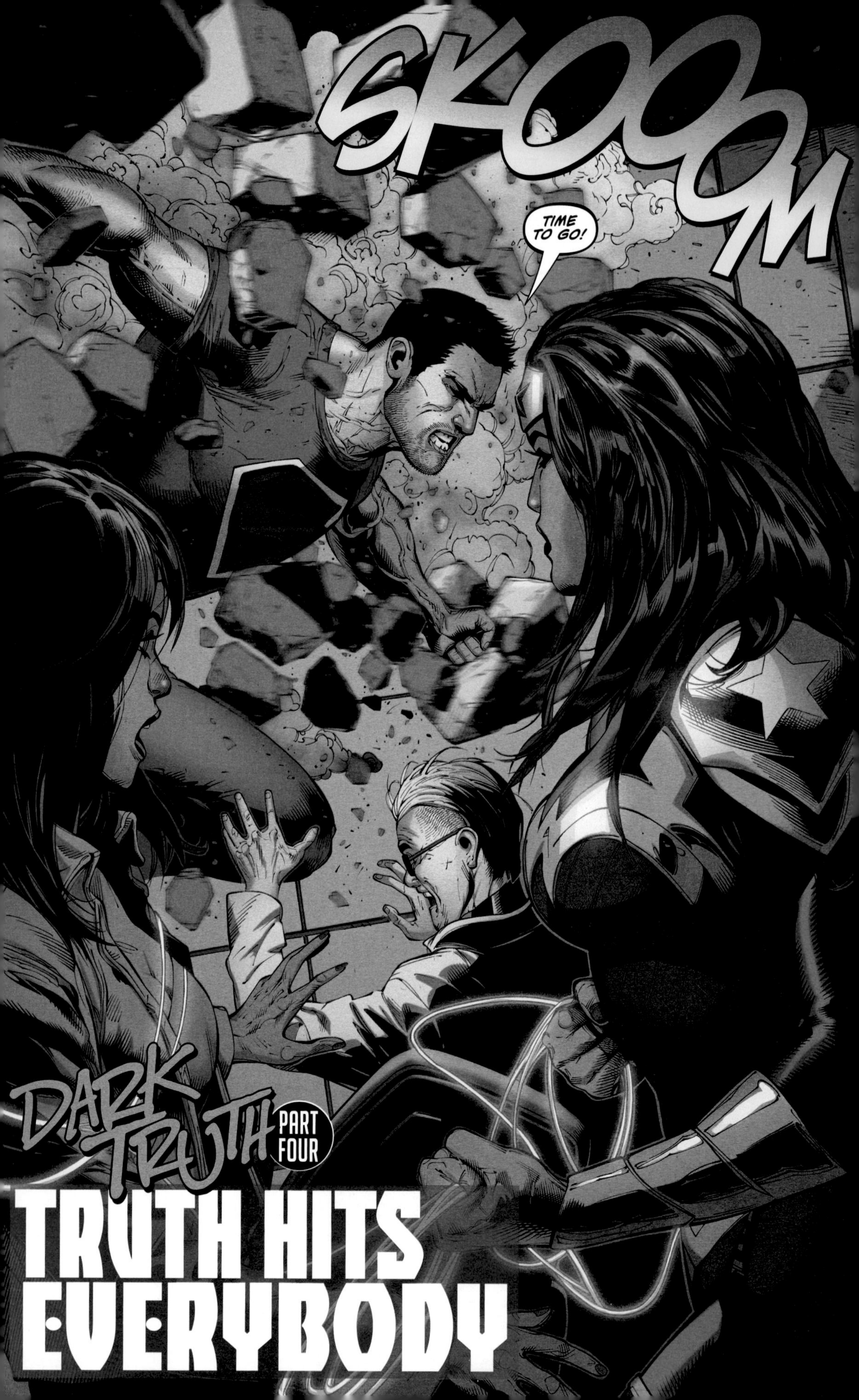
SKOOOM
TIME TO GO!
DARK TRUTH PART FOUR
TRUTH HITS EVERYBODY

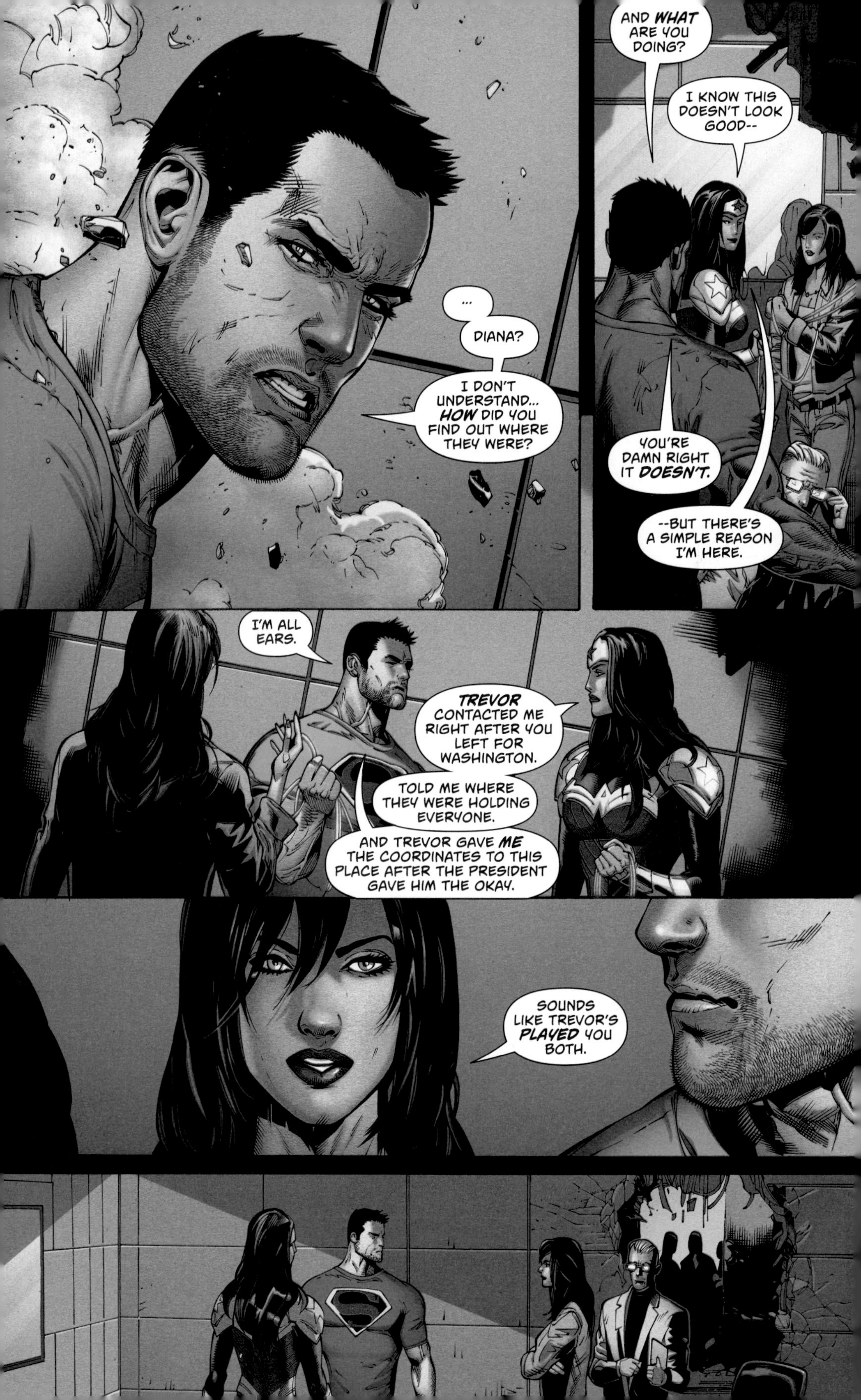
...
DIANA?
I DON'T UNDERSTAND... HOW DID YOU FIND OUT WHERE THEY WERE?
AND WHAT ARE YOU DOING?
I KNOW THIS DOESN'T LOOK GOOD--
YOU'RE DAMN RIGHT IT DOESN'T.
--BUT THERE'S A SIMPLE REASON I'M HERE.
I'M ALL EARS.
TREVOR CONTACTED ME RIGHT AFTER YOU LEFT FOR WASHINGTON.
TOLD ME WHERE THEY WERE HOLDING EVERYONE.
AND TREVOR GAVE ME THE COORDINATES TO THIS PLACE AFTER THE PRESIDENT GAVE HIM THE OKAY.
SOUNDS LIKE TREVOR'S PLAYED YOU BOTH.

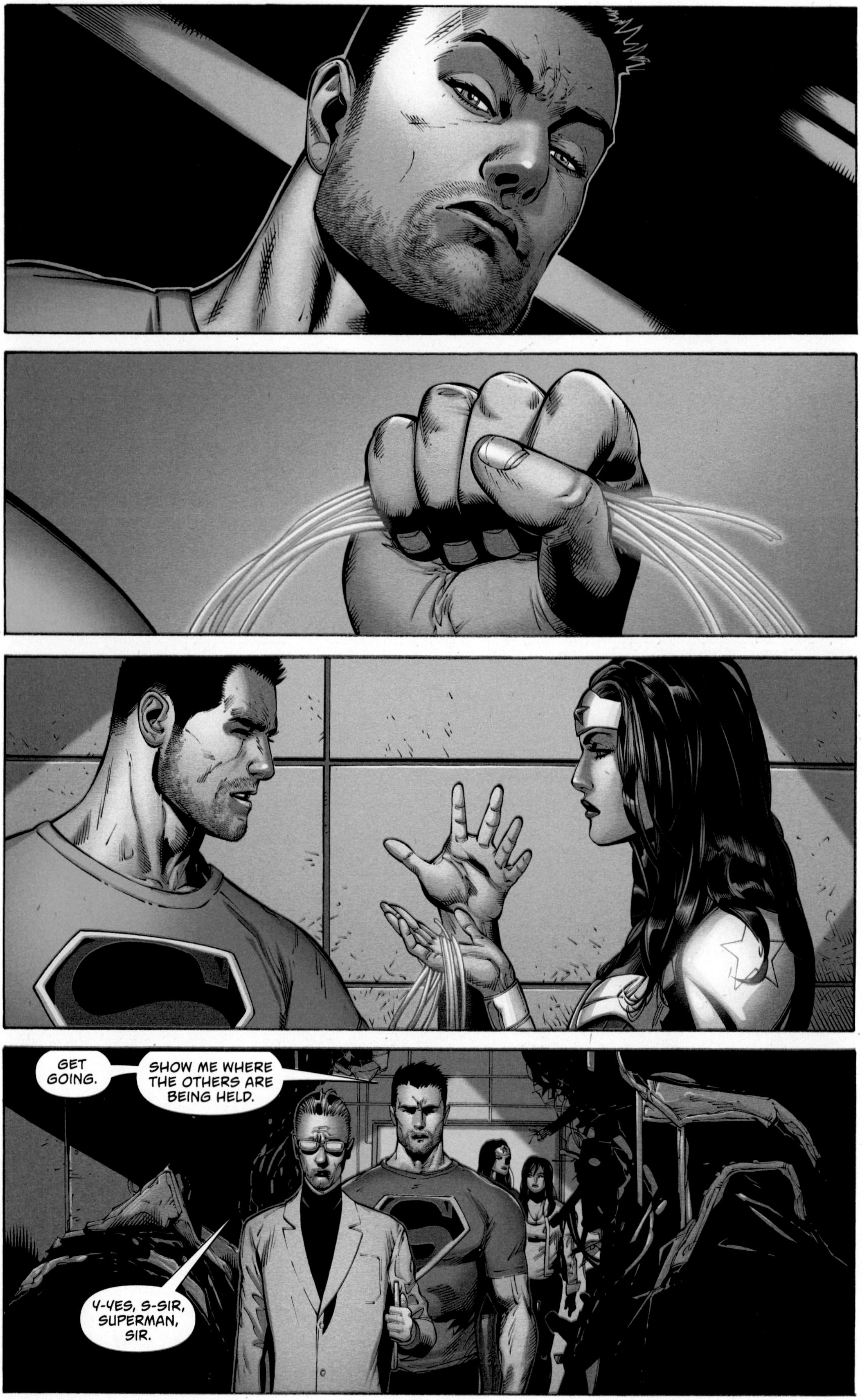
GET GOING.
SHOW ME WHERE THE OTHERS ARE BEING HELD.
Y-YES, S-SIR, SUPERMAN, SIR.

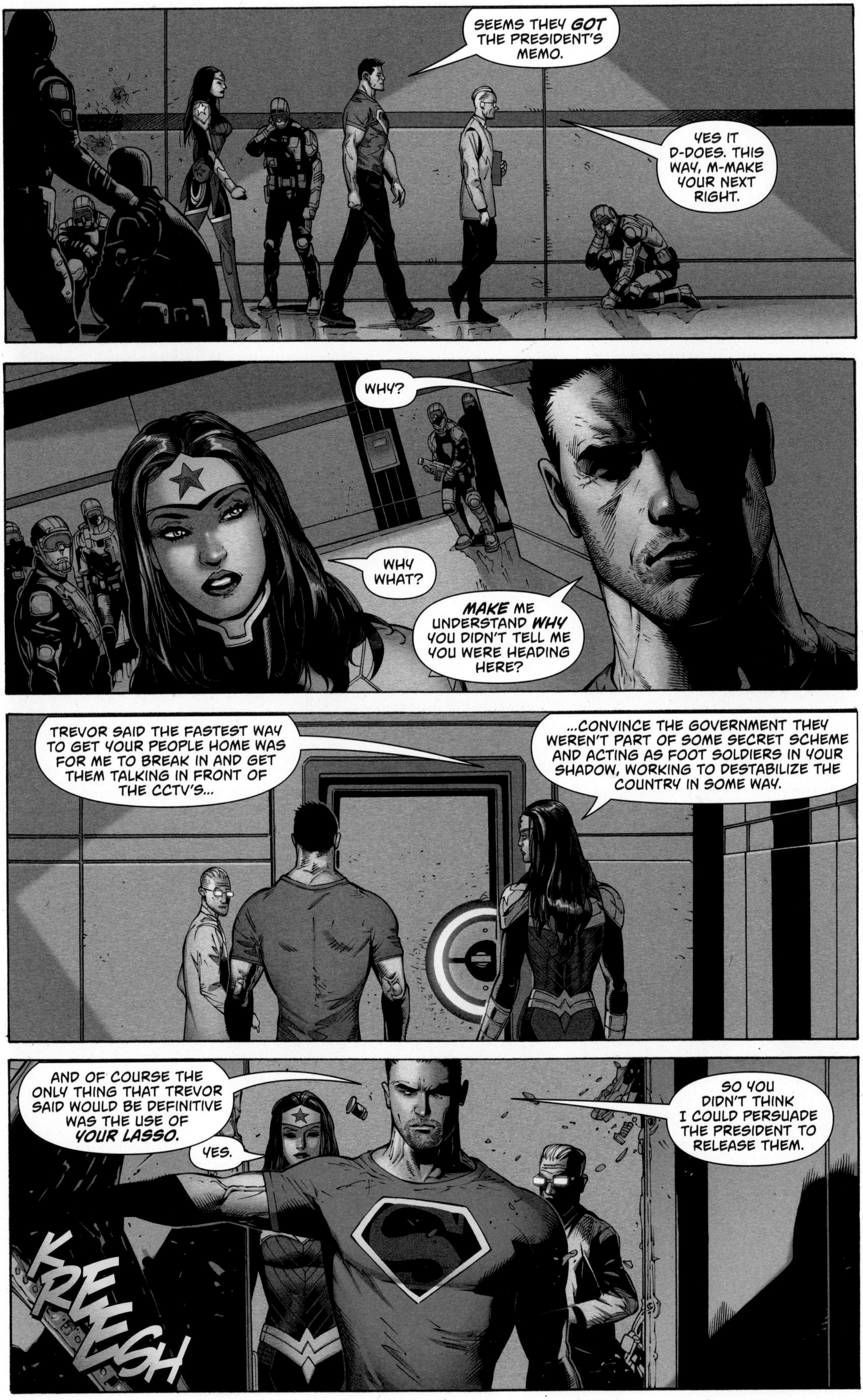
SEEMS THEY GOT THE PRESIDENT'S MEMO.
YES IT D-DOES. THIS WAY, M-MAKE YOUR NEXT RIGHT.
WHY?
WHY WHAT?
MAKE ME UNDERSTAND WHY YOU DIDN'T TELL ME YOU WERE HEADING HERE?
TREVOR SAID THE FASTEST WAY TO GET YOUR PEOPLE HOME WAS FOR ME TO BREAK IN AND GET THEM TALKING IN FRONT OF THE CCTV'S...
...CONVINCE THE GOVERNMENT THEY WEREN'T PART OF SOME SECRET SCHEME AND ACTING AS FOOT SOLDIERS IN YOUR SHADOW, WORKING TO DESTABILIZE THE COUNTRY IN SOME WAY.
AND OF COURSE THE ONLY THING THAT TREVOR SAID WOULD BE DEFINITIVE WAS THE USE OF YOUR LASSO.
YES.
SO YOU DIDN'T THINK I COULD PERSUADE THE PRESIDENT TO RELEASE THEM.
KREESH

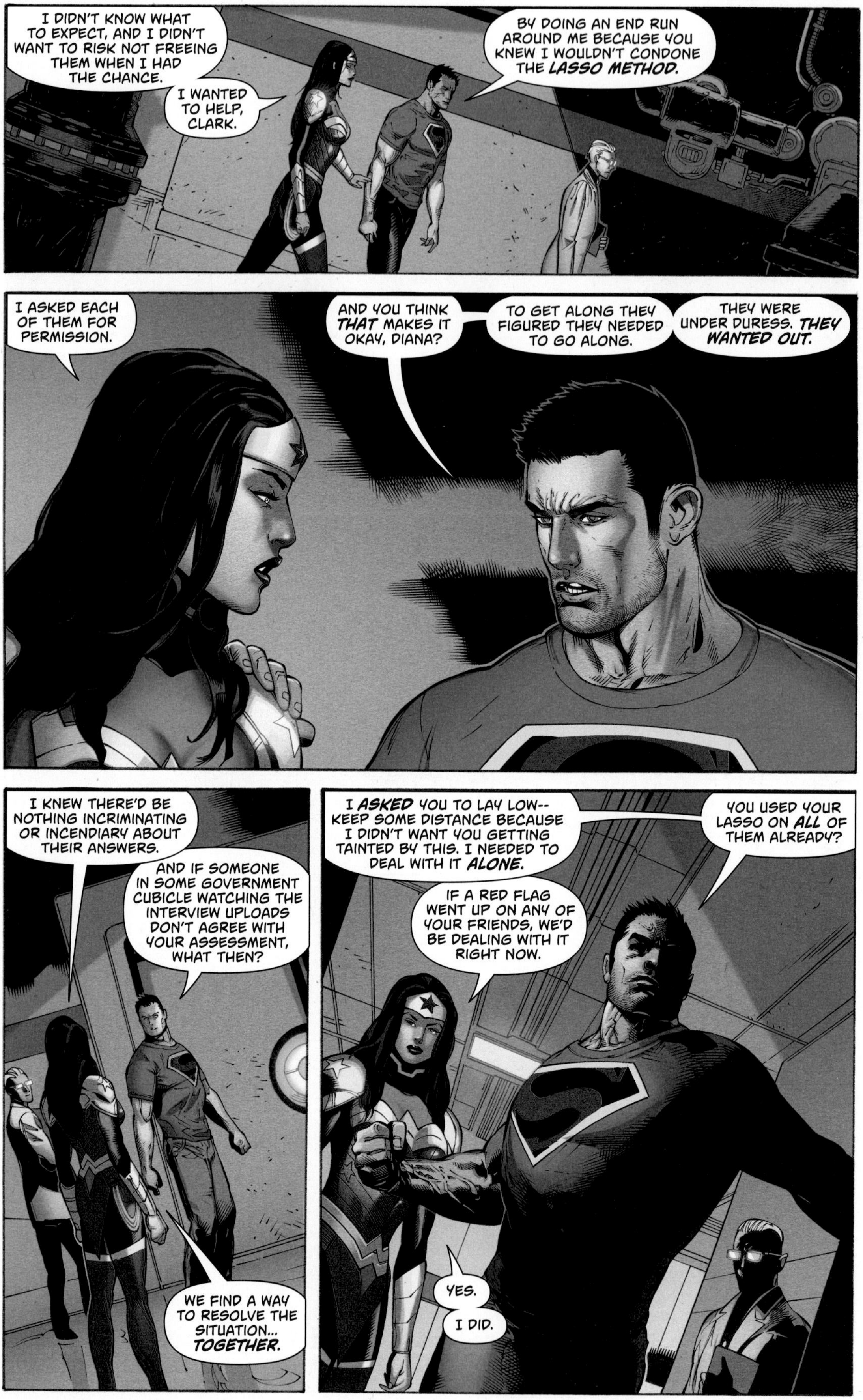
I DIDN'T KNOW WHAT TO EXPECT, AND I DIDN'T WANT TO RISK NOT FREEING THEM WHEN I HAD THE CHANCE.
I WANTED TO HELP, CLARK.
BY DOING AN END RUN AROUND ME BECAUSE YOU KNEW I WOULDN'T CONDONE THE LASSO METHOD.
I ASKED EACH OF THEM FOR PERMISSION.
AND YOU THINK THAT MAKES IT OKAY, DIANA?
TO GET ALONG THEY FIGURED THEY NEEDED TO GO ALONG.
THEY WERE UNDER DURESS. THEY WANTED OUT.
I KNEW THERE'D BE NOTHING INCRIMINATING OR INCENDIARY ABOUT THEIR ANSWERS.
AND IF SOMEONE IN SOME GOVERNMENT CUBICLE WATCHING THE INTERVIEW UPLOADS DON'T AGREE WITH YOUR ASSESSMENT, WHAT THEN?
WE FIND A WAY TO RESOLVE THE SITUATION... TOGETHER.
I ASKED YOU TO LAY LOW--KEEP SOME DISTANCE BECAUSE I DIDN'T WANT YOU GETTING TAINTED BY THIS. I NEEDED TO DEAL WITH IT ALONE.
IF A RED FLAG WENT UP ON ANY OF YOUR FRIENDS, WE'D BE DEALING WITH IT RIGHT NOW.
YOU USED YOUR LASSO ON ALL OF THEM ALREADY?
YES.
I DID.

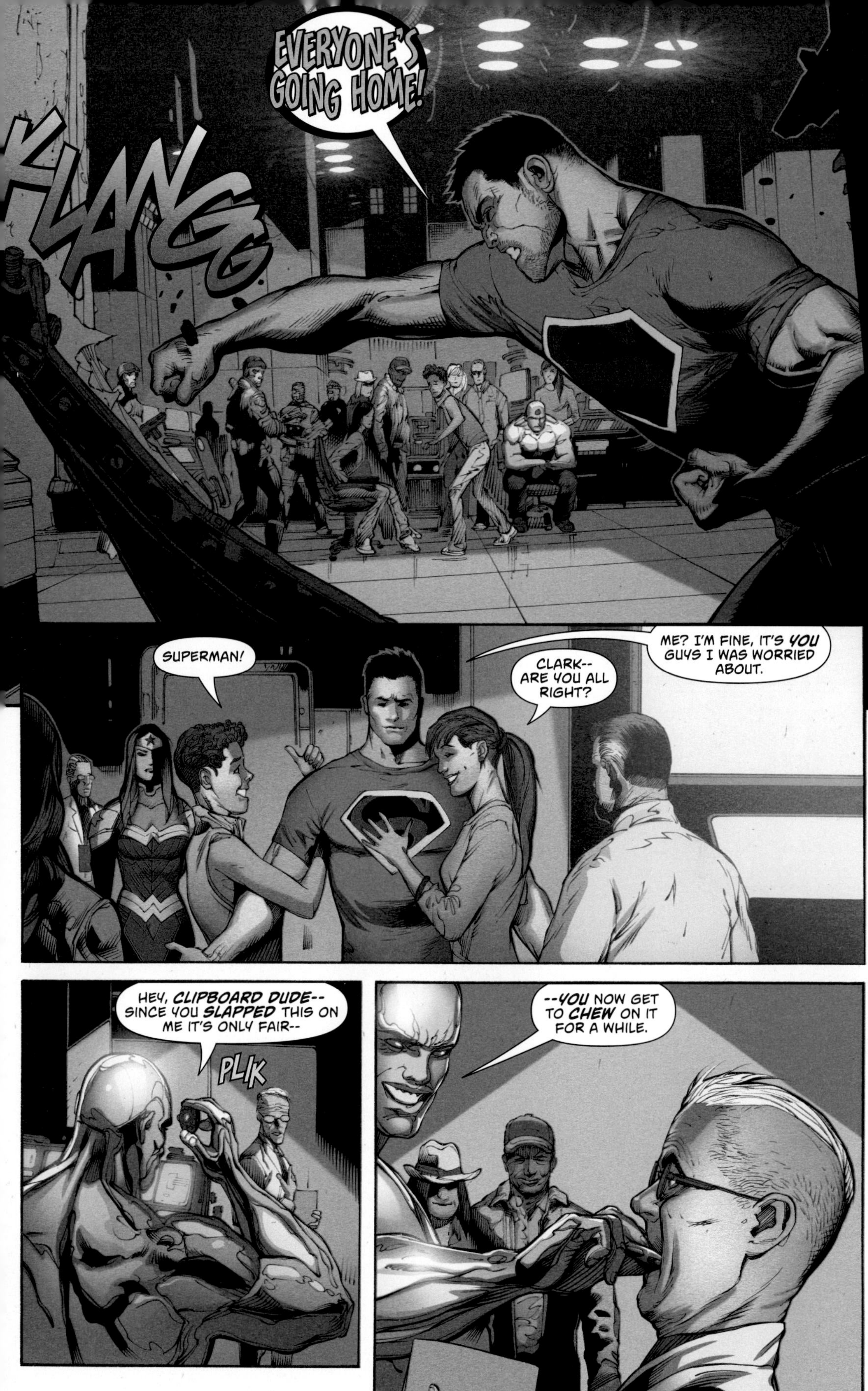
KLANGG
EVERYONE'S GOING HOME!
SUPERMAN!
CLARK-- ARE YOU ALL RIGHT?
ME? I'M FINE, IT'S YOU GUYS I WAS WORRIED ABOUT.
HEY, CLIPBOARD DUDE-- SINCE YOU SLAPPED THIS ON ME IT'S ONLY FAIR--
PLIK
--YOU NOW GET TO CHEW ON IT FOR A WHILE.

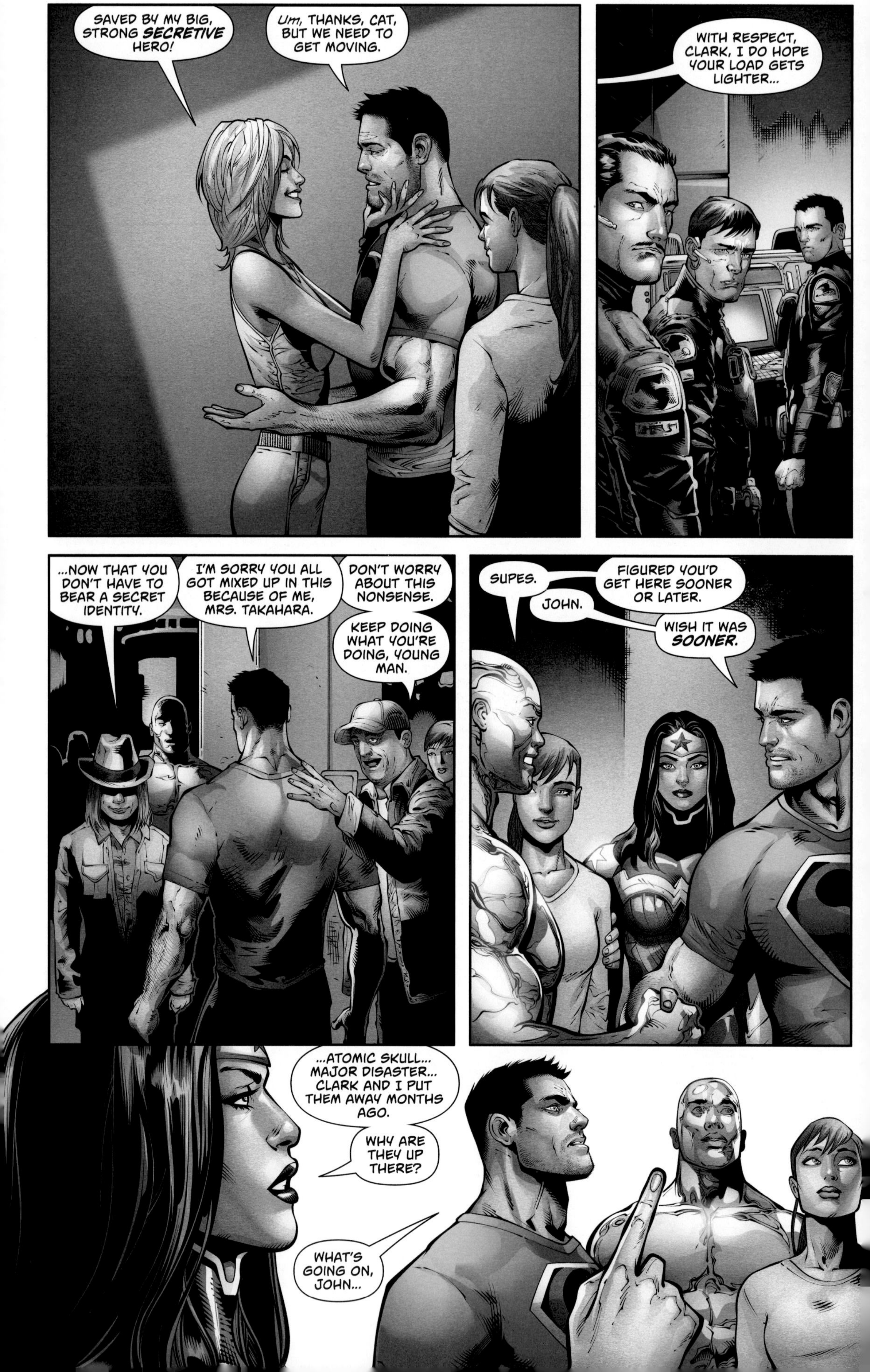
SAVED BY MY BIG, STRONG SECRETIVE HERO!
Um, THANKS, CAT, BUT WE NEED TO GET MOVING.
WITH RESPECT, CLARK, I DO HOPE YOUR LOAD GETS LIGHTER...
...NOW THAT YOU DON'T HAVE TO BEAR A SECRET IDENTITY.
I'M SORRY YOU ALL GOT MIXED UP IN THIS BECAUSE OF ME, MRS. TAKAHARA.
DON'T WORRY ABOUT THIS NONSENSE.
KEEP DOING WHAT YOU'RE DOING, YOUNG MAN.
SUPES.
JOHN.
FIGURED YOU'D GET HERE SOONER OR LATER.
WISH IT WAS SOONER.
...ATOMIC SKULL... MAJOR DISASTER... CLARK AND I PUT THEM AWAY MONTHS AGO.
WHY ARE THEY UP THERE?
WHAT'S GOING ON, JOHN...

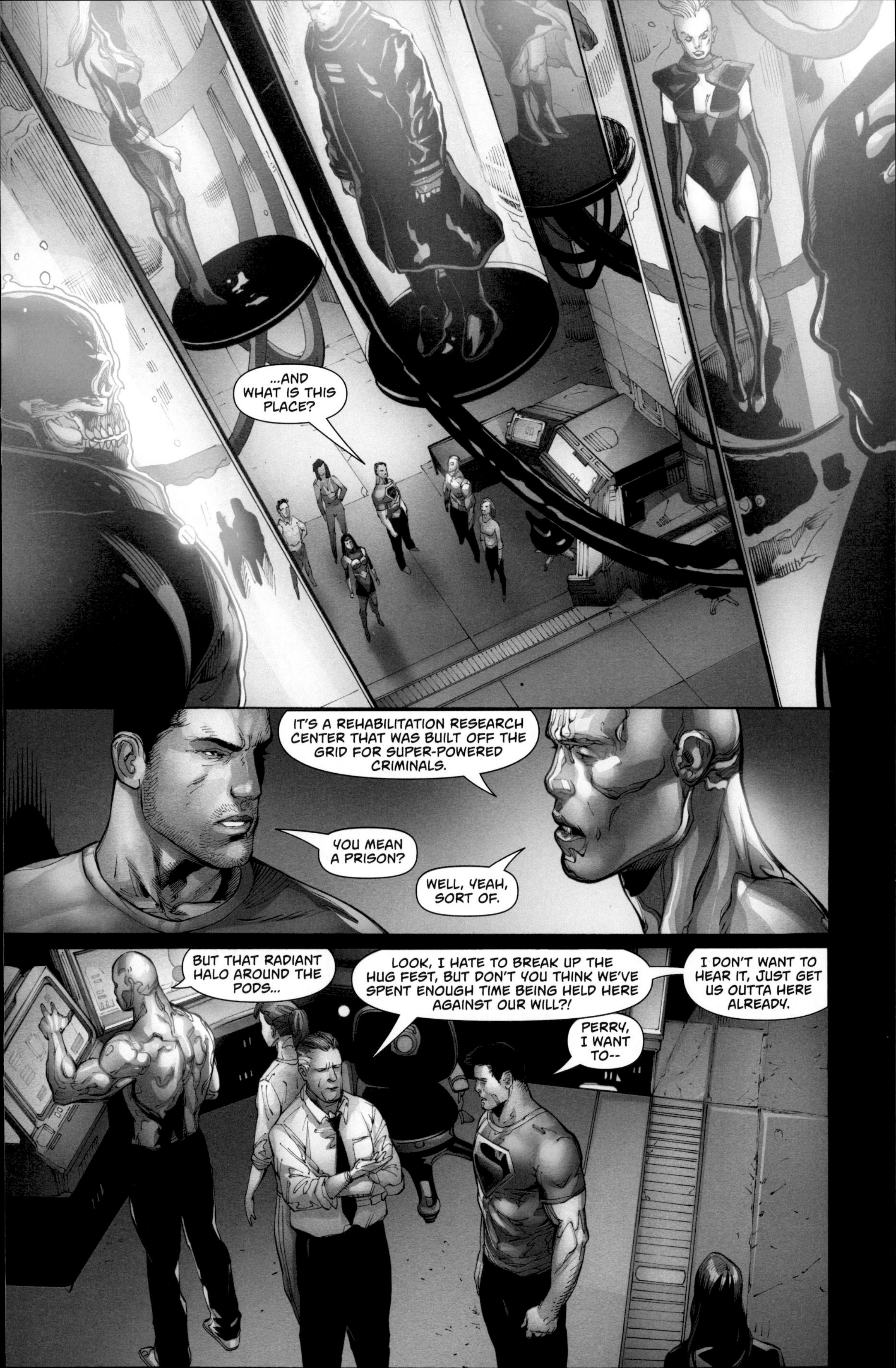
...AND WHAT IS THIS PLACE?
IT'S A REHABILITATION RESEARCH CENTER THAT WAS BUILT OFF THE GRID FOR SUPER-POWERED CRIMINALS.
YOU MEAN A PRISON?
WELL, YEAH, SORT OF.
BUT THAT RADIANT HALO AROUND THE PODS...
LOOK, I HATE TO BREAK UP THE HUG FEST, BUT DON'T YOU THINK WE'VE SPENT ENOUGH TIME BEING HELD HERE AGAINST OUR WILL?!
PERRY, I WANT TO--
I DON'T WANT TO HEAR IT, JUST GET US OUTTA HERE ALREADY.

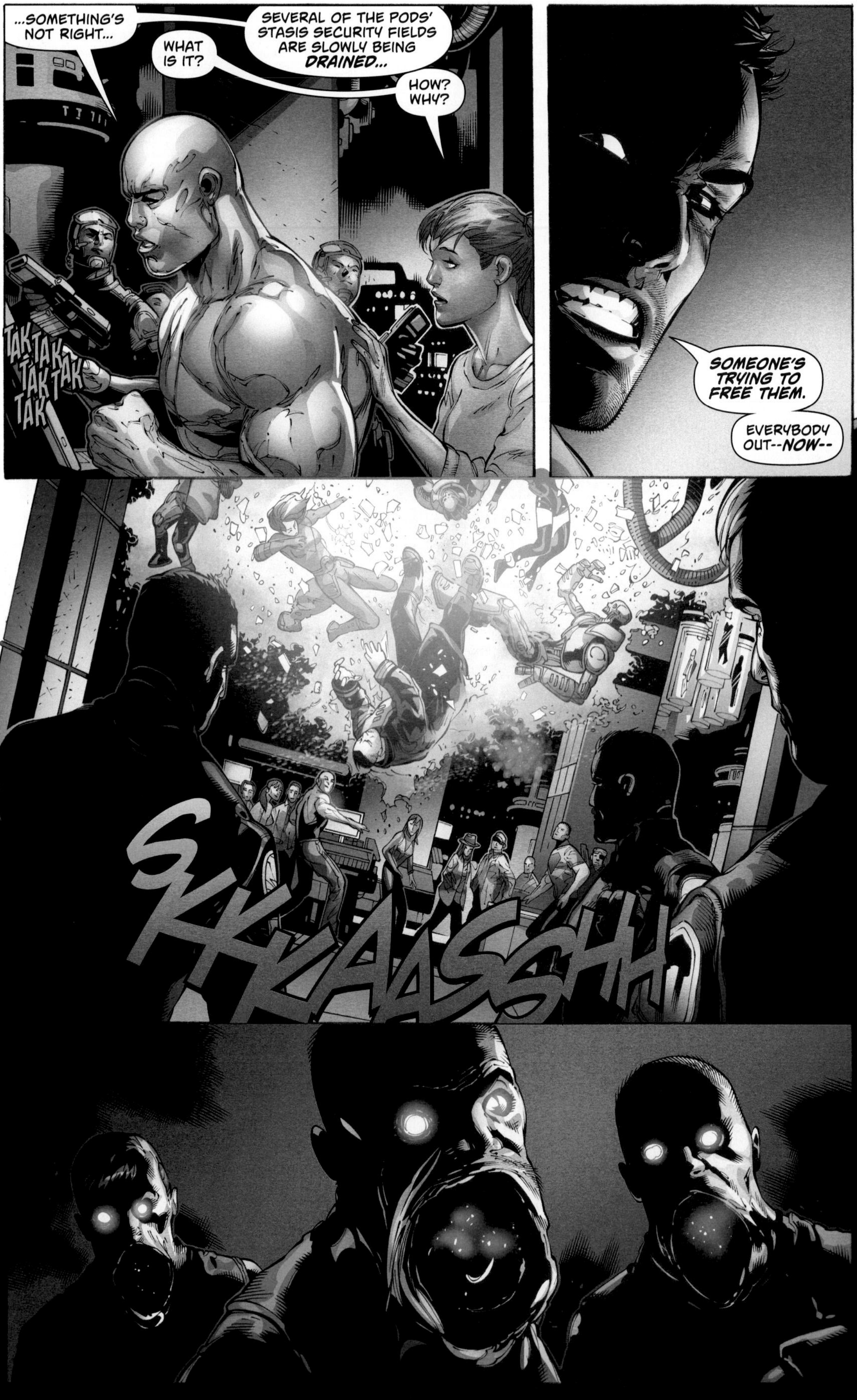
...SOMETHING'S NOT RIGHT...
WHAT IS IT?
SEVERAL OF THE PODS' STASIS SECURITY FIELDS ARE SLOWLY BEING DRAINED...
HOW? WHY?
TAK TAK TAK TAK TAK TAK
SOMEONE'S TRYING TO FREE THEM.
EVERYBODY OUT--NOW--
SKKAASSHH

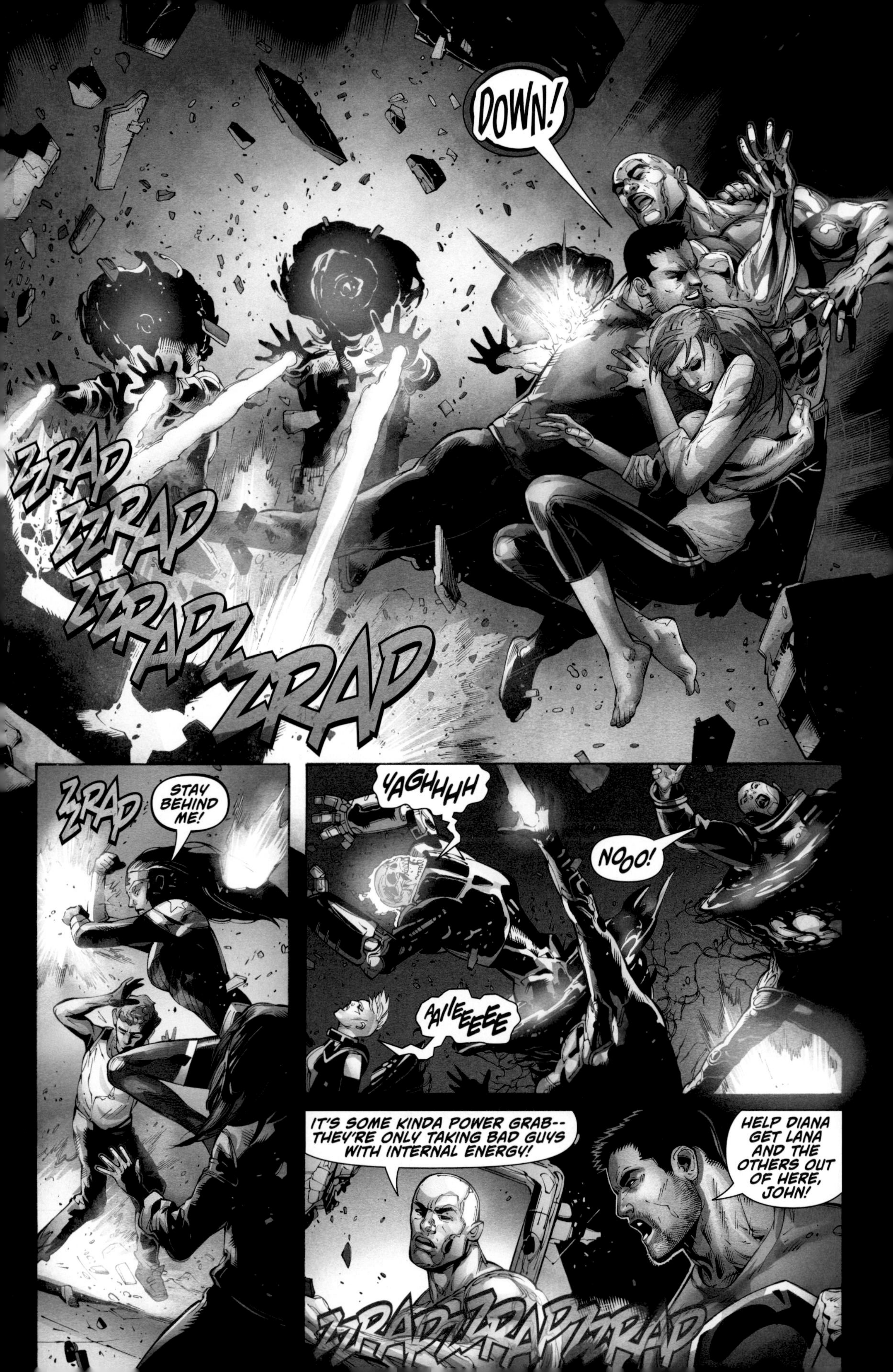
DOWN!
ZZRAD
ZZRAD
ZZRAD
ZZRAD
ZZRAD
STAY BEHIND ME!
YAGHHHH
NOOO!
AAIIEEEEE
IT'S SOME KINDA POWER GRAB-- THEY'RE ONLY TAKING BAD GUYS WITH INTERNAL ENERGY!
HELP DIANA GET LANA AND THE OTHERS OUT OF HERE, JOHN!
ZZRAD ZZRAD ZZRAD ZZRAD

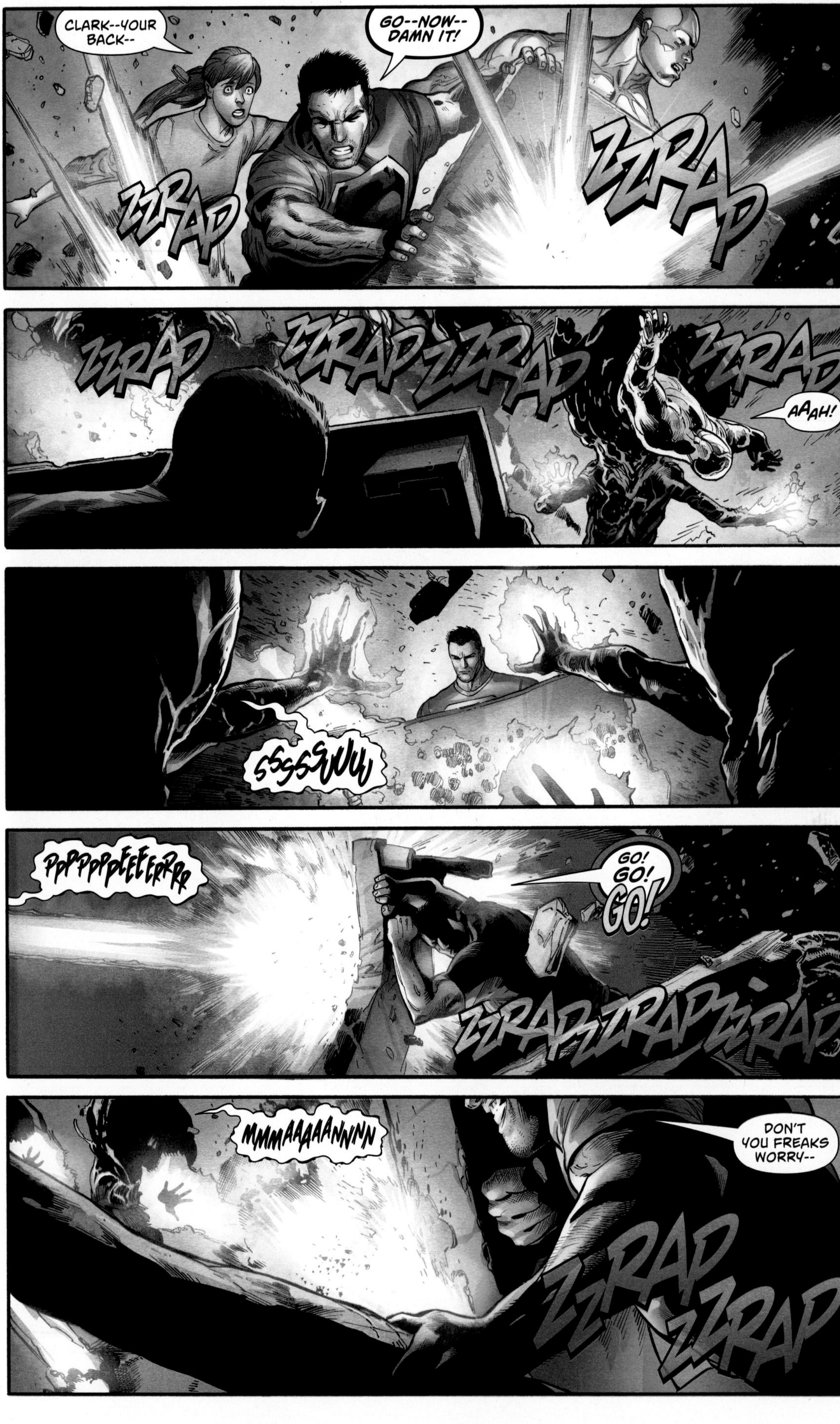

CLARK--YOUR BACK--
GO--NOW--DAMN IT!
ZZRAP
ZZRAP
ZZRAP
ZZRAP ZZRAP
ZZRAD
AAAH!
SSSSSUUUU
PPPPPPPEEEERRR
GO! GO! GO!
ZZRAPZZRAPZZRAP
MMMAAAAANNNN
DON'T YOU FREAKS WORRY--
ZZRAP
ZZRAP

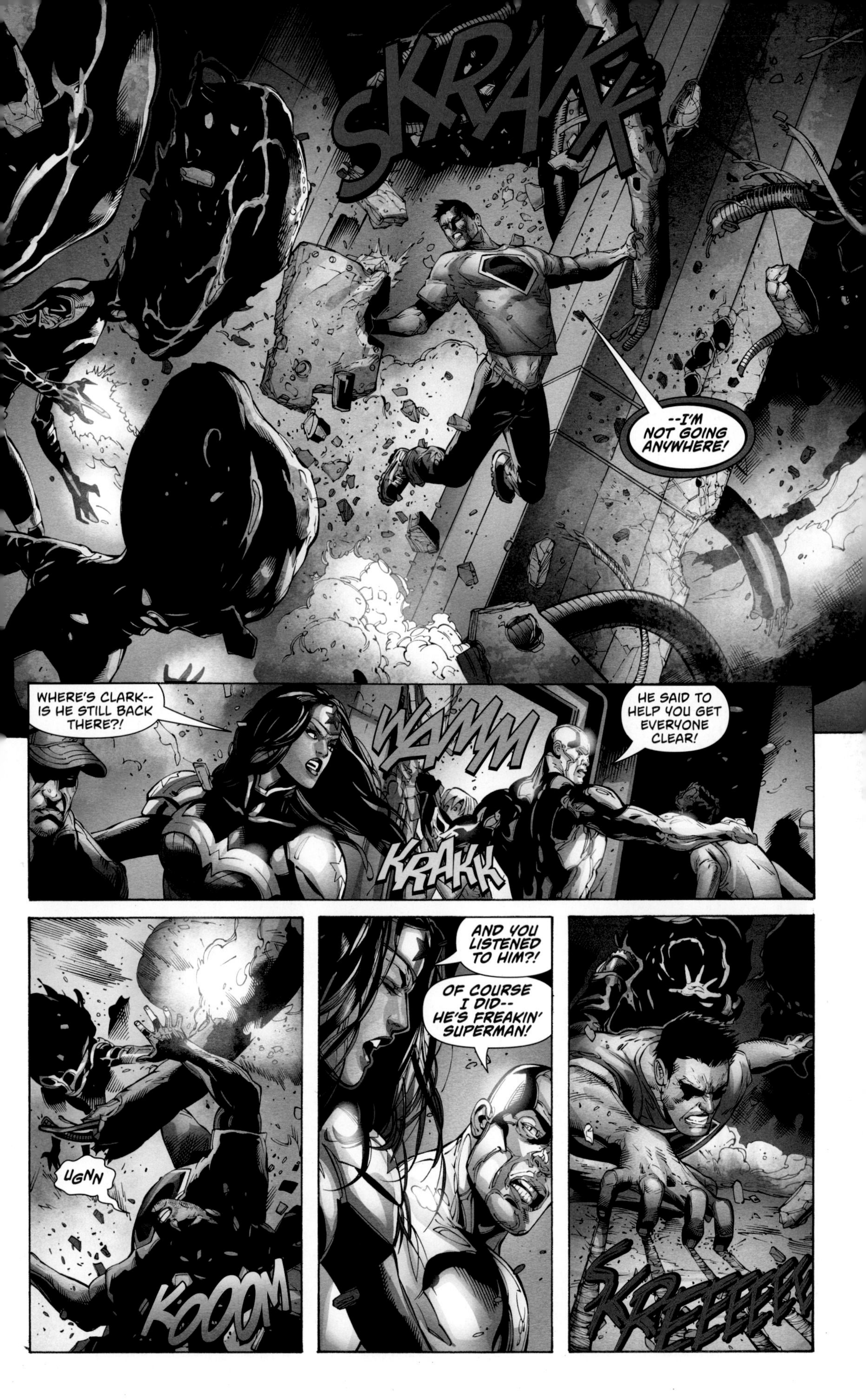
SKRAKK
--I'M NOT GOING ANYWHERE!
WHERE'S CLARK-- IS HE STILL BACK THERE?!
WAMM
HE SAID TO HELP YOU GET EVERYONE CLEAR!
KRAKK
UGNN
KOOOM
AND YOU LISTENED TO HIM?!
OF COURSE I DID-- HE'S FREAKIN' SUPERMAN!
SKREEEEEE

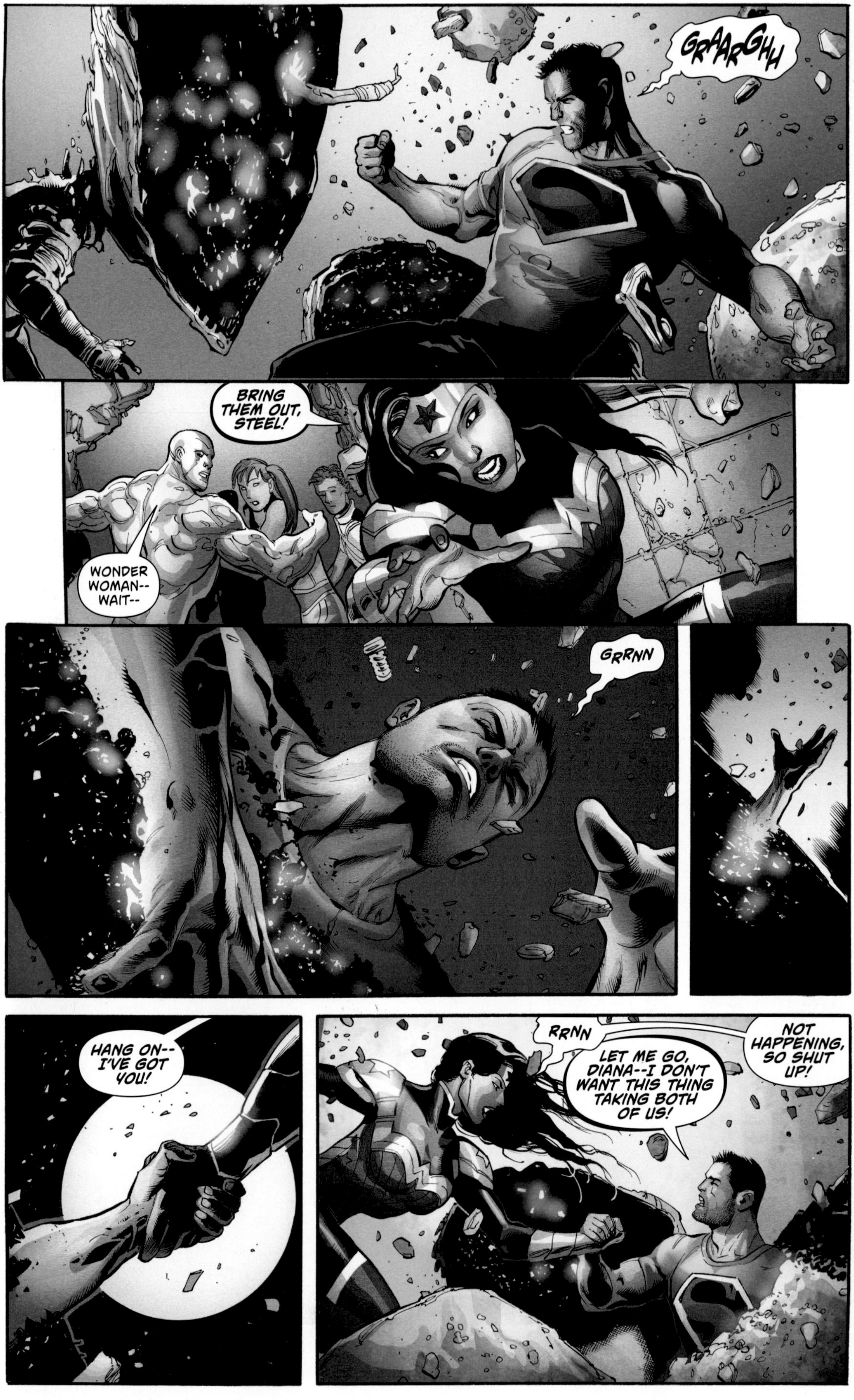
GRAARGHH
BRING THEM OUT, STEEL!
WONDER WOMAN-- WAIT--
GRRNN
HANG ON-- I'VE GOT YOU!
RRNN
LET ME GO, DIANA--I DON'T WANT THIS THING TAKING BOTH OF US!
NOT HAPPENING, SO SHUT UP!

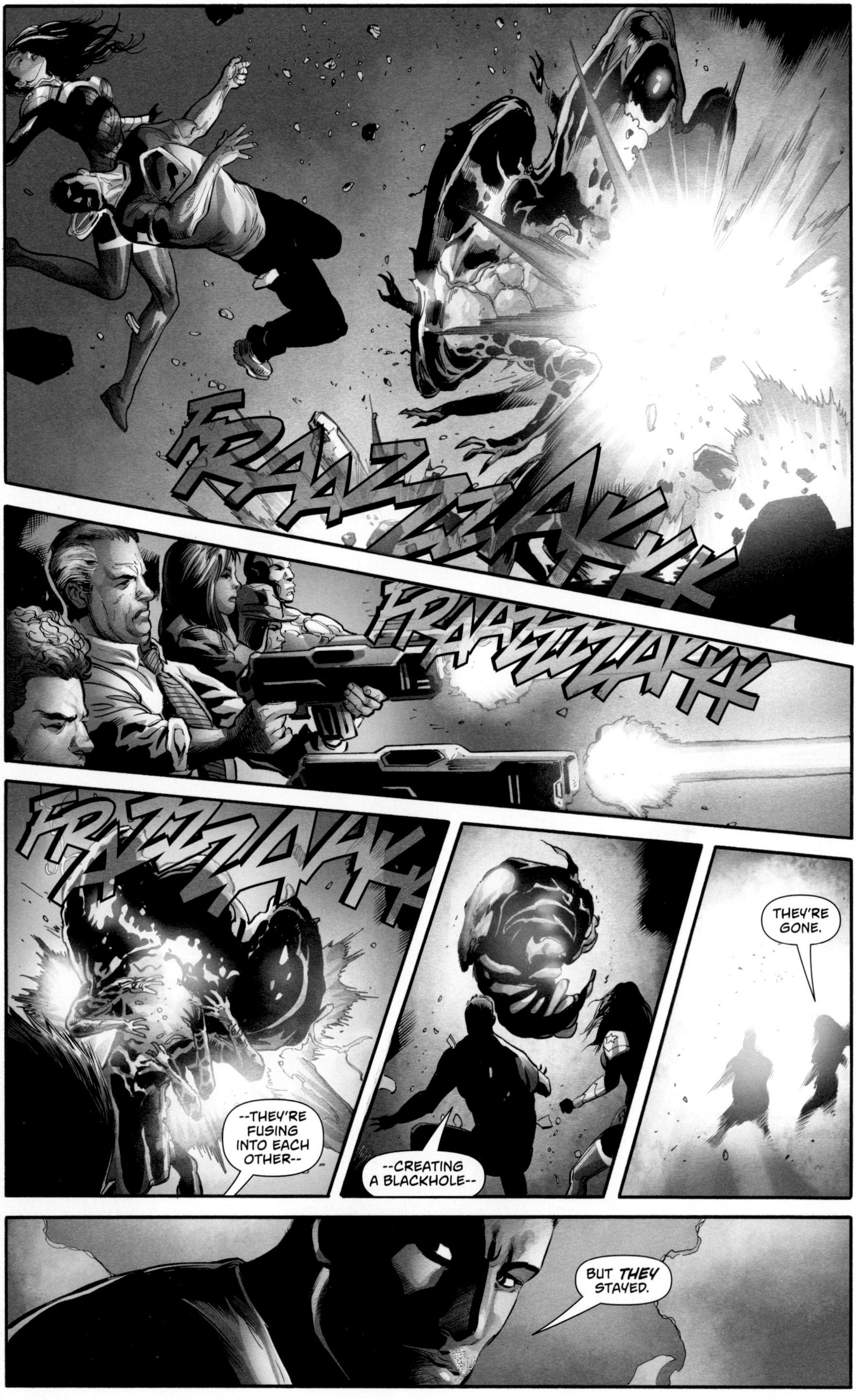
--THEY'RE FUSING INTO EACH OTHER--
--CREATING A BLACKHOLE--
THEY'RE GONE.
BUT *THEY* STAYED.

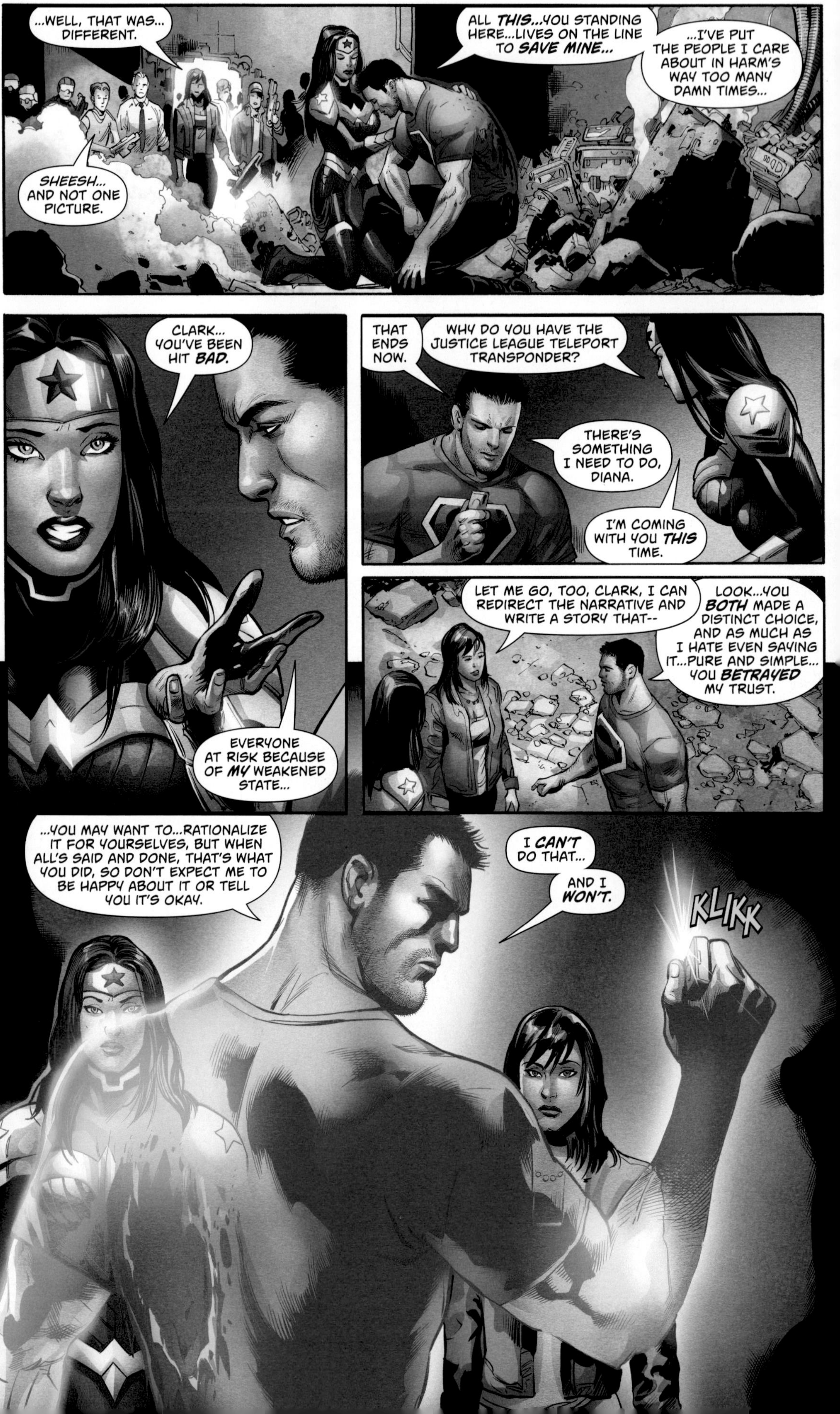
...WELL, THAT WAS... DIFFERENT.
SHEESH... AND NOT ONE PICTURE.
ALL THIS...YOU STANDING HERE...LIVES ON THE LINE TO SAVE MINE...
...I'VE PUT THE PEOPLE I CARE ABOUT IN HARM'S WAY TOO MANY DAMN TIMES...
CLARK... YOU'VE BEEN HIT BAD.
EVERYONE AT RISK BECAUSE OF MY WEAKENED STATE...
THAT ENDS NOW.
WHY DO YOU HAVE THE JUSTICE LEAGUE TELEPORT TRANSPONDER?
THERE'S SOMETHING I NEED TO DO, DIANA.
I'M COMING WITH YOU THIS TIME.
LET ME GO, TOO, CLARK, I CAN REDIRECT THE NARRATIVE AND WRITE A STORY THAT--
LOOK...YOU BOTH MADE A DISTINCT CHOICE, AND AS MUCH AS I HATE EVEN SAYING IT...PURE AND SIMPLE... YOU BETRAYED MY TRUST.
...YOU MAY WANT TO...RATIONALIZE IT FOR YOURSELVES, BUT WHEN ALL'S SAID AND DONE, THAT'S WHAT YOU DID, SO DON'T EXPECT ME TO BE HAPPY ABOUT IT OR TELL YOU IT'S OKAY.
I CAN'T DO THAT...
AND I WON'T.
KLIKK

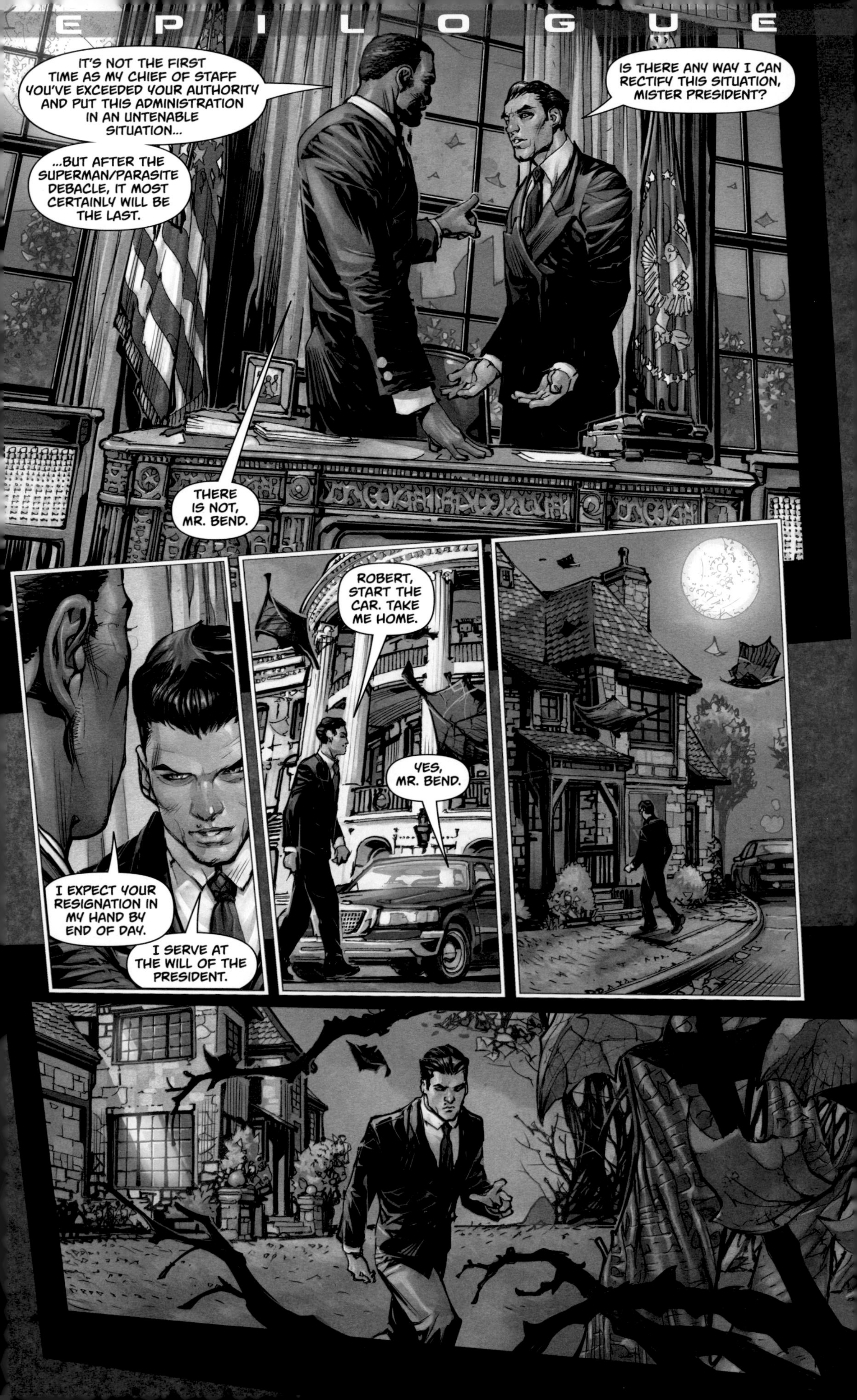
EPILOGUE
IT'S NOT THE FIRST TIME AS MY CHIEF OF STAFF YOU'VE EXCEEDED YOUR AUTHORITY AND PUT THIS ADMINISTRATION IN AN UNTENABLE SITUATION...
...BUT AFTER THE SUPERMAN/PARASITE DEBACLE, IT MOST CERTAINLY WILL BE THE LAST.
IS THERE ANY WAY I CAN RECTIFY THIS SITUATION, MISTER PRESIDENT?
THERE IS NOT, MR. BEND.
I EXPECT YOUR RESIGNATION IN MY HAND BY END OF DAY.
I SERVE AT THE WILL OF THE PRESIDENT.
ROBERT, START THE CAR. TAKE ME HOME.
YES, MR. BEND.

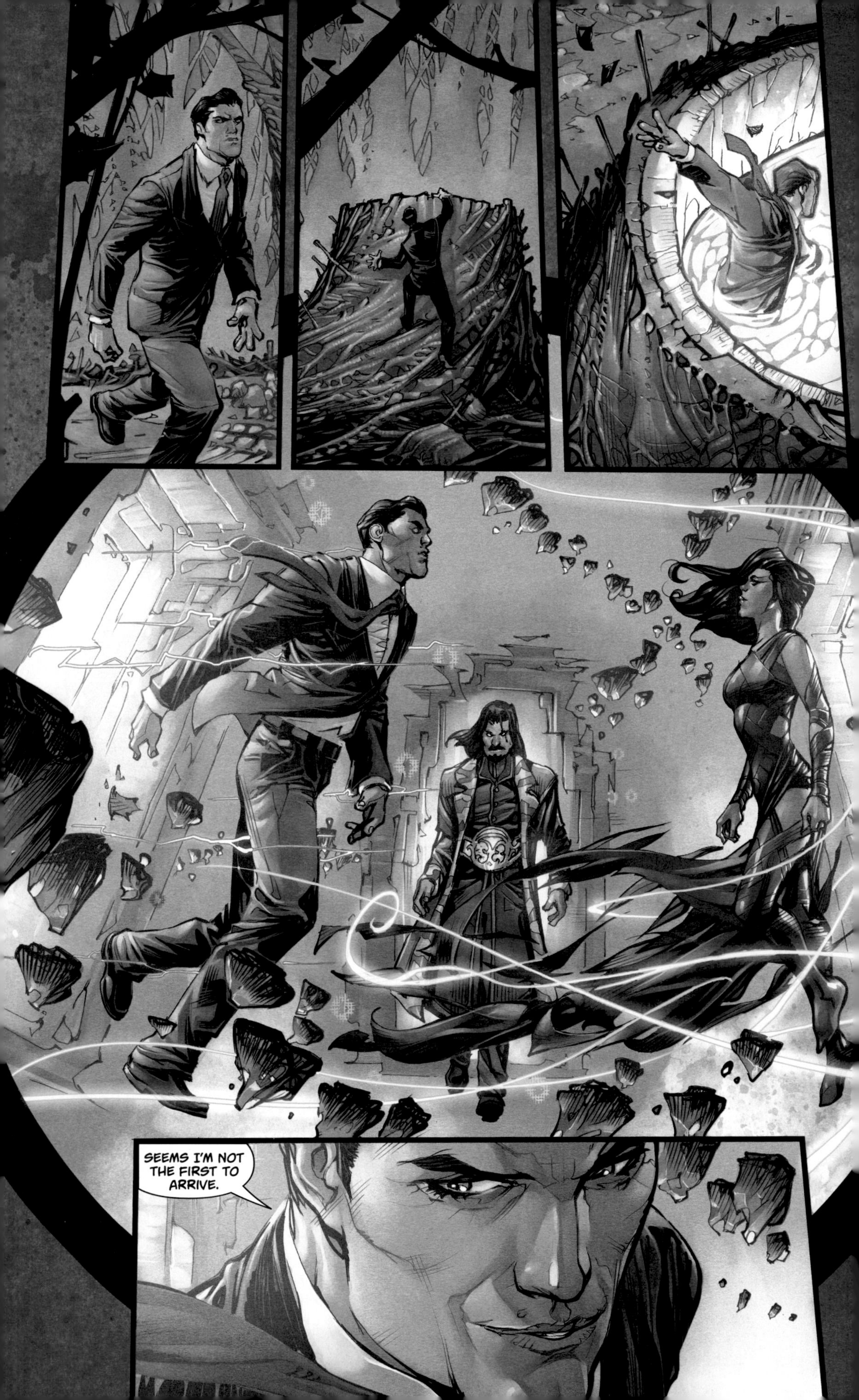
SEEMS I'M NOT THE FIRST TO ARRIVE.

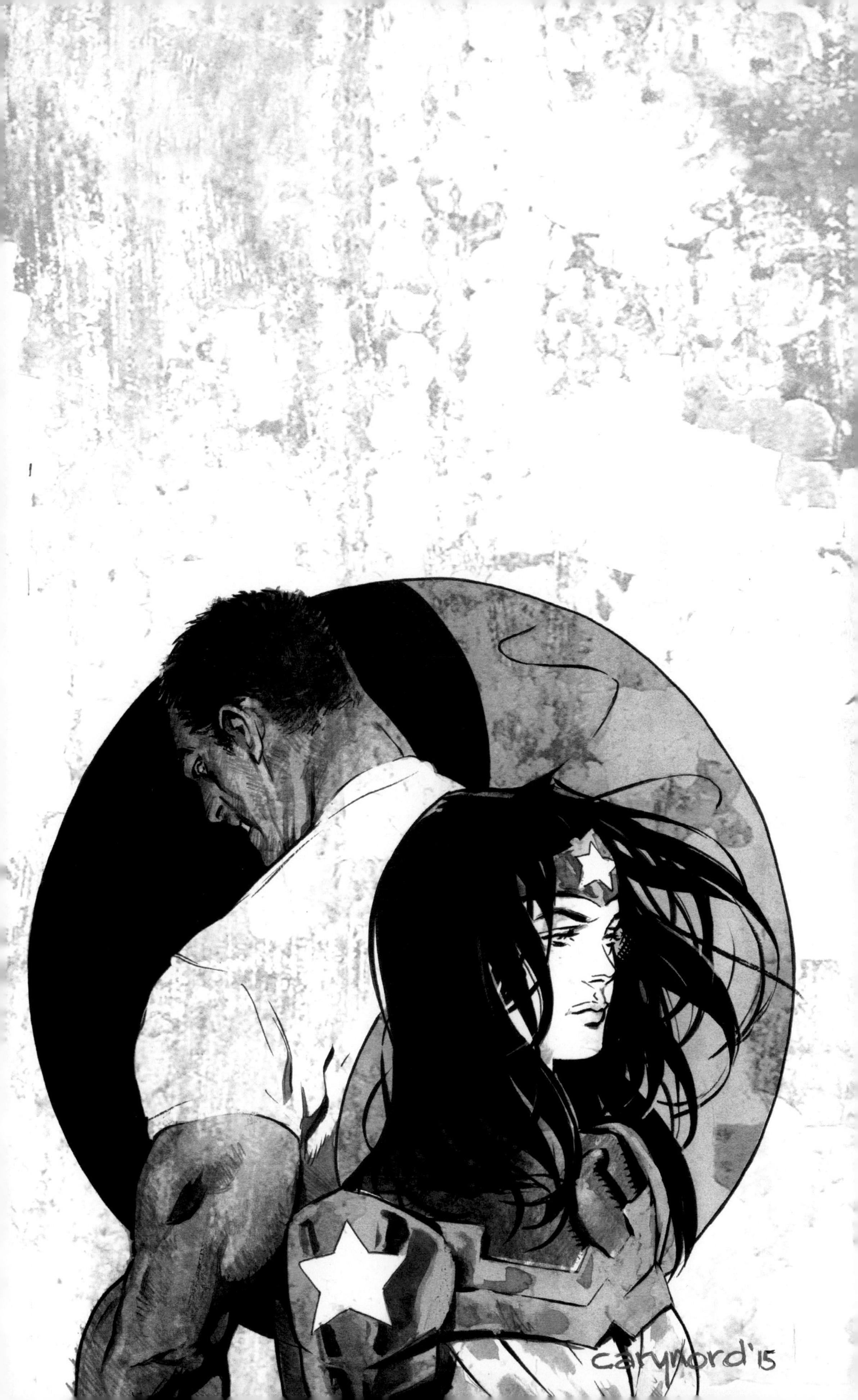
carynord'15

HEART OF THE SUN

PETER J. TOMASI writer **DOUG MAHNKE** penciller **JAIME MENDOZA SEAN PARSONS JOHNNY DESJARDINS** inkers **WIL QUINTANA** colorist **ROB LEIGH** letterer cover by **CARY NORD**

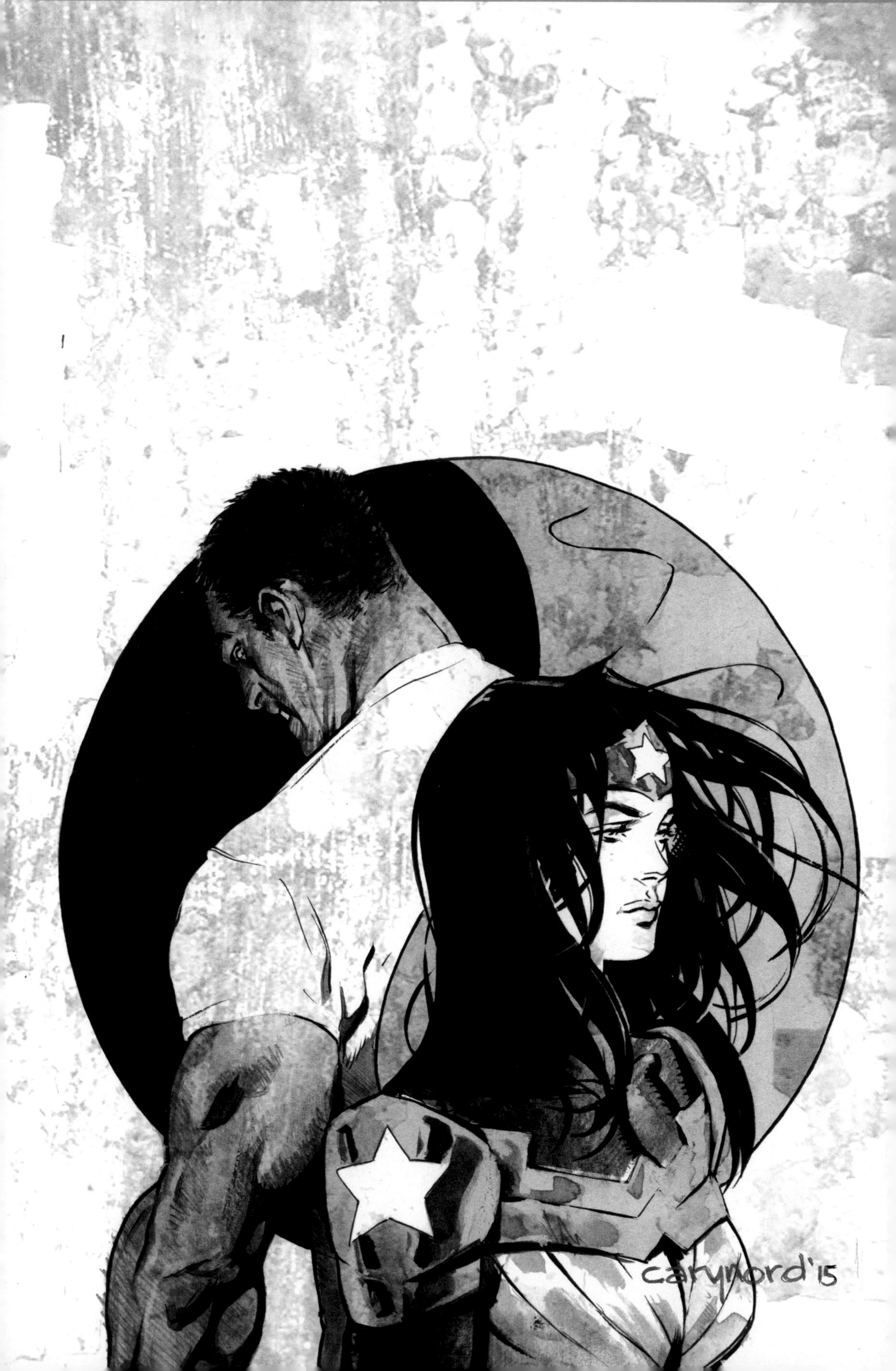
carynord'15

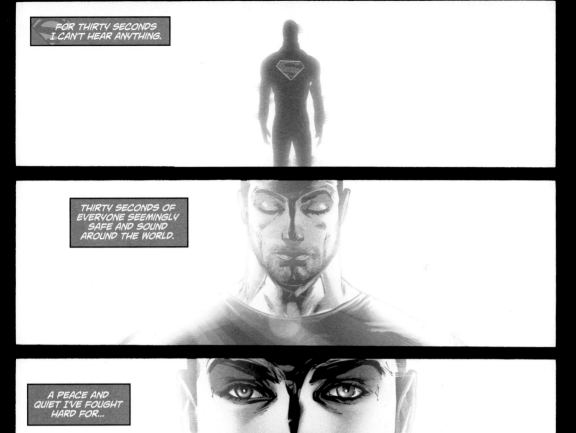

FOR THIRTY SECONDS I CAN'T HEAR ANYTHING.

THIRTY SECONDS OF EVERYONE SEEMINGLY SAFE AND SOUND AROUND THE WORLD.

A PEACE AND QUIET I'VE FOUGHT HARD FOR...

...BUT I KNOW IT'S AN ILLUSION...

...A FLEETING MOMENT OF SERENITY THAT ONLY LASTS AS LONG AS IT TAKES FOR MY ATOMS TO BE BROKEN APART AND REARRANGED BY THIS TRANSPORTER.

THEN THE BLOOD ON MY HANDS MAKES THE LAST FEW WEEKS COME RUSHING BACK...

...MY SECRET IDENTITY BLOWN, MY POWERS SOMEHOW BEING DRAINED, TRUST BROKEN BETWEEN DIANA AND ME, MY FRIENDS PUT IN HARM'S WAY-- RISKING THEIR LIVES TO SAVE MINE...

...EVERYTHING'S UPSIDE DOWN, BUT THAT ENDS TODAY BECAUSE...

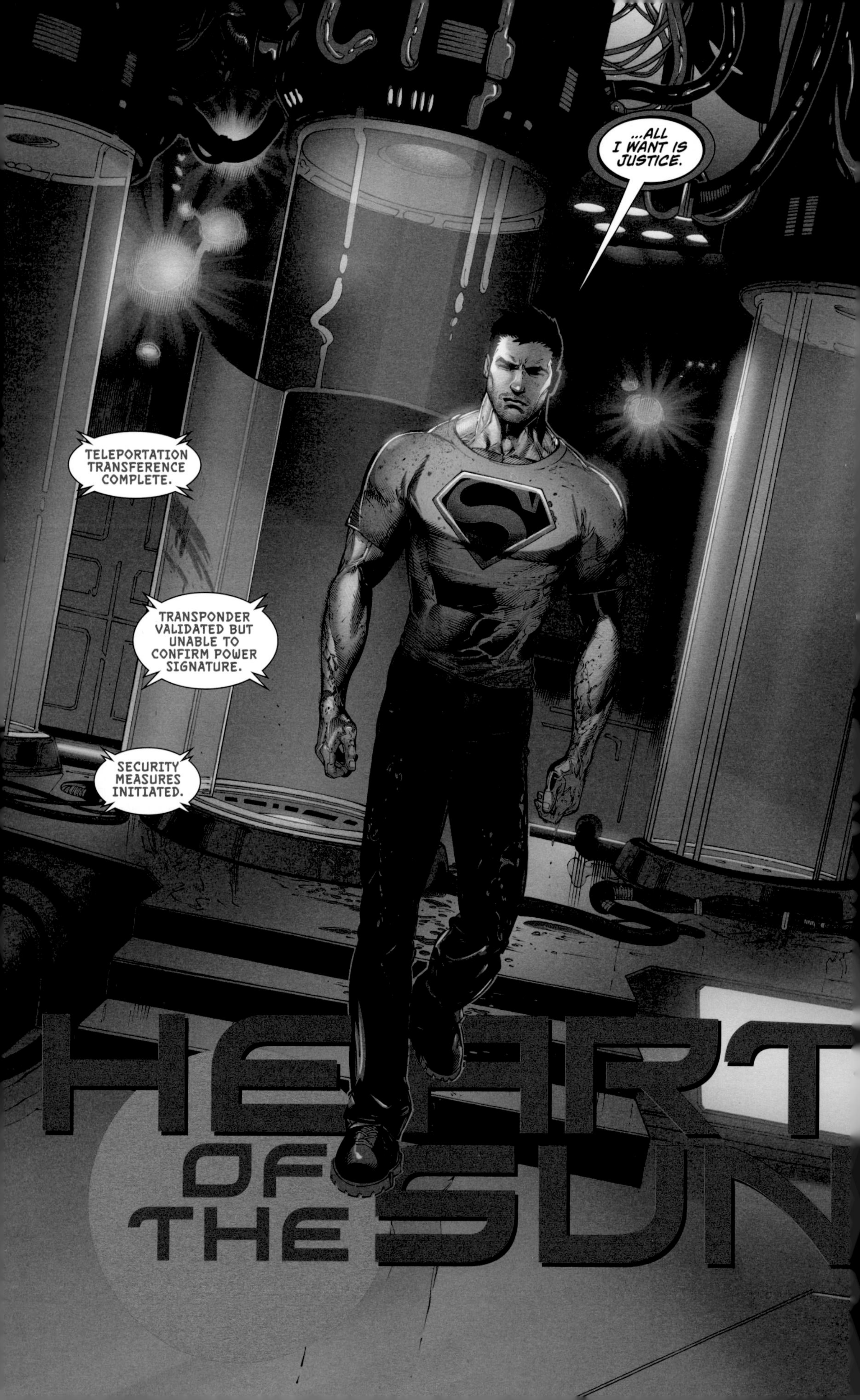

...ALL I WANT IS JUSTICE.
TELEPORTATION TRANSFERENCE COMPLETE.
TRANSPONDER VALIDATED BUT UNABLE TO CONFIRM POWER SIGNATURE.
SECURITY MEASURES INITIATED.
HEART OF THE SUN

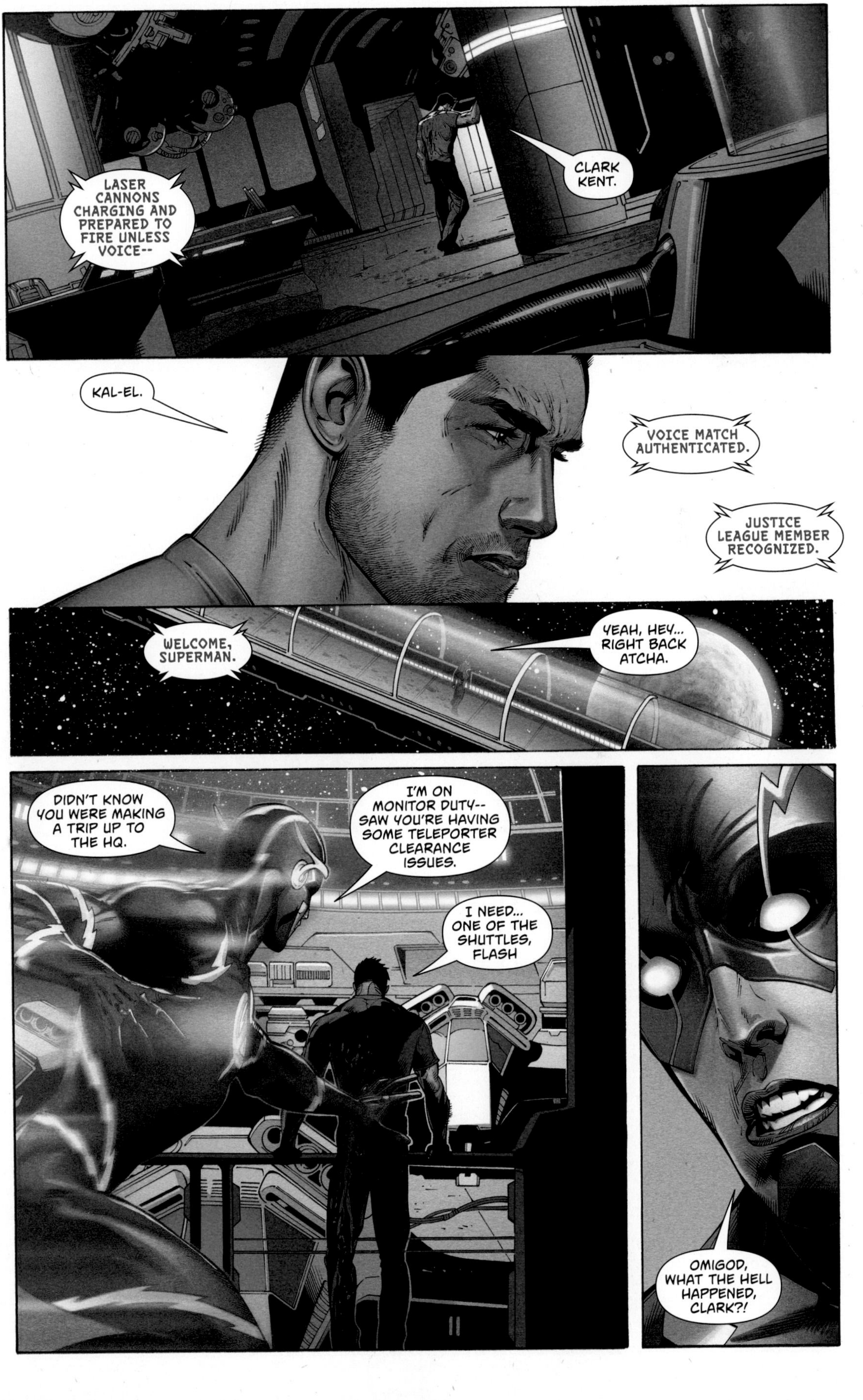
LASER CANNONS CHARGING AND PREPARED TO FIRE UNLESS VOICE--
CLARK KENT.
KAL-EL.
VOICE MATCH AUTHENTICATED.
JUSTICE LEAGUE MEMBER RECOGNIZED.
WELCOME, SUPERMAN.
YEAH, HEY... RIGHT BACK ATCHA.
DIDN'T KNOW YOU WERE MAKING A TRIP UP TO THE HQ.
I'M ON MONITOR DUTY-- SAW YOU'RE HAVING SOME TELEPORTER CLEARANCE ISSUES.
I NEED... ONE OF THE SHUTTLES, FLASH
OMIGOD, WHAT THE HELL HAPPENED, CLARK?!

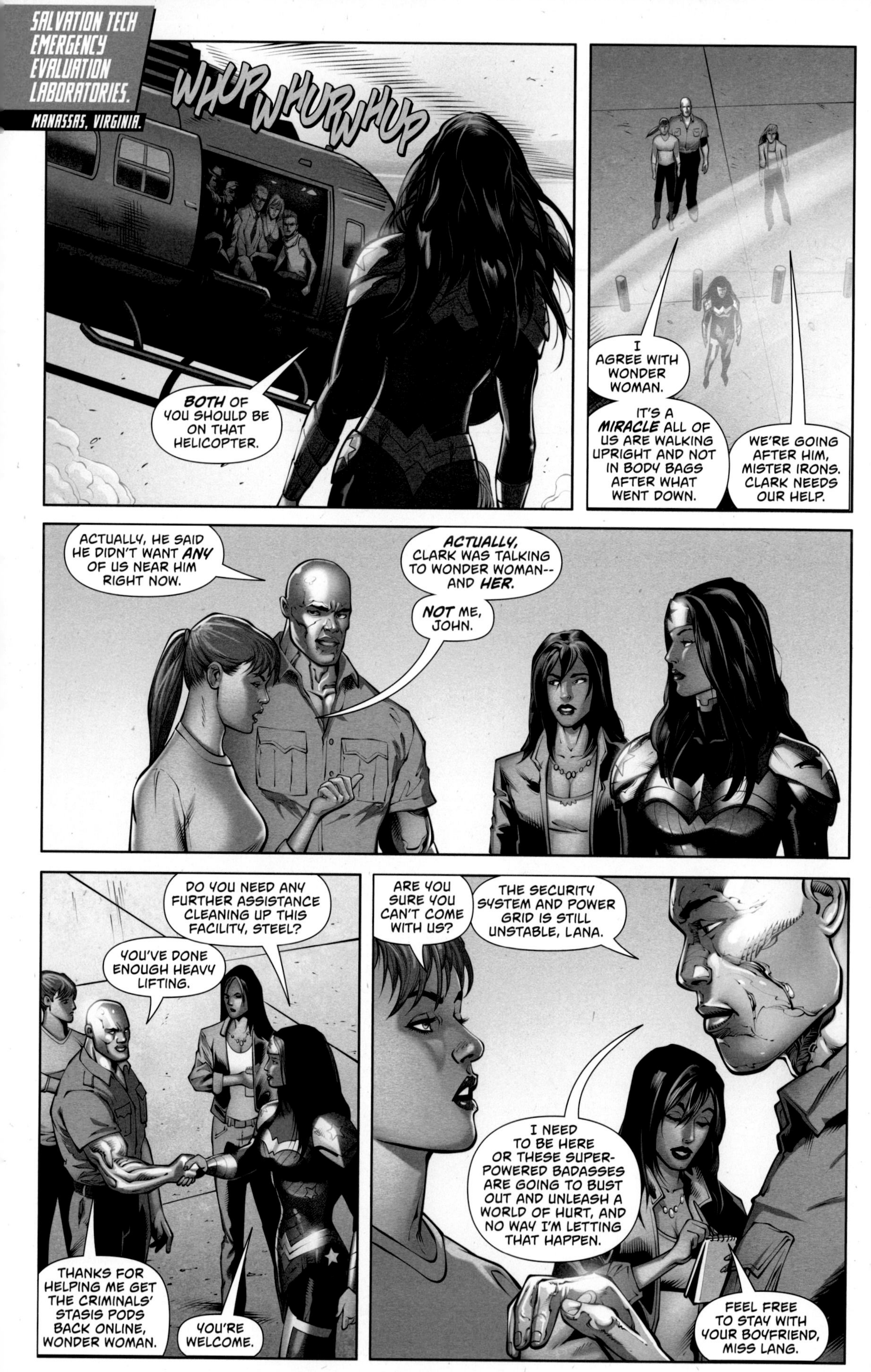
SALVATION TECH EMERGENCY EVALUATION LABORATORIES.
MANASSAS, VIRGINIA.
WHUP WHUP WHUP
BOTH OF YOU SHOULD BE ON THAT HELICOPTER.
I AGREE WITH WONDER WOMAN.
IT'S A MIRACLE ALL OF US ARE WALKING UPRIGHT AND NOT IN BODY BAGS AFTER WHAT WENT DOWN.
WE'RE GOING AFTER HIM, MISTER IRONS. CLARK NEEDS OUR HELP.
ACTUALLY, HE SAID HE DIDN'T WANT ANY OF US NEAR HIM RIGHT NOW.
ACTUALLY, CLARK WAS TALKING TO WONDER WOMAN-- AND HER.
NOT ME, JOHN.
DO YOU NEED ANY FURTHER ASSISTANCE CLEANING UP THIS FACILITY, STEEL?
YOU'VE DONE ENOUGH HEAVY LIFTING.
THANKS FOR HELPING ME GET THE CRIMINALS' STASIS PODS BACK ONLINE, WONDER WOMAN.
YOU'RE WELCOME.
ARE YOU SURE YOU CAN'T COME WITH US?
THE SECURITY SYSTEM AND POWER GRID IS STILL UNSTABLE, LANA.
I NEED TO BE HERE OR THESE SUPER-POWERED BADASSES ARE GOING TO BUST OUT AND UNLEASH A WORLD OF HURT, AND NO WAY I'M LETTING THAT HAPPEN.
FEEL FREE TO STAY WITH YOUR BOYFRIEND, MISS LANG.

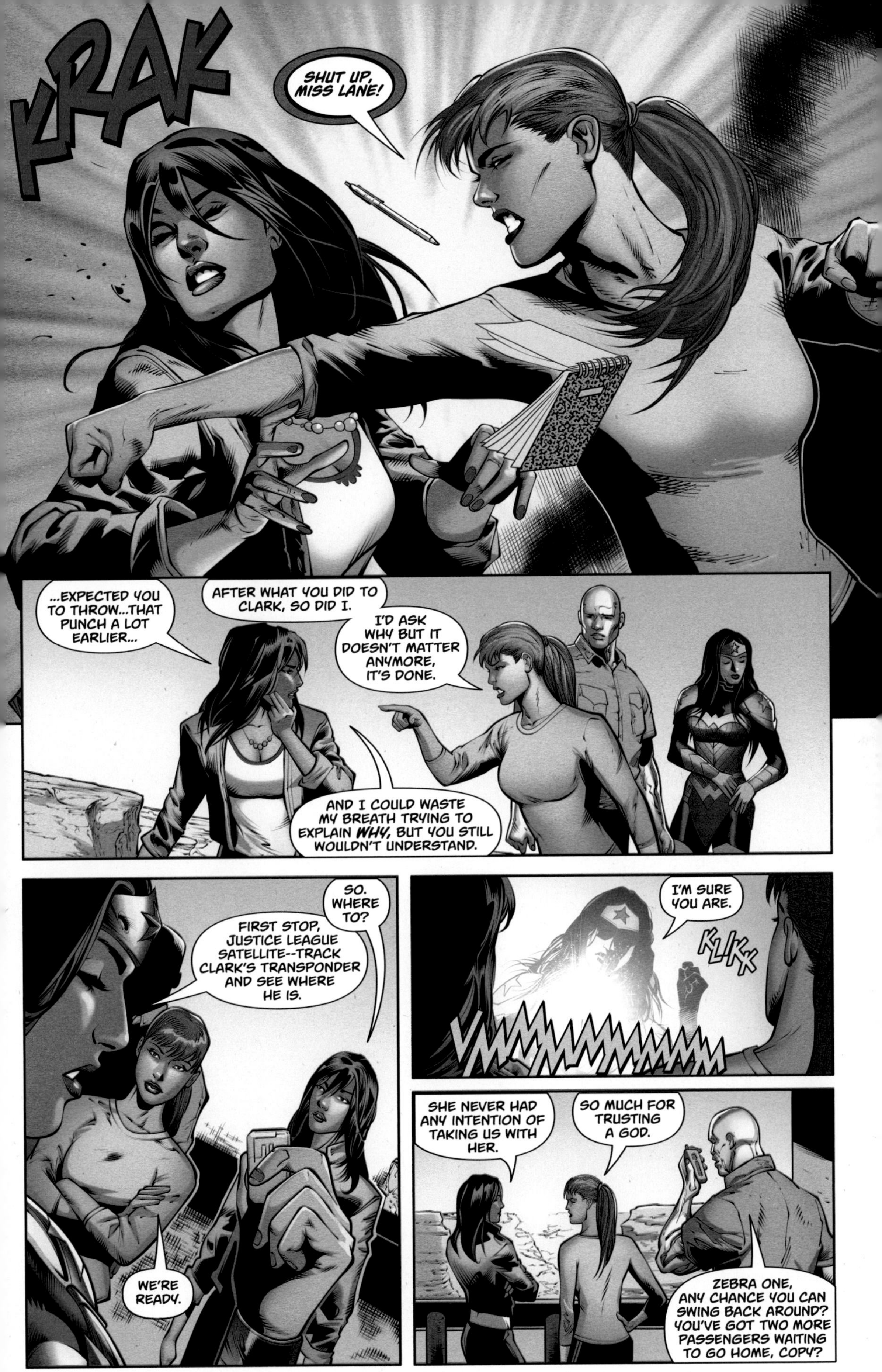
KRAK
SHUT UP, MISS LANE!
...EXPECTED YOU TO THROW...THAT PUNCH A LOT EARLIER...
AFTER WHAT YOU DID TO CLARK, SO DID I.
I'D ASK WHY BUT IT DOESN'T MATTER ANYMORE, IT'S DONE.
AND I COULD WASTE MY BREATH TRYING TO EXPLAIN *WHY*, BUT YOU STILL WOULDN'T UNDERSTAND.
SO. WHERE TO?
FIRST STOP, JUSTICE LEAGUE SATELLITE--TRACK CLARK'S TRANSPONDER AND SEE WHERE HE IS.
WE'RE READY.
I'M SURE YOU ARE.
KLIKK
VMMMMMMMMM
SHE NEVER HAD ANY INTENTION OF TAKING US WITH HER.
SO MUCH FOR TRUSTING A GOD.
ZEBRA ONE, ANY CHANCE YOU CAN SWING BACK AROUND? YOU'VE GOT TWO MORE PASSENGERS WAITING TO GO HOME, COPY?

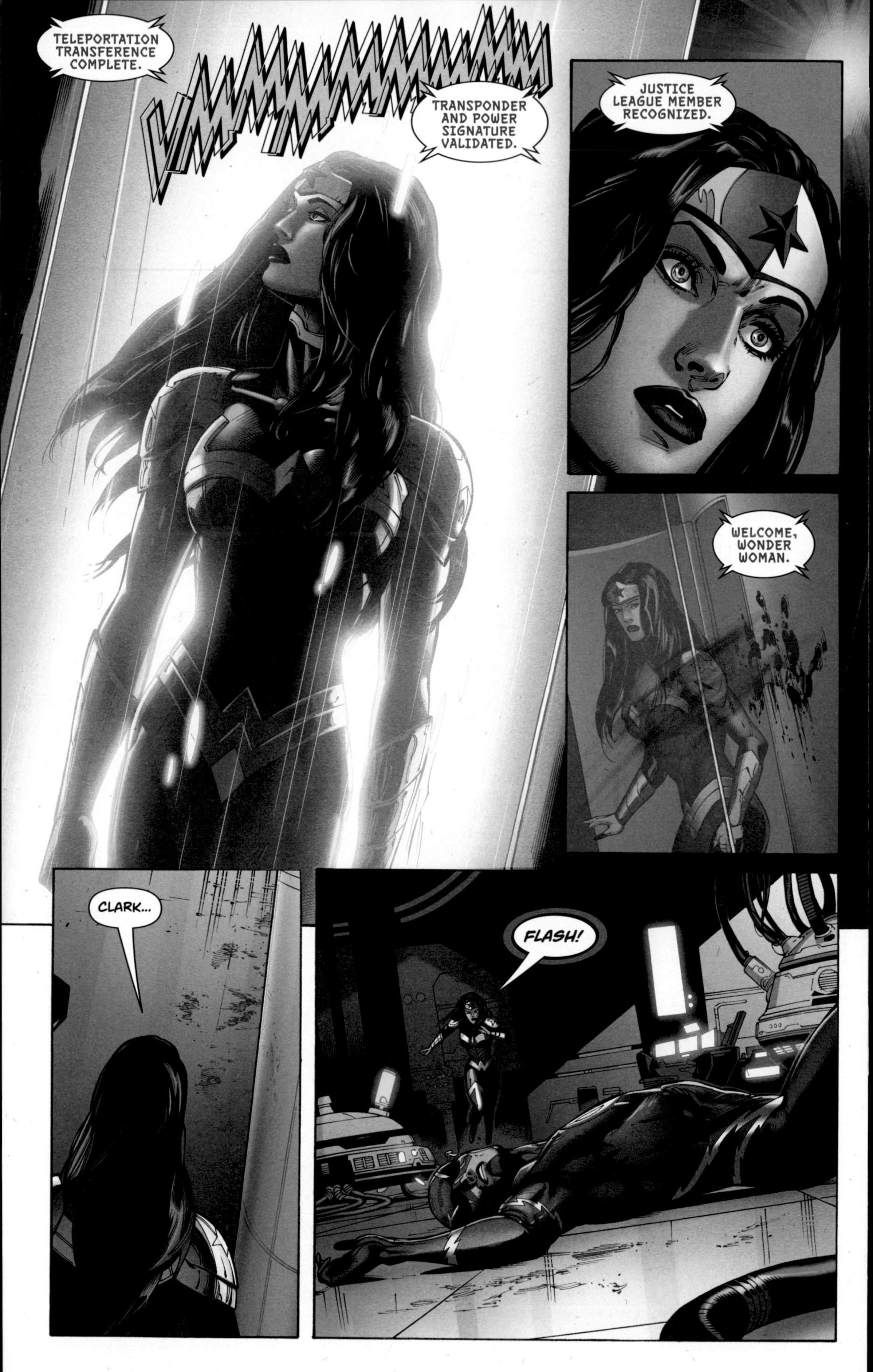
TELEPORTATION TRANSFERENCE COMPLETE.
TRANSPONDER AND POWER SIGNATURE VALIDATED.
JUSTICE LEAGUE MEMBER RECOGNIZED.
WELCOME, WONDER WOMAN.
CLARK...
FLASH!

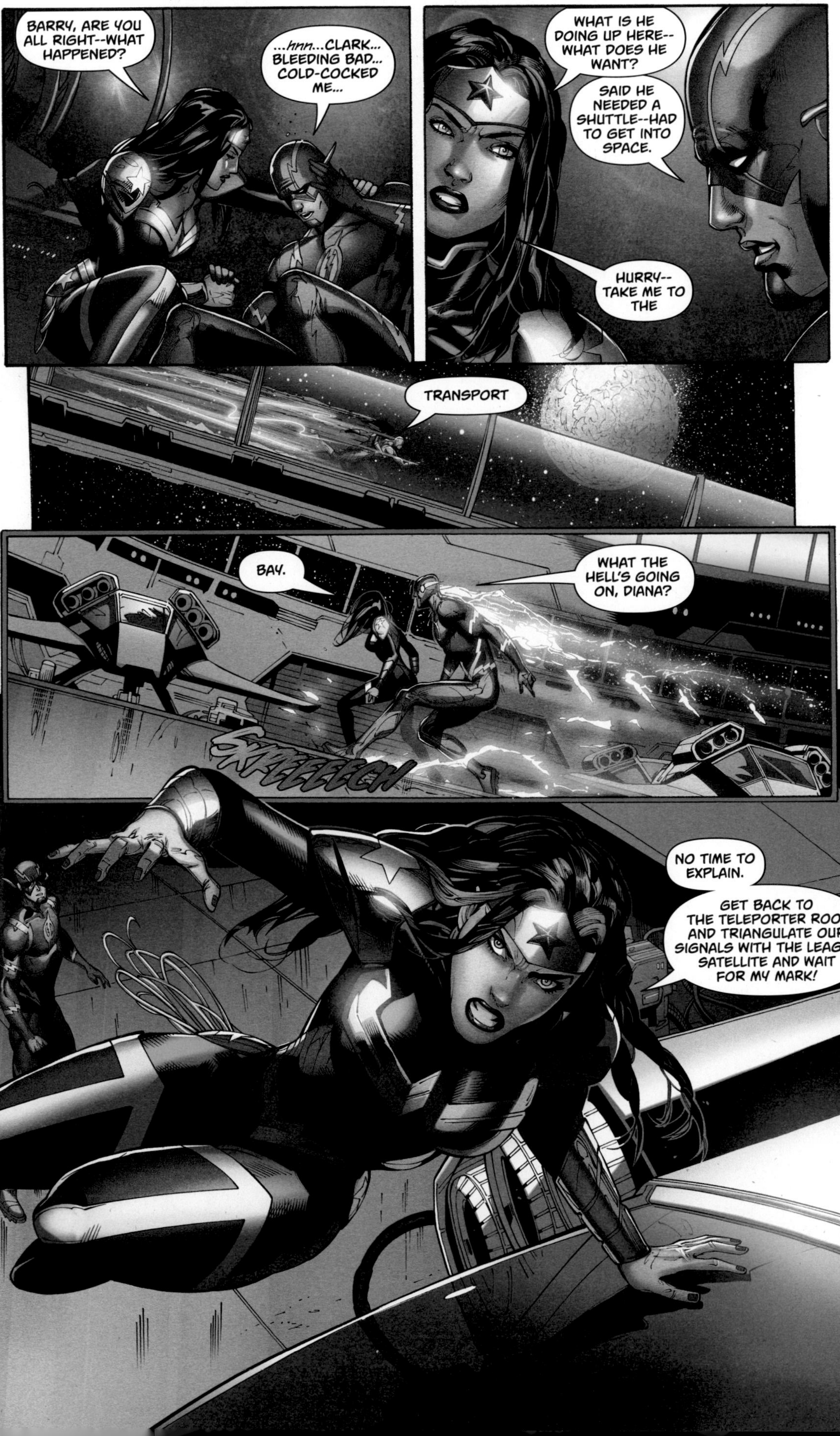
BARRY, ARE YOU ALL RIGHT--WHAT HAPPENED?
...hnn...CLARK... BLEEDING BAD... COLD-COCKED ME...
WHAT IS HE DOING UP HERE-- WHAT DOES HE WANT?
SAID HE NEEDED A SHUTTLE--HAD TO GET INTO SPACE.
HURRY-- TAKE ME TO THE
TRANSPORT
BAY.
WHAT THE HELL'S GOING ON, DIANA?
SKREEEEECH
NO TIME TO EXPLAIN.
GET BACK TO THE TELEPORTER ROOM AND TRIANGULATE OUR SIGNALS WITH THE LEAGUE SATELLITE AND WAIT FOR MY MARK!

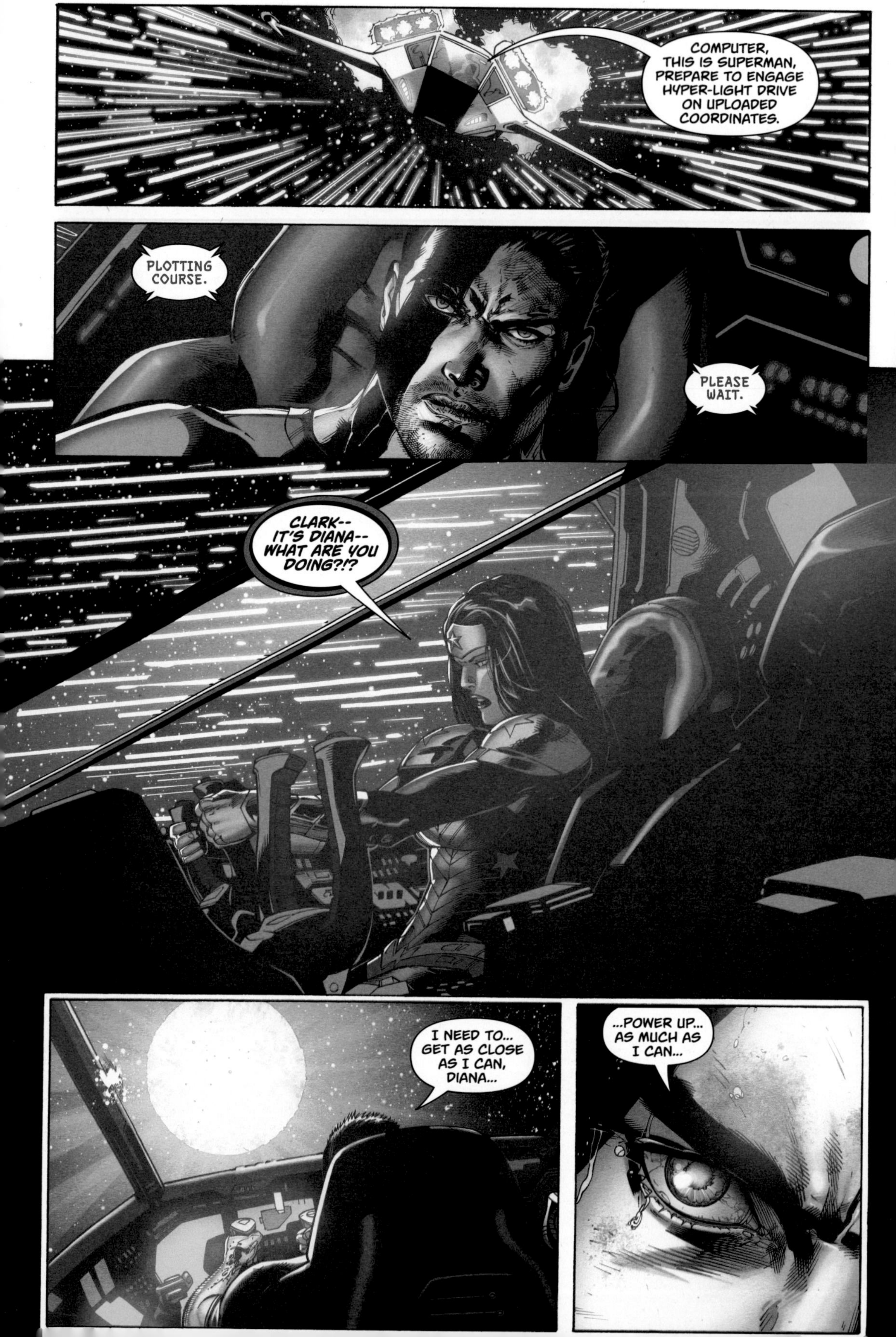
COMPUTER, THIS IS SUPERMAN, PREPARE TO ENGAGE HYPER-LIGHT DRIVE ON UPLOADED COORDINATES.
PLOTTING COURSE.
PLEASE WAIT.
CLARK-- IT'S DIANA-- WHAT ARE YOU DOING?!?
I NEED TO... GET AS CLOSE AS I CAN, DIANA...
...POWER UP... AS MUCH AS I CAN...

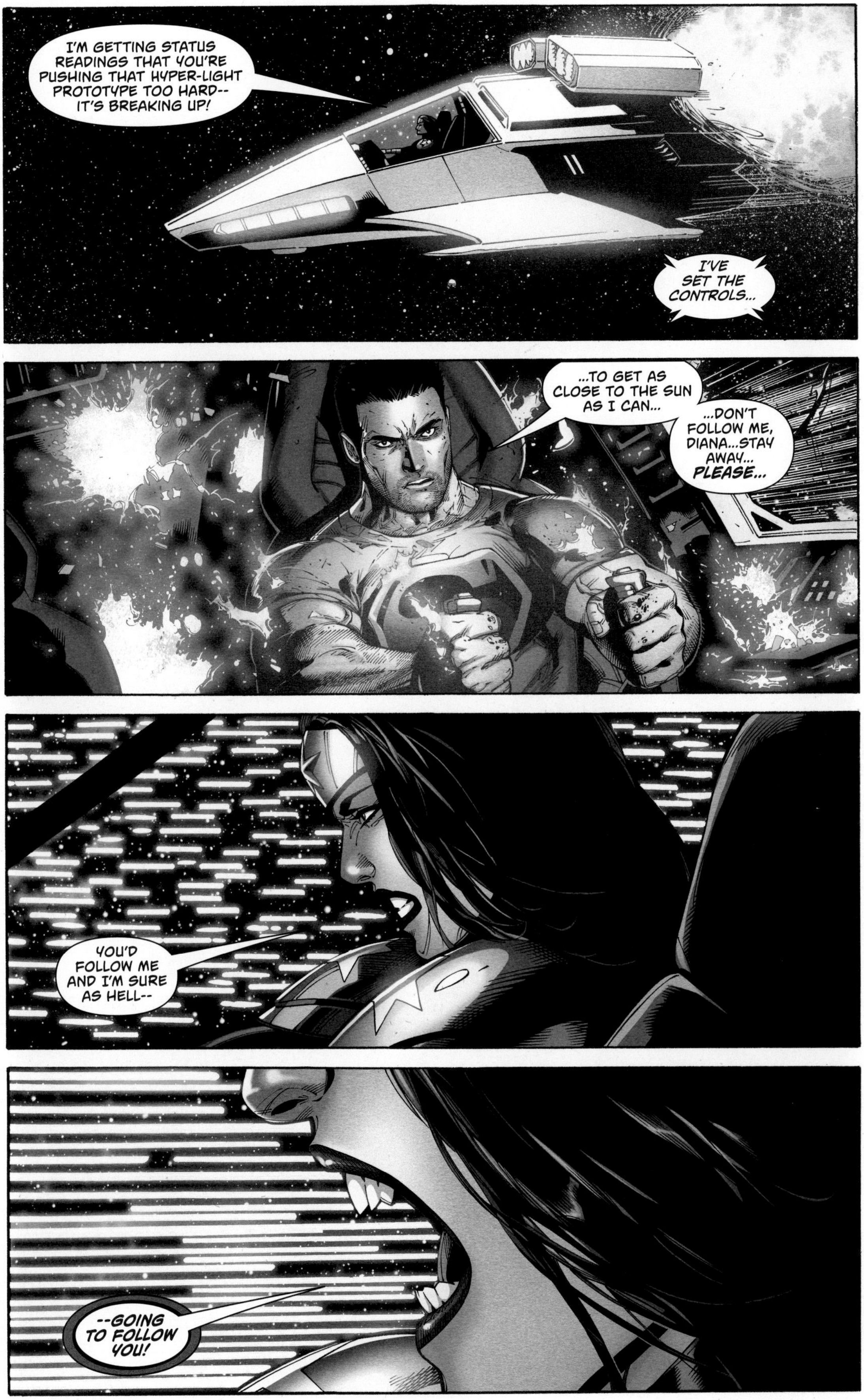
I'M GETTING STATUS READINGS THAT YOU'RE PUSHING THAT HYPER-LIGHT PROTOTYPE TOO HARD-- IT'S BREAKING UP!
I'VE SET THE CONTROLS...
...TO GET AS CLOSE TO THE SUN AS I CAN...
...DON'T FOLLOW ME, DIANA...STAY AWAY... PLEASE...
YOU'D FOLLOW ME AND I'M SURE AS HELL--
--GOING TO FOLLOW YOU!

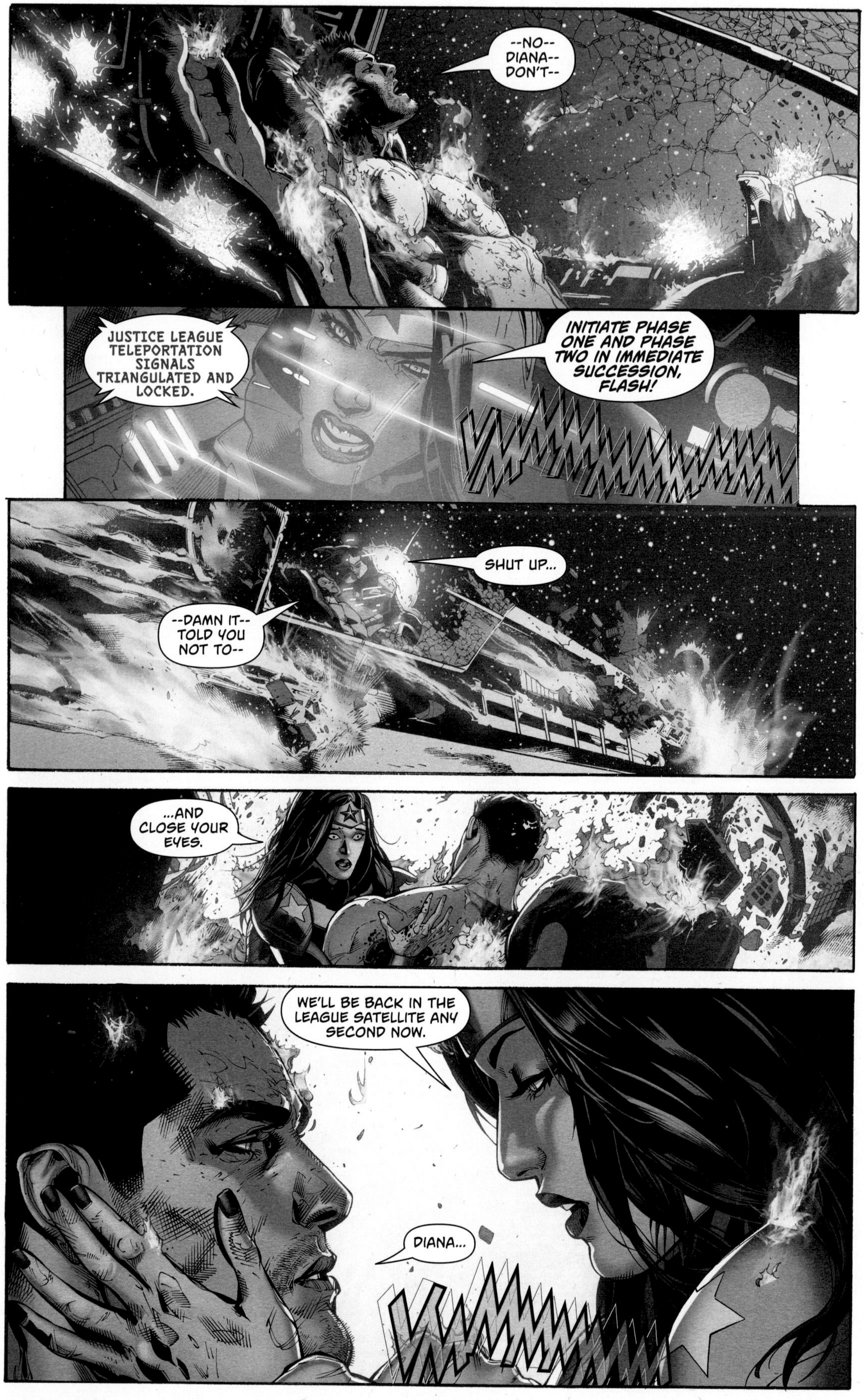
--NO-- DIANA-- DON'T--
JUSTICE LEAGUE TELEPORTATION SIGNALS TRIANGULATED AND LOCKED.
INITIATE PHASE ONE AND PHASE TWO IN IMMEDIATE SUCCESSION, FLASH!
SHUT UP...
--DAMN IT-- TOLD YOU NOT TO--
...AND CLOSE YOUR EYES.
WE'LL BE BACK IN THE LEAGUE SATELLITE ANY SECOND NOW.
DIANA...

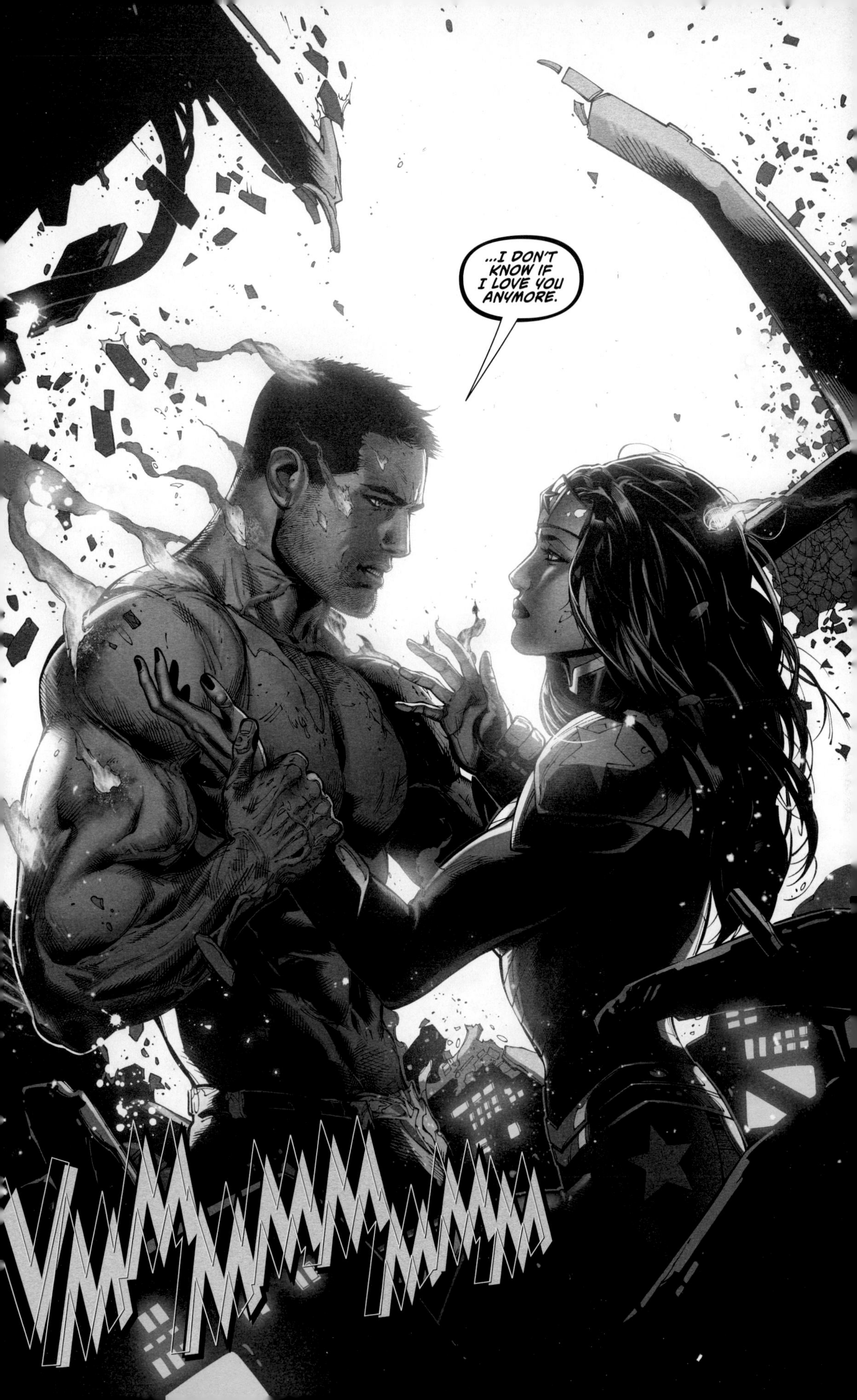
...I DON'T KNOW IF I LOVE YOU ANYMORE.

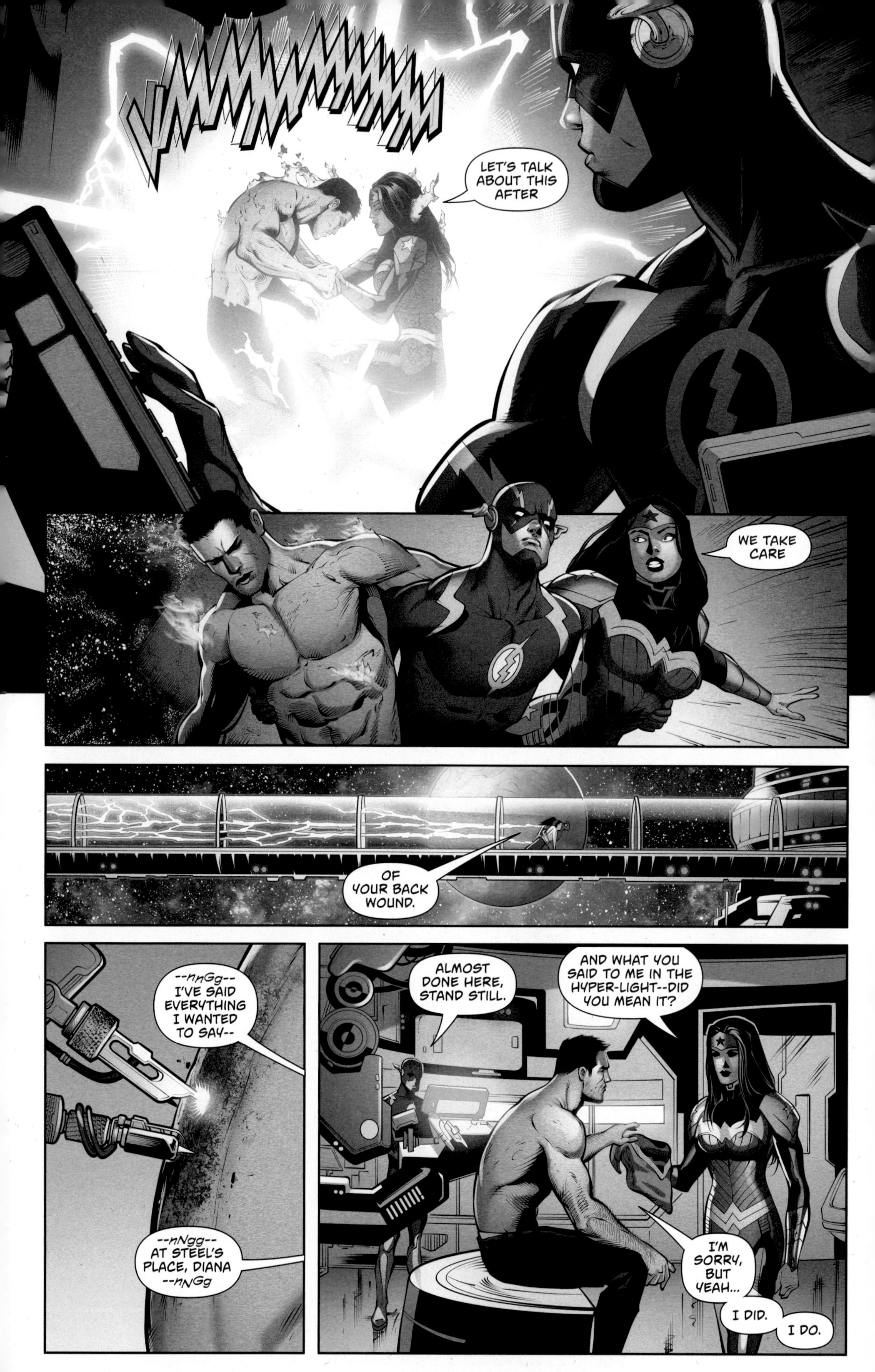

LET'S TALK ABOUT THIS AFTER
WE TAKE CARE
OF YOUR BACK WOUND.
--nnGg-- I'VE SAID EVERYTHING I WANTED TO SAY--
--nNgg-- AT STEEL'S PLACE, DIANA --nNGg
ALMOST DONE HERE, STAND STILL.
AND WHAT YOU SAID TO ME IN THE HYPER-LIGHT--DID YOU MEAN IT?
I'M SORRY, BUT YEAH...
I DID.
I DO.

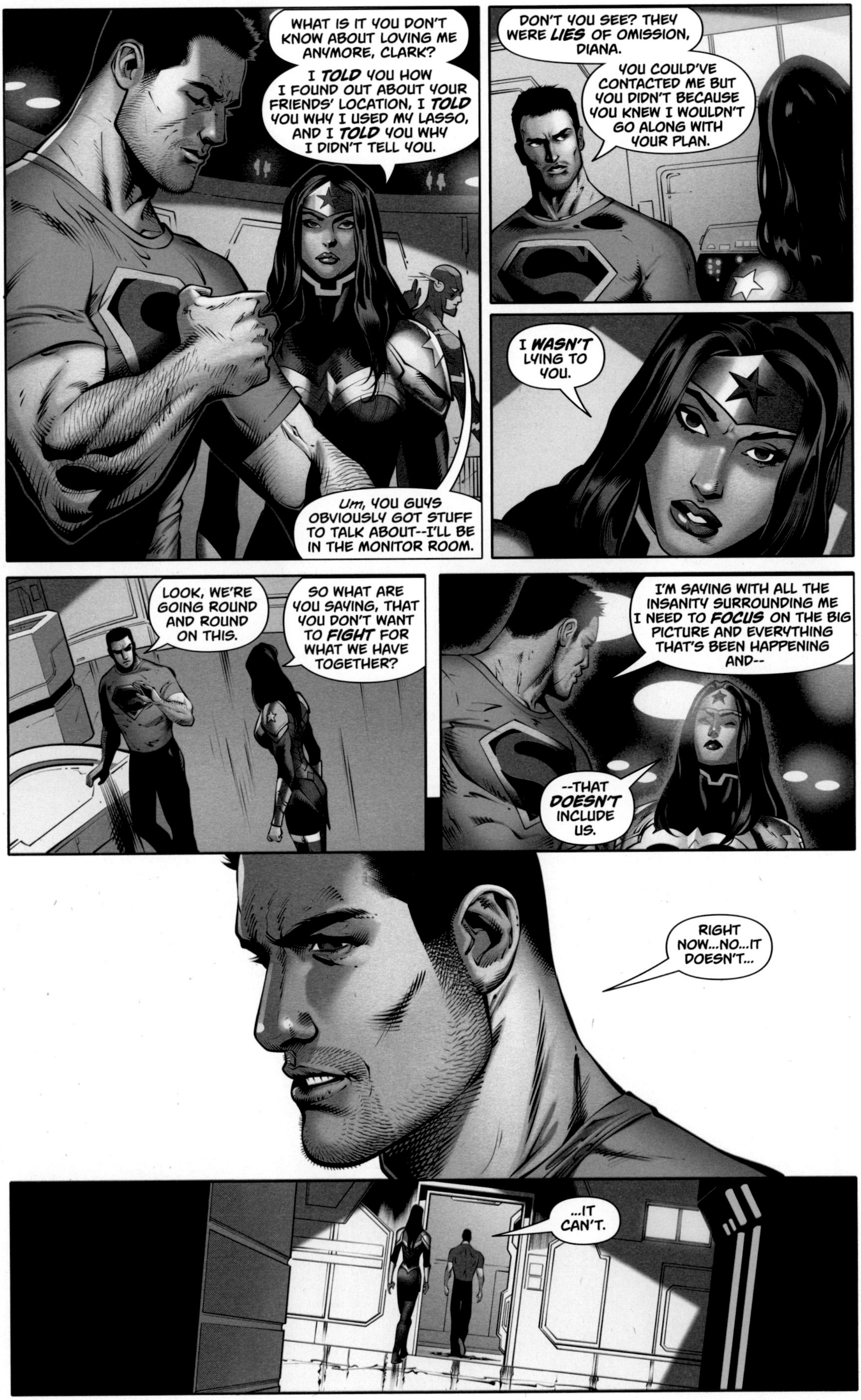
WHAT IS IT YOU DON'T KNOW ABOUT LOVING ME ANYMORE, CLARK?
I TOLD YOU HOW I FOUND OUT ABOUT YOUR FRIENDS' LOCATION, I TOLD YOU WHY I USED MY LASSO, AND I TOLD YOU WHY I DIDN'T TELL YOU.
Um, YOU GUYS OBVIOUSLY GOT STUFF TO TALK ABOUT--I'LL BE IN THE MONITOR ROOM.
DON'T YOU SEE? THEY WERE LIES OF OMISSION, DIANA.
YOU COULD'VE CONTACTED ME BUT YOU DIDN'T BECAUSE YOU KNEW I WOULDN'T GO ALONG WITH YOUR PLAN.
I WASN'T LYING TO YOU.
LOOK, WE'RE GOING ROUND AND ROUND ON THIS.
SO WHAT ARE YOU SAYING, THAT YOU DON'T WANT TO FIGHT FOR WHAT WE HAVE TOGETHER?
I'M SAYING WITH ALL THE INSANITY SURROUNDING ME I NEED TO FOCUS ON THE BIG PICTURE AND EVERYTHING THAT'S BEEN HAPPENING AND--
--THAT DOESN'T INCLUDE US.
RIGHT NOW...NO...IT DOESN'T...
...IT CAN'T.

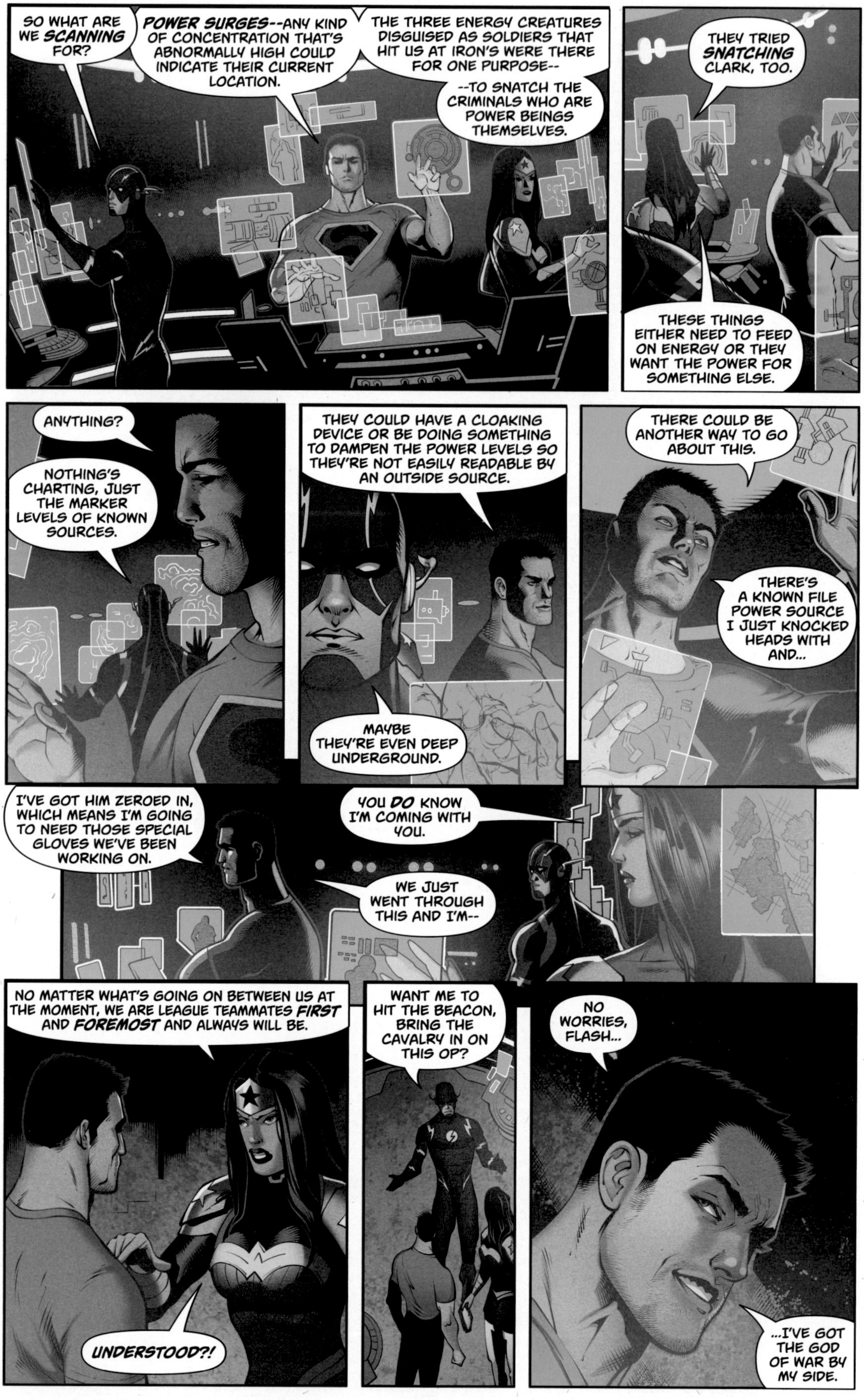
SO WHAT ARE WE SCANNING FOR?
POWER SURGES--ANY KIND OF CONCENTRATION THAT'S ABNORMALLY HIGH COULD INDICATE THEIR CURRENT LOCATION.
THE THREE ENERGY CREATURES DISGUISED AS SOLDIERS THAT HIT US AT IRON'S WERE THERE FOR ONE PURPOSE--
--TO SNATCH THE CRIMINALS WHO ARE POWER BEINGS THEMSELVES.
THEY TRIED SNATCHING CLARK, TOO.
THESE THINGS EITHER NEED TO FEED ON ENERGY OR THEY WANT THE POWER FOR SOMETHING ELSE.
ANYTHING?
NOTHING'S CHARTING, JUST THE MARKER LEVELS OF KNOWN SOURCES.
THEY COULD HAVE A CLOAKING DEVICE OR BE DOING SOMETHING TO DAMPEN THE POWER LEVELS SO THEY'RE NOT EASILY READABLE BY AN OUTSIDE SOURCE.
MAYBE THEY'RE EVEN DEEP UNDERGROUND.
THERE COULD BE ANOTHER WAY TO GO ABOUT THIS.
THERE'S A KNOWN FILE POWER SOURCE I JUST KNOCKED HEADS WITH AND...
I'VE GOT HIM ZEROED IN, WHICH MEANS I'M GOING TO NEED THOSE SPECIAL GLOVES WE'VE BEEN WORKING ON.
YOU DO KNOW I'M COMING WITH YOU.
WE JUST WENT THROUGH THIS AND I'M--
NO MATTER WHAT'S GOING ON BETWEEN US AT THE MOMENT, WE ARE LEAGUE TEAMMATES FIRST AND FOREMOST AND ALWAYS WILL BE.
UNDERSTOOD?!
WANT ME TO HIT THE BEACON, BRING THE CAVALRY IN ON THIS OP?
NO WORRIES, FLASH...
...I'VE GOT THE GOD OF WAR BY MY SIDE.

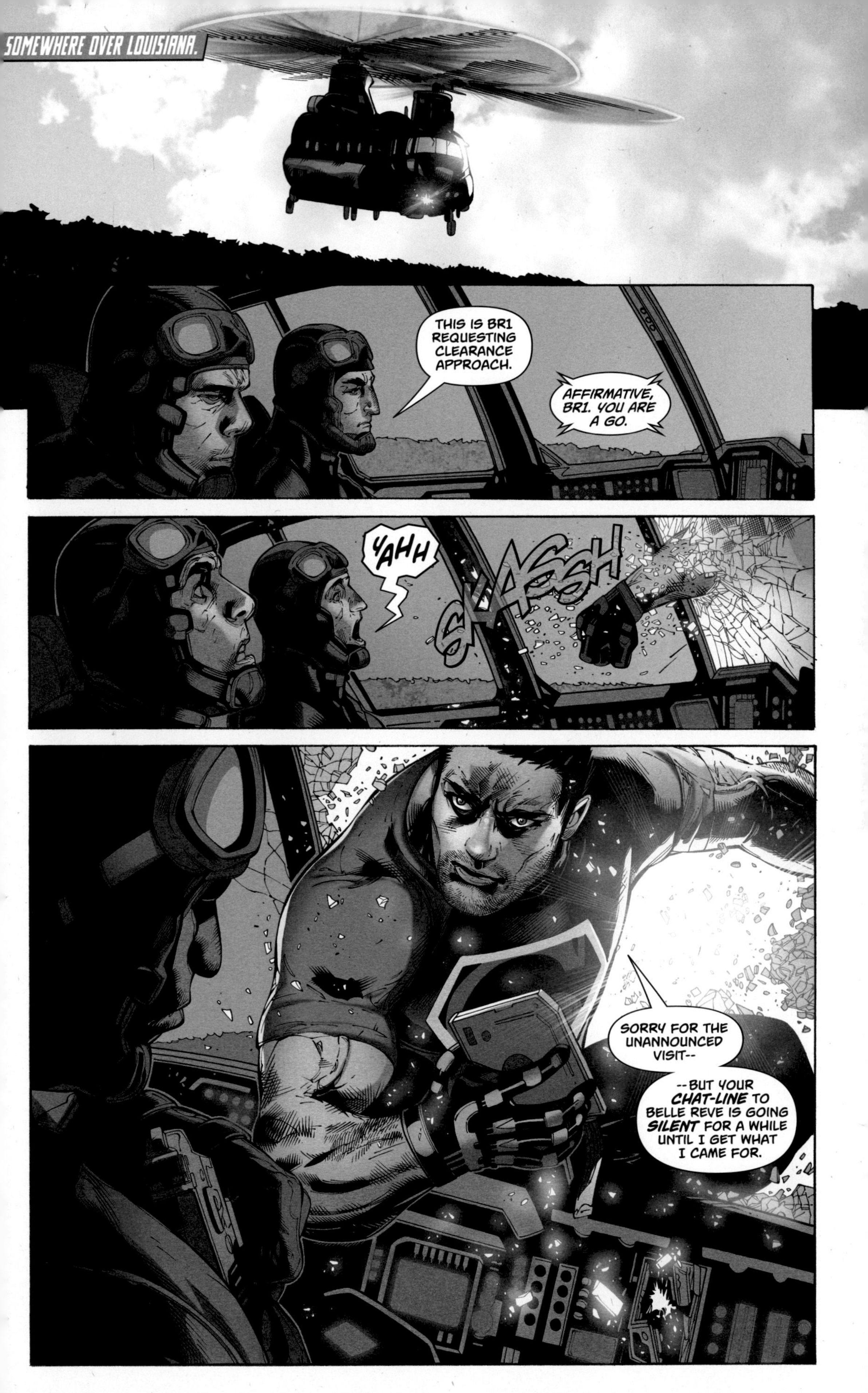
SOMEWHERE OVER LOUISIANA.
THIS IS BR1 REQUESTING CLEARANCE APPROACH.
AFFIRMATIVE, BR1. YOU ARE A GO.
YAHH
SKASSH
SORRY FOR THE UNANNOUNCED VISIT--
--BUT YOUR CHAT-LINE TO BELLE REVE IS GOING SILENT FOR A WHILE UNTIL I GET WHAT I CAME FOR.

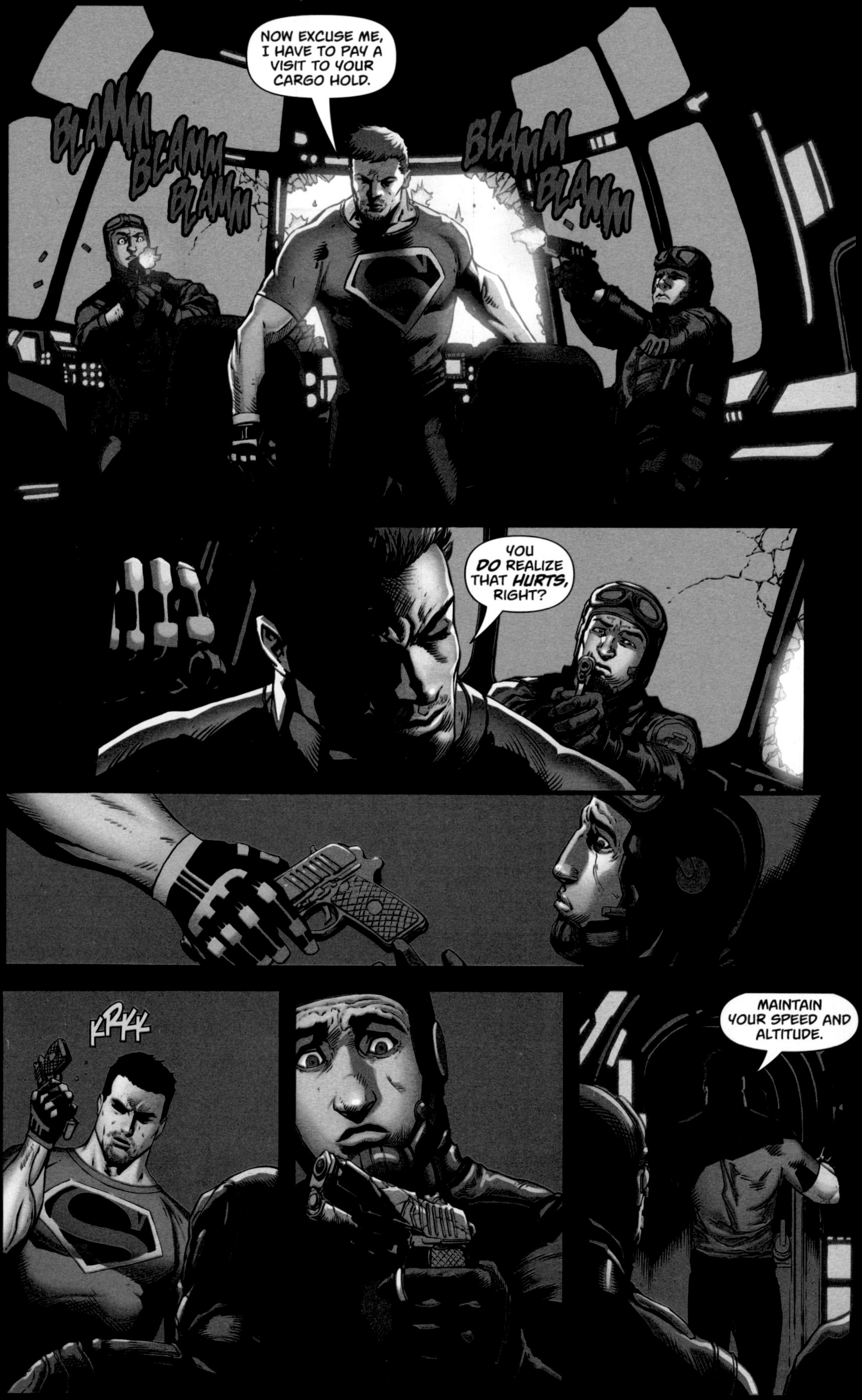
NOW EXCUSE ME, I HAVE TO PAY A VISIT TO YOUR CARGO HOLD.
BLAMM BLAMM BLAMM
BLAMM BLAMM
YOU DO REALIZE THAT HURTS, RIGHT?
KRKK
MAINTAIN YOUR SPEED AND ALTITUDE.

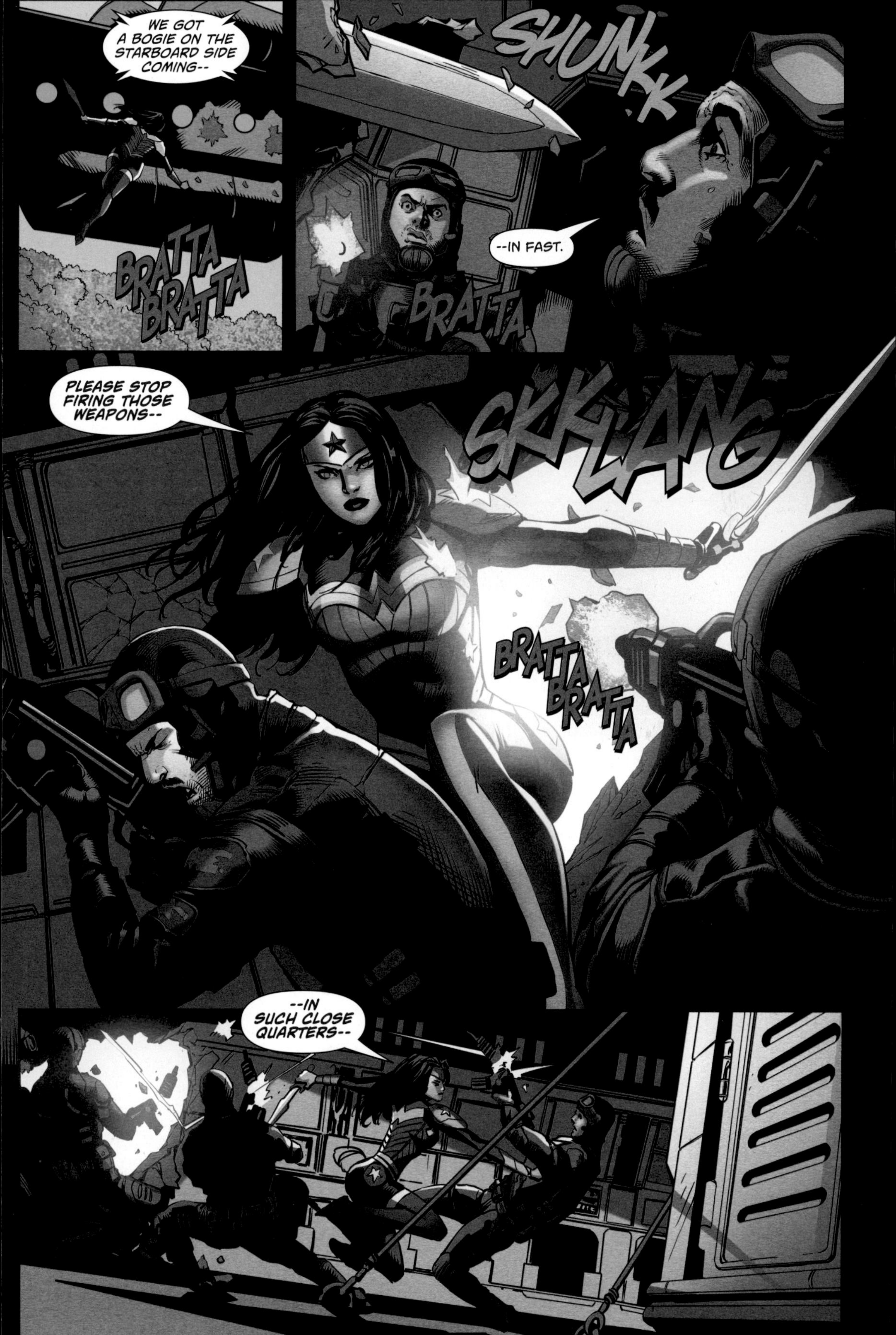
WE GOT A BOGIE ON THE STARBOARD SIDE COMING--
BRATTA BRATTA
SHUNKK
--IN FAST.
BRATTA
PLEASE STOP FIRING THOSE WEAPONS--
SKKLANG
BRATTA BRATTA
--IN SUCH CLOSE QUARTERS--

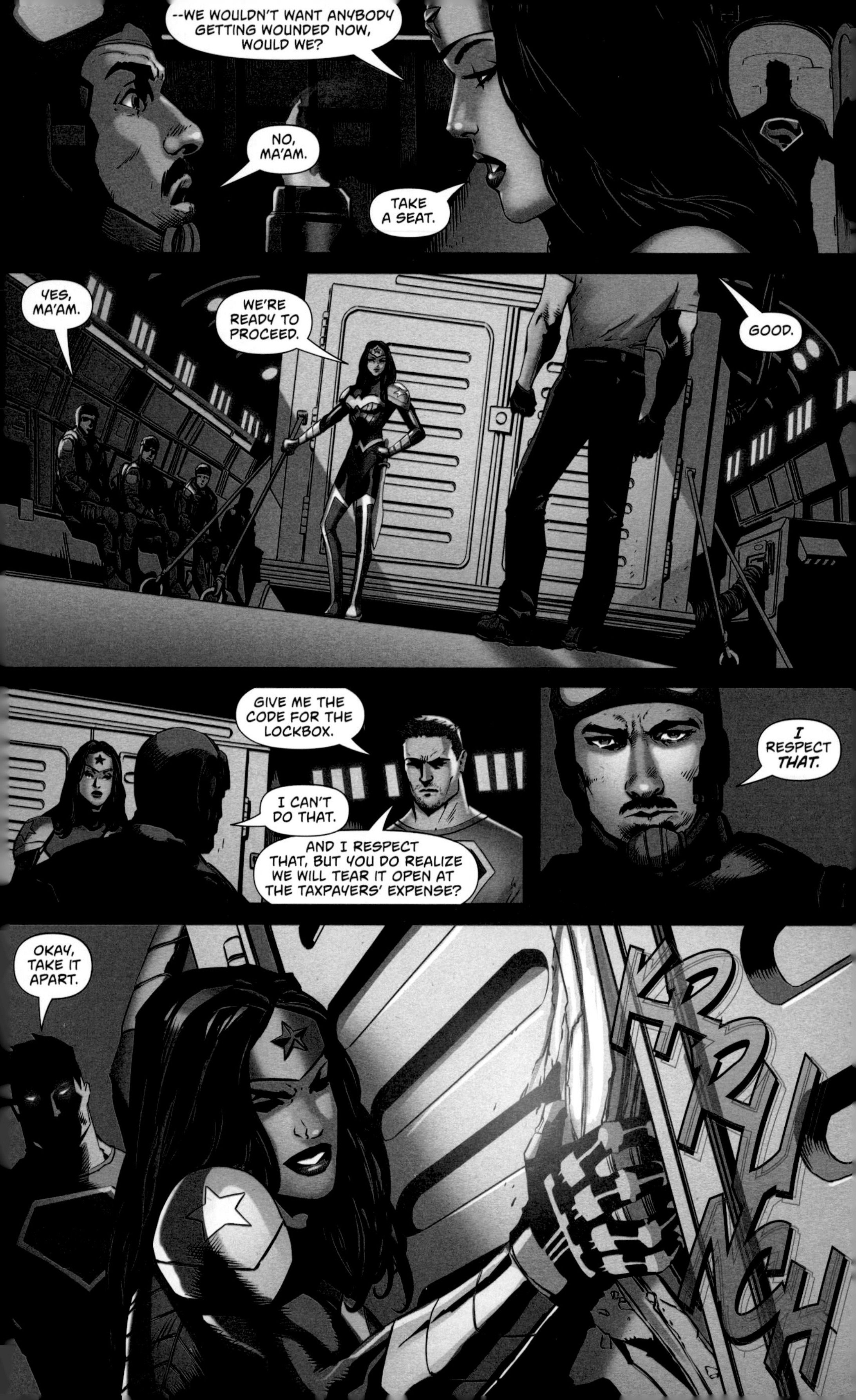
--WE WOULDN'T WANT ANYBODY GETTING WOUNDED NOW, WOULD WE?
NO, MA'AM.
TAKE A SEAT.
YES, MA'AM.
WE'RE READY TO PROCEED.
GOOD.
GIVE ME THE CODE FOR THE LOCKBOX.
I CAN'T DO THAT.
AND I RESPECT THAT, BUT YOU DO REALIZE WE WILL TEAR IT OPEN AT THE TAXPAYERS' EXPENSE?
I RESPECT *THAT.*
OKAY, TAKE IT APART.

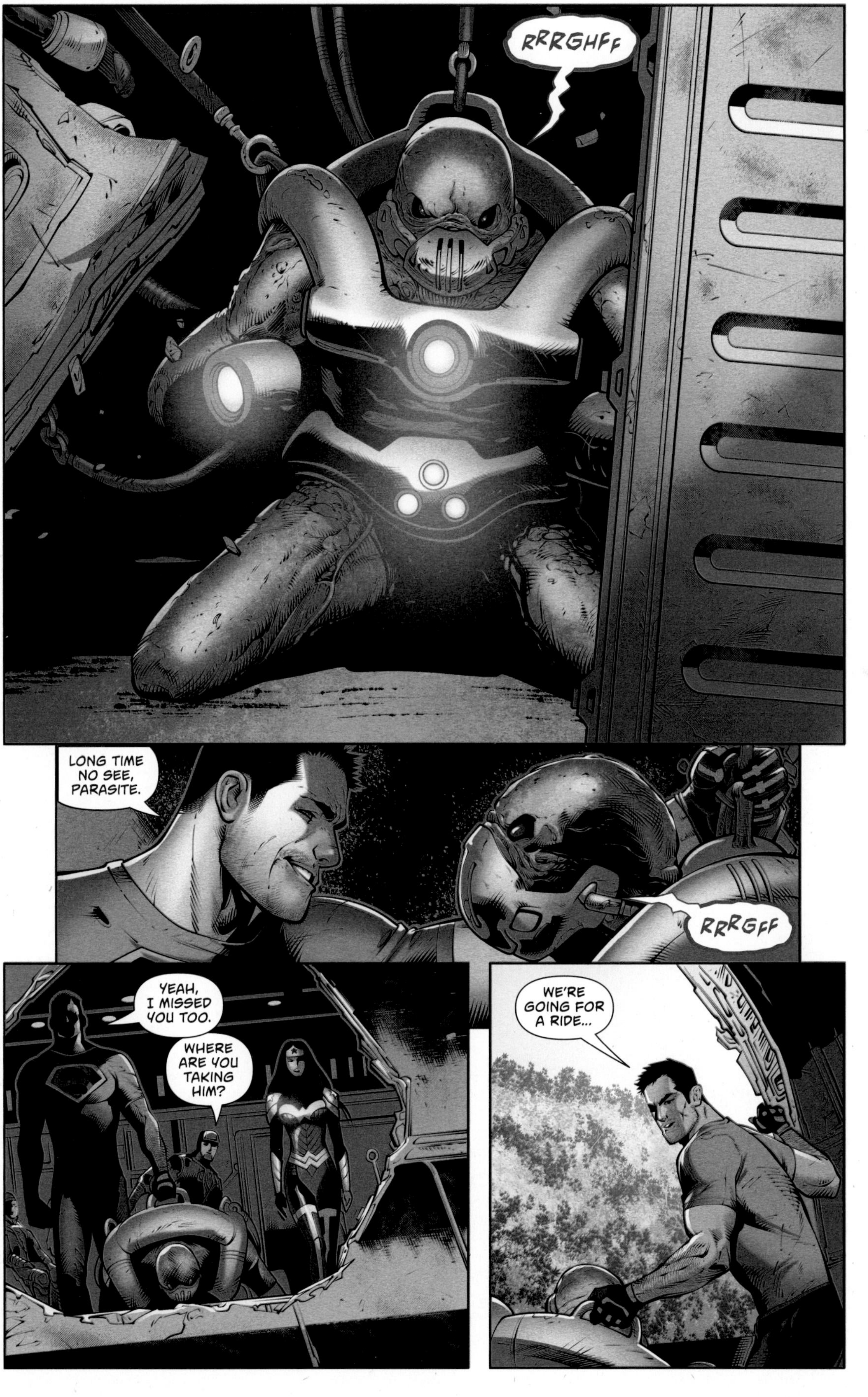
RRRGHFF
LONG TIME NO SEE, PARASITE.
RRRGFF
YEAH, I MISSED YOU TOO.
WHERE ARE YOU TAKING HIM?
WE'RE GOING FOR A RIDE...

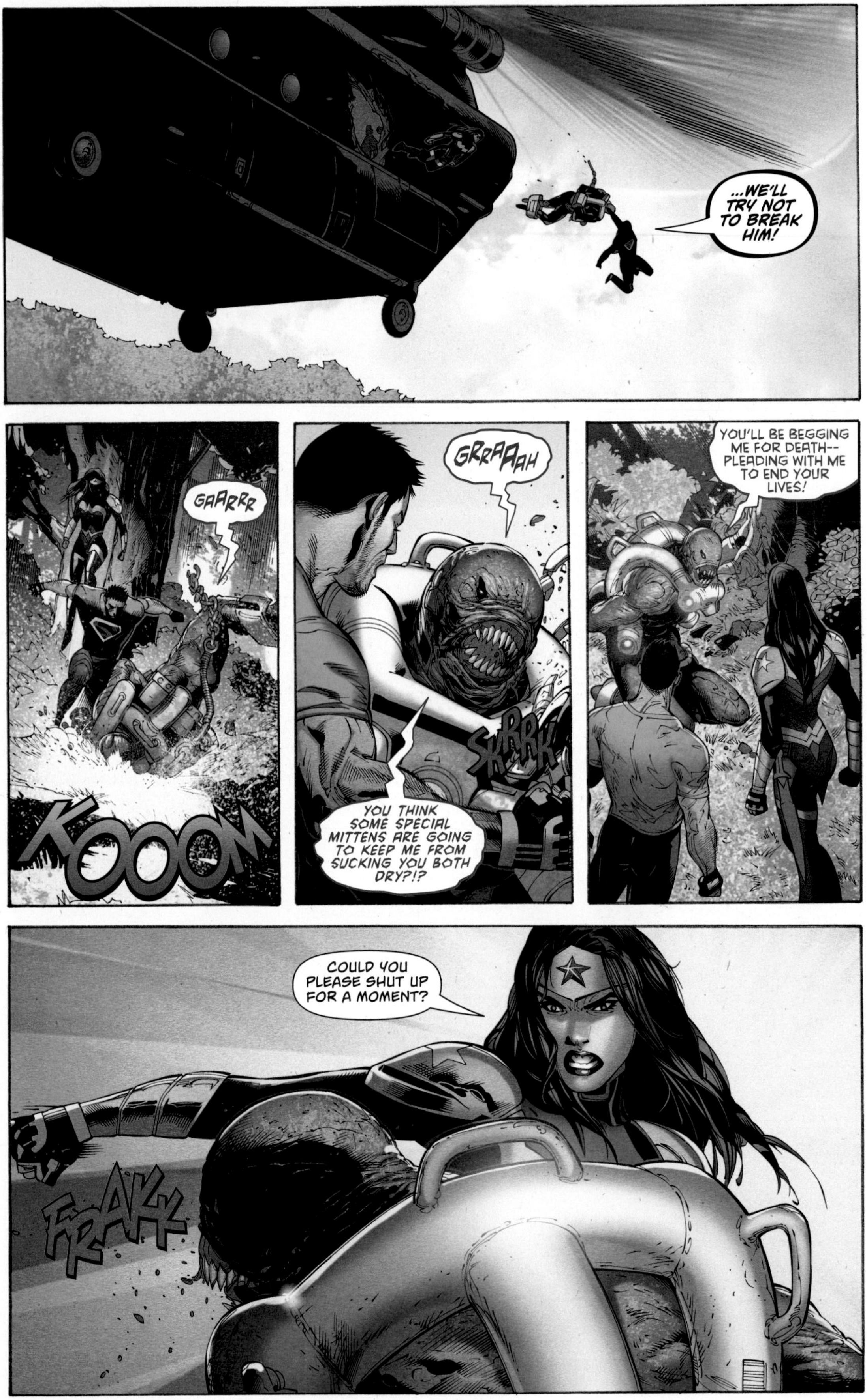
...WE'LL TRY NOT TO BREAK HIM!
GAARRR
KOOOM
GRRAAAH
YOU THINK SOME SPECIAL MITTENS ARE GOING TO KEEP ME FROM SUCKING YOU BOTH DRY?!?
SKRRK
YOU'LL BE BEGGING ME FOR DEATH-- PLEADING WITH ME TO END YOUR LIVES!
COULD YOU PLEASE SHUT UP FOR A MOMENT?
FRAKK

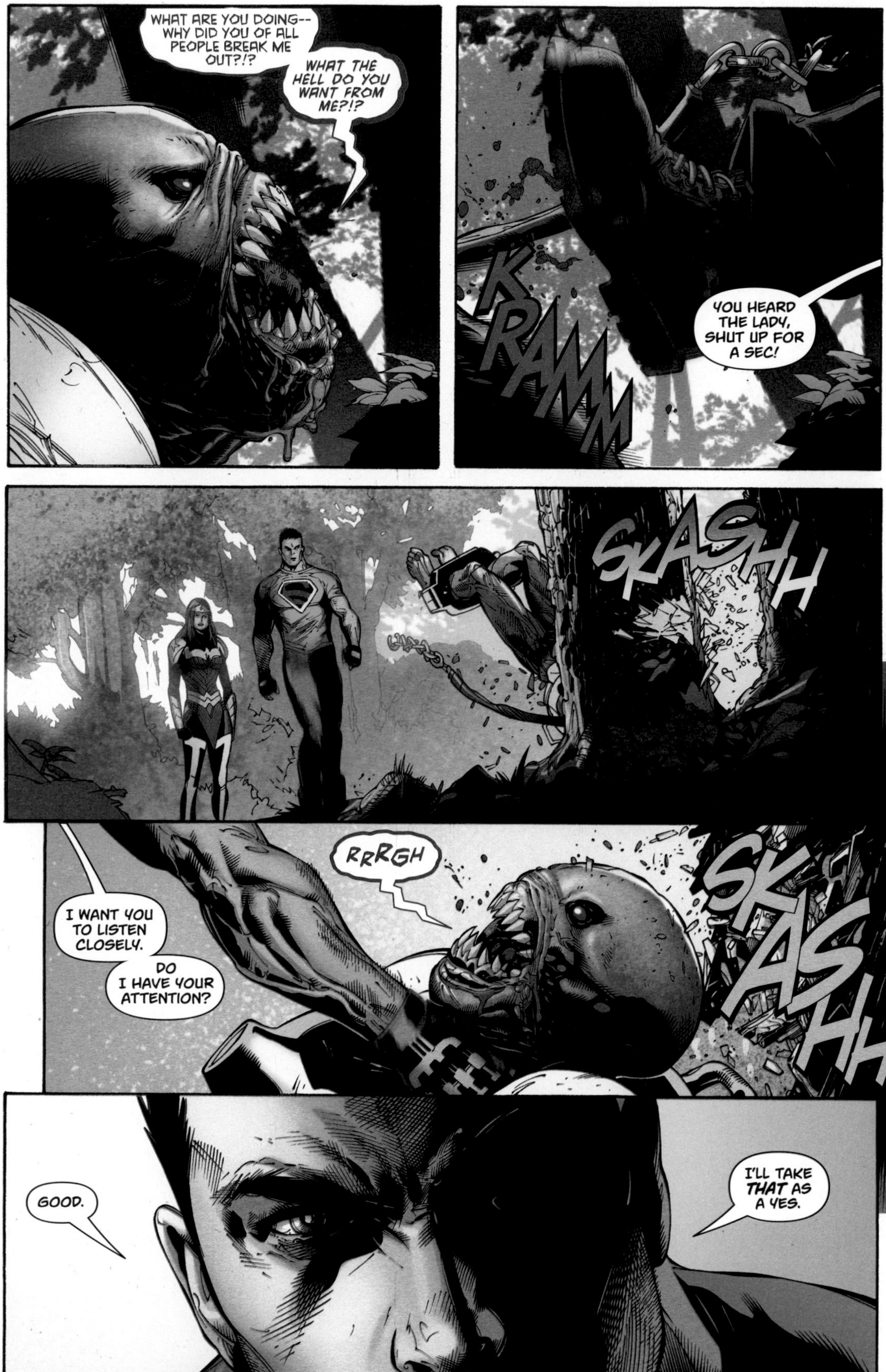
WHAT ARE YOU DOING-- WHY DID YOU OF ALL PEOPLE BREAK ME OUT?!?
WHAT THE HELL DO YOU WANT FROM ME?!?
KRAMM
YOU HEARD THE LADY, SHUT UP FOR A SEC!
SKASHH
RRRGH
I WANT YOU TO LISTEN CLOSELY.
DO I HAVE YOUR ATTENTION?
SKASHH
GOOD.
I'LL TAKE *THAT* AS A YES.

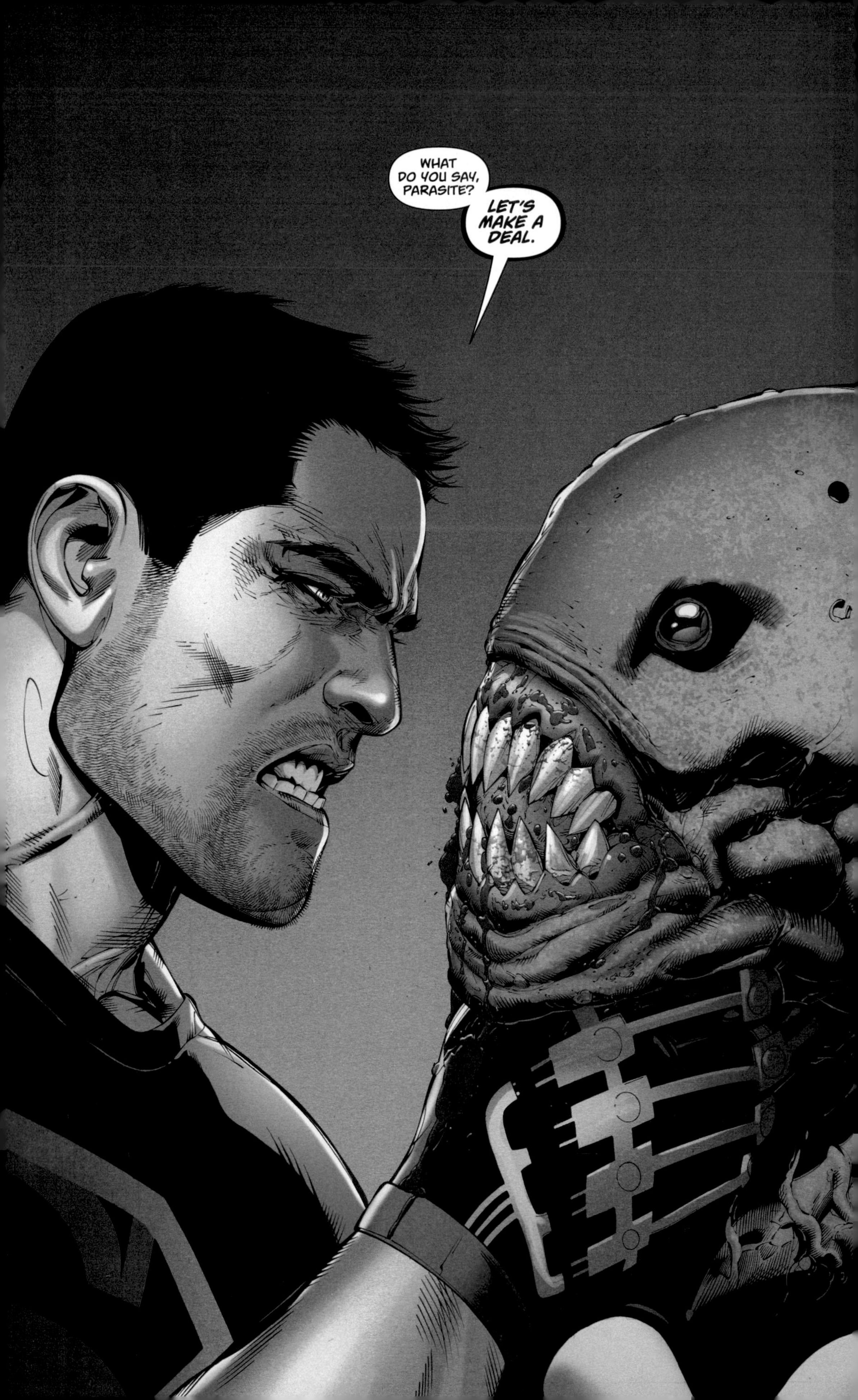
WHAT DO YOU SAY, PARASITE?
LET'S MAKE A DEAL.

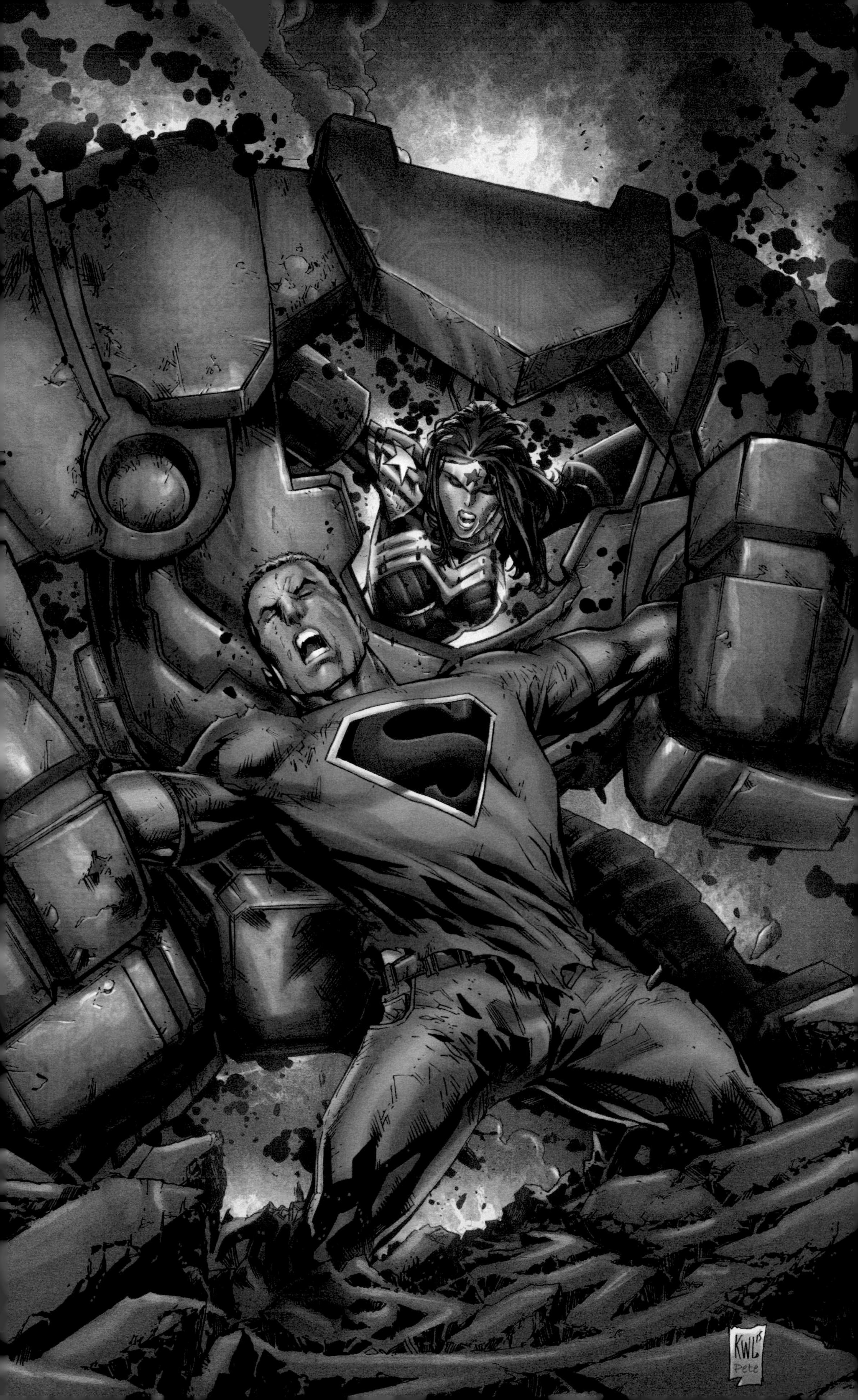

RAVENOUS

PETER J. TOMASI writer DOUG MAHNKE penciller JAIME MENDOZA MARK IRWIN KEITH CHAMPAGNE DOUG MAHNKE inkers WIL QUINTANA colorist TRAVIS LANHAM letterer cover by ED BENES & PETE PANTAZIS

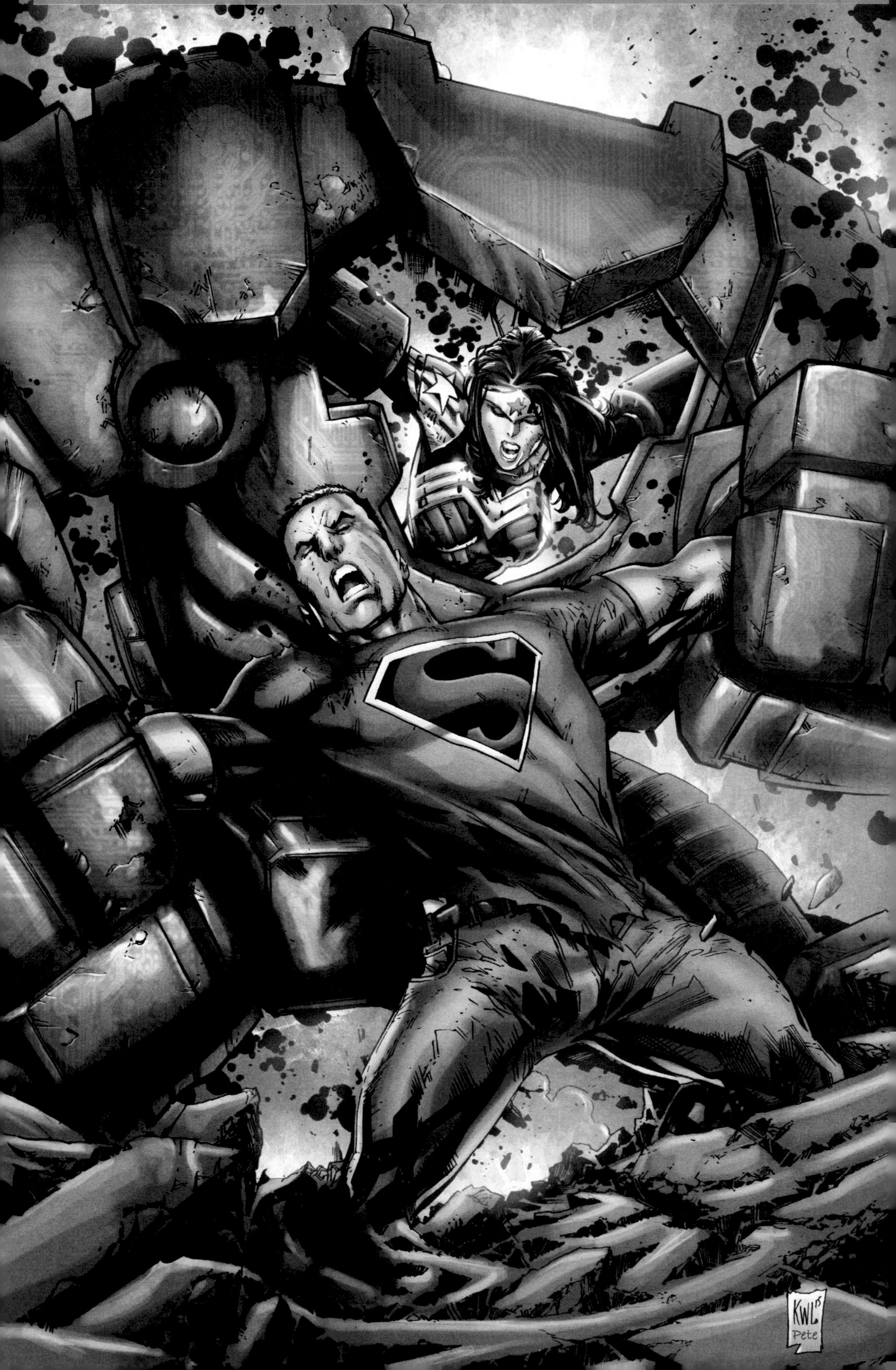
KWL 15
Pete

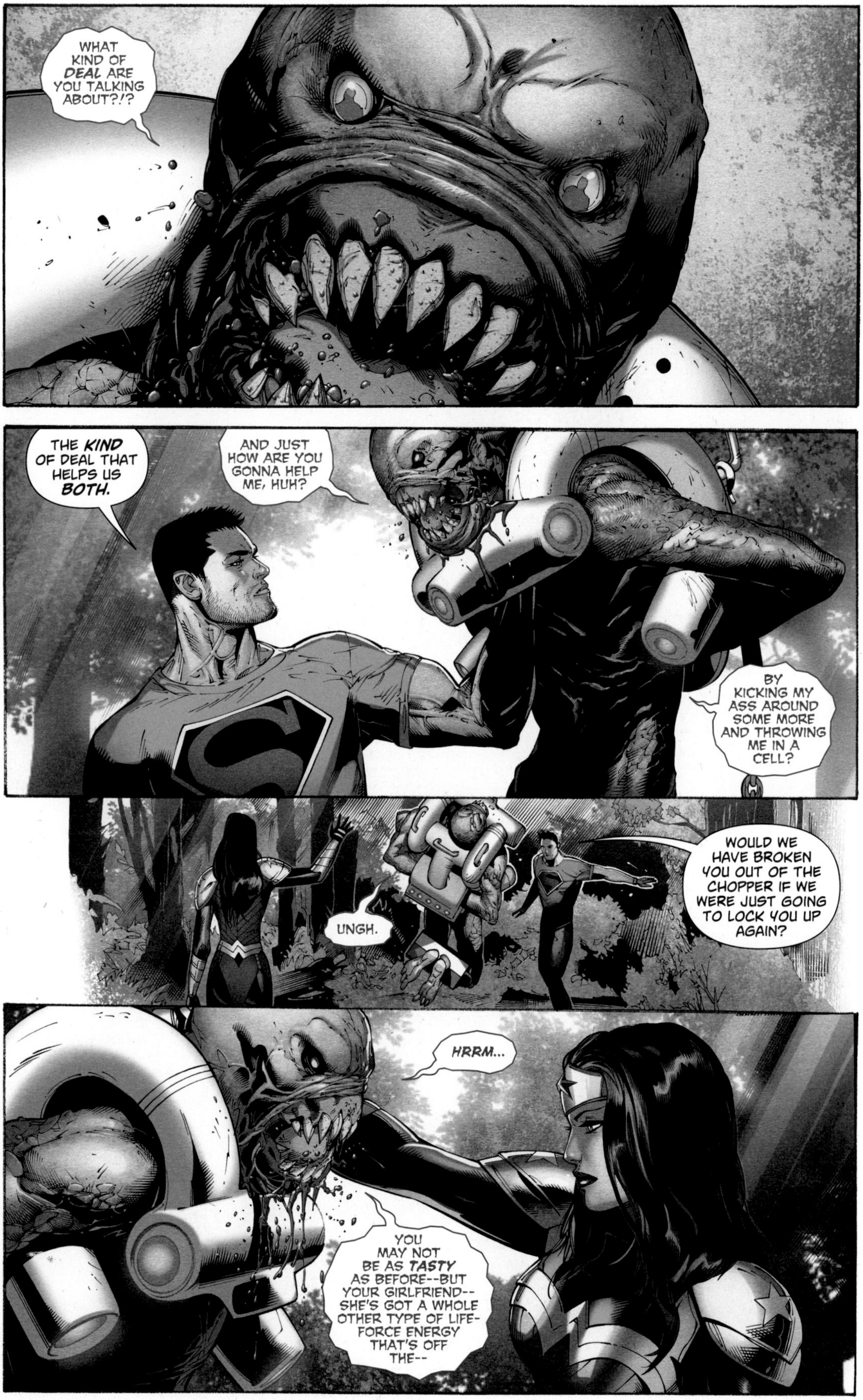

WHAT KIND OF DEAL ARE YOU TALKING ABOUT?!?
THE KIND OF DEAL THAT HELPS US BOTH.
AND JUST HOW ARE YOU GONNA HELP ME, HUH?
BY KICKING MY ASS AROUND SOME MORE AND THROWING ME IN A CELL?
UNGH.
WOULD WE HAVE BROKEN YOU OUT OF THE CHOPPER IF WE WERE JUST GOING TO LOCK YOU UP AGAIN?
HRRM...
YOU MAY NOT BE AS TASTY AS BEFORE--BUT YOUR GIRLFRIEND--SHE'S GOT A WHOLE OTHER TYPE OF LIFE-FORCE ENERGY THAT'S OFF THE--

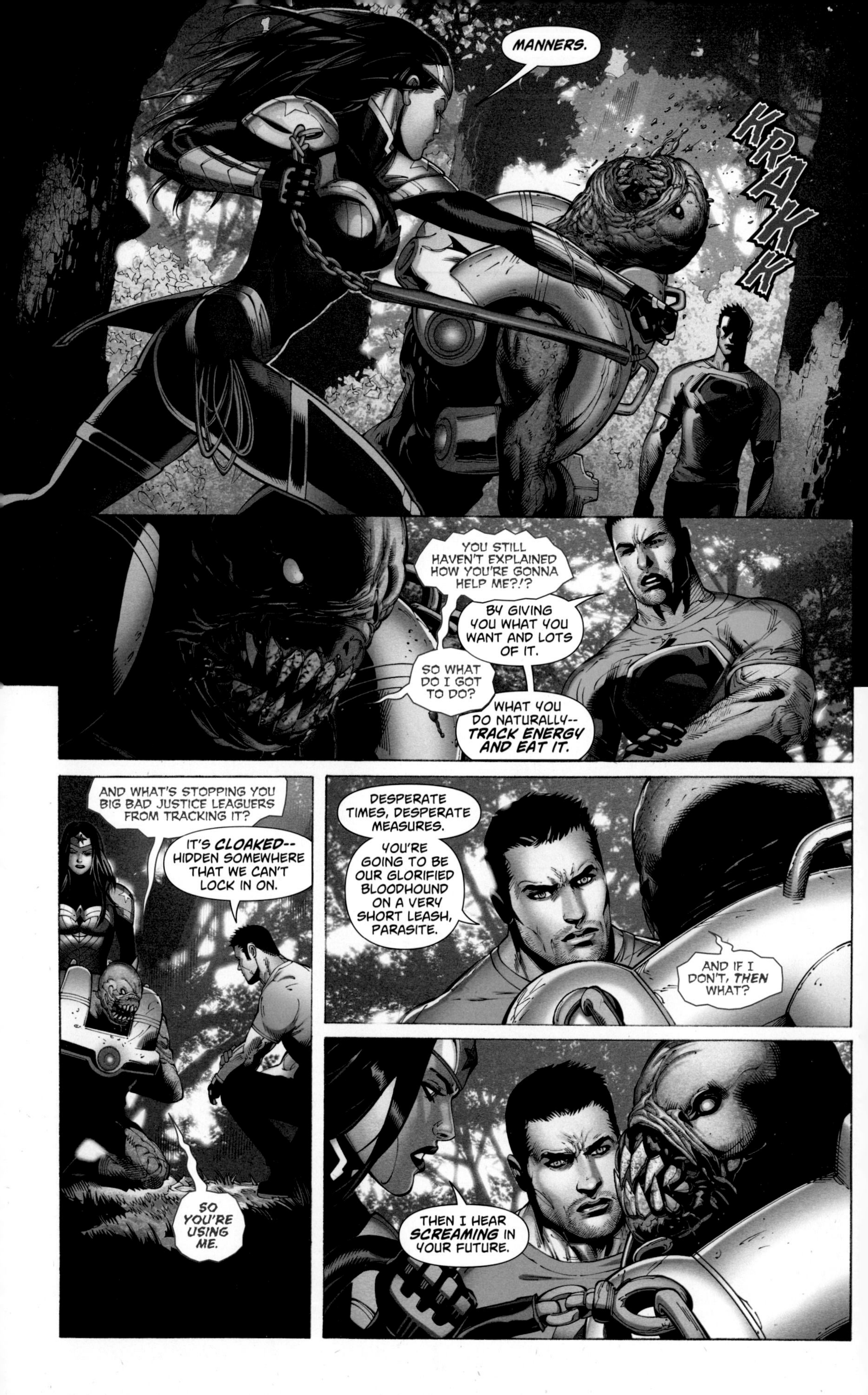
MANNERS.
KRAKK
YOU STILL HAVEN'T EXPLAINED HOW YOU'RE GONNA HELP ME?!?
BY GIVING YOU WHAT YOU WANT AND LOTS OF IT.
SO WHAT DO I GOT TO DO?
WHAT YOU DO NATURALLY-- TRACK ENERGY AND EAT IT.
AND WHAT'S STOPPING YOU BIG BAD JUSTICE LEAGUERS FROM TRACKING IT?
IT'S CLOAKED-- HIDDEN SOMEWHERE THAT WE CAN'T LOCK IN ON.
SO YOU'RE USING ME.
DESPERATE TIMES, DESPERATE MEASURES.
YOU'RE GOING TO BE OUR GLORIFIED BLOODHOUND ON A VERY SHORT LEASH, PARASITE.
AND IF I DON'T, THEN WHAT?
THEN I HEAR SCREAMING IN YOUR FUTURE.

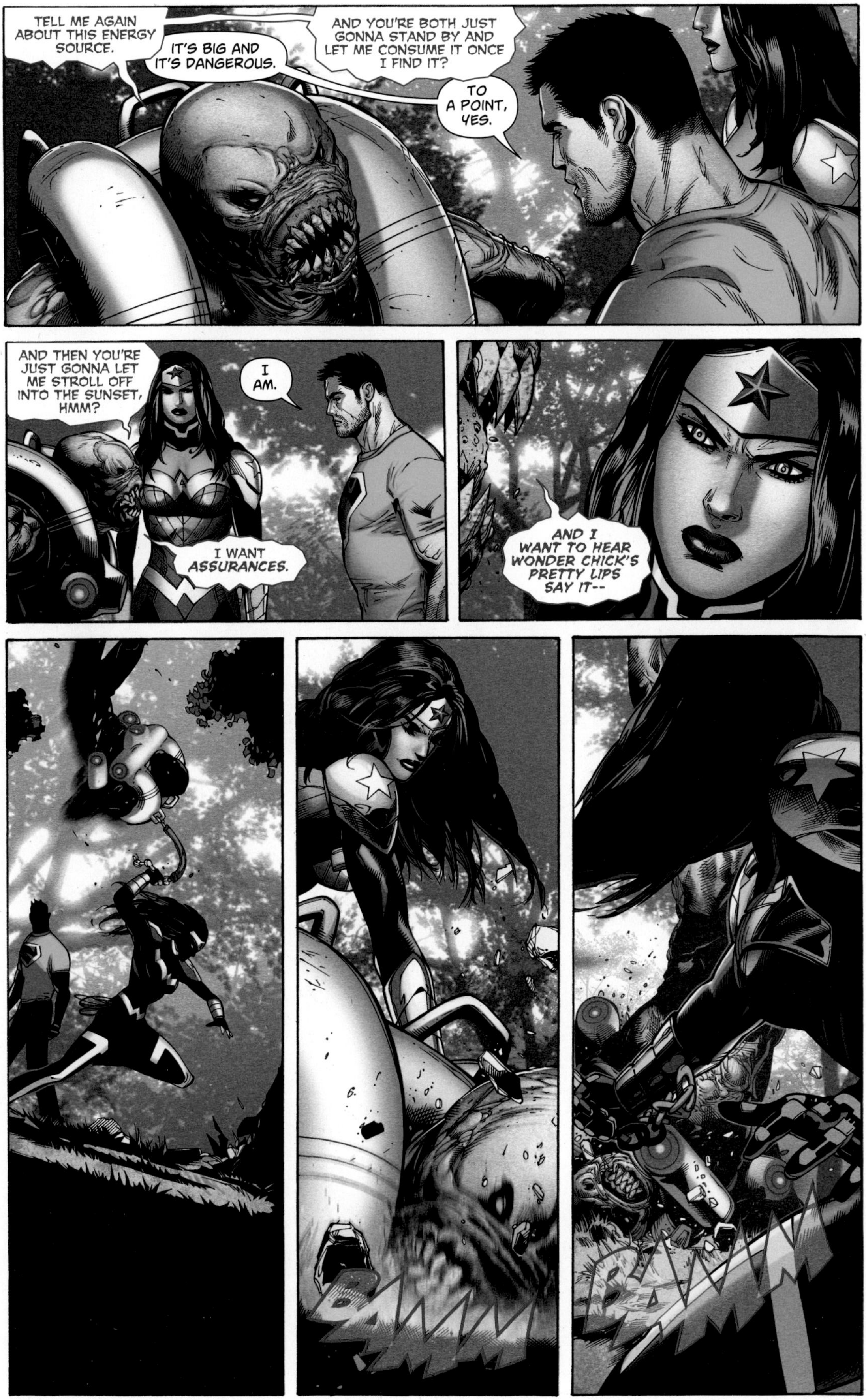
TELL ME AGAIN ABOUT THIS ENERGY SOURCE.
IT'S BIG AND IT'S DANGEROUS.
AND YOU'RE BOTH JUST GONNA STAND BY AND LET ME CONSUME IT ONCE I FIND IT?
TO A POINT, YES.
AND THEN YOU'RE JUST GONNA LET ME STROLL OFF INTO THE SUNSET, HMM?
I AM.
I WANT ASSURANCES.
AND I WANT TO HEAR WONDER CHICK'S PRETTY LIPS SAY IT--
BAMM
BAMM

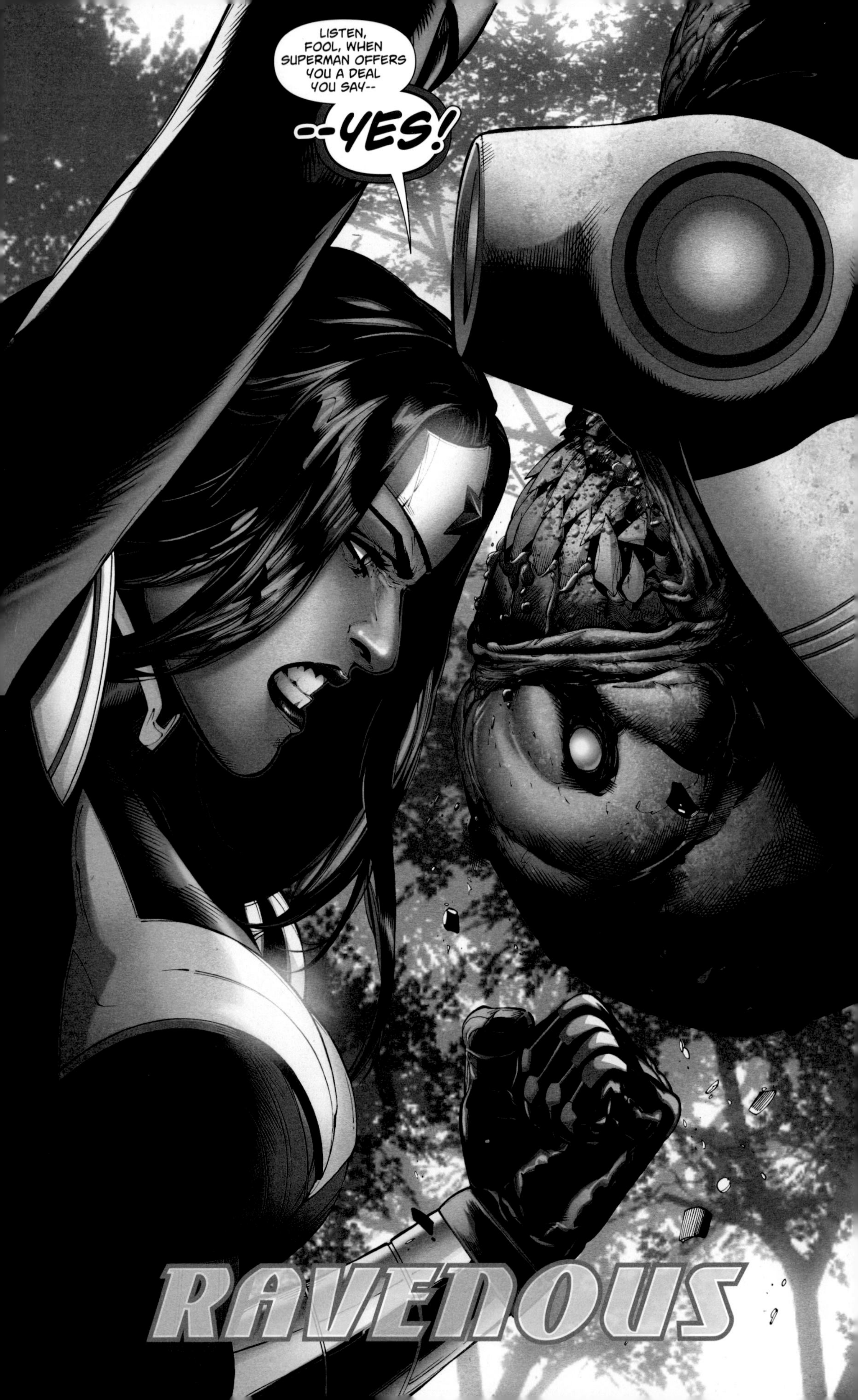
LISTEN, FOOL, WHEN SUPERMAN OFFERS YOU A DEAL YOU SAY--
--YES!
RAVENOUS

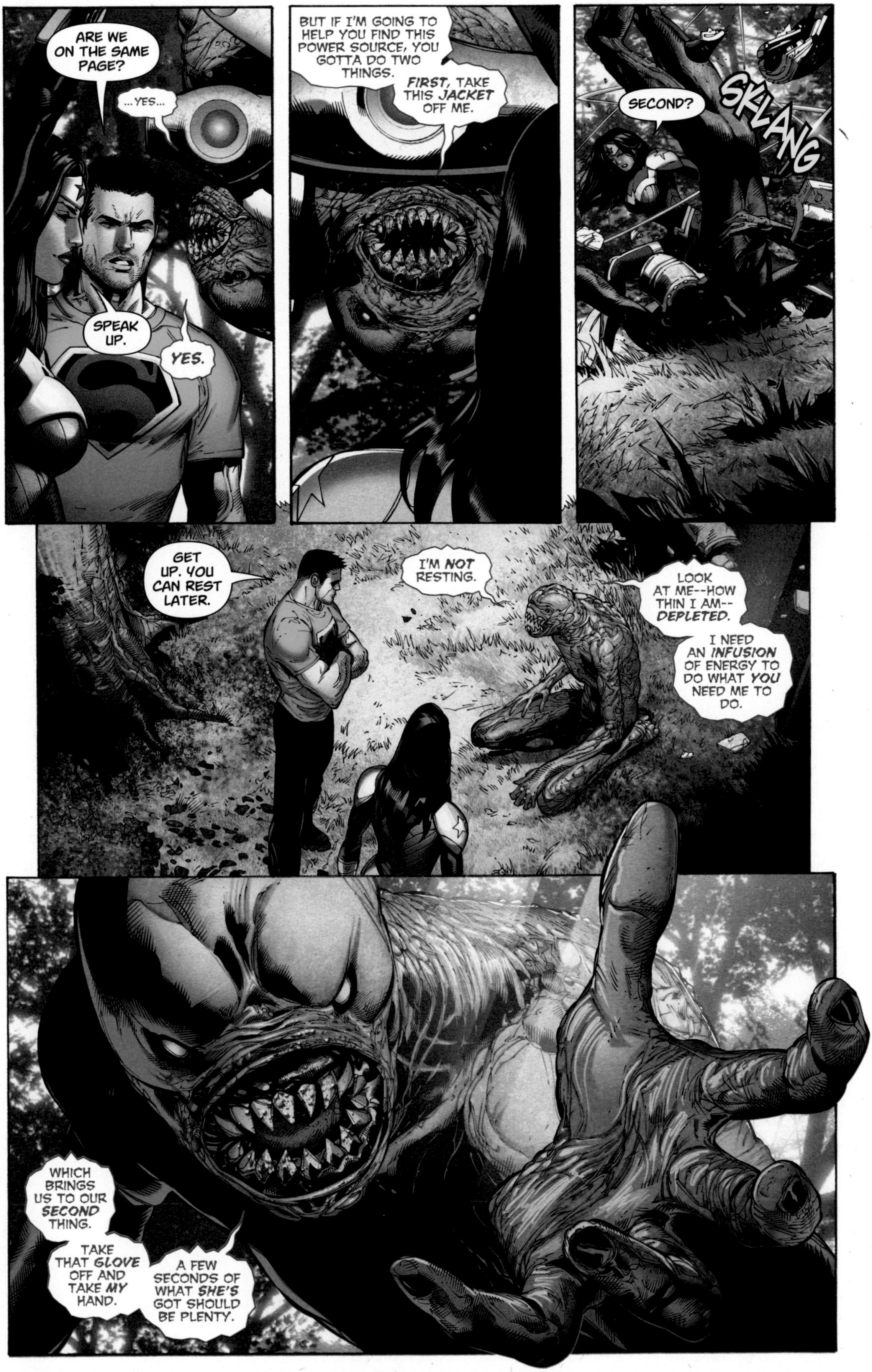
ARE WE ON THE SAME PAGE?
...YES...
SPEAK UP.
YES.
BUT IF I'M GOING TO HELP YOU FIND THIS POWER SOURCE, YOU GOTTA DO TWO THINGS.
FIRST, TAKE THIS JACKET OFF ME.
SECOND?
SKLANG
GET UP. YOU CAN REST LATER.
I'M NOT RESTING.
LOOK AT ME--HOW THIN I AM--DEPLETED.
I NEED AN INFUSION OF ENERGY TO DO WHAT YOU NEED ME TO DO.
WHICH BRINGS US TO OUR SECOND THING.
TAKE THAT GLOVE OFF AND TAKE MY HAND.
A FEW SECONDS OF WHAT SHE'S GOT SHOULD BE PLENTY.

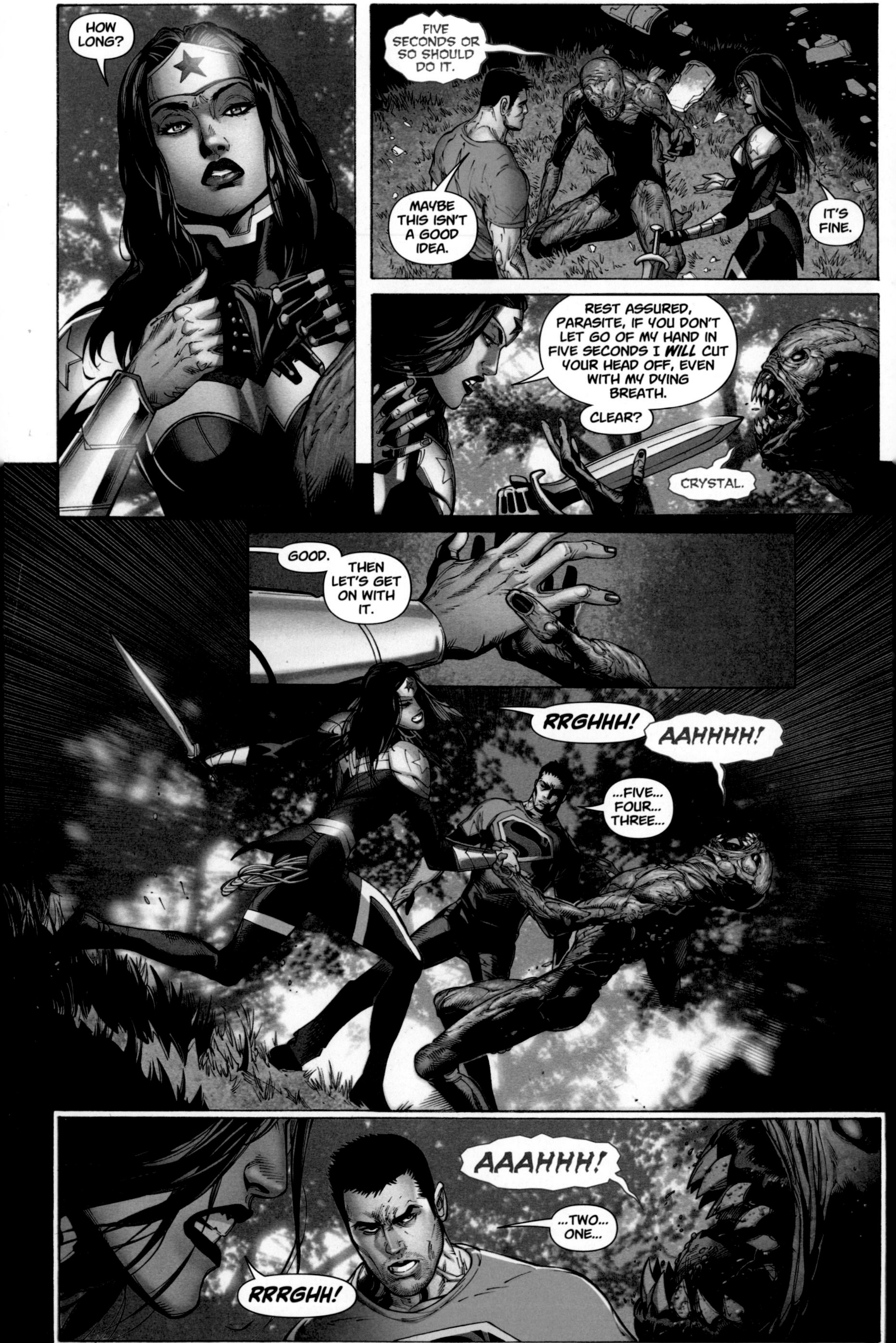
HOW LONG?
FIVE SECONDS OR SO SHOULD DO IT.
MAYBE THIS ISN'T A GOOD IDEA.
IT'S FINE.
REST ASSURED, PARASITE, IF YOU DON'T LET GO OF MY HAND IN FIVE SECONDS I WILL CUT YOUR HEAD OFF, EVEN WITH MY DYING BREATH.
CLEAR?
CRYSTAL.
GOOD.
THEN LET'S GET ON WITH IT.
RRGHHH!
AAHHHH!
...FIVE... FOUR... THREE...
AAAHHH!
...TWO... ONE...
RRRGHH!

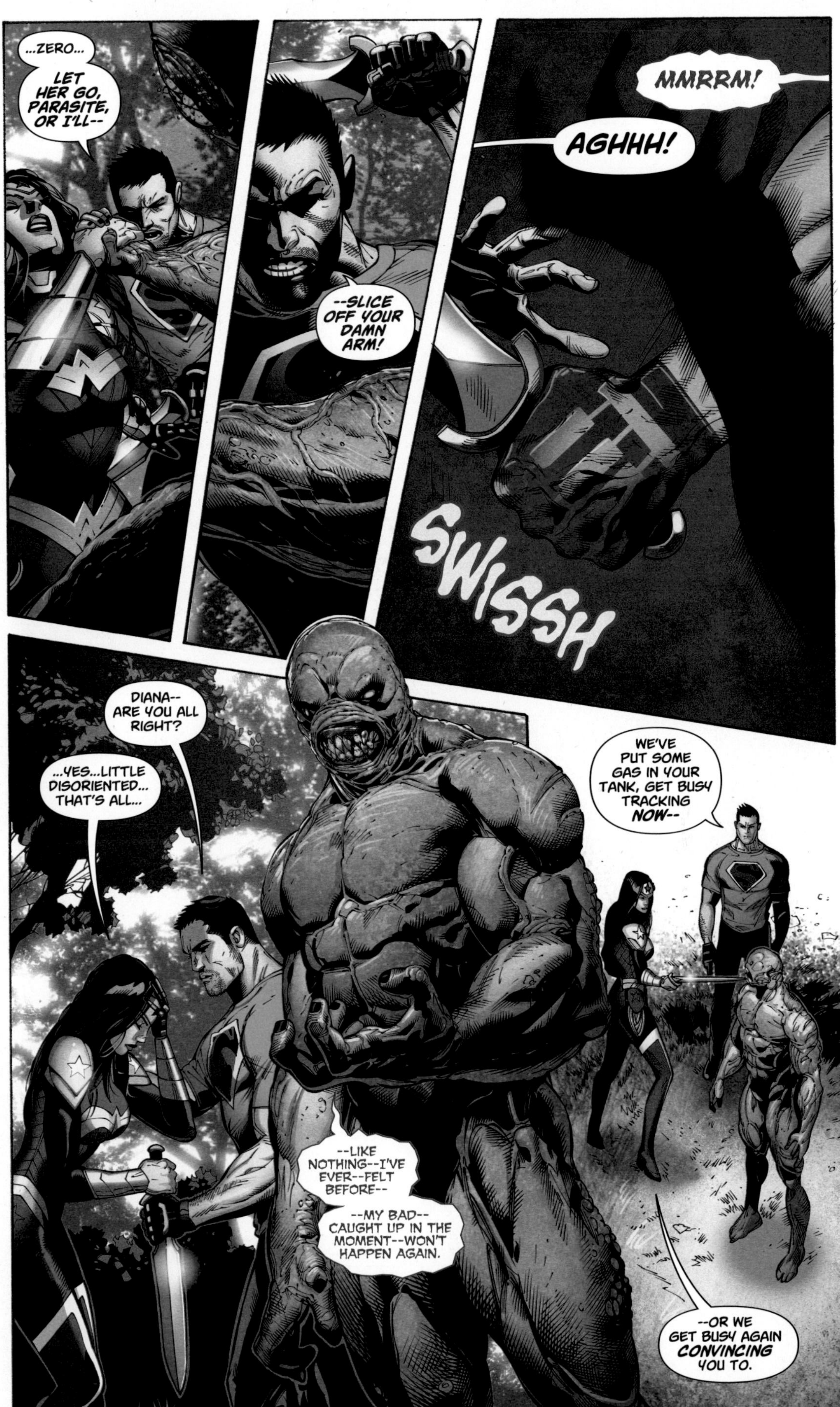
...ZERO...
LET HER GO, PARASITE, OR I'LL--
--SLICE OFF YOUR DAMN ARM!
MMRRM!
AGHHH!
SWISSH
DIANA-- ARE YOU ALL RIGHT?
...YES...LITTLE DISORIENTED... THAT'S ALL...
--LIKE NOTHING--I'VE EVER--FELT BEFORE--
--MY BAD-- CAUGHT UP IN THE MOMENT--WON'T HAPPEN AGAIN.
WE'VE PUT SOME GAS IN YOUR TANK, GET BUSY TRACKING NOW--
--OR WE GET BUSY AGAIN CONVINCING YOU TO.

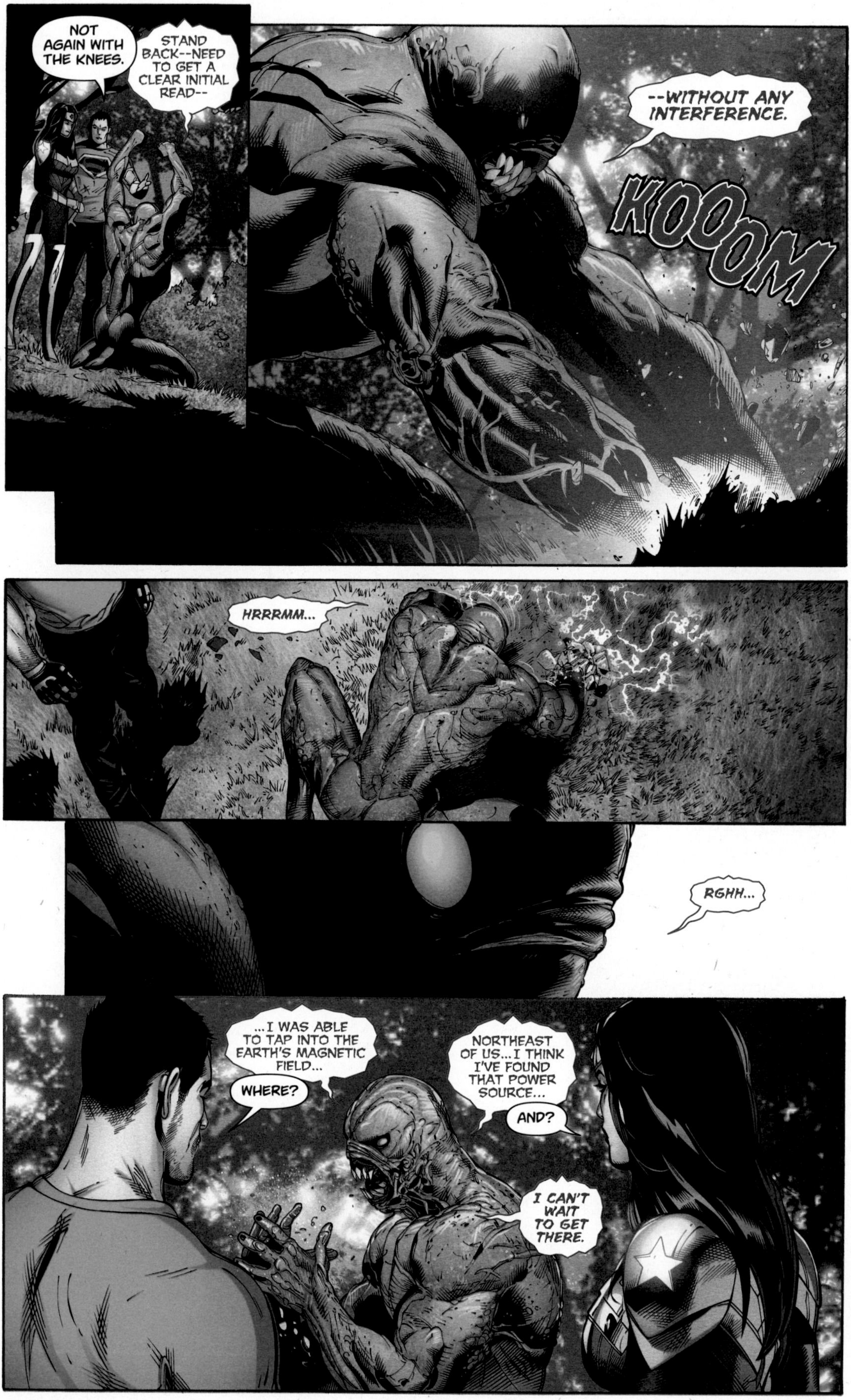
NOT AGAIN WITH THE KNEES.
STAND BACK--NEED TO GET A CLEAR INITIAL READ--
--WITHOUT ANY INTERFERENCE.
KOOOM
HRRRMM...
RGHH...
...I WAS ABLE TO TAP INTO THE EARTH'S MAGNETIC FIELD...
WHERE?
NORTHEAST OF US...I THINK I'VE FOUND THAT POWER SOURCE...
AND?
I CAN'T WAIT TO GET THERE.

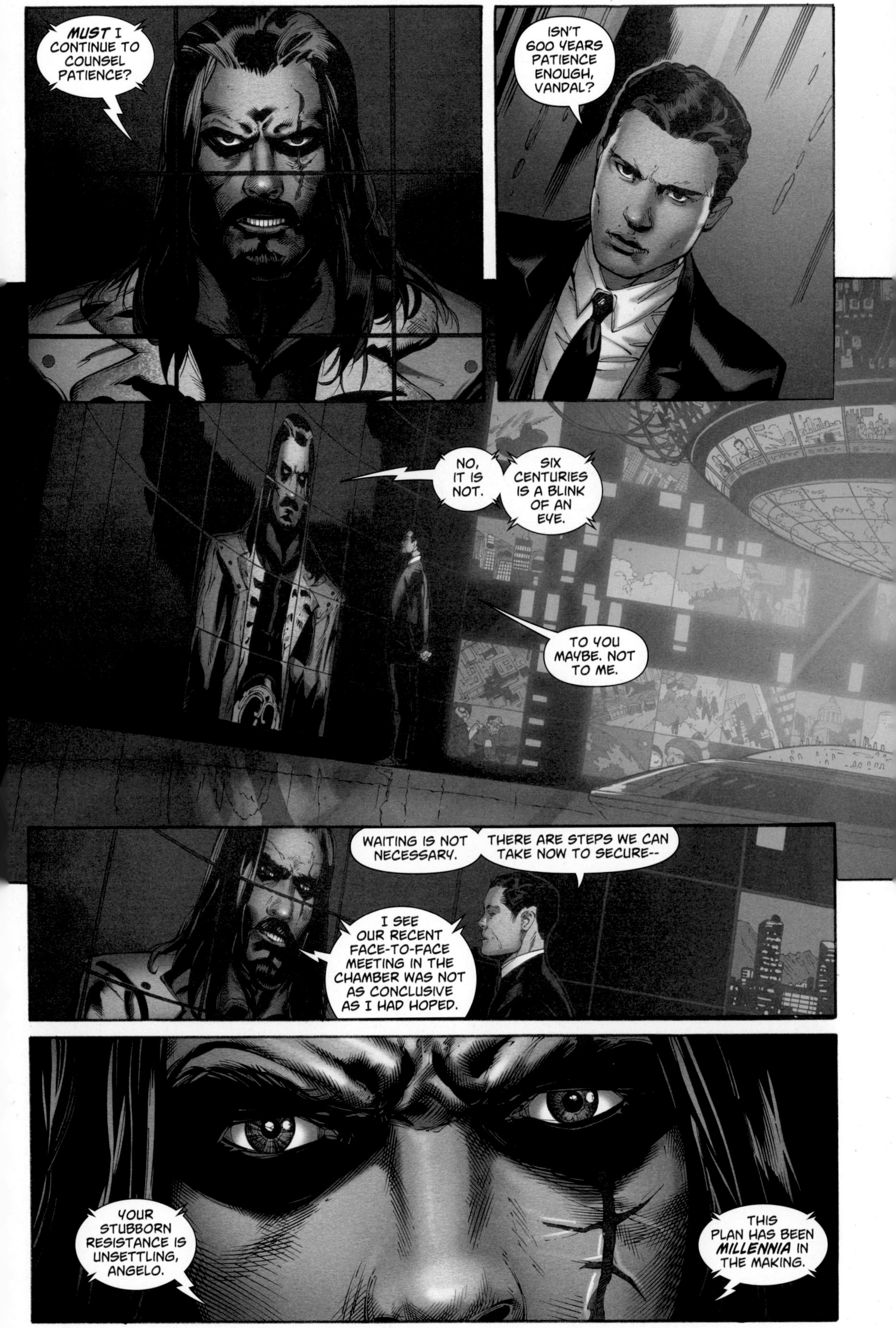
MUST I CONTINUE TO COUNSEL PATIENCE?
ISN'T 600 YEARS PATIENCE ENOUGH, VANDAL?
NO, IT IS NOT.
SIX CENTURIES IS A BLINK OF AN EYE.
TO YOU MAYBE. NOT TO ME.
WAITING IS NOT NECESSARY.
THERE ARE STEPS WE CAN TAKE NOW TO SECURE--
I SEE OUR RECENT FACE-TO-FACE MEETING IN THE CHAMBER WAS NOT AS CONCLUSIVE AS I HAD HOPED.
YOUR STUBBORN RESISTANCE IS UNSETTLING, ANGELO.
THIS PLAN HAS BEEN MILLENNIA IN THE MAKING.

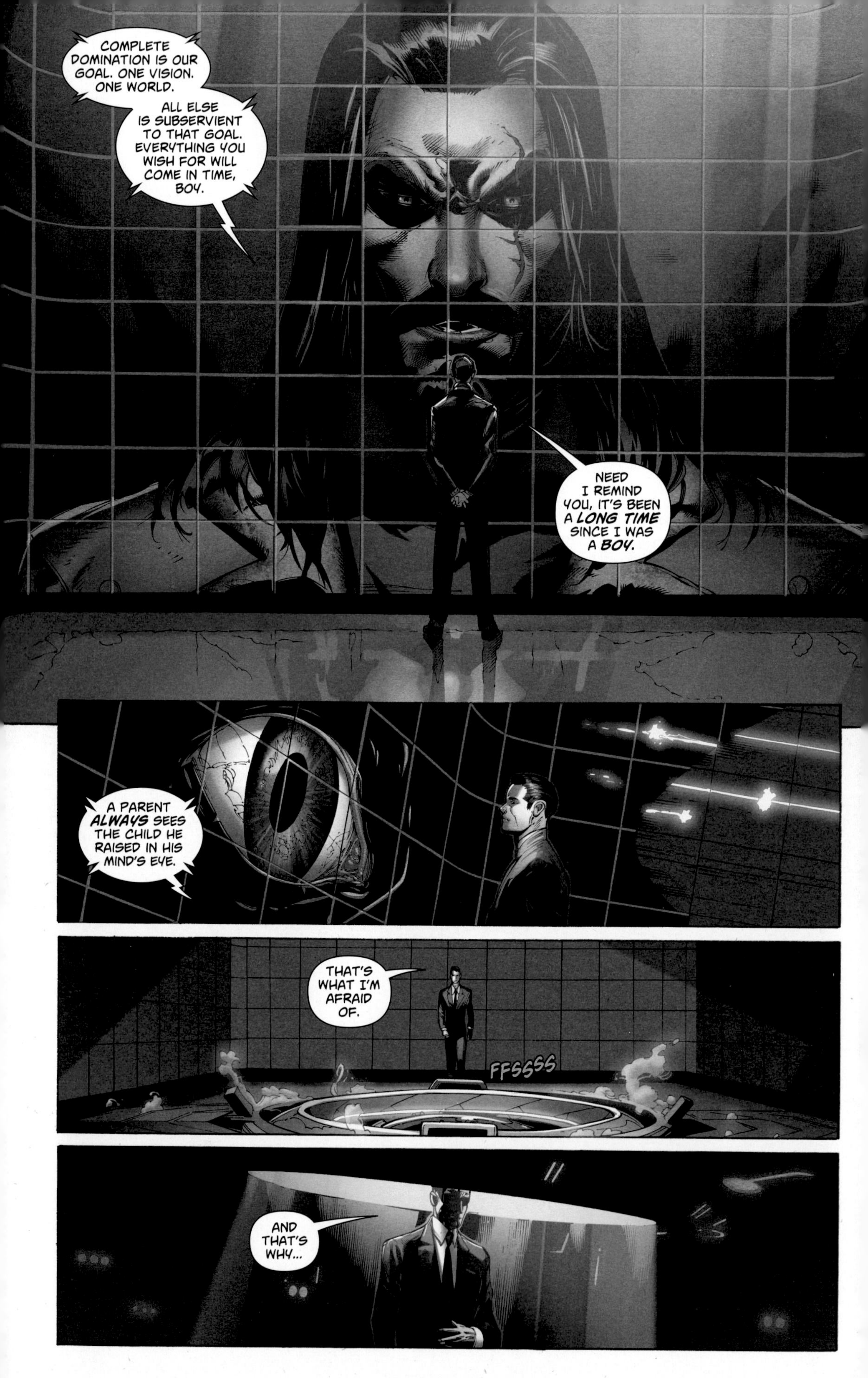
COMPLETE DOMINATION IS OUR GOAL. ONE VISION. ONE WORLD.
ALL ELSE IS SUBSERVIENT TO THAT GOAL. EVERYTHING YOU WISH FOR WILL COME IN TIME, BOY.
NEED I REMIND YOU, IT'S BEEN A LONG TIME SINCE I WAS A BOY.
A PARENT ALWAYS SEES THE CHILD HE RAISED IN HIS MIND'S EYE.
THAT'S WHAT I'M AFRAID OF.
FFSSSS
AND THAT'S WHY...

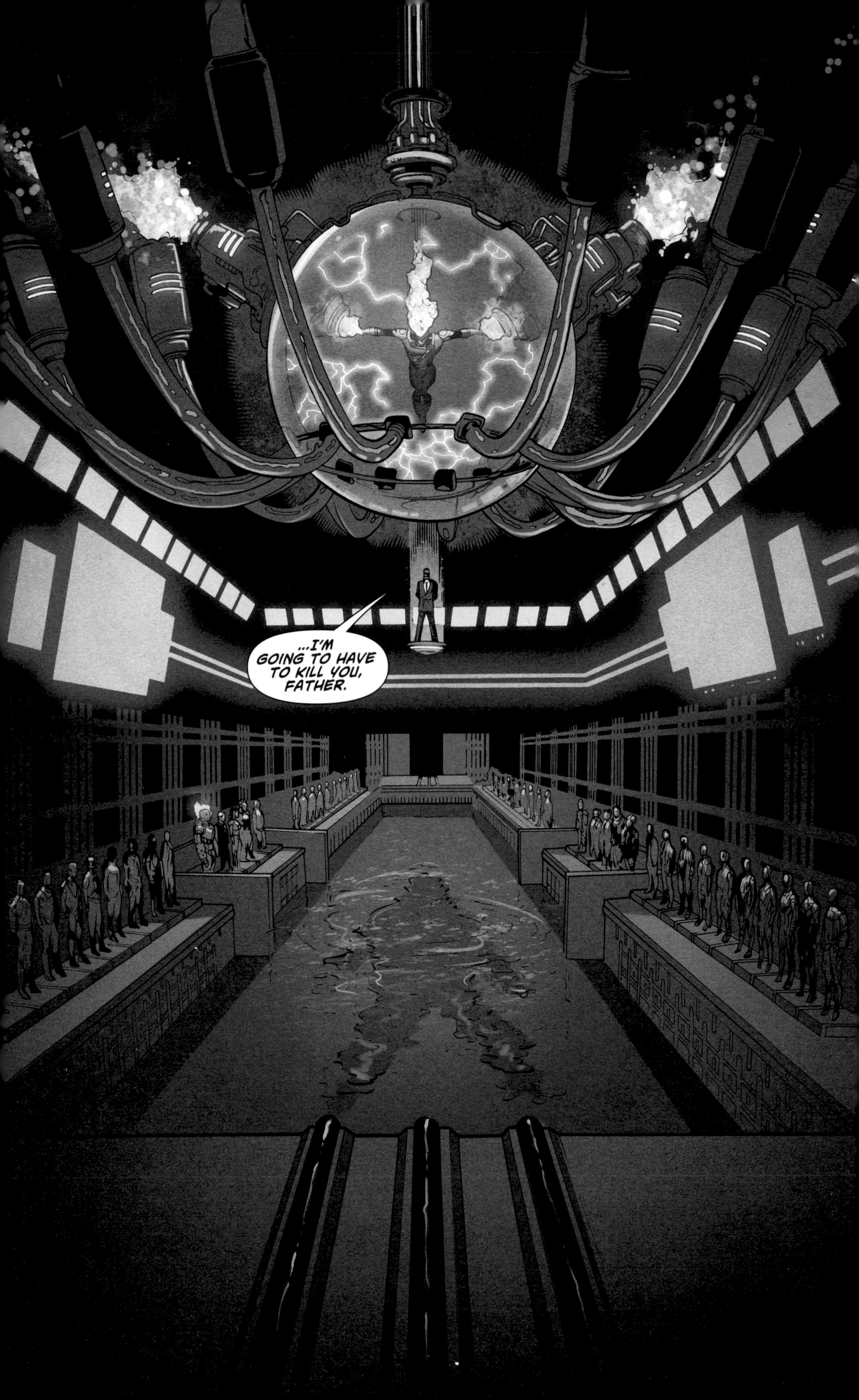
...I'M GOING TO HAVE TO KILL YOU, FATHER.

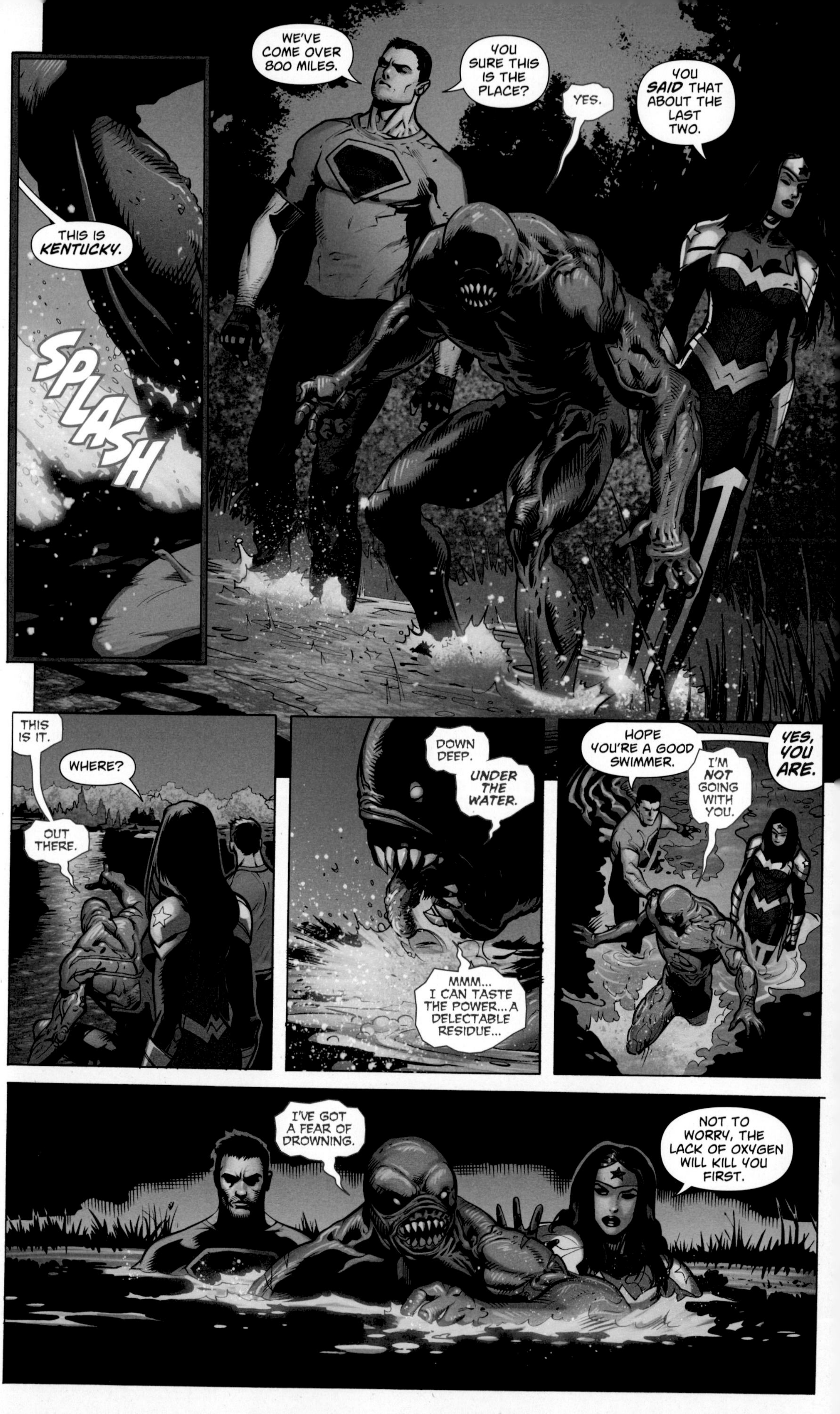
THIS IS KENTUCKY.
SPLASH
WE'VE COME OVER 800 MILES.
YOU SURE THIS IS THE PLACE?
YES.
YOU SAID THAT ABOUT THE LAST TWO.
THIS IS IT.
WHERE?
OUT THERE.
DOWN DEEP.
UNDER THE WATER.
MMM... I CAN TASTE THE POWER...A DELECTABLE RESIDUE...
HOPE YOU'RE A GOOD SWIMMER.
I'M NOT GOING WITH YOU.
YES, YOU ARE.
I'VE GOT A FEAR OF DROWNING.
NOT TO WORRY, THE LACK OF OXYGEN WILL KILL YOU FIRST.

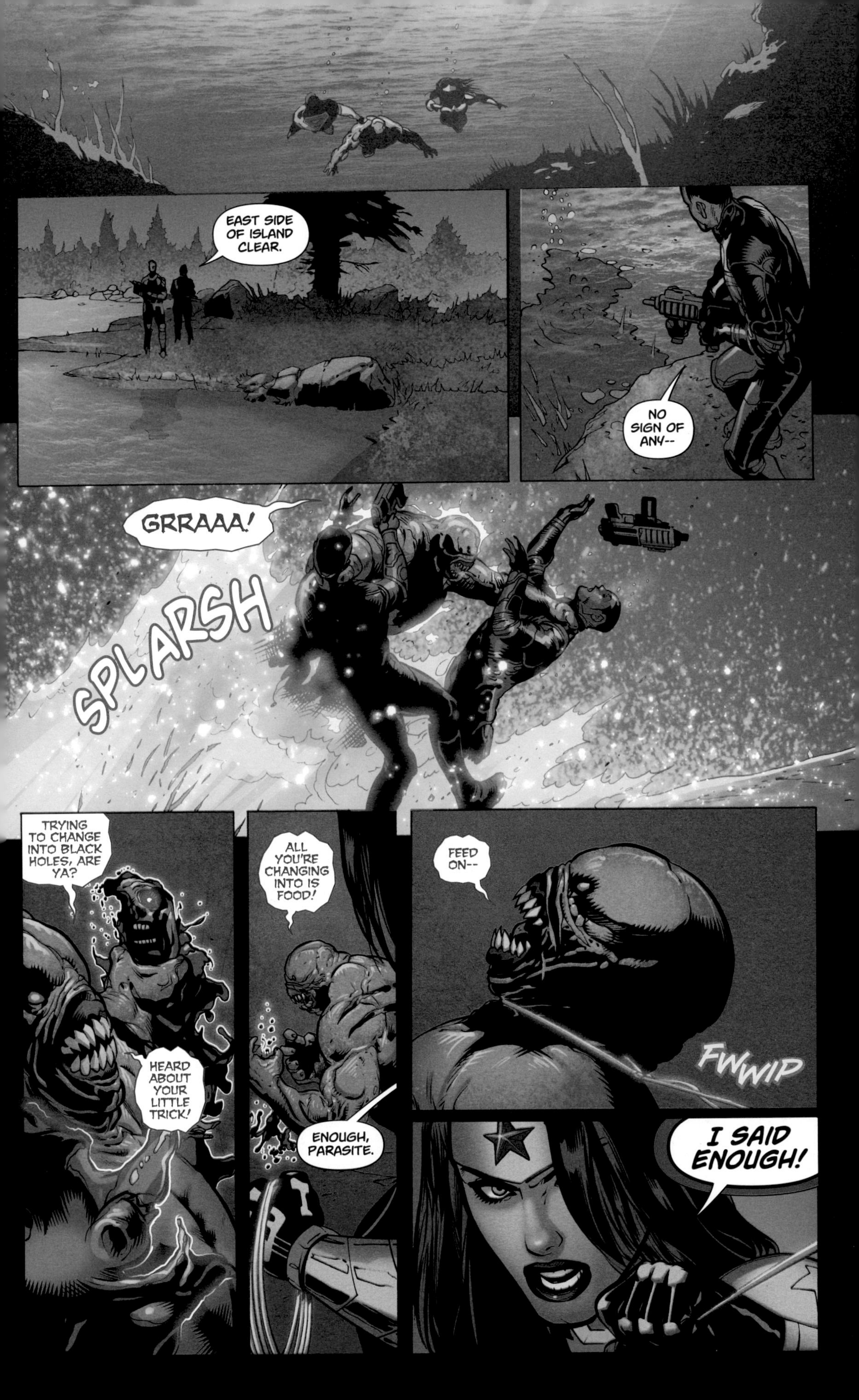
EAST SIDE OF ISLAND CLEAR.
NO SIGN OF ANY--
GRRAAA!
SPLARSH
TRYING TO CHANGE INTO BLACK HOLES, ARE YA?
HEARD ABOUT YOUR LITTLE TRICK!
ALL YOU'RE CHANGING INTO IS FOOD!
ENOUGH, PARASITE.
FEED ON--
FWWIP
I SAID ENOUGH!

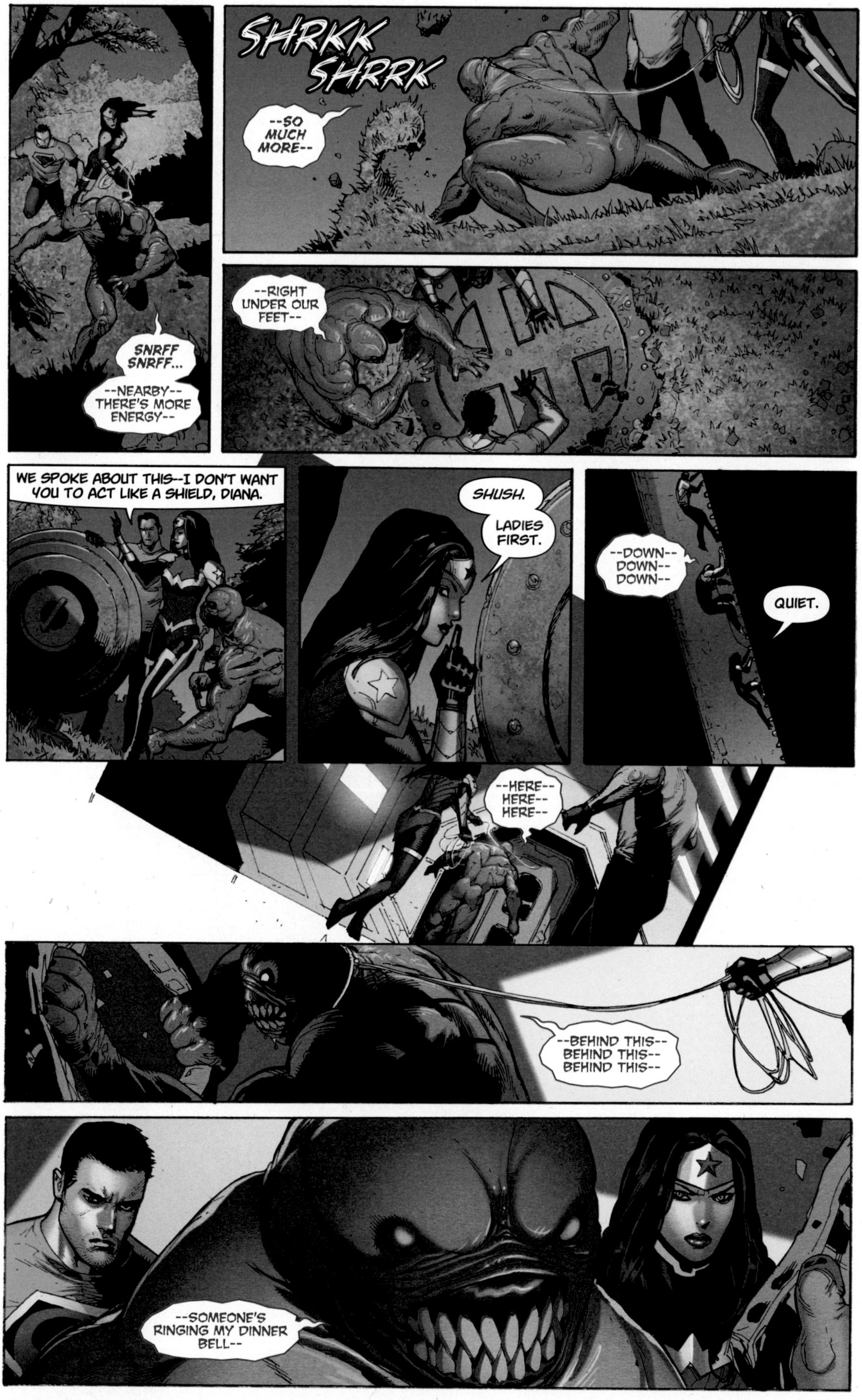
SNRFF SNRFF...
--NEARBY-- THERE'S MORE ENERGY--
SHRKK SHRRK
--SO MUCH MORE--
--RIGHT UNDER OUR FEET--
WE SPOKE ABOUT THIS--I DON'T WANT YOU TO ACT LIKE A SHIELD, DIANA.
SHUSH.
LADIES FIRST.
--DOWN-- DOWN-- DOWN--
QUIET.
--HERE-- HERE-- HERE--
--BEHIND THIS-- BEHIND THIS-- BEHIND THIS--
--SOMEONE'S RINGING MY DINNER BELL--

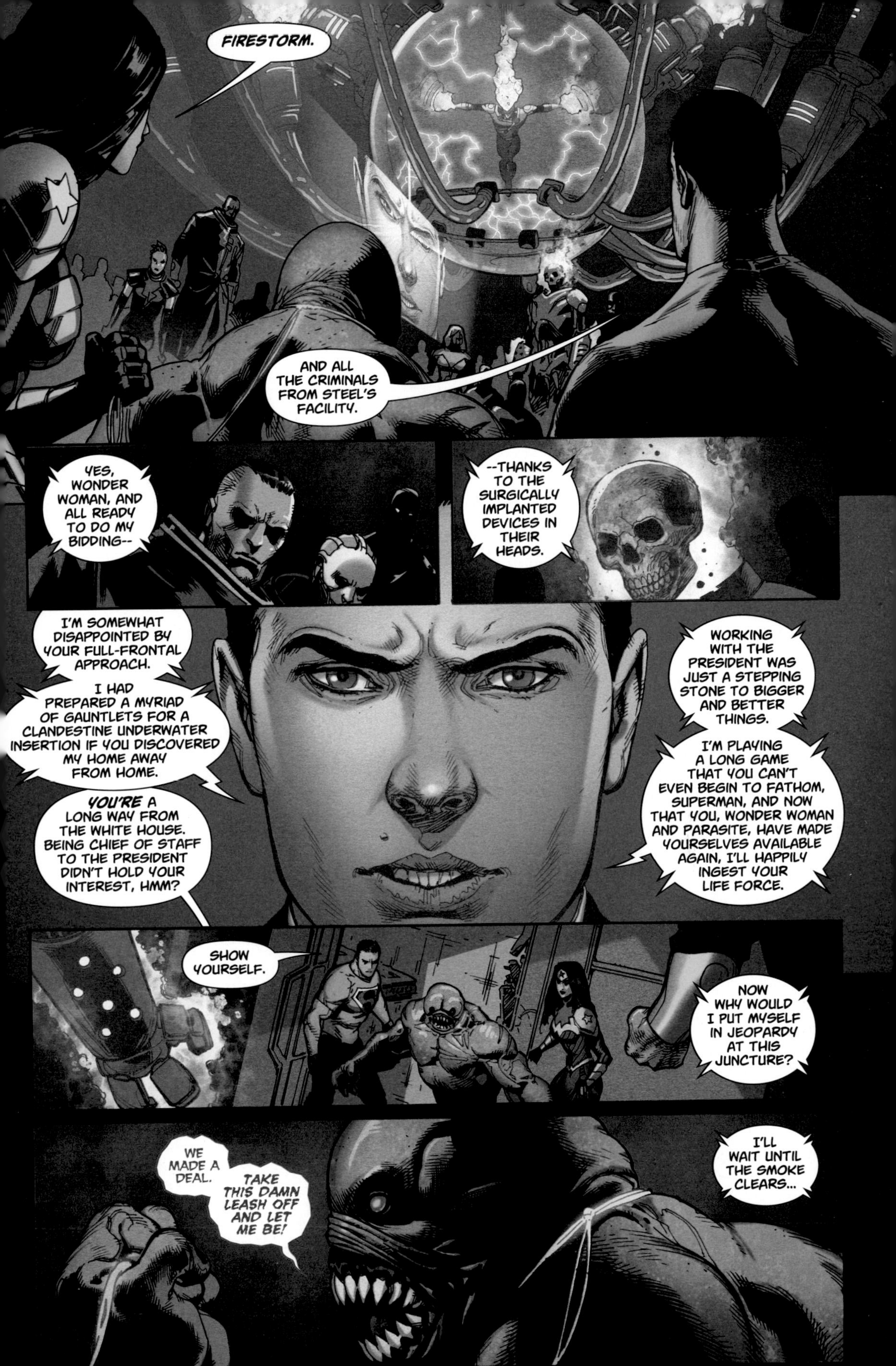
FIRESTORM.
AND ALL THE CRIMINALS FROM STEEL'S FACILITY.
YES, WONDER WOMAN, AND ALL READY TO DO MY BIDDING--
--THANKS TO THE SURGICALLY IMPLANTED DEVICES IN THEIR HEADS.
I'M SOMEWHAT DISAPPOINTED BY YOUR FULL-FRONTAL APPROACH.
I HAD PREPARED A MYRIAD OF GAUNTLETS FOR A CLANDESTINE UNDERWATER INSERTION IF YOU DISCOVERED MY HOME AWAY FROM HOME.
YOU'RE A LONG WAY FROM THE WHITE HOUSE. BEING CHIEF OF STAFF TO THE PRESIDENT DIDN'T HOLD YOUR INTEREST, HMM?
WORKING WITH THE PRESIDENT WAS JUST A STEPPING STONE TO BIGGER AND BETTER THINGS.
I'M PLAYING A LONG GAME THAT YOU CAN'T EVEN BEGIN TO FATHOM, SUPERMAN, AND NOW THAT YOU, WONDER WOMAN AND PARASITE, HAVE MADE YOURSELVES AVAILABLE AGAIN, I'LL HAPPILY INGEST YOUR LIFE FORCE.
SHOW YOURSELF.
NOW WHY WOULD I PUT MYSELF IN JEOPARDY AT THIS JUNCTURE?
WE MADE A DEAL.
TAKE THIS DAMN LEASH OFF AND LET ME BE!
I'LL WAIT UNTIL THE SMOKE CLEARS...

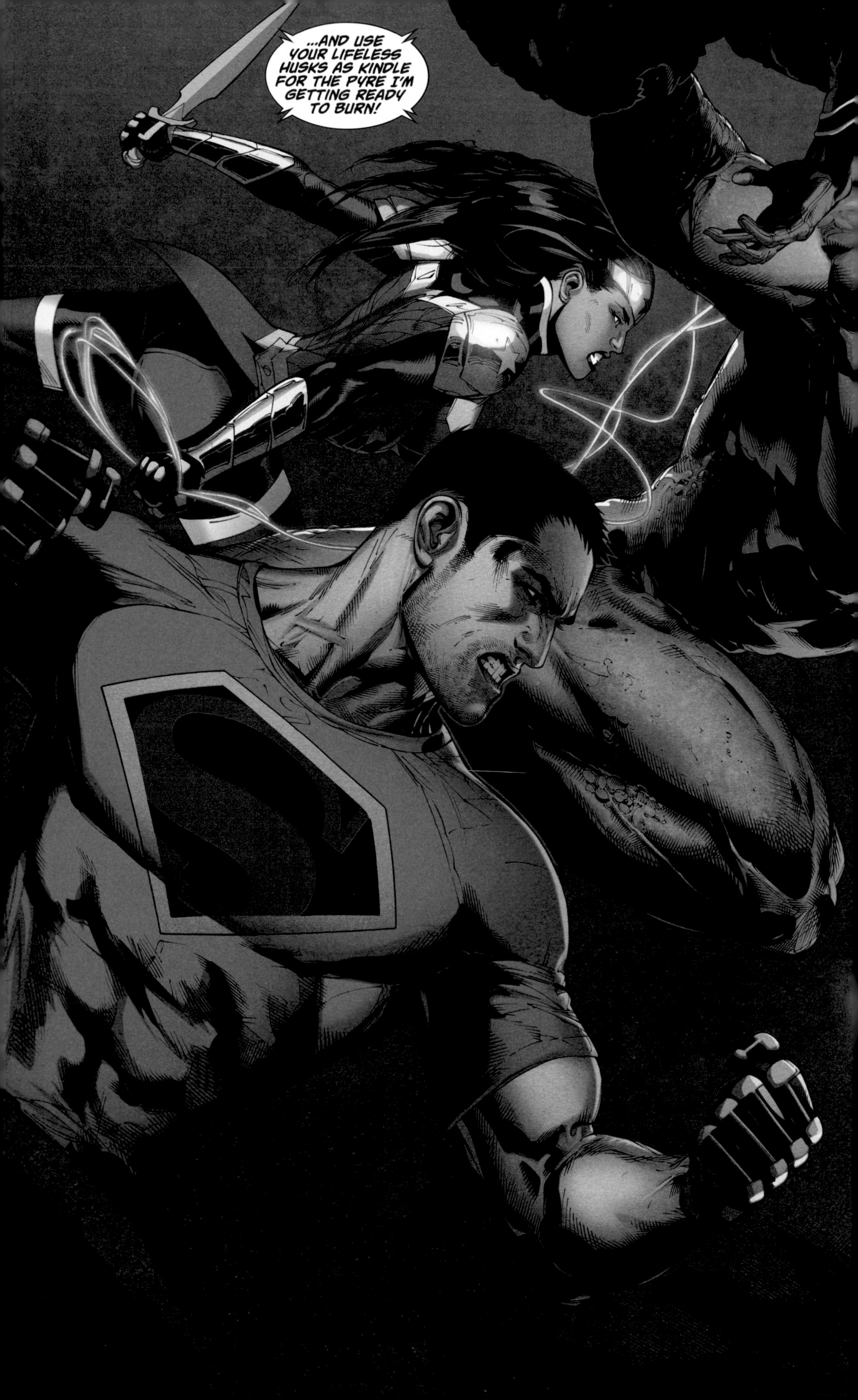
...AND USE YOUR LIFELESS HUSKS AS KINDLE FOR THE PYRE I'M GETTING READY TO BURN!

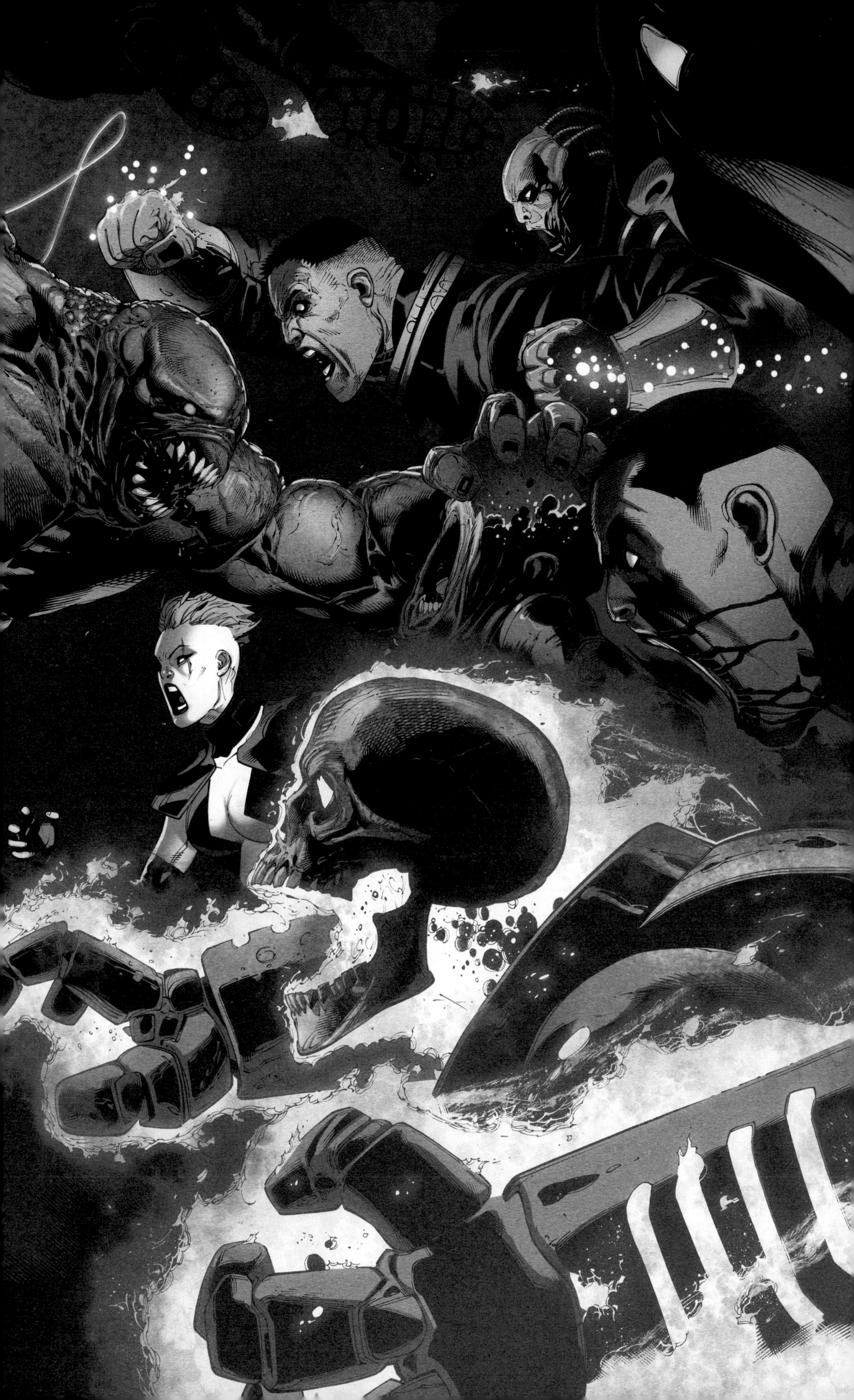

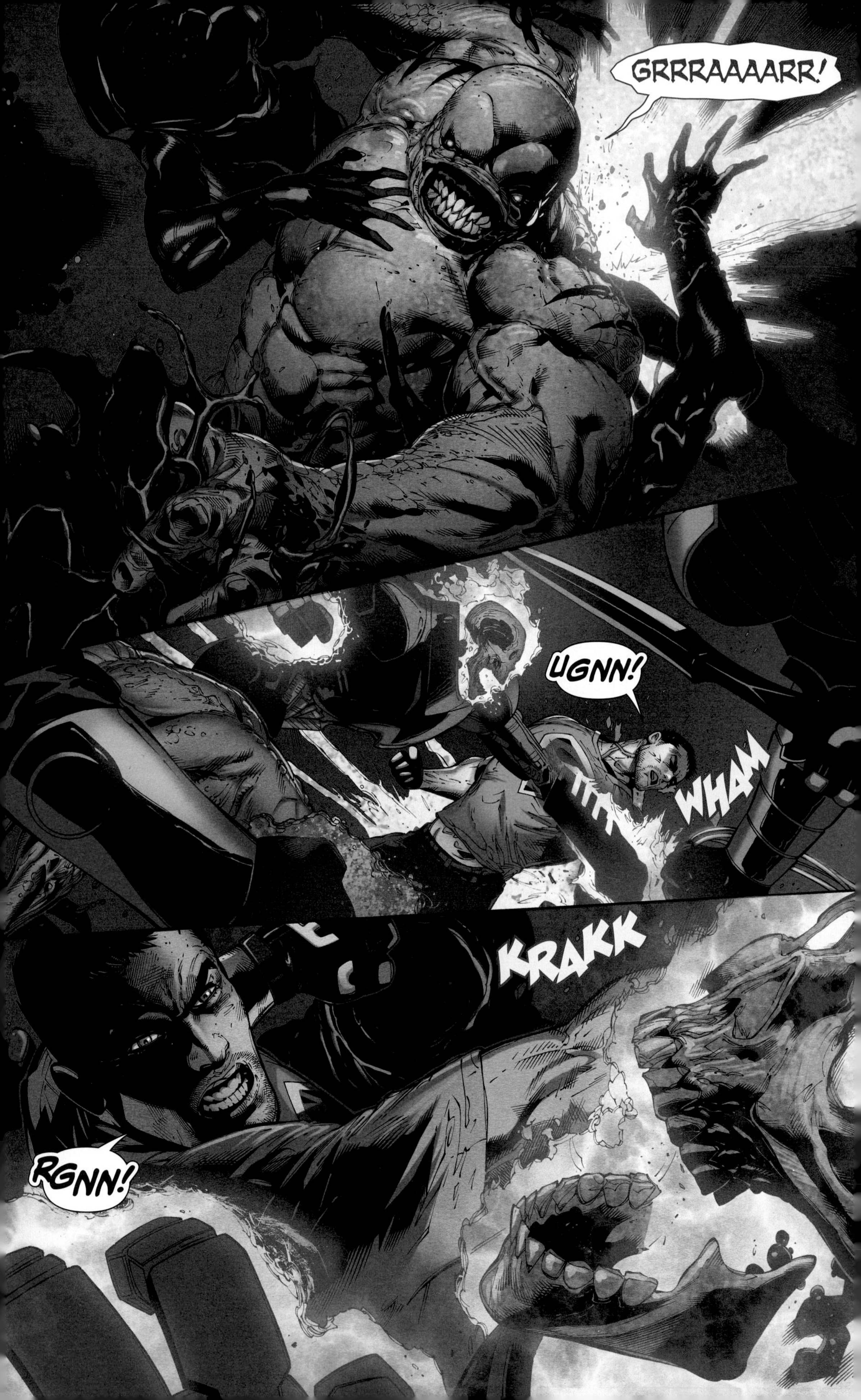
GRRRAAAARR!
UGNN!
WHAM
KRAKK
RGNN!

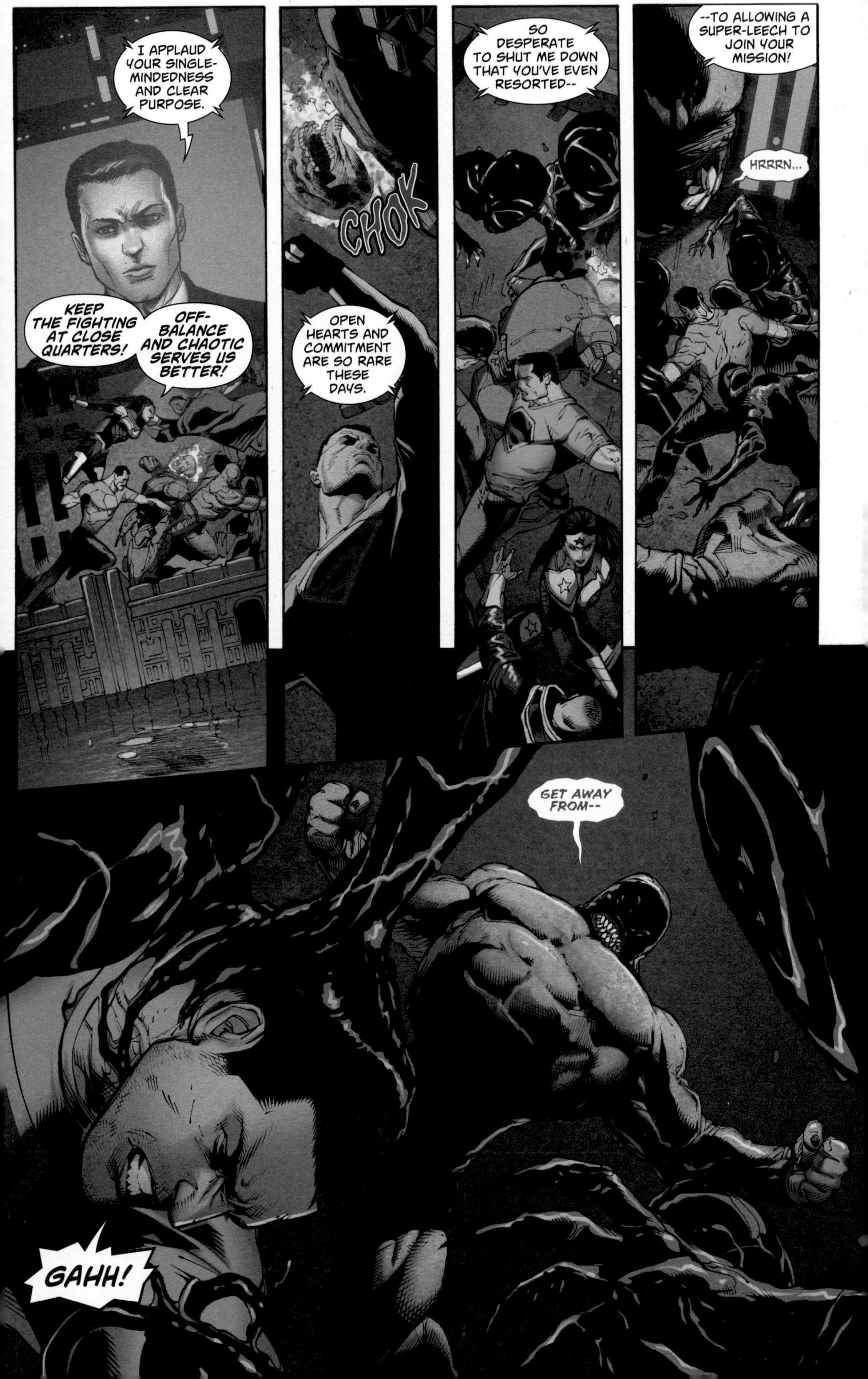
I APPLAUD YOUR SINGLE-MINDEDNESS AND CLEAR PURPOSE.
KEEP THE FIGHTING AT CLOSE QUARTERS!
OFF-BALANCE AND CHAOTIC SERVES US BETTER!
CHOK
OPEN HEARTS AND COMMITMENT ARE SO RARE THESE DAYS.
SO DESPERATE TO SHUT ME DOWN THAT YOU'VE EVEN RESORTED--
--TO ALLOWING A SUPER-LEECH TO JOIN YOUR MISSION!
HRRRN...
GET AWAY FROM--
GAHH!

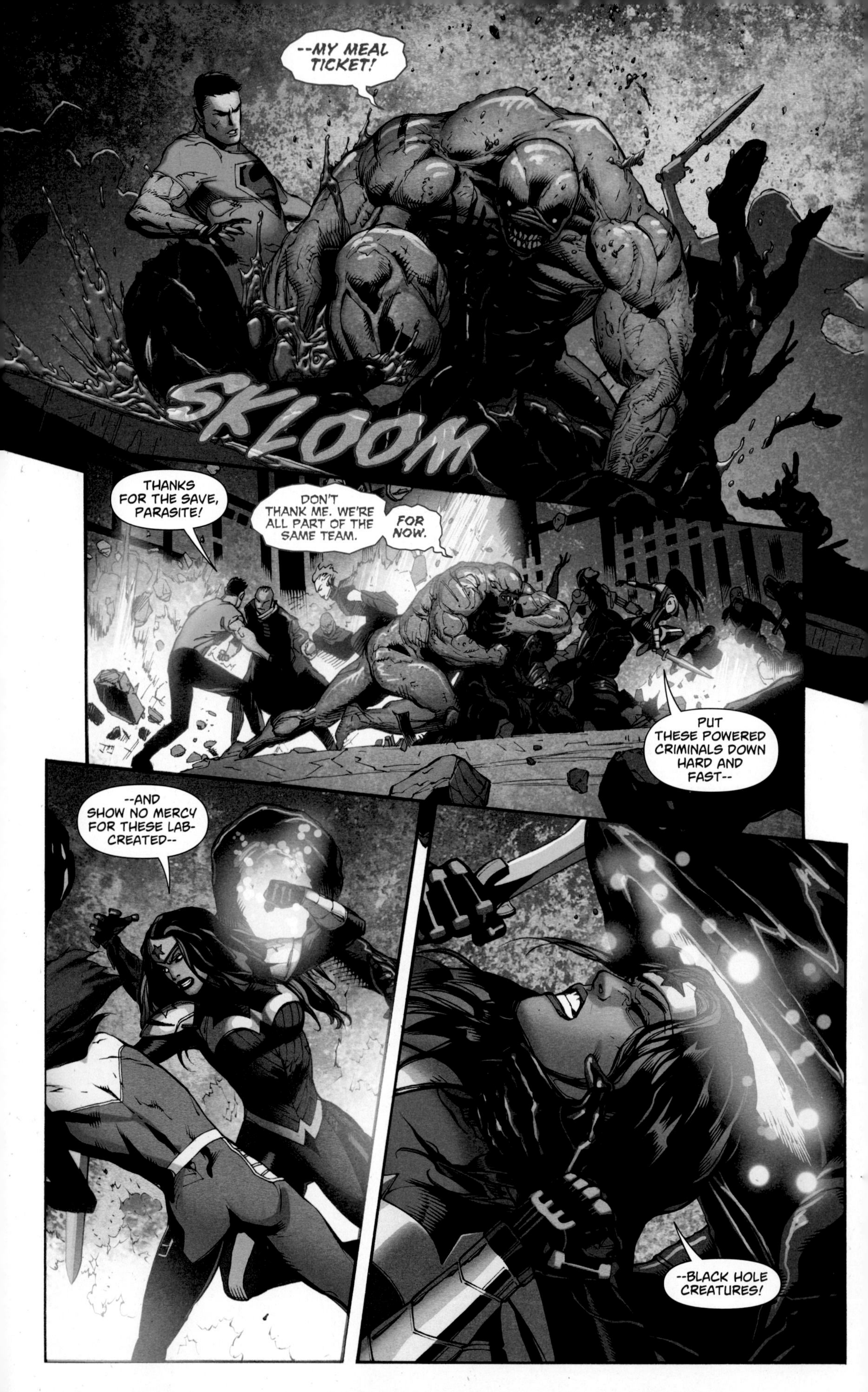
--MY MEAL TICKET!
SKLOOM
THANKS FOR THE SAVE, PARASITE!
DON'T THANK ME. WE'RE ALL PART OF THE SAME TEAM.
FOR NOW.
PUT THESE POWERED CRIMINALS DOWN HARD AND FAST--
--AND SHOW NO MERCY FOR THESE LAB-CREATED--
--BLACK HOLE CREATURES!

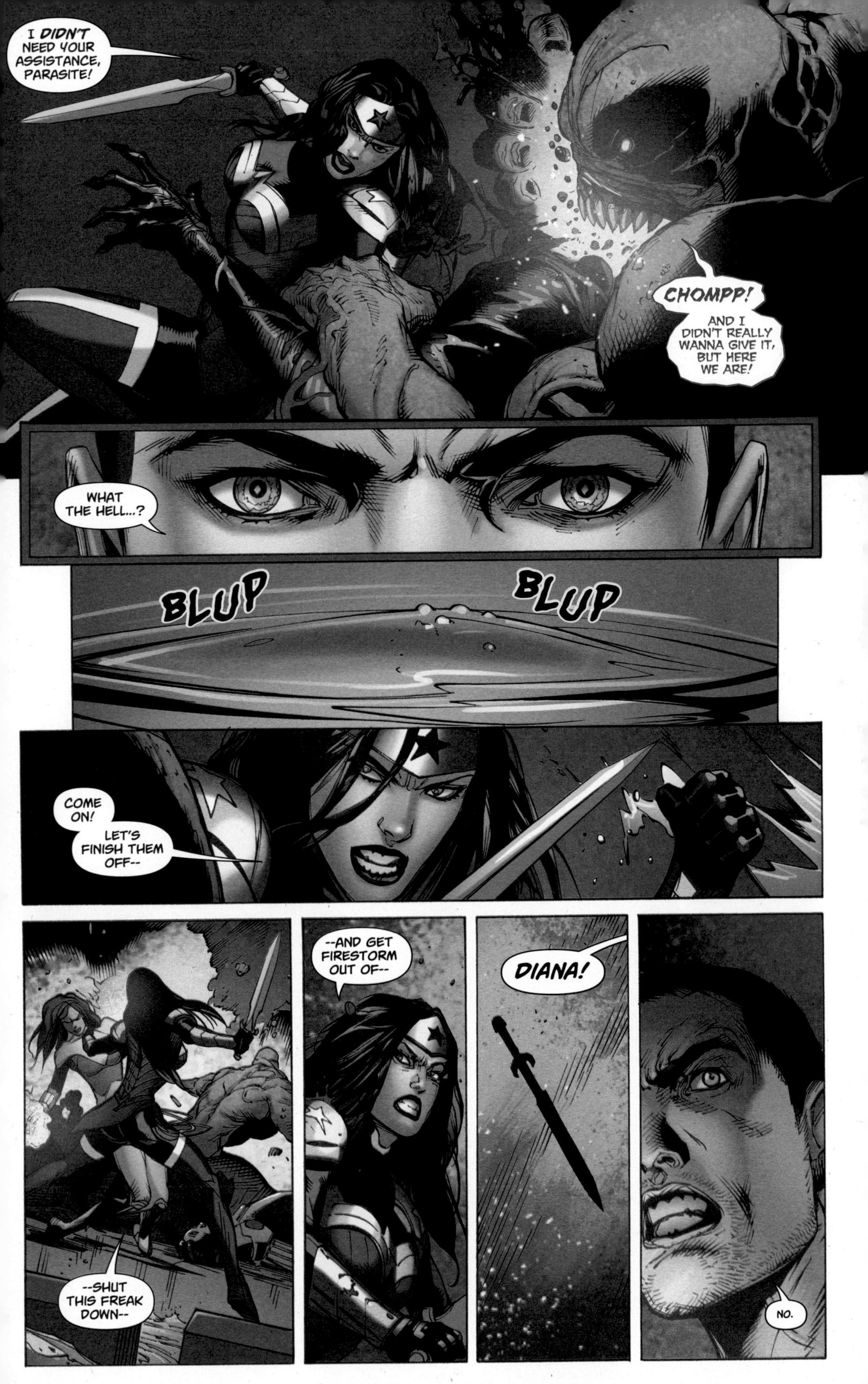
I DIDN'T NEED YOUR ASSISTANCE, PARASITE!
CHOMPP!
AND I DIDN'T REALLY WANNA GIVE IT, BUT HERE WE ARE!
WHAT THE HELL...?
BLUP
BLUP
COME ON!
LET'S FINISH THEM OFF--
--SHUT THIS FREAK DOWN--
--AND GET FIRESTORM OUT OF--
DIANA!
NO.

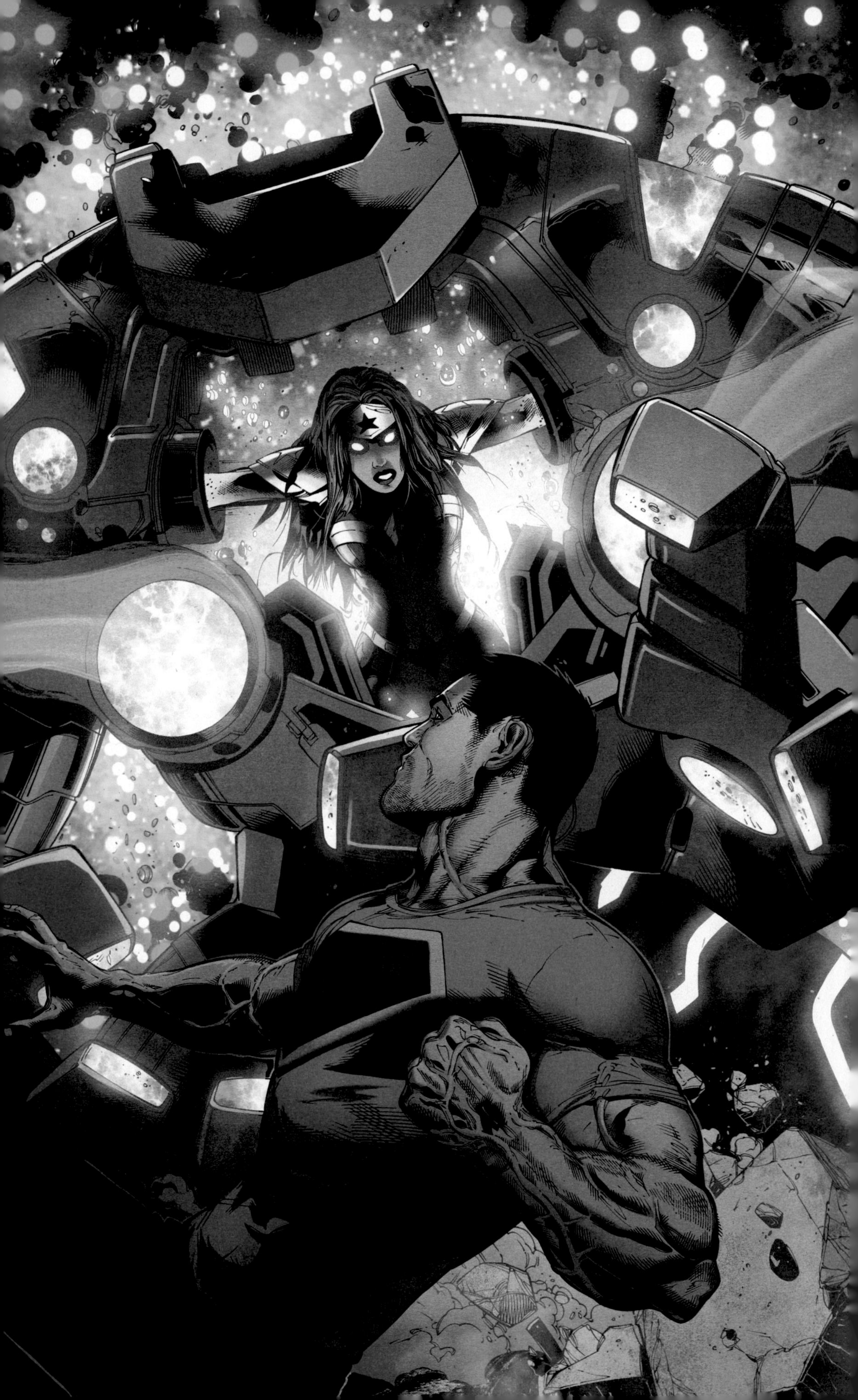

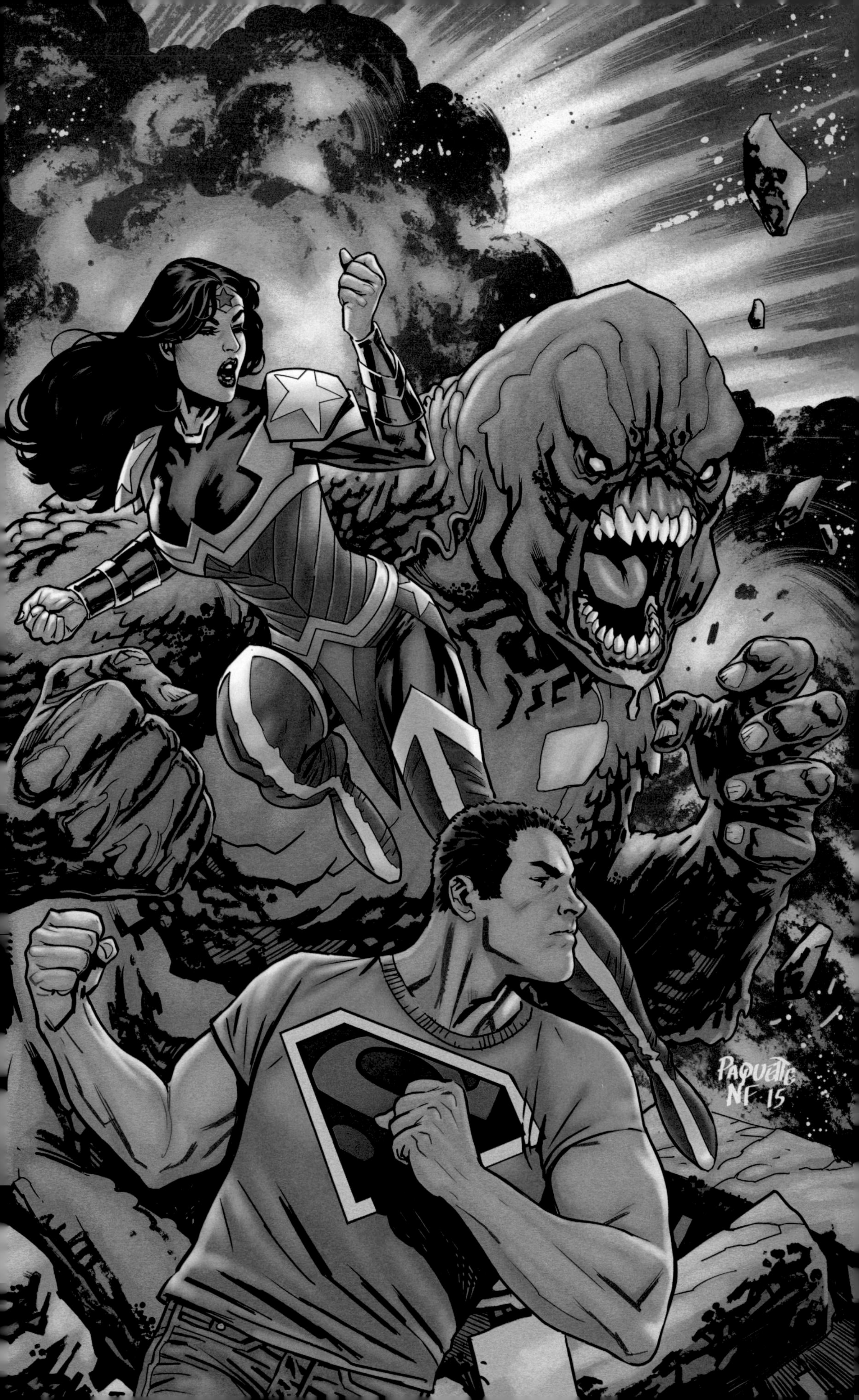
PAQUETTE
NF 15

POWER HUNGRY

PETER J. TOMASI writer ARDIAN SYAF TOM DERENICK pencillers TOM DERENICK JAIME MENDOZA JORDI TARRAGONA MARK IRWIN inkers WIL QUINTANA colorist
TOM NAPOLITANO letterer cover by YANICK PAQUETTE & NATHAN FAIRBAIRN

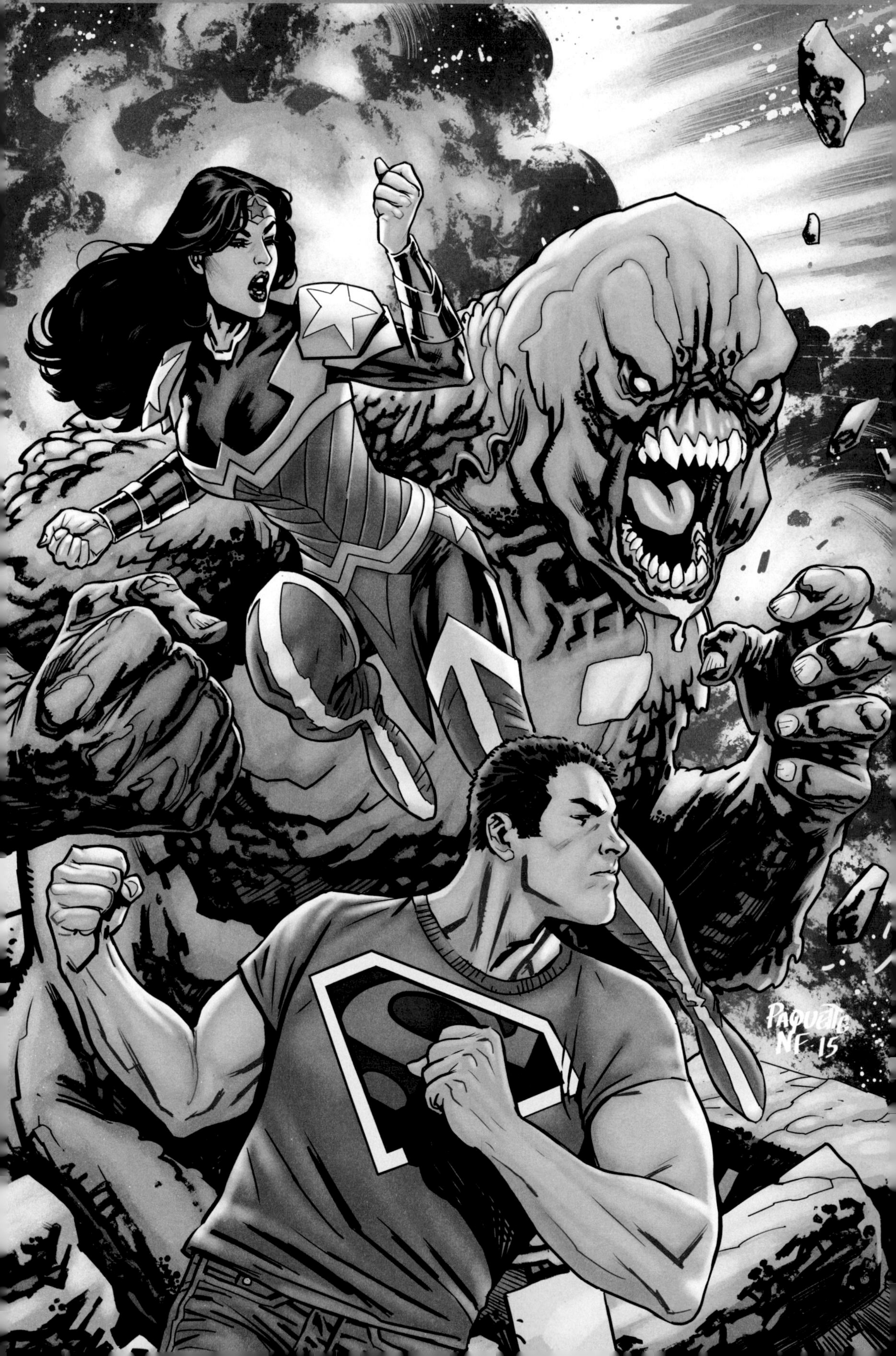
PAQUETTE
NF 15

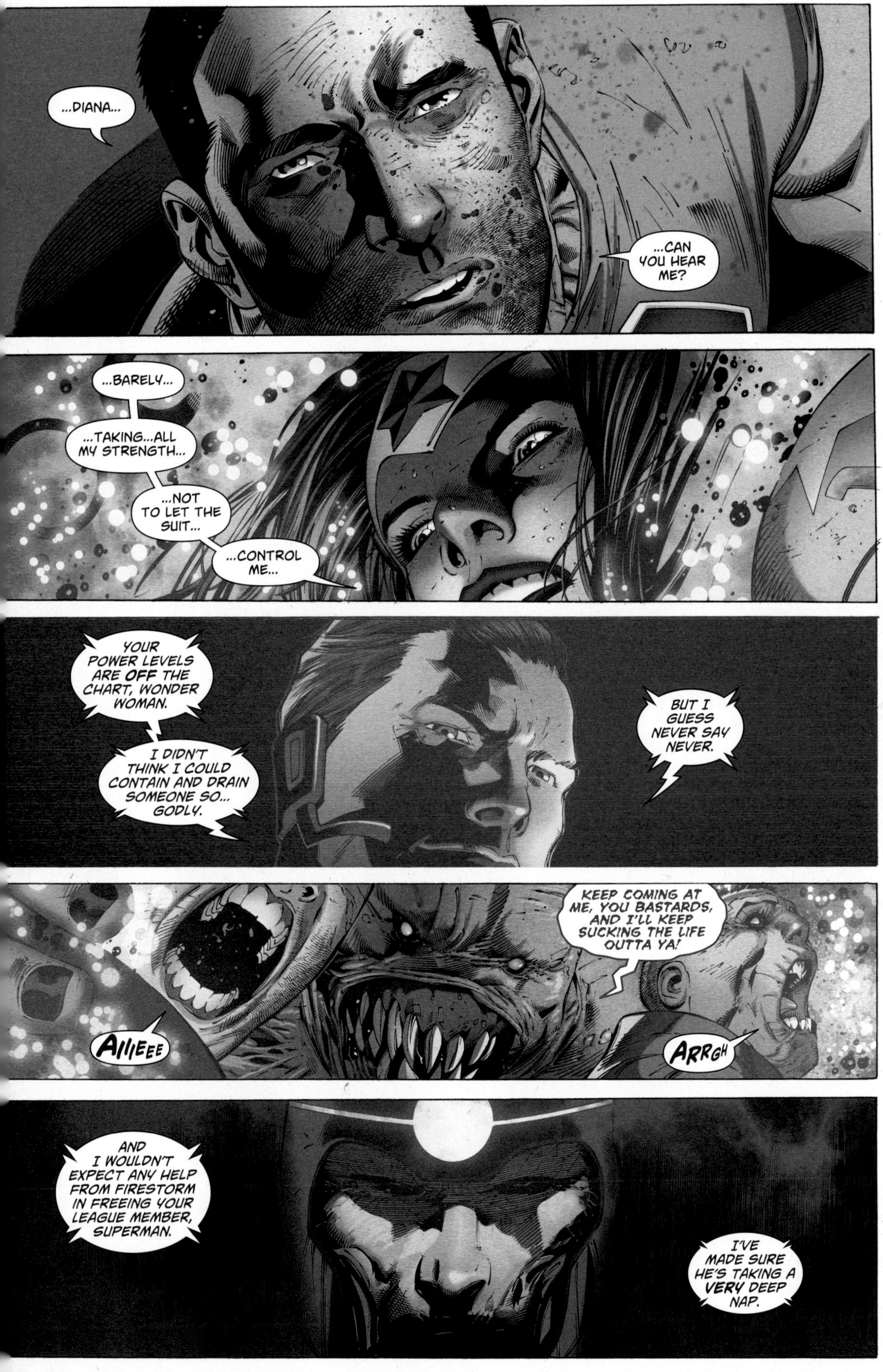
...DIANA...
...CAN YOU HEAR ME?
...BARELY...
...TAKING...ALL MY STRENGTH...
...NOT TO LET THE SUIT...
...CONTROL ME...
YOUR POWER LEVELS ARE OFF THE CHART, WONDER WOMAN.
I DIDN'T THINK I COULD CONTAIN AND DRAIN SOMEONE SO... GODLY.
BUT I GUESS NEVER SAY NEVER.
AIIIEEE
KEEP COMING AT ME, YOU BASTARDS, AND I'LL KEEP SUCKING THE LIFE OUTTA YA!
ARRGH
AND I WOULDN'T EXPECT ANY HELP FROM FIRESTORM IN FREEING YOUR LEAGUE MEMBER, SUPERMAN.
I'VE MADE SURE HE'S TAKING A VERY DEEP NAP.

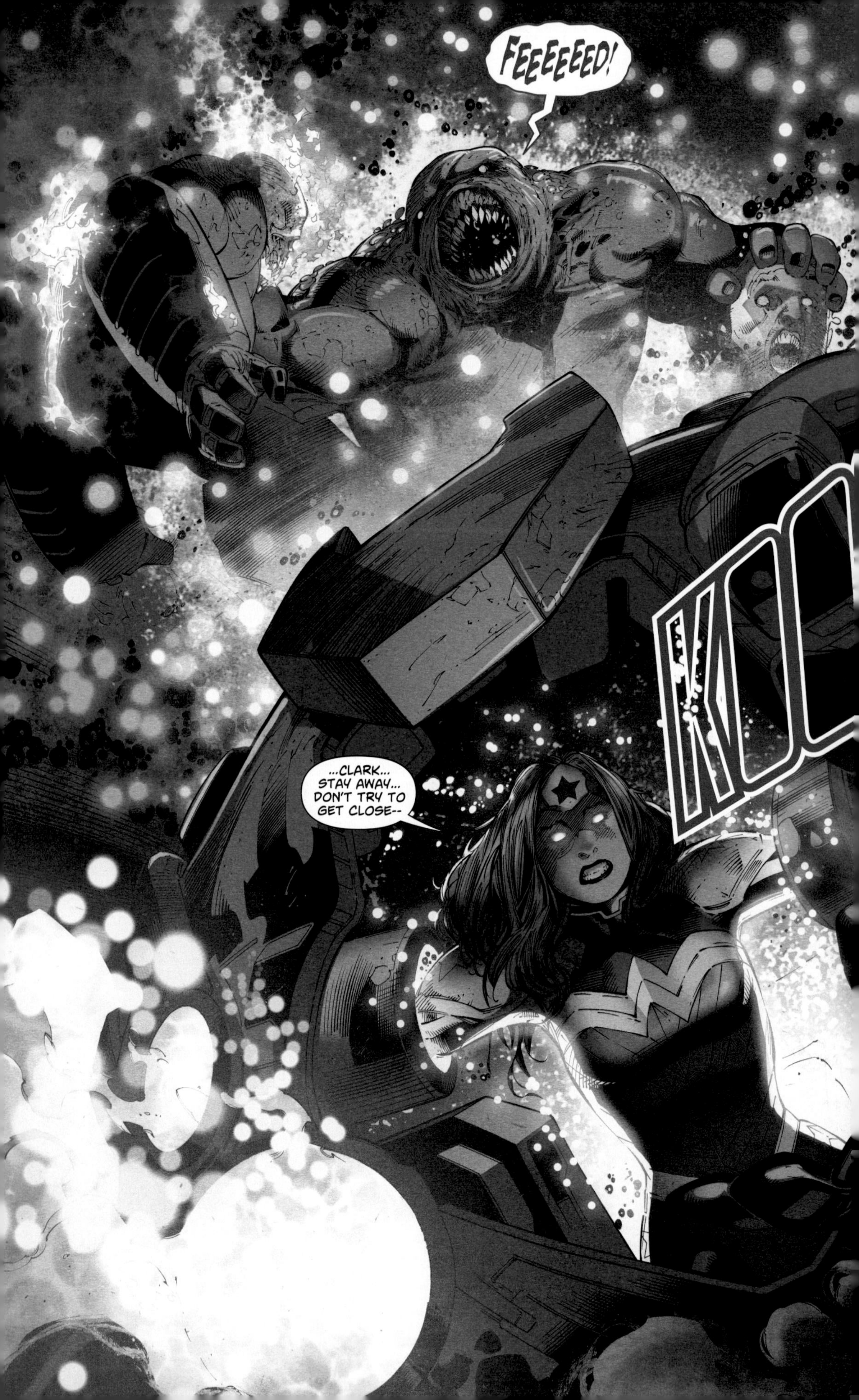
FEEEEEED!
...CLARK... STAY AWAY... DON'T TRY TO GET CLOSE--

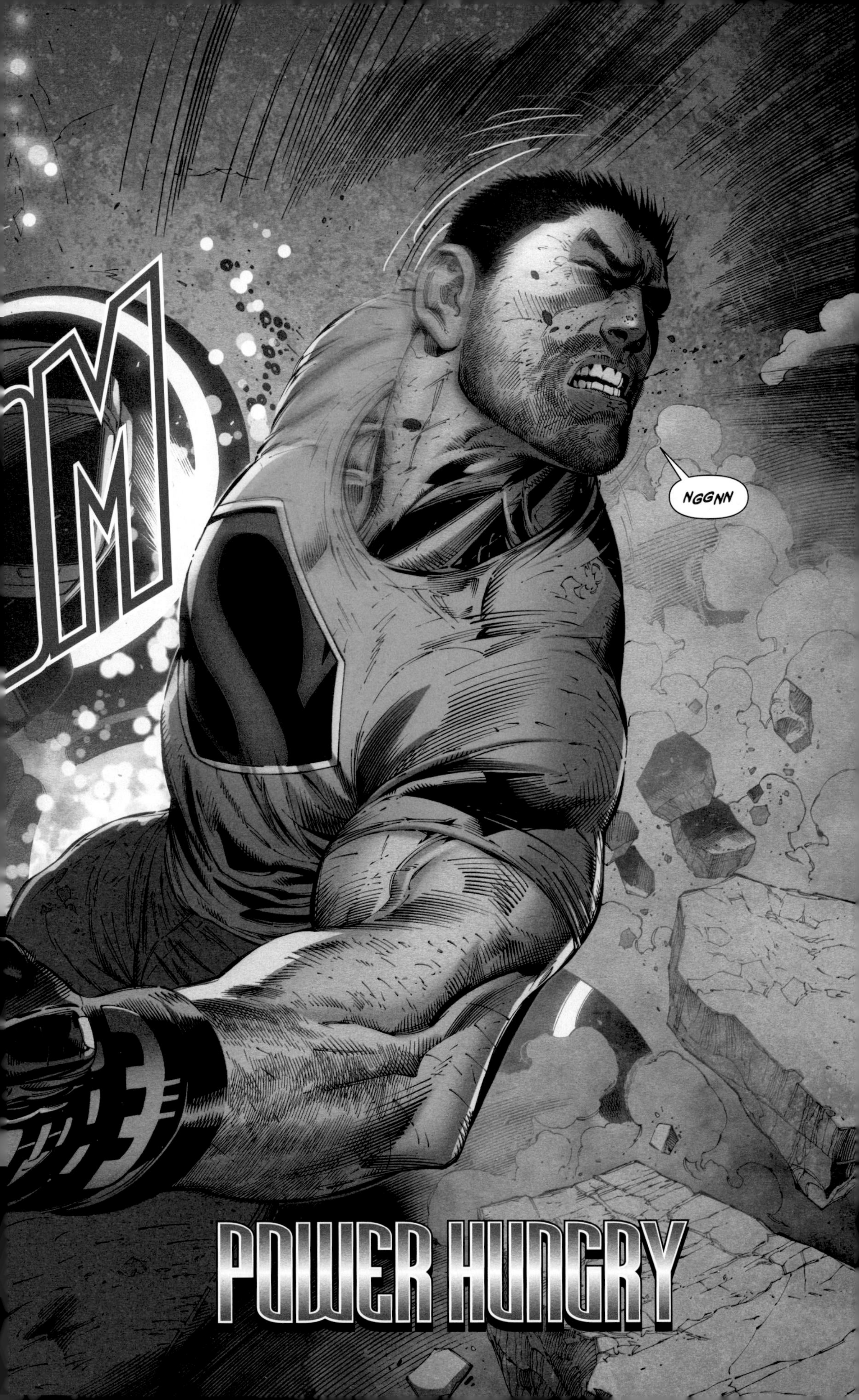
NGGNN
POWER HUNGRY

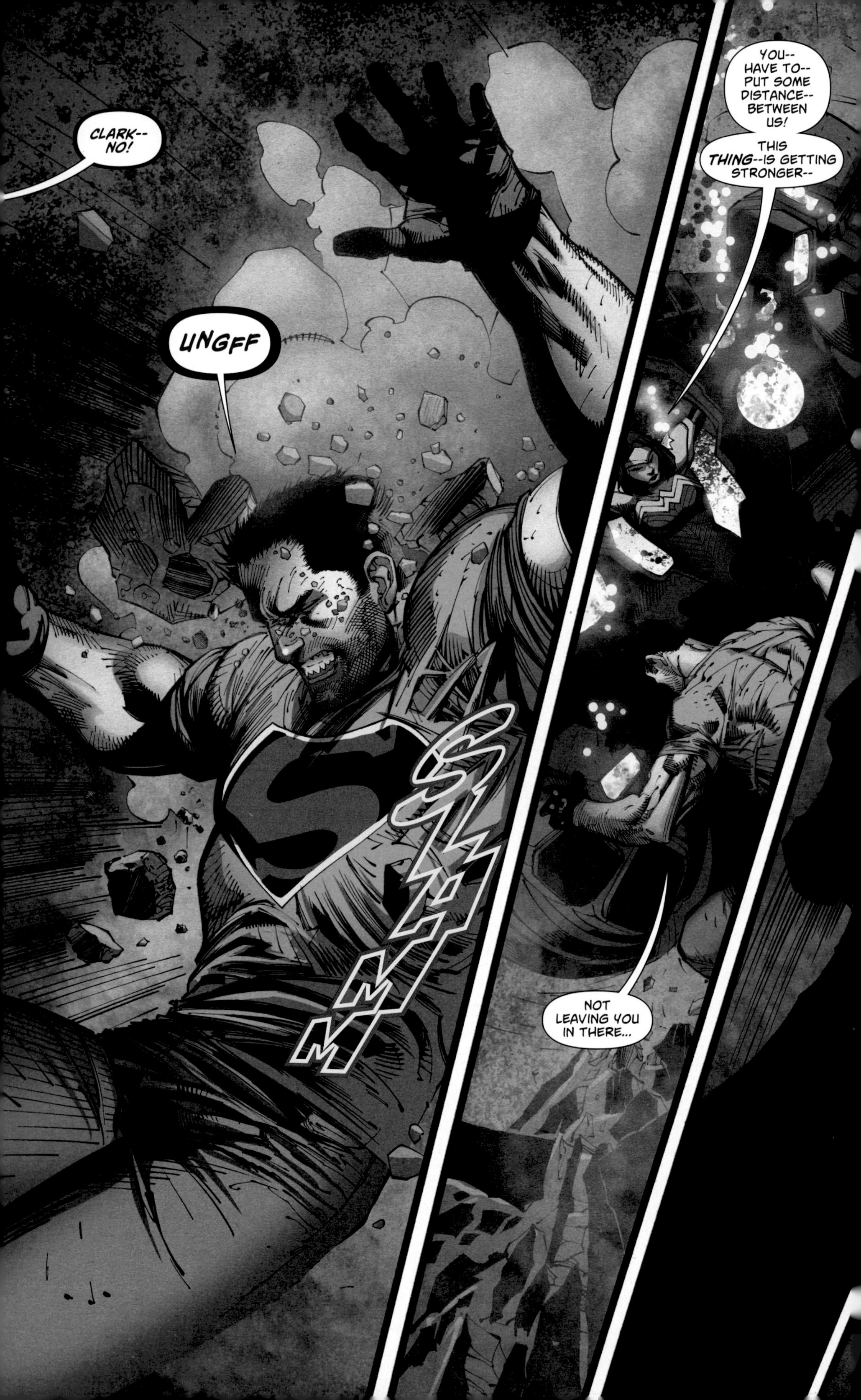
CLARK-- NO!
UNGFF
YOU-- HAVE TO-- PUT SOME DISTANCE-- BETWEEN US!
THIS THING--IS GETTING STRONGER--
SLAMM
NOT LEAVING YOU IN THERE...

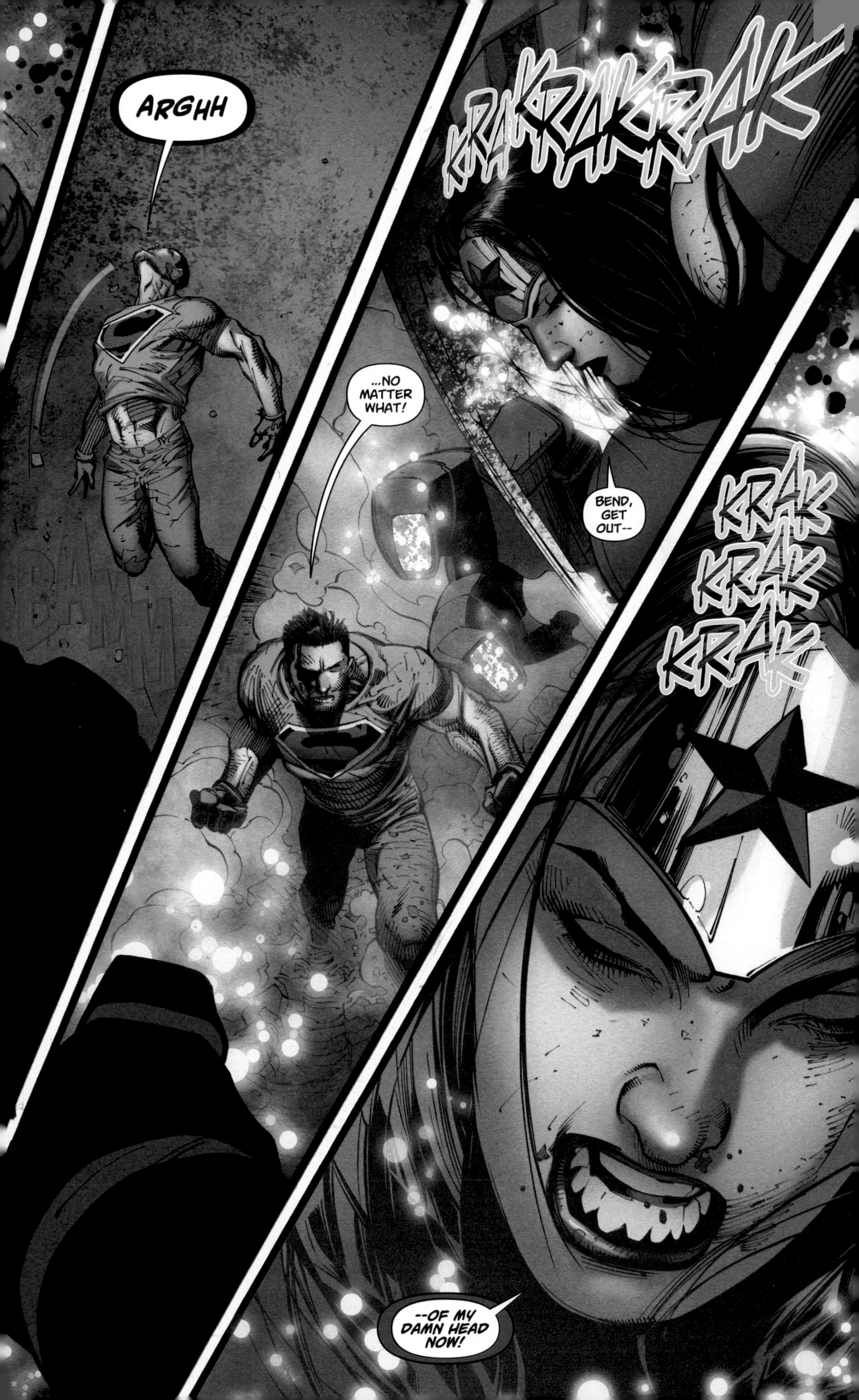
ARGHH
BAMM
...NO MATTER WHAT!
KRAKKRAKKRAK
BEND, GET OUT--
KRAK
KRAK
KRAK
--OF MY DAMN HEAD NOW!

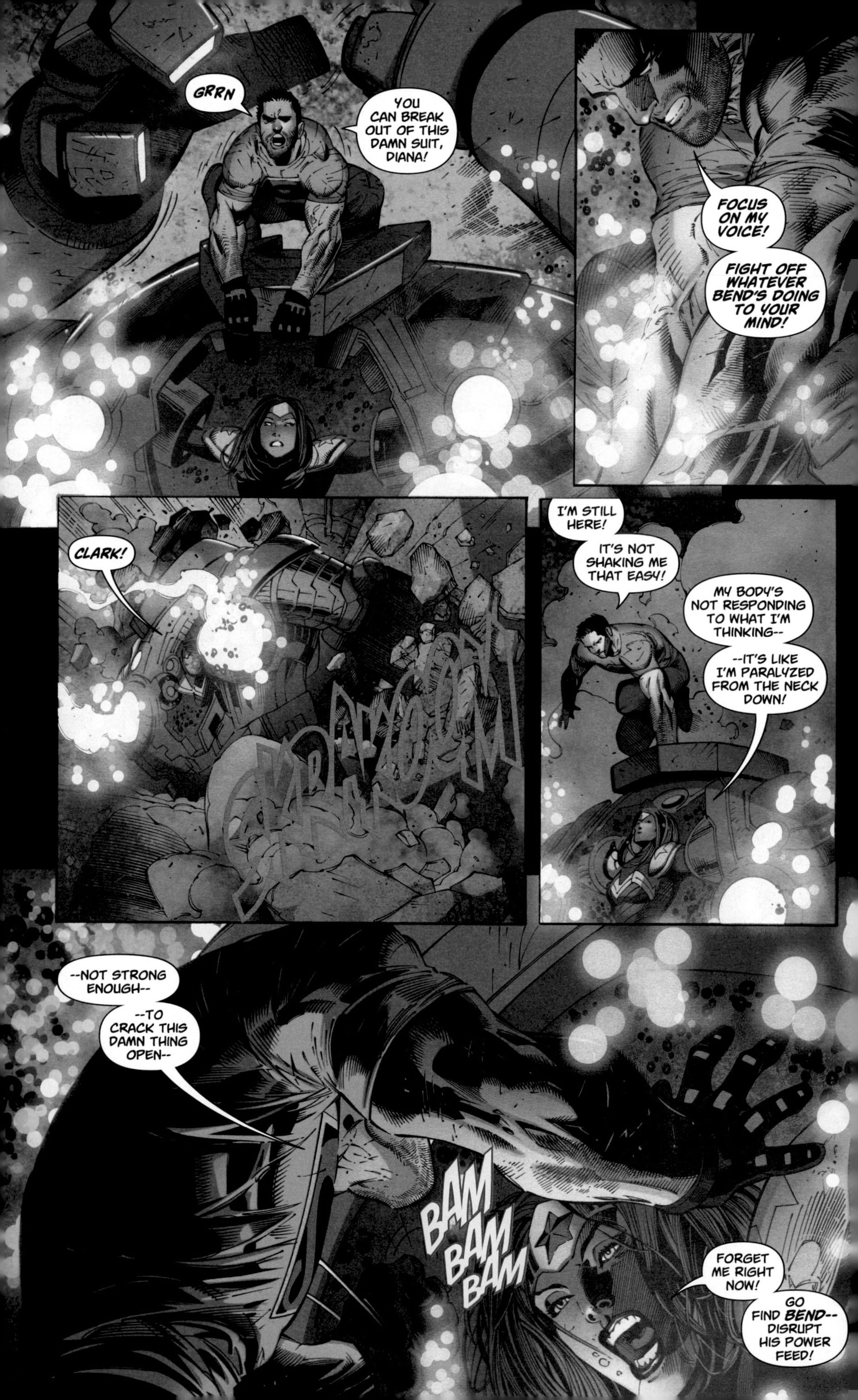
GRRN
YOU CAN BREAK OUT OF THIS DAMN SUIT, DIANA!
FOCUS ON MY VOICE!
FIGHT OFF WHATEVER BEND'S DOING TO YOUR MIND!
CLARK!
KRA-KOOOM
I'M STILL HERE!
IT'S NOT SHAKING ME THAT EASY!
MY BODY'S NOT RESPONDING TO WHAT I'M THINKING--
--IT'S LIKE I'M PARALYZED FROM THE NECK DOWN!
--NOT STRONG ENOUGH--
--TO CRACK THIS DAMN THING OPEN--
BAM BAM BAM
FORGET ME RIGHT NOW!
GO FIND BEND-- DISRUPT HIS POWER FEED!

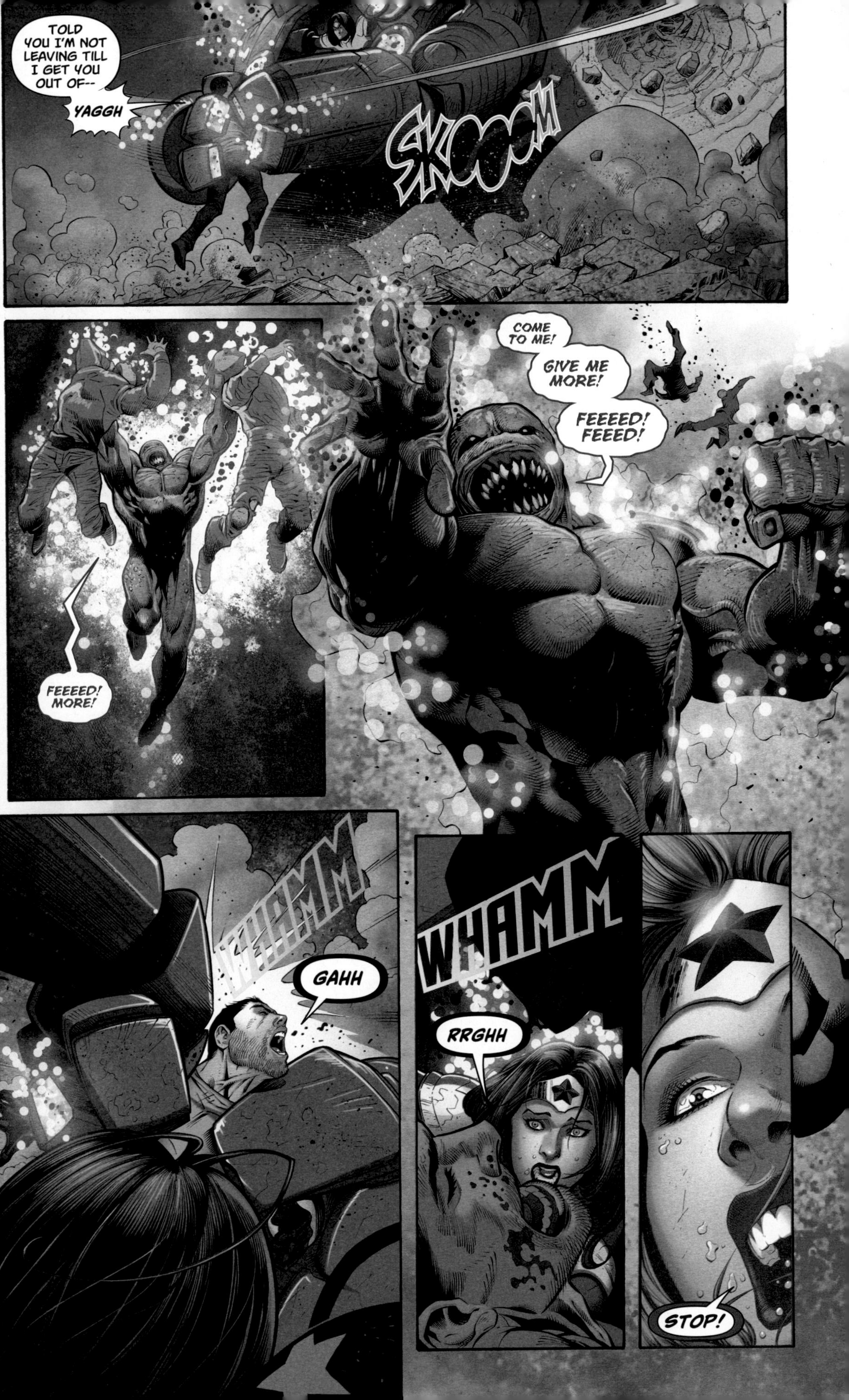
TOLD YOU I'M NOT LEAVING TILL I GET YOU OUT OF--
YAGGH
SKOOOM
FEEEED! MORE!
COME TO ME!
GIVE ME MORE!
FEEEED! FEEED!
WHAMM
GAHH
WHAMM
RRGHH
STOP!

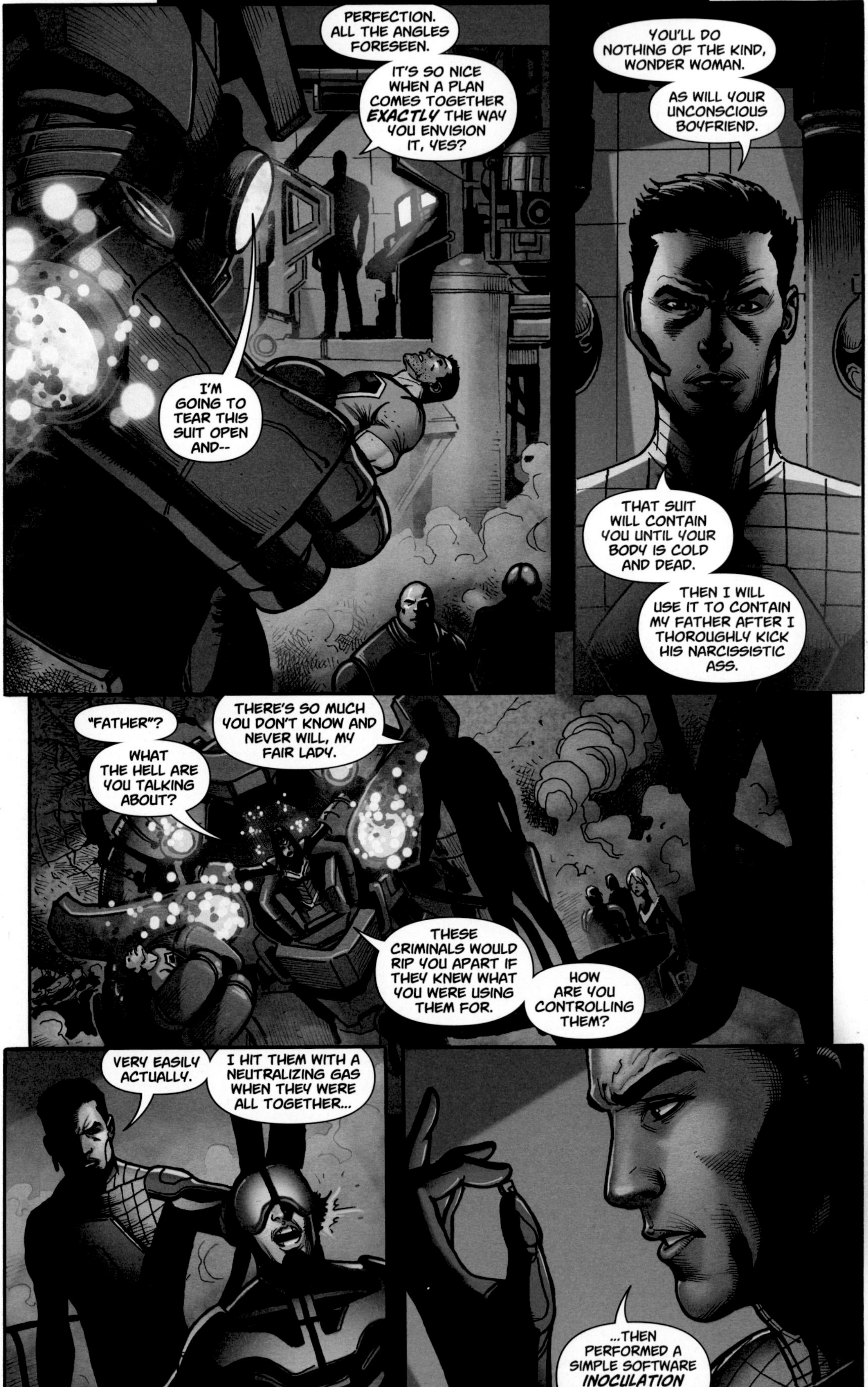
PERFECTION. ALL THE ANGLES FORESEEN.
IT'S SO NICE WHEN A PLAN COMES TOGETHER *EXACTLY* THE WAY YOU ENVISION IT, YES?
I'M GOING TO TEAR THIS SUIT OPEN AND--
YOU'LL DO NOTHING OF THE KIND, WONDER WOMAN.
AS WILL YOUR UNCONSCIOUS BOYFRIEND.
THAT SUIT WILL CONTAIN YOU UNTIL YOUR BODY IS COLD AND DEAD.
THEN I WILL USE IT TO CONTAIN MY FATHER AFTER I THOROUGHLY KICK HIS NARCISSISTIC ASS.
"FATHER"?
WHAT THE HELL ARE YOU TALKING ABOUT?
THERE'S SO MUCH YOU DON'T KNOW AND NEVER WILL, MY FAIR LADY.
THESE CRIMINALS WOULD RIP YOU APART IF THEY KNEW WHAT YOU WERE USING THEM FOR.
HOW ARE YOU CONTROLLING THEM?
VERY EASILY ACTUALLY.
I HIT THEM WITH A NEUTRALIZING GAS WHEN THEY WERE ALL TOGETHER...
...THEN PERFORMED A SIMPLE SOFTWARE *INOCULATION* INTO THEIR OH-SO-PLIANT MINDS.

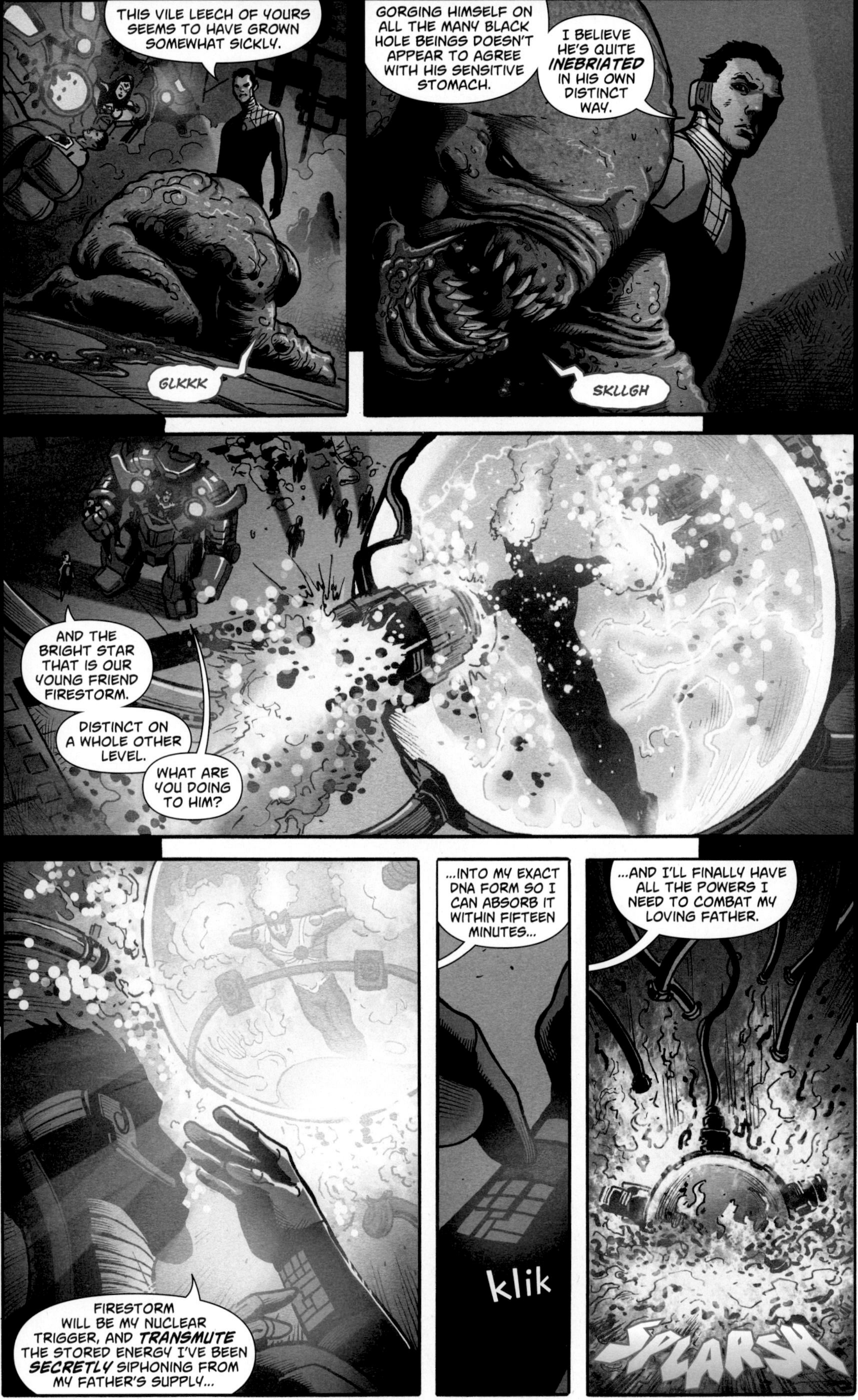
THIS VILE LEECH OF YOURS SEEMS TO HAVE GROWN SOMEWHAT SICKLY.
GLKKK
GORGING HIMSELF ON ALL THE MANY BLACK HOLE BEINGS DOESN'T APPEAR TO AGREE WITH HIS SENSITIVE STOMACH.
I BELIEVE HE'S QUITE INEBRIATED IN HIS OWN DISTINCT WAY.
SKLLGH
AND THE BRIGHT STAR THAT IS OUR YOUNG FRIEND FIRESTORM.
DISTINCT ON A WHOLE OTHER LEVEL.
WHAT ARE YOU DOING TO HIM?
FIRESTORM WILL BE MY NUCLEAR TRIGGER, AND TRANSMUTE THE STORED ENERGY I'VE BEEN SECRETLY SIPHONING FROM MY FATHER'S SUPPLY...
...INTO MY EXACT DNA FORM SO I CAN ABSORB IT WITHIN FIFTEEN MINUTES...
klik
...AND I'LL FINALLY HAVE ALL THE POWERS I NEED TO COMBAT MY LOVING FATHER.
SPLARSH

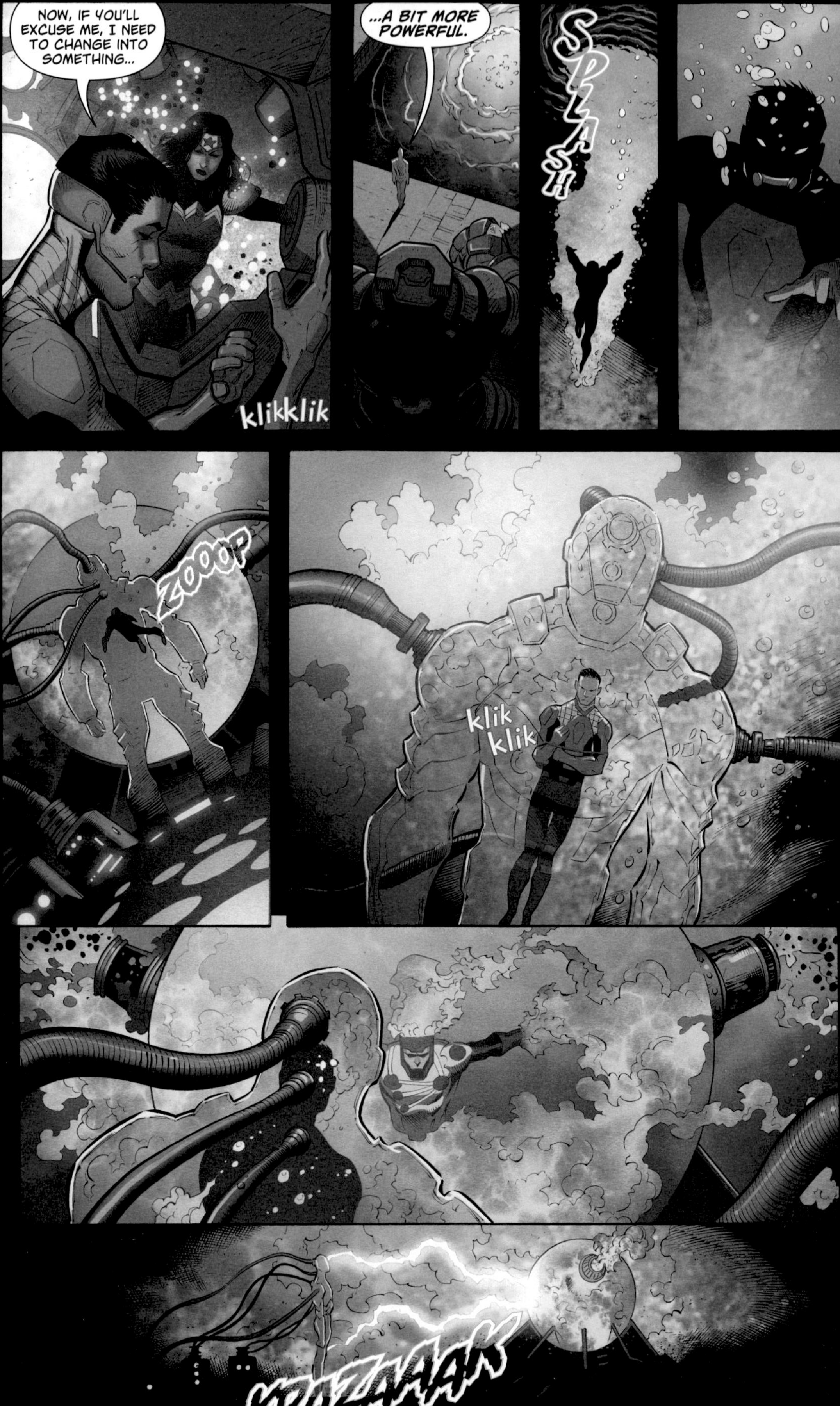
NOW, IF YOU'LL EXCUSE ME, I NEED TO CHANGE INTO SOMETHING...
klikklik
...A BIT MORE POWERFUL.
SPLASH
ZOOOP
klik klik
KRAZAAAK

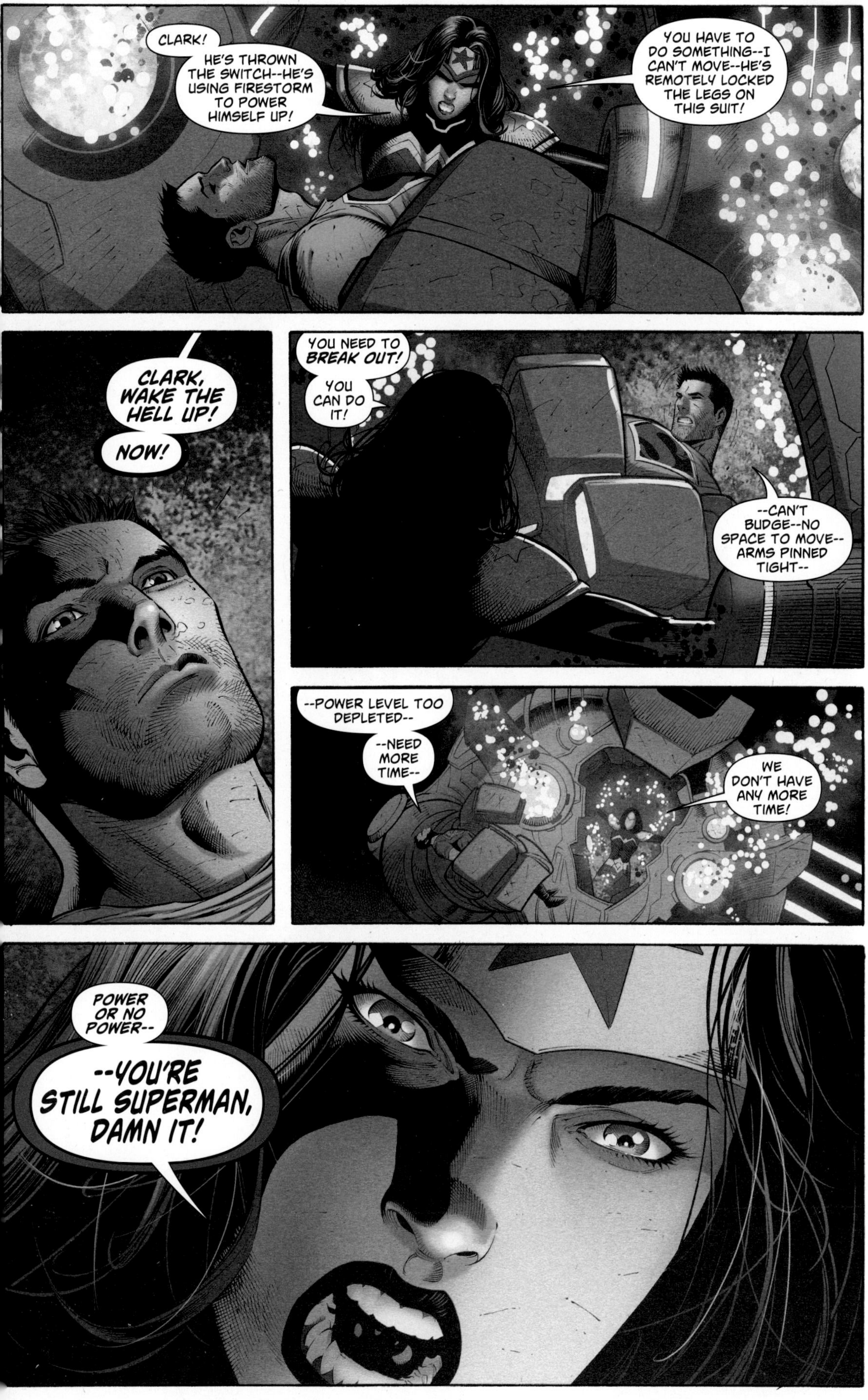
CLARK!
HE'S THROWN THE SWITCH--HE'S USING FIRESTORM TO POWER HIMSELF UP!
YOU HAVE TO DO SOMETHING--I CAN'T MOVE--HE'S REMOTELY LOCKED THE LEGS ON THIS SUIT!
CLARK, WAKE THE HELL UP!
NOW!
YOU NEED TO BREAK OUT!
YOU CAN DO IT!
--CAN'T BUDGE--NO SPACE TO MOVE--ARMS PINNED TIGHT--
--POWER LEVEL TOO DEPLETED--
--NEED MORE TIME--
WE DON'T HAVE ANY MORE TIME!
POWER OR NO POWER--
--YOU'RE STILL SUPERMAN, DAMN IT!

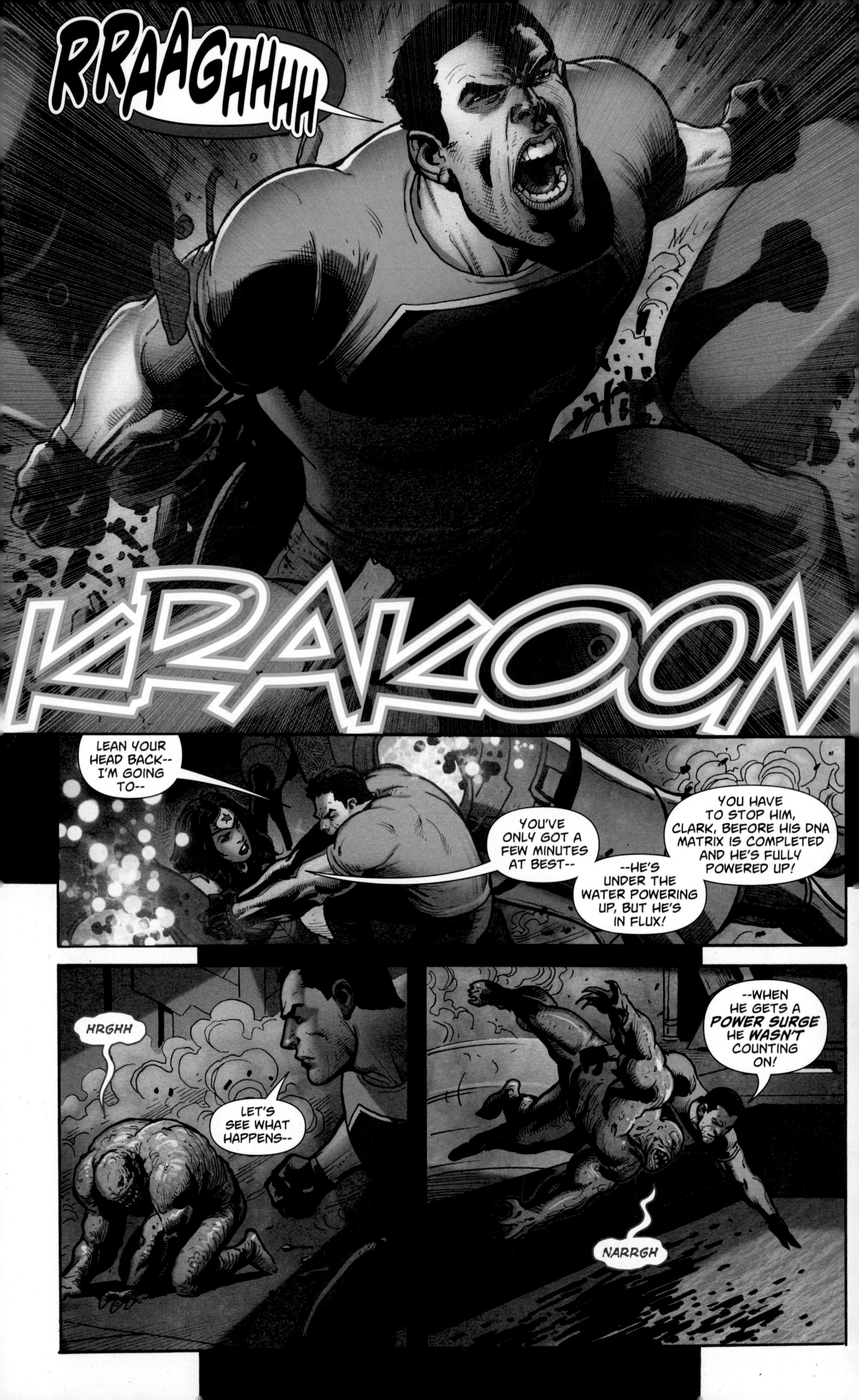
RRAAGHHHH
KRAKOOM
LEAN YOUR HEAD BACK-- I'M GOING TO--
YOU'VE ONLY GOT A FEW MINUTES AT BEST--
--HE'S UNDER THE WATER POWERING UP, BUT HE'S IN FLUX!
YOU HAVE TO STOP HIM, CLARK, BEFORE HIS DNA MATRIX IS COMPLETED AND HE'S FULLY POWERED UP!
HRGHH
LET'S SEE WHAT HAPPENS--
--WHEN HE GETS A POWER SURGE HE WASN'T COUNTING ON!
NARRGH

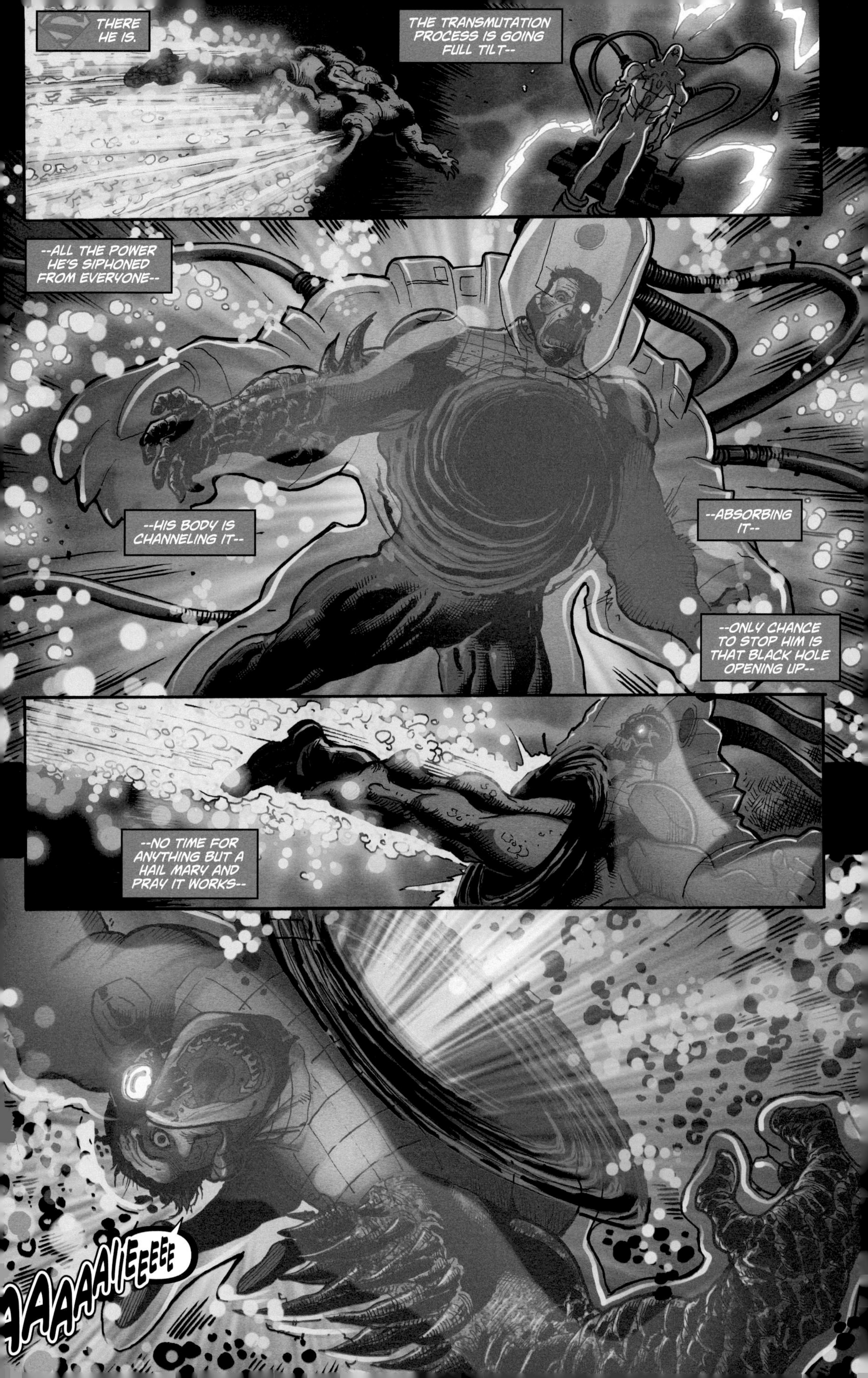
THERE HE IS.
THE TRANSMUTATION PROCESS IS GOING FULL TILT--
--ALL THE POWER HE'S SIPHONED FROM EVERYONE--
--HIS BODY IS CHANNELING IT--
--ABSORBING IT--
--ONLY CHANCE TO STOP HIM IS THAT BLACK HOLE OPENING UP--
--NO TIME FOR ANYTHING BUT A HAIL MARY AND PRAY IT WORKS--
AAAAAIIEEEEE

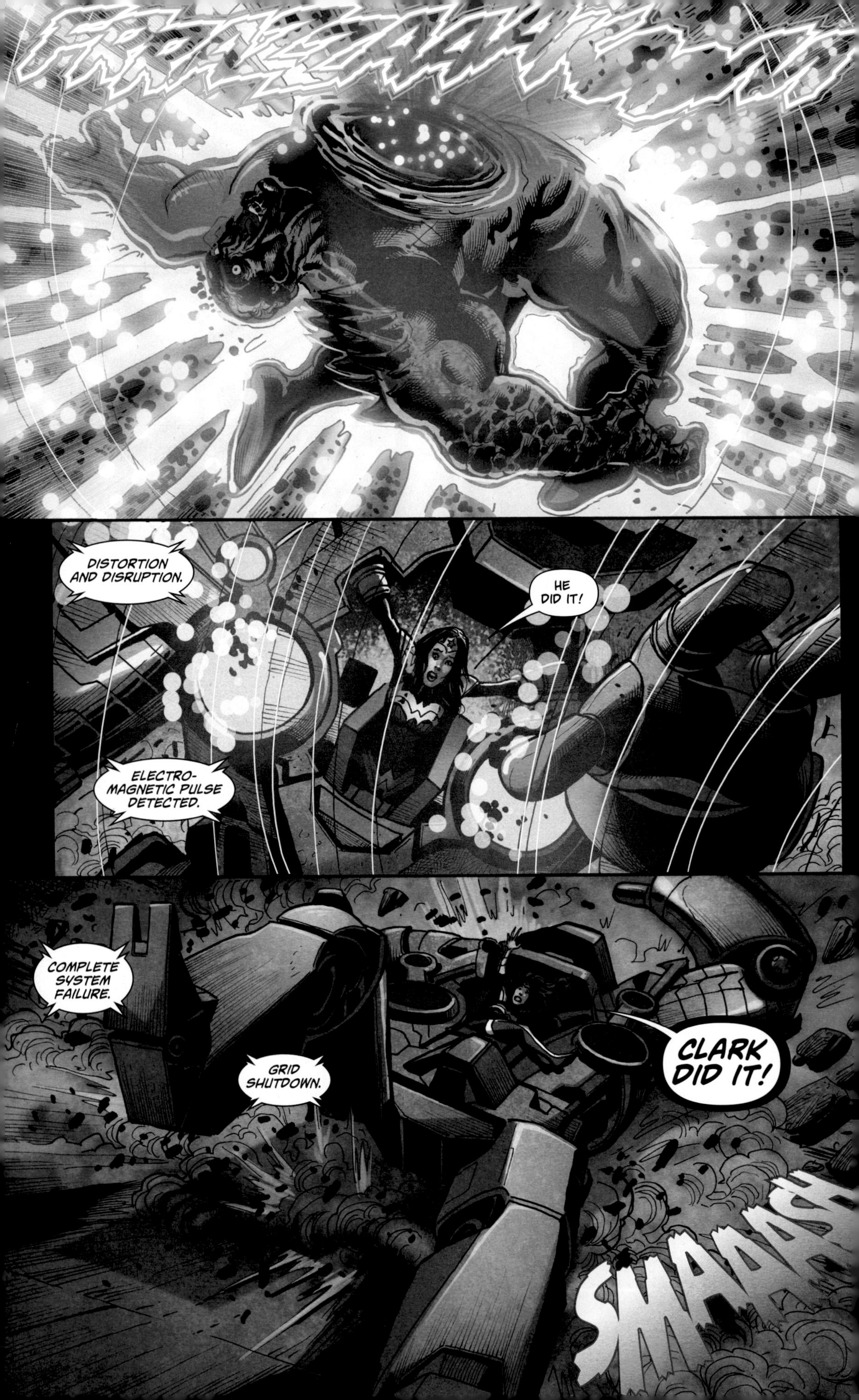
DISTORTION AND DISRUPTION.
HE DID IT!
ELECTRO-MAGNETIC PULSE DETECTED.
COMPLETE SYSTEM FAILURE.
GRID SHUTDOWN.
CLARK DID IT!

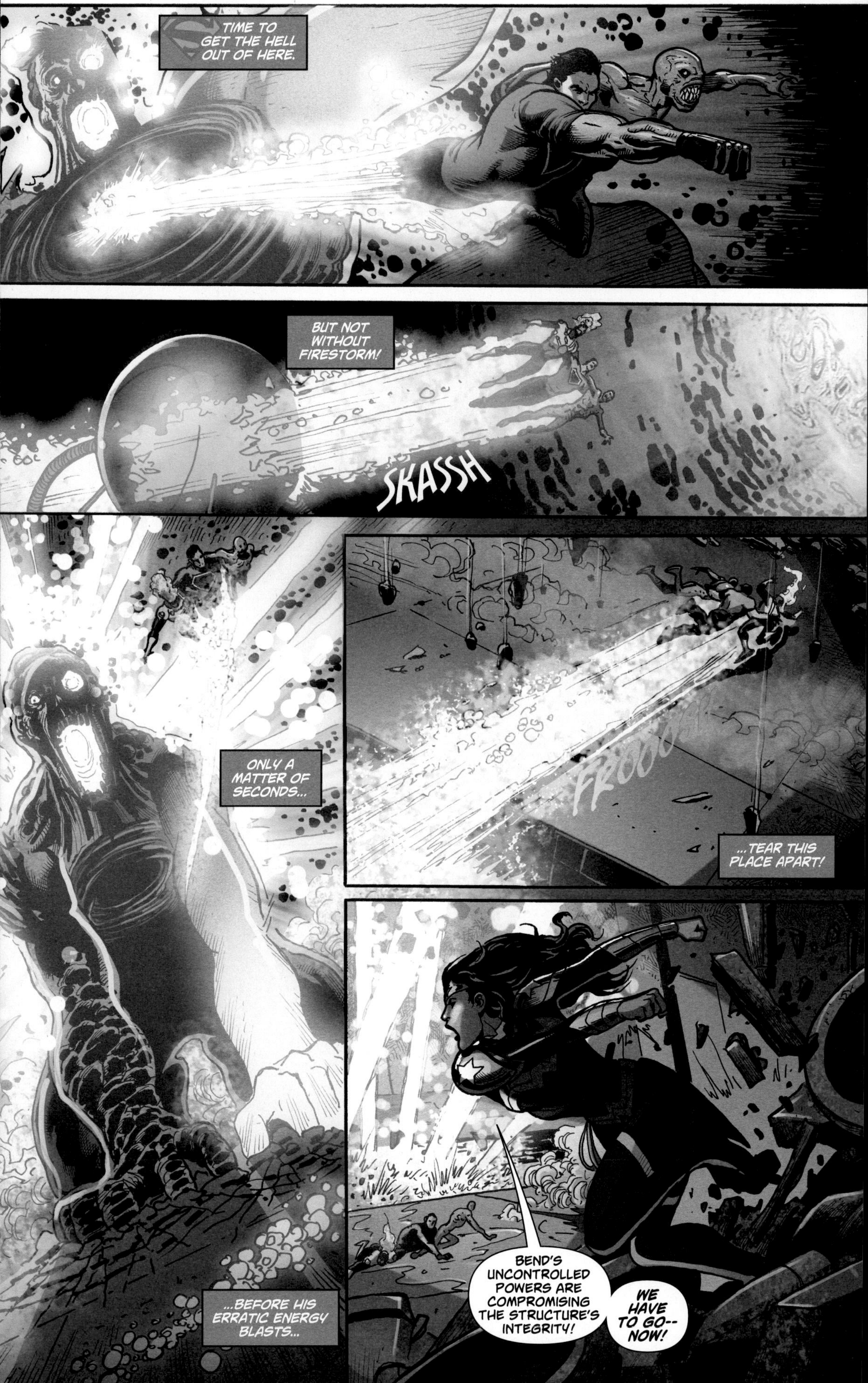

TIME TO GET THE HELL OUT OF HERE.
BUT NOT WITHOUT FIRESTORM!
SKASSH
ONLY A MATTER OF SECONDS...
...BEFORE HIS ERRATIC ENERGY BLASTS...
...TEAR THIS PLACE APART!
BEND'S UNCONTROLLED POWERS ARE COMPROMISING THE STRUCTURE'S INTEGRITY!
WE HAVE TO GO-- NOW!

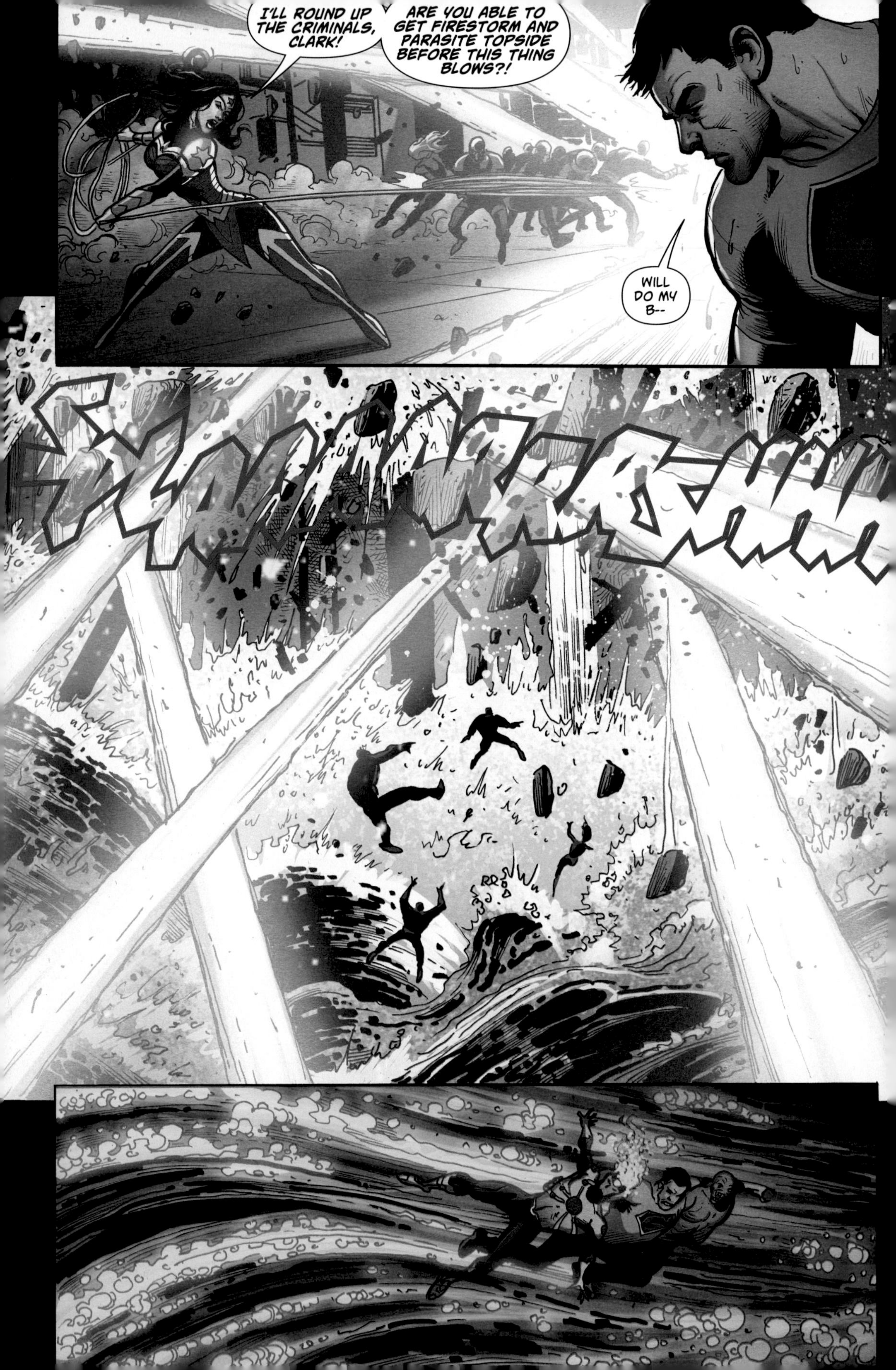
I'LL ROUND UP THE CRIMINALS, CLARK!
ARE YOU ABLE TO GET FIRESTORM AND PARASITE TOPSIDE BEFORE THIS THING BLOWS?!
WILL DO MY B--

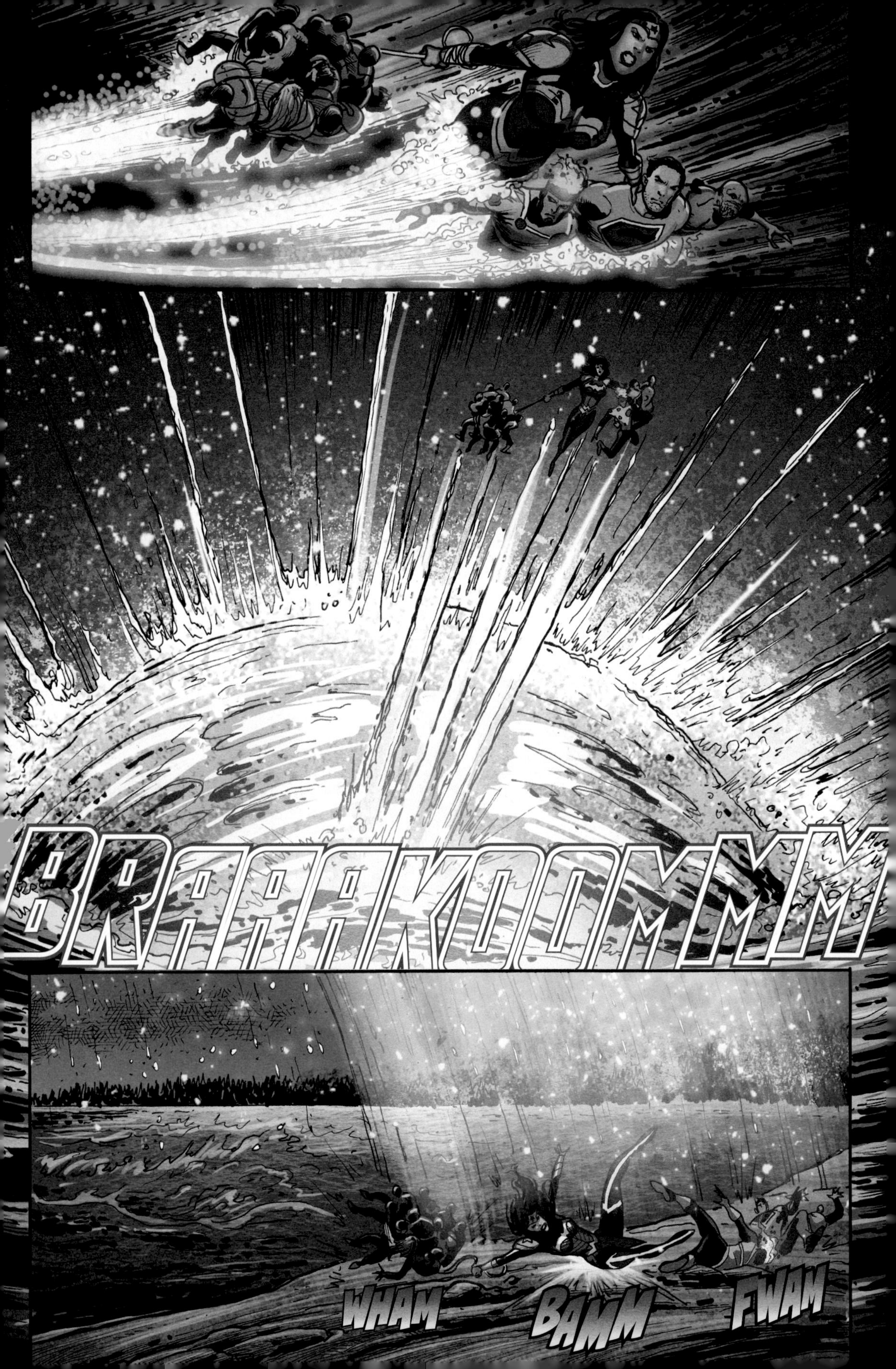
BRAAAKOOMMMM
WHAM
BAMM
FWAM

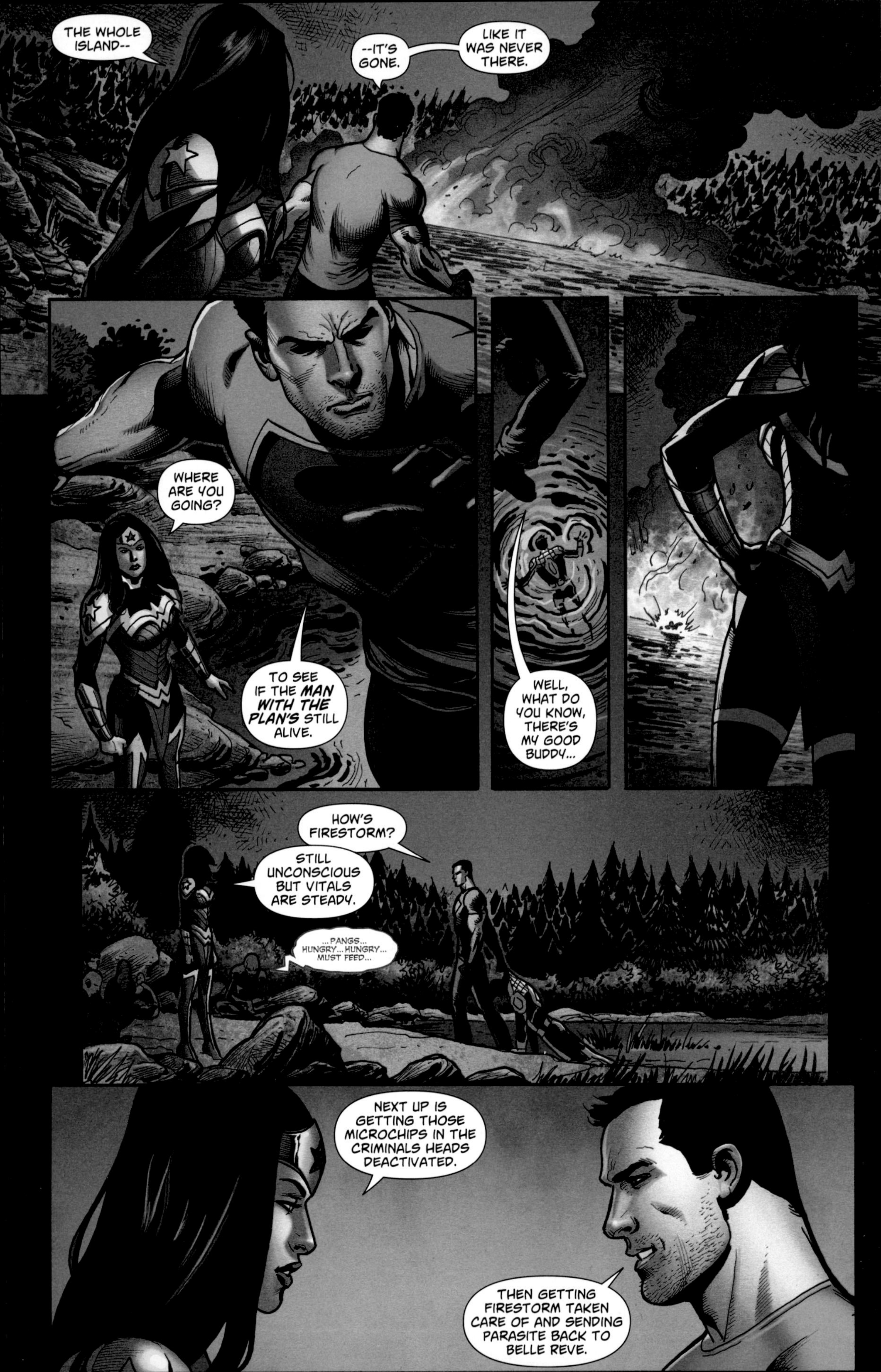
THE WHOLE ISLAND--
--IT'S GONE.
LIKE IT WAS NEVER THERE.
WHERE ARE YOU GOING?
TO SEE IF THE MAN WITH THE PLAN'S STILL ALIVE.
WELL, WHAT DO YOU KNOW, THERE'S MY GOOD BUDDY...
HOW'S FIRESTORM?
STILL UNCONSCIOUS BUT VITALS ARE STEADY.
...PANGS... HUNGRY... HUNGRY... MUST FEED...
NEXT UP IS GETTING THOSE MICROCHIPS IN THE CRIMINALS HEADS DEACTIVATED.
THEN GETTING FIRESTORM TAKEN CARE OF AND SENDING PARASITE BACK TO BELLE REVE.

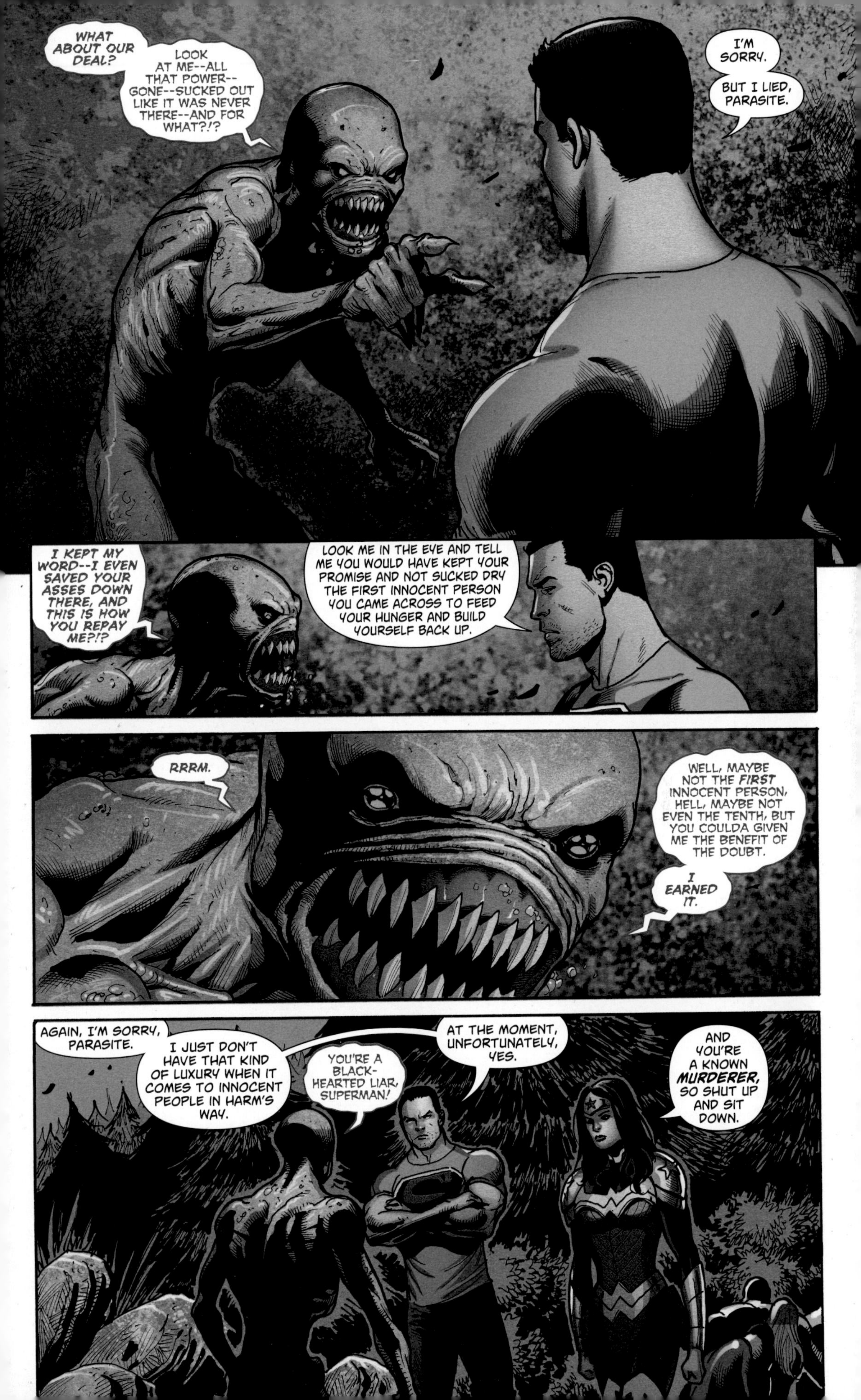
WHAT ABOUT OUR DEAL?
LOOK AT ME--ALL THAT POWER--GONE--SUCKED OUT LIKE IT WAS NEVER THERE--AND FOR WHAT?!?
I'M SORRY.
BUT I LIED, PARASITE.
I KEPT MY WORD--I EVEN SAVED YOUR ASSES DOWN THERE, AND THIS IS HOW YOU REPAY ME?!?
LOOK ME IN THE EYE AND TELL ME YOU WOULD HAVE KEPT YOUR PROMISE AND NOT SUCKED DRY THE FIRST INNOCENT PERSON YOU CAME ACROSS TO FEED YOUR HUNGER AND BUILD YOURSELF BACK UP.
RRRM.
WELL, MAYBE NOT THE FIRST INNOCENT PERSON, HELL, MAYBE NOT EVEN THE TENTH, BUT YOU COULDA GIVEN ME THE BENEFIT OF THE DOUBT.
I EARNED IT.
AGAIN, I'M SORRY, PARASITE.
I JUST DON'T HAVE THAT KIND OF LUXURY WHEN IT COMES TO INNOCENT PEOPLE IN HARM'S WAY.
YOU'RE A BLACK-HEARTED LIAR, SUPERMAN!
AT THE MOMENT, UNFORTUNATELY, YES.
AND YOU'RE A KNOWN MURDERER, SO SHUT UP AND SIT DOWN.

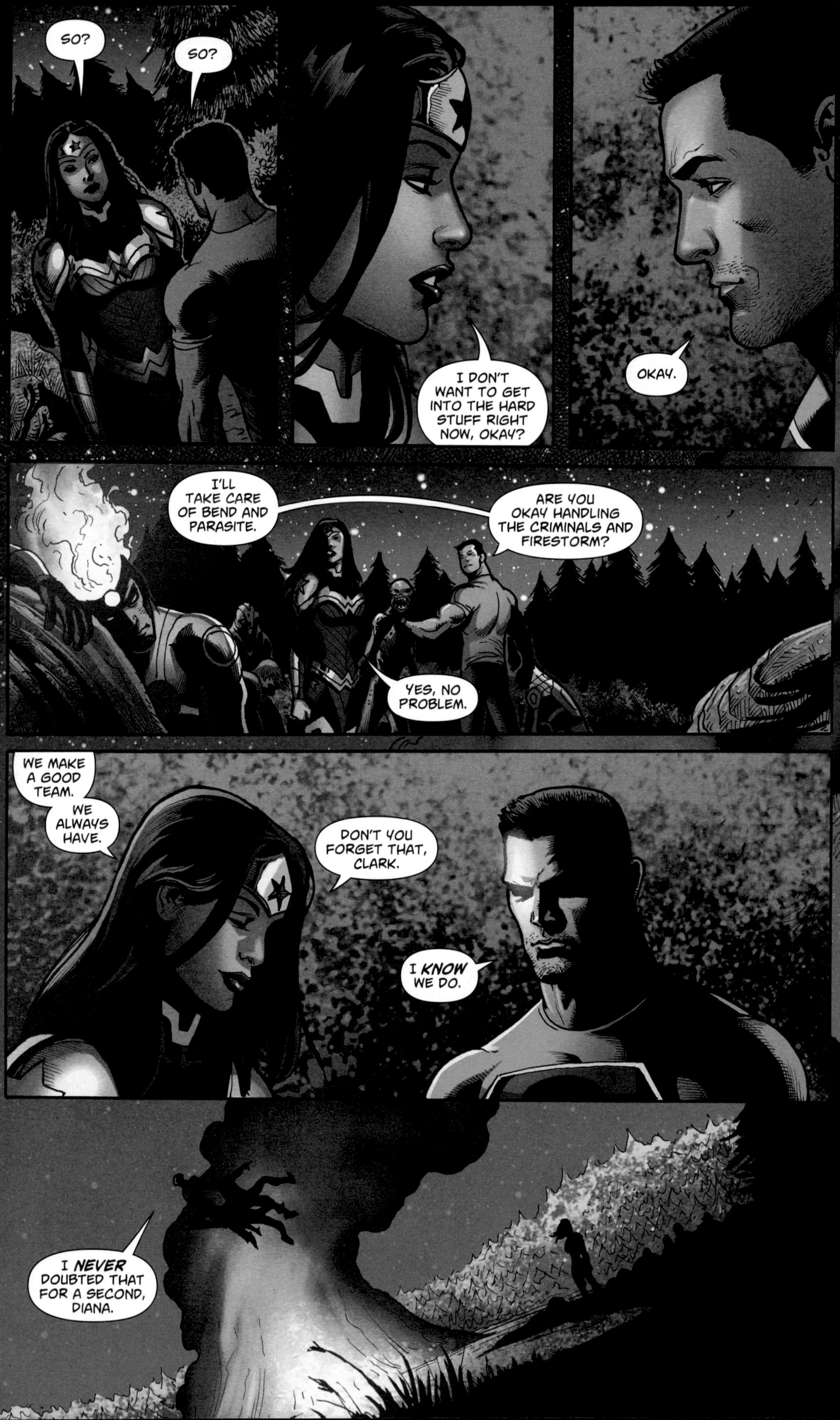
SO?
SO?
I DON'T WANT TO GET INTO THE HARD STUFF RIGHT NOW, OKAY?
OKAY.
I'LL TAKE CARE OF BEND AND PARASITE.
ARE YOU OKAY HANDLING THE CRIMINALS AND FIRESTORM?
YES, NO PROBLEM.
WE MAKE A GOOD TEAM.
WE ALWAYS HAVE.
DON'T YOU FORGET THAT, CLARK.
I *KNOW* WE DO.
I *NEVER* DOUBTED THAT FOR A SECOND, DIANA.

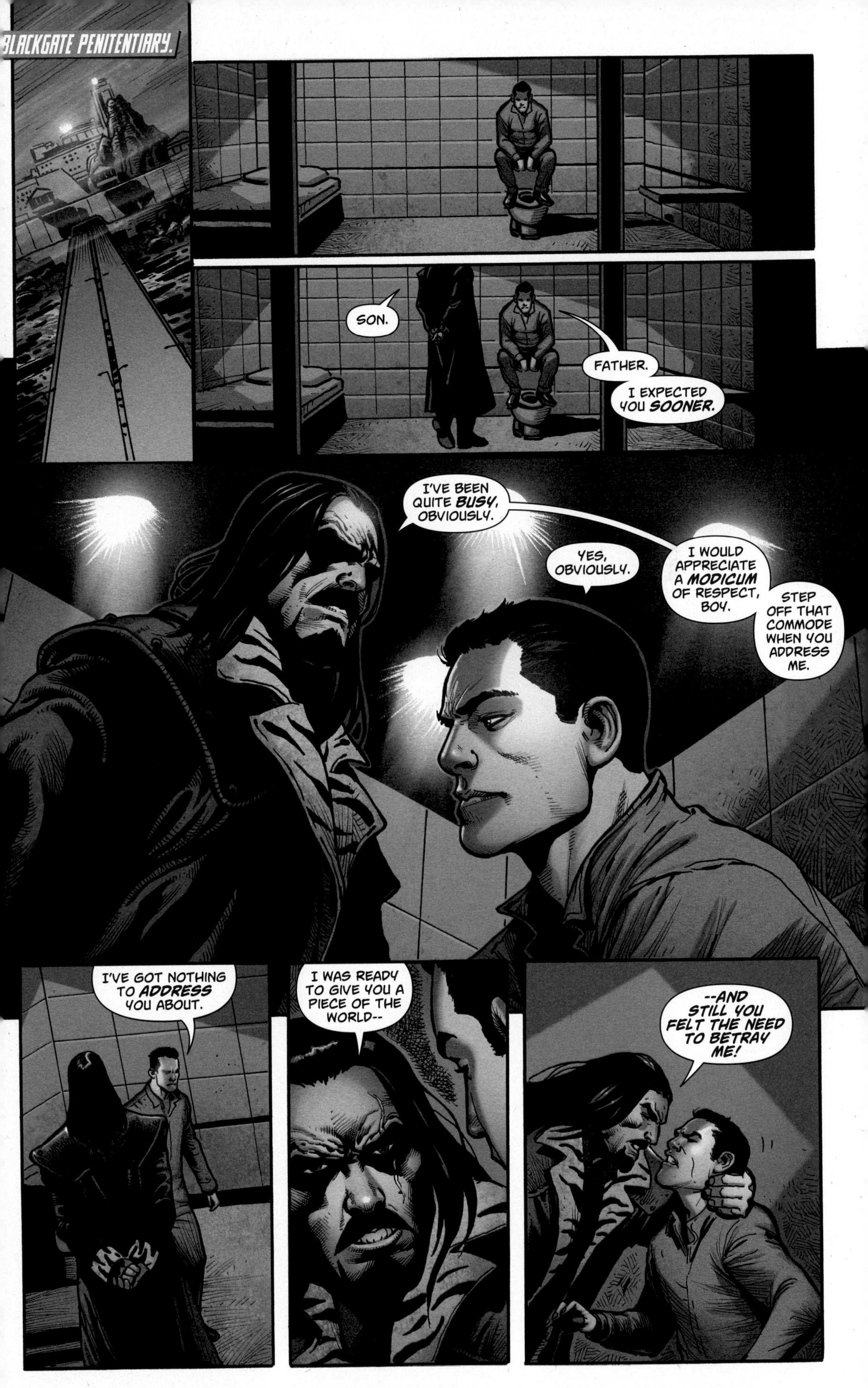
BLACKGATE PENITENTIARY.
SON.
FATHER.
I EXPECTED YOU SOONER.
I'VE BEEN QUITE BUSY, OBVIOUSLY.
YES, OBVIOUSLY.
I WOULD APPRECIATE A MODICUM OF RESPECT, BOY.
STEP OFF THAT COMMODE WHEN YOU ADDRESS ME.
I'VE GOT NOTHING TO ADDRESS YOU ABOUT.
I WAS READY TO GIVE YOU A PIECE OF THE WORLD--
--AND STILL YOU FELT THE NEED TO BETRAY ME!

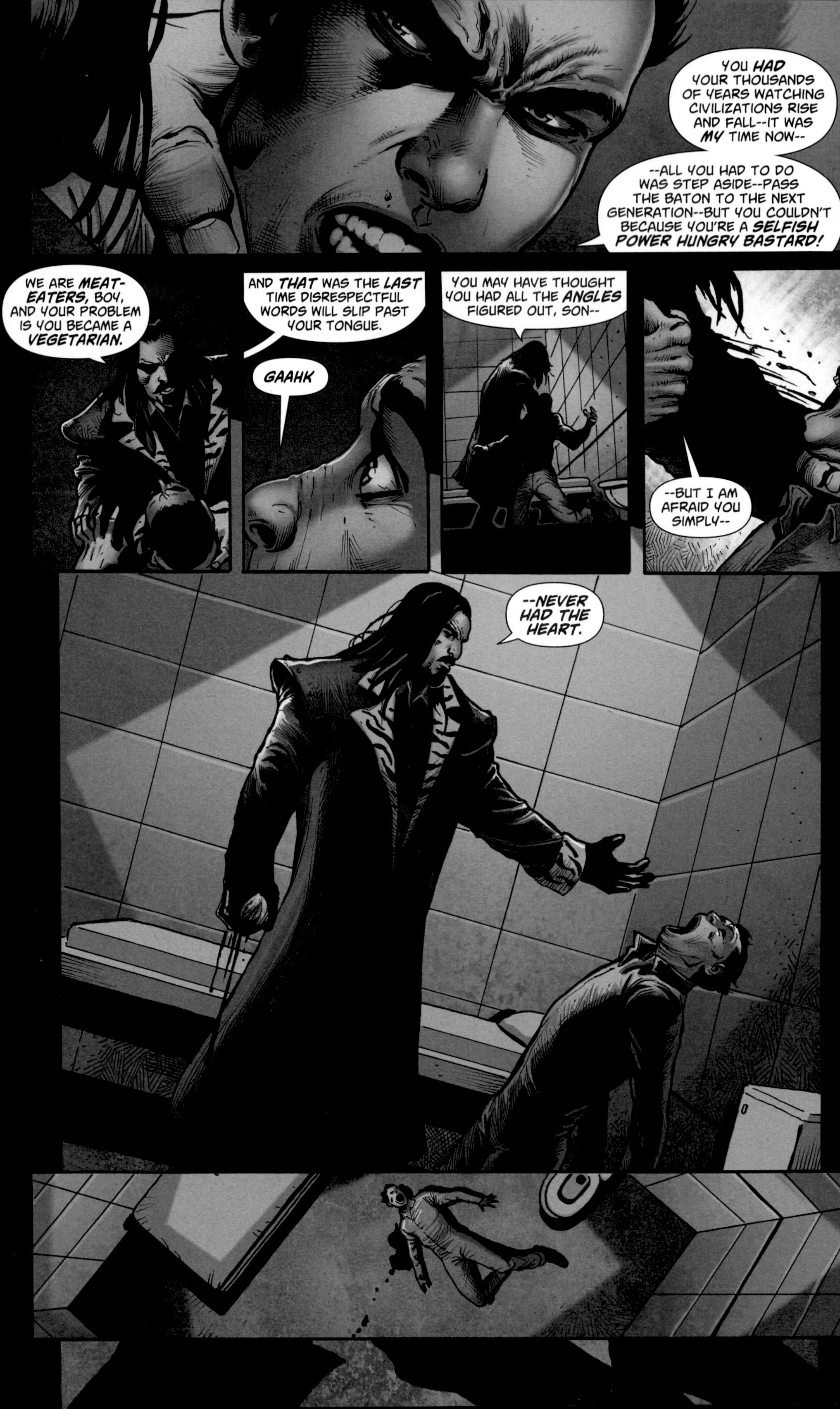
YOU HAD YOUR THOUSANDS OF YEARS WATCHING CIVILIZATIONS RISE AND FALL--IT WAS MY TIME NOW--
--ALL YOU HAD TO DO WAS STEP ASIDE--PASS THE BATON TO THE NEXT GENERATION--BUT YOU COULDN'T BECAUSE YOU'RE A SELFISH POWER HUNGRY BASTARD!
WE ARE MEAT-EATERS, BOY, AND YOUR PROBLEM IS YOU BECAME A VEGETARIAN.
AND THAT WAS THE LAST TIME DISRESPECTFUL WORDS WILL SLIP PAST YOUR TONGUE.
GAAHK
YOU MAY HAVE THOUGHT YOU HAD ALL THE ANGLES FIGURED OUT, SON--
--BUT I AM AFRAID YOU SIMPLY--
--NEVER HAD THE HEART.

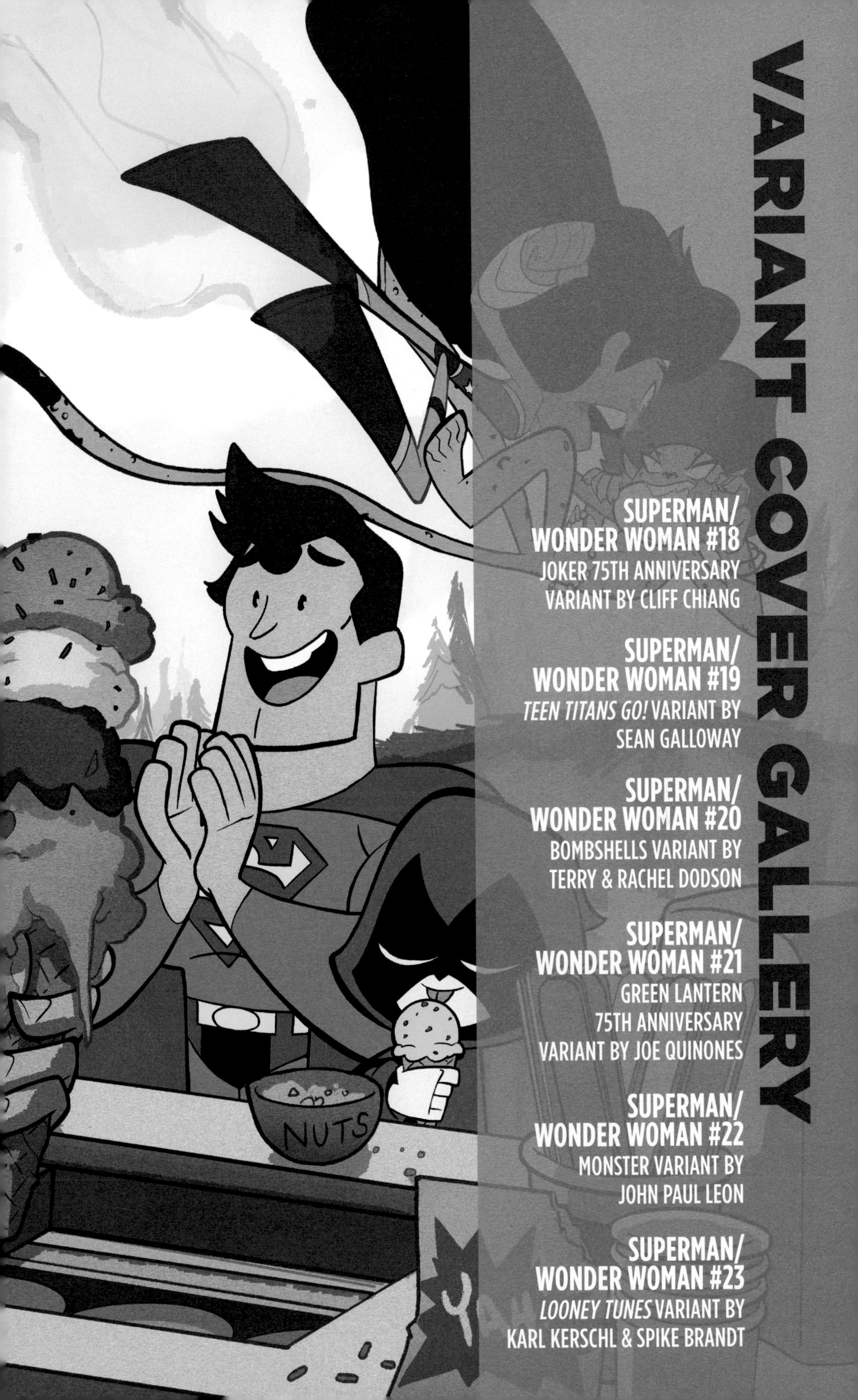
NUTS

VARIANT COVER GALLERY

SUPERMAN/ WONDER WOMAN #18
JOKER 75TH ANNIVERSARY VARIANT BY CLIFF CHIANG

SUPERMAN/ WONDER WOMAN #19
TEEN TITANS GO! VARIANT BY SEAN GALLOWAY

SUPERMAN/ WONDER WOMAN #20
BOMBSHELLS VARIANT BY TERRY & RACHEL DODSON

SUPERMAN/ WONDER WOMAN #21
GREEN LANTERN 75TH ANNIVERSARY VARIANT BY JOE QUINONES

SUPERMAN/ WONDER WOMAN #22
MONSTER VARIANT BY JOHN PAUL LEON

SUPERMAN/ WONDER WOMAN #23
LOONEY TUNES VARIANT BY KARL KERSCHL & SPIKE BRANDT

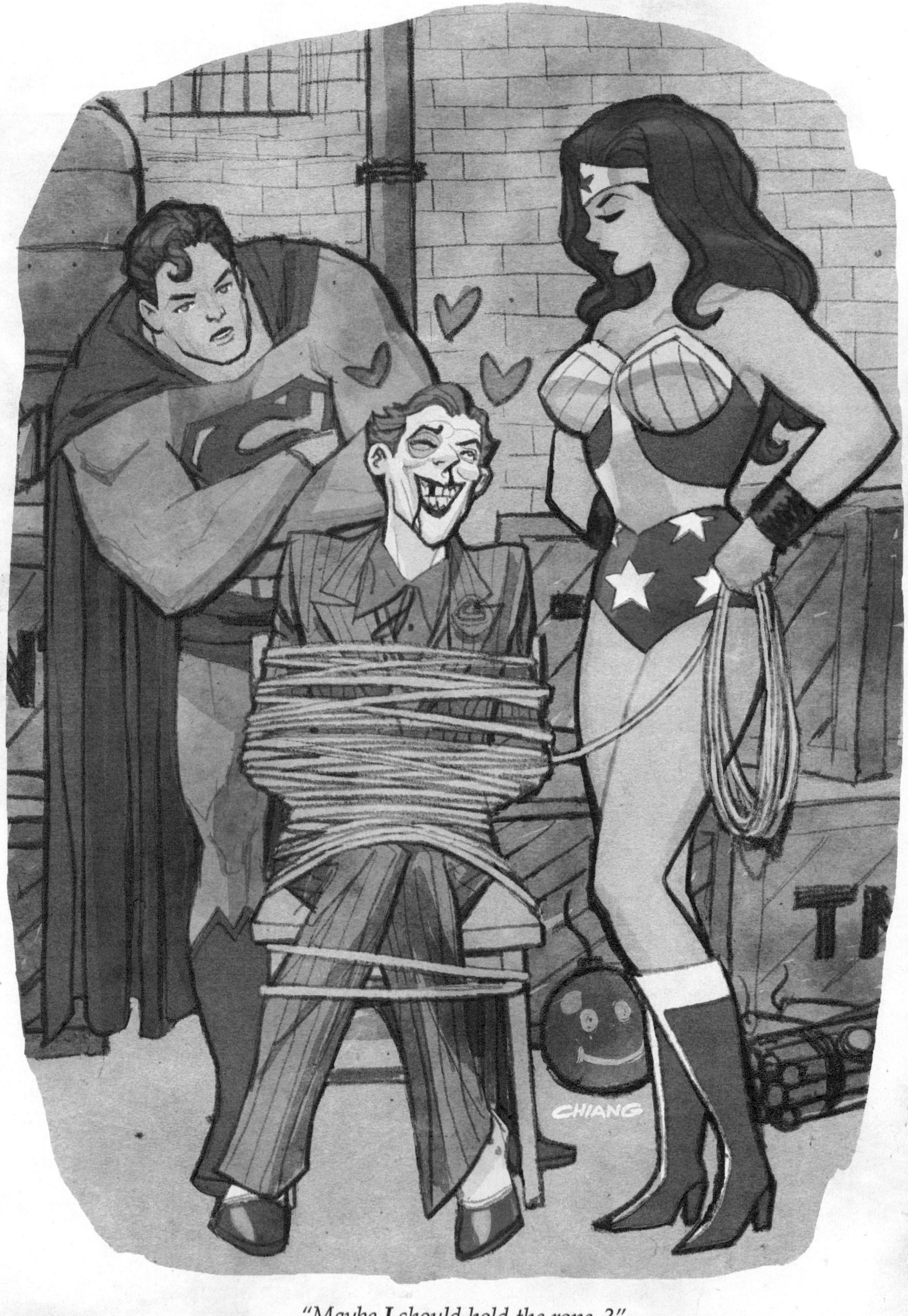

CHIANG

*"Maybe **I** should hold the rope..?"*

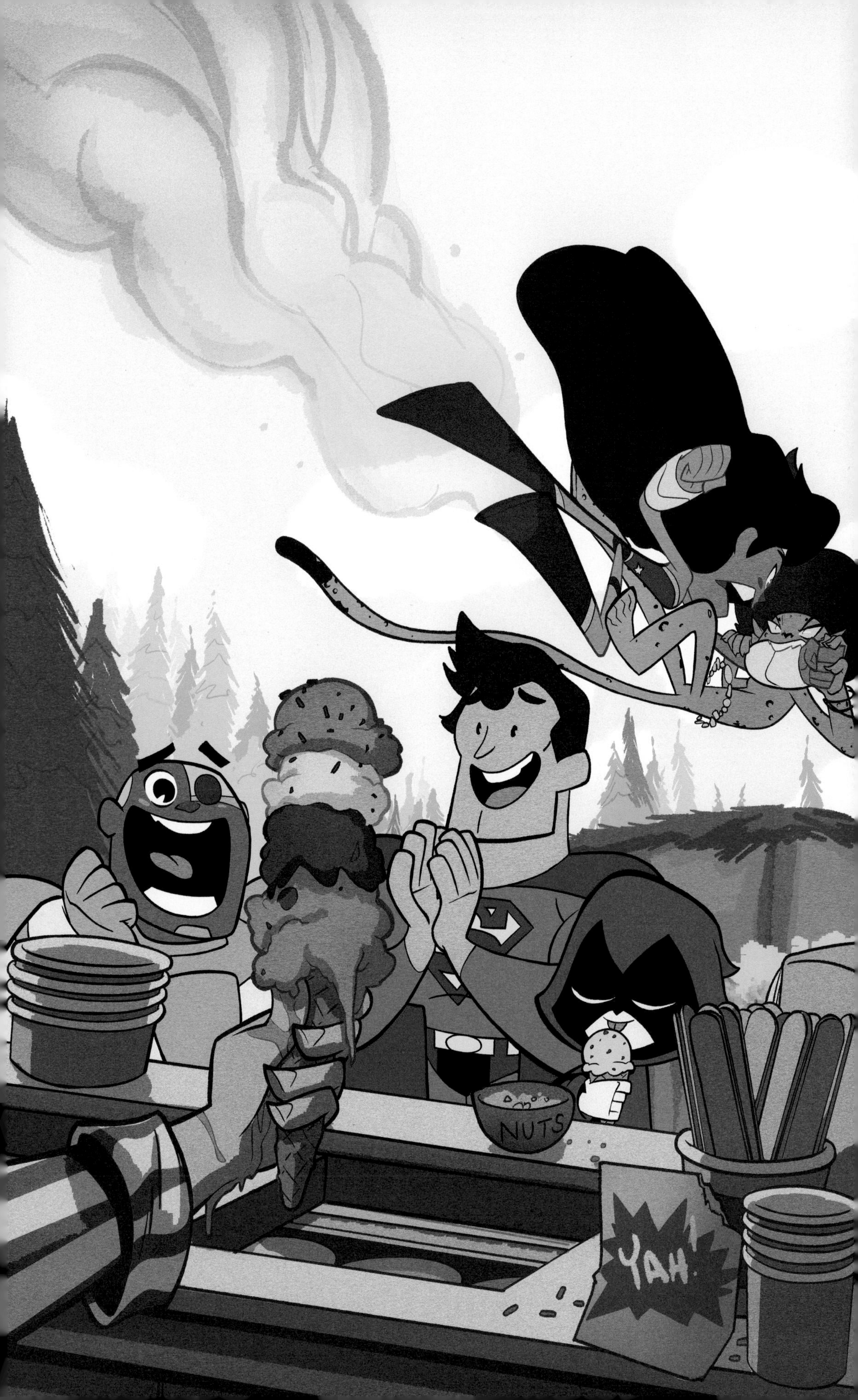
NUTS
YAH!

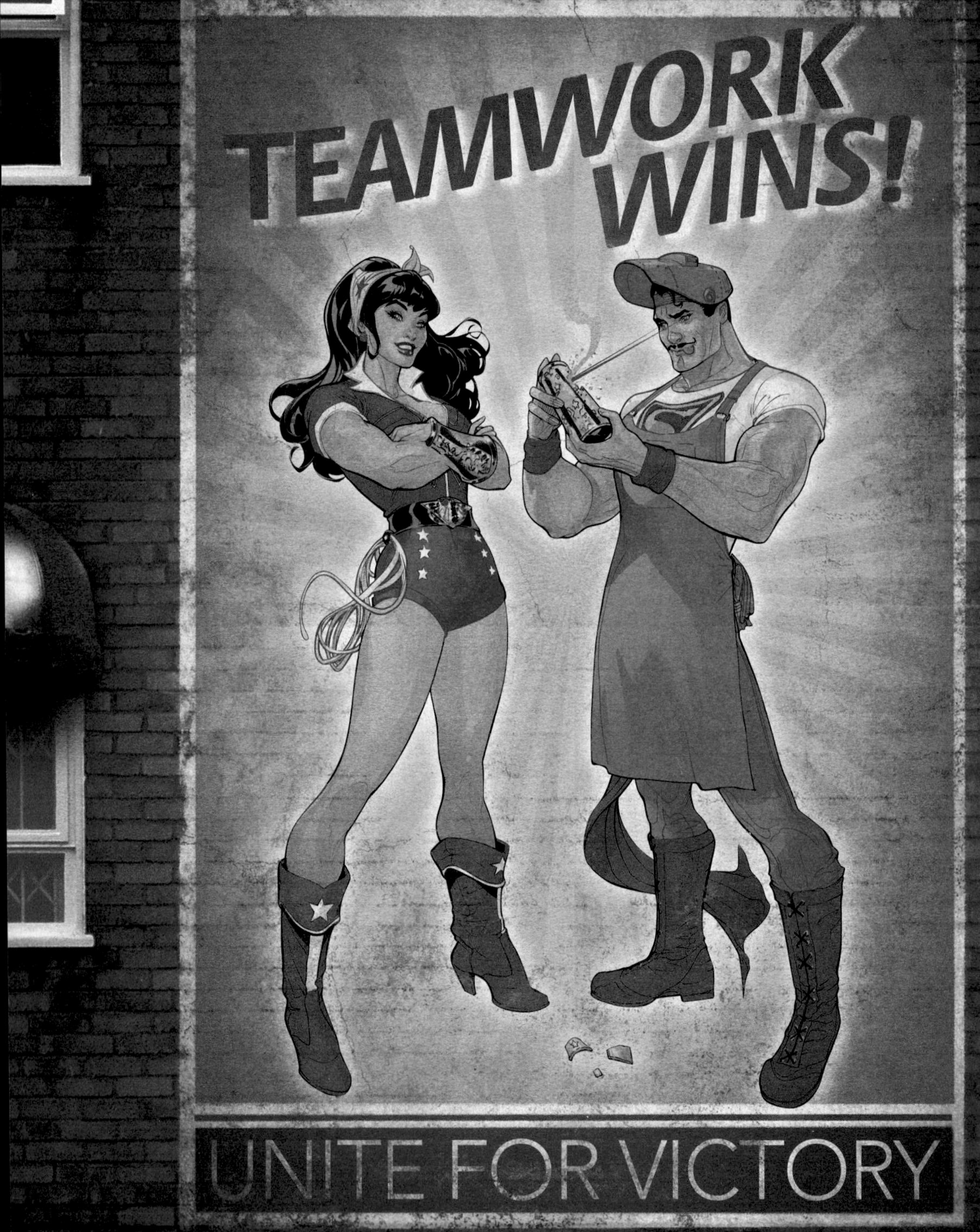
TEAMWORK WINS!
UNITE FOR VICTORY

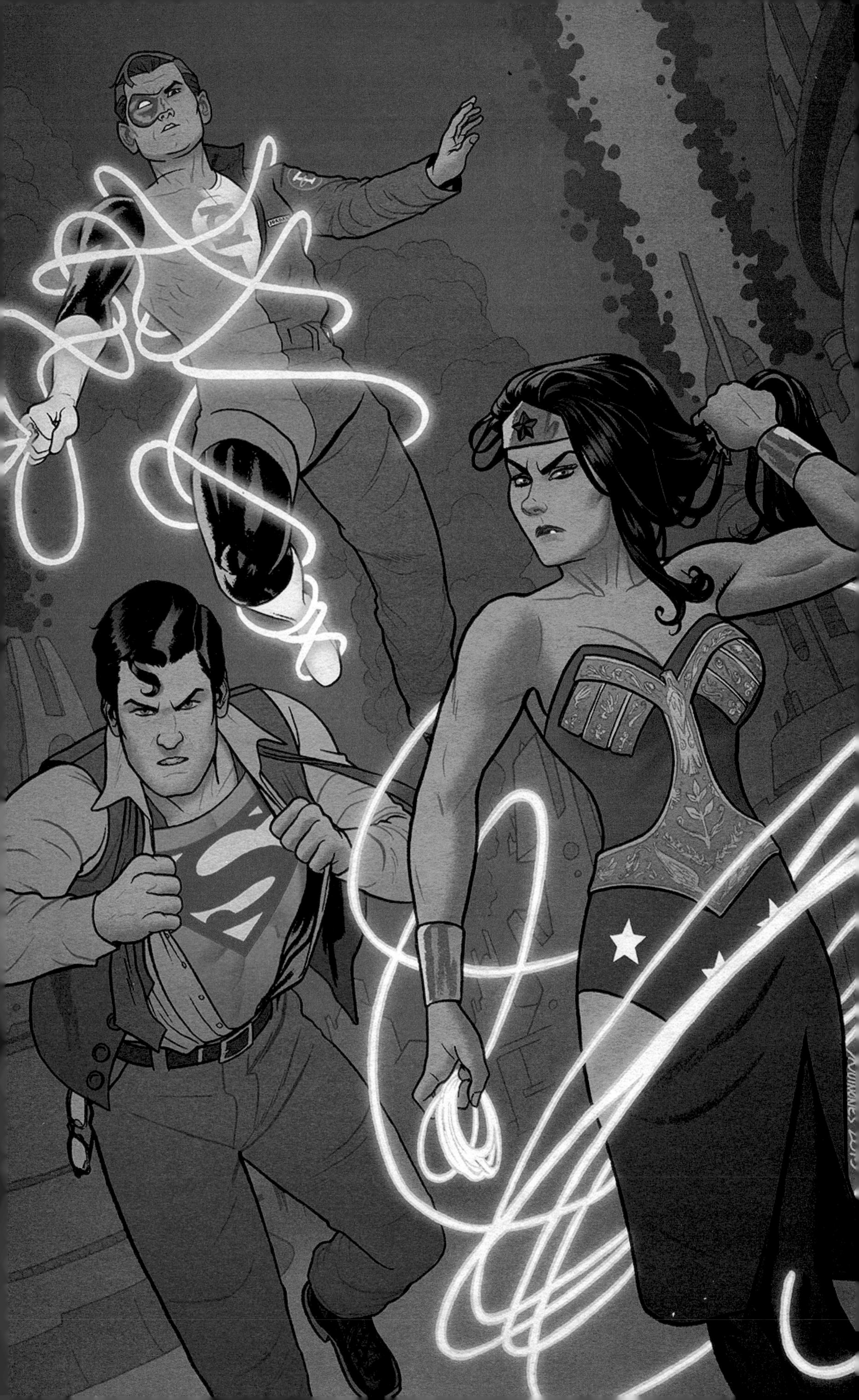

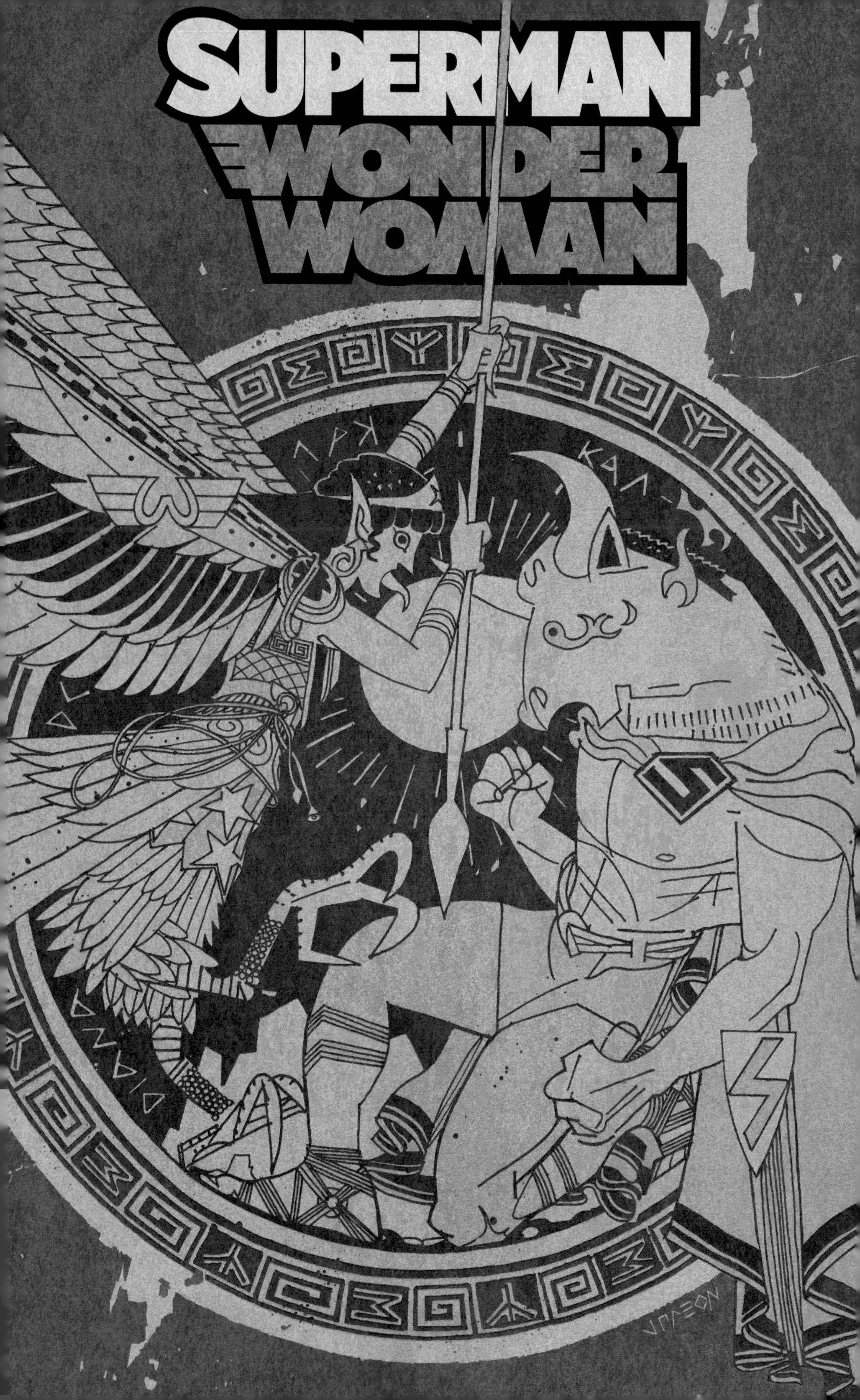
SUPERMAN
WONDER
WOMAN

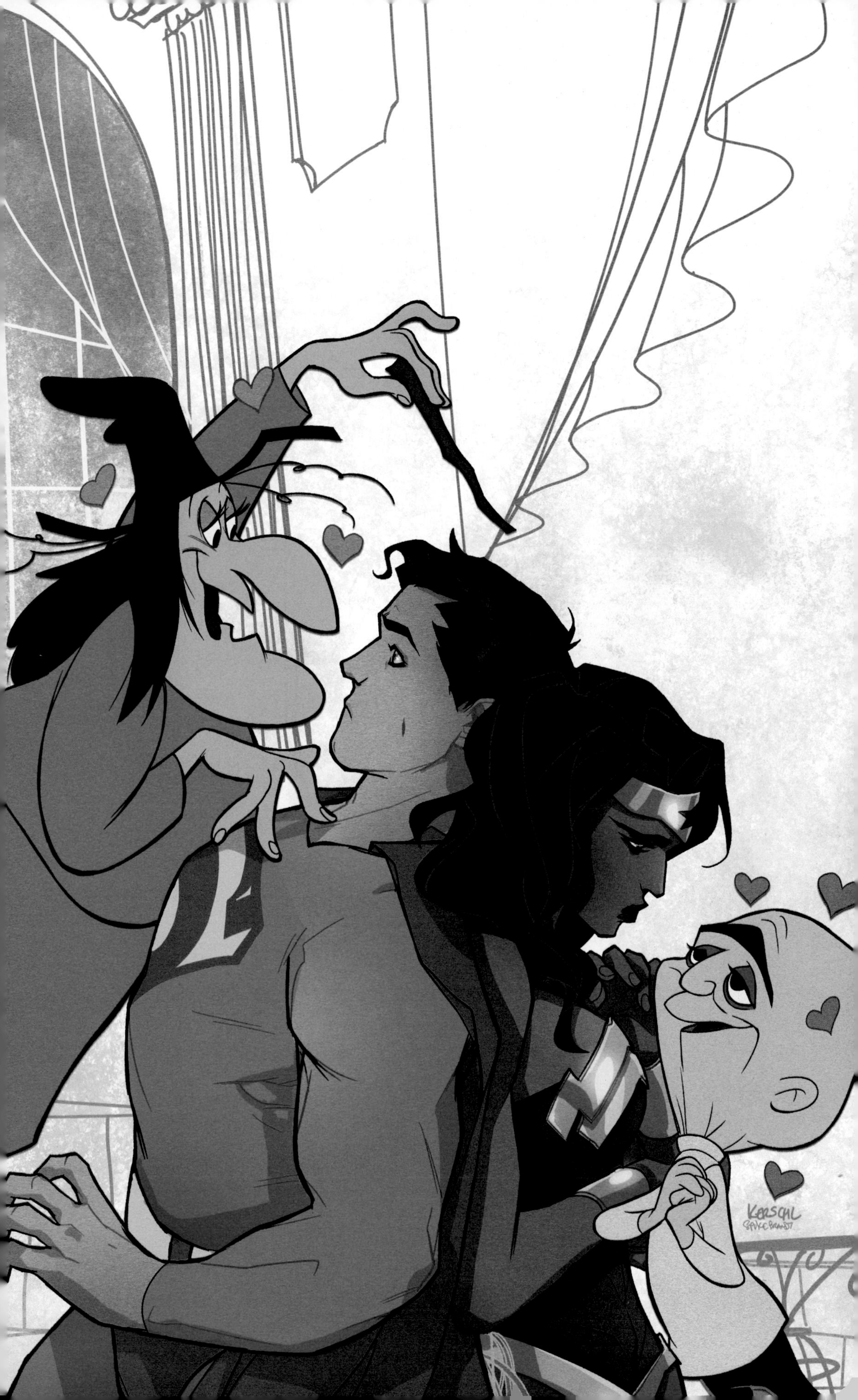
KERSCHL

TRUTH PREVIEW

PETER J. TOMASI writer **PAULO SIQUEIRA** artist **HI-FI** colorist **ROB LEIGH** letterer

In the spring of 2015, this preview to the DARK TRUTH story arc was released as an online teaser. Ultimately, the scenes in the preview were retold in SUPERMAN/WONDER WOMAN #22—with some scenes excised, and other parts of the story told with a different tone. Here you will find the confrontation between Superman and the Flash that ultimately took place "off camera" in the printed comic, and a different spin on the scene between Superman and Wonder Woman.

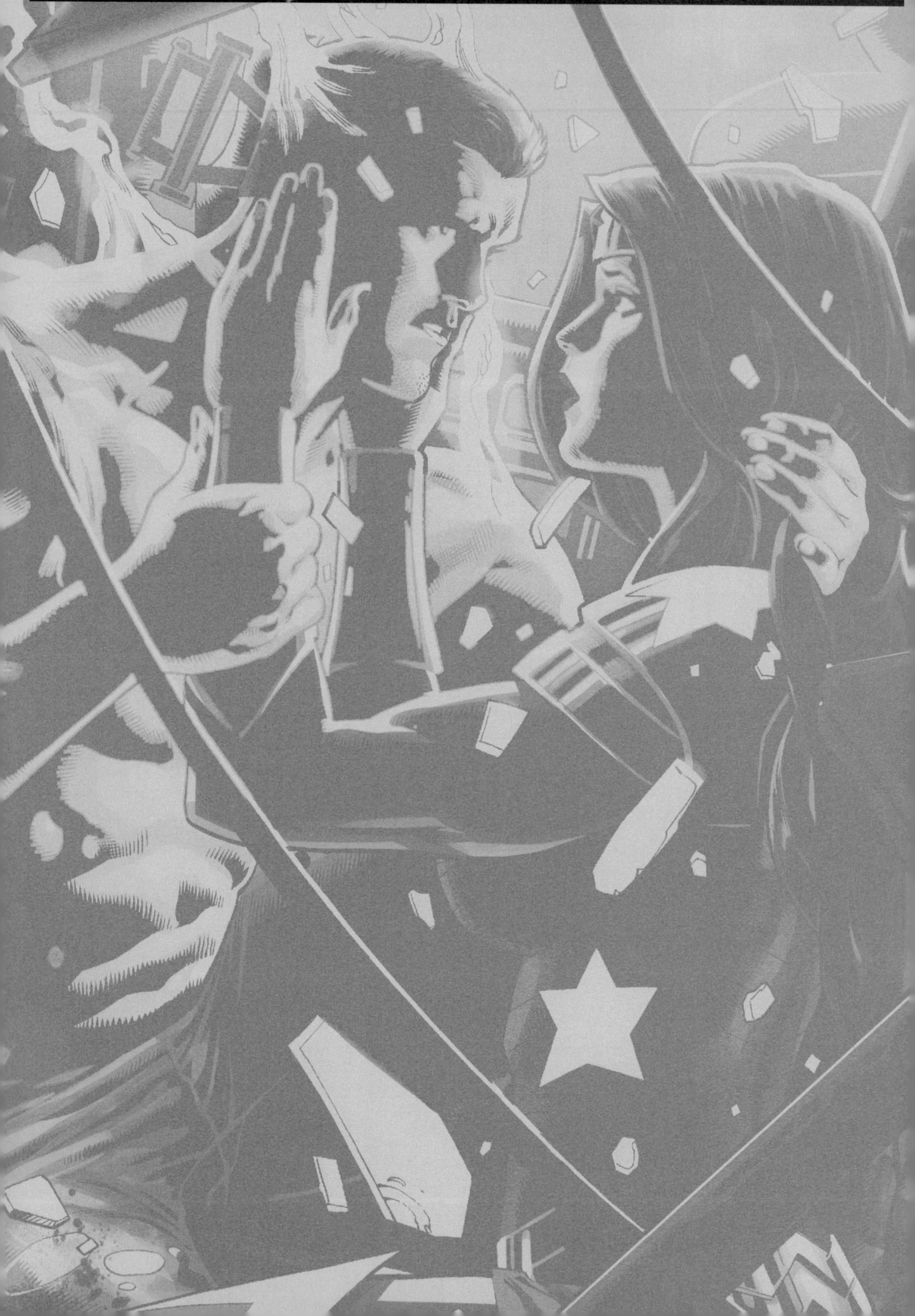

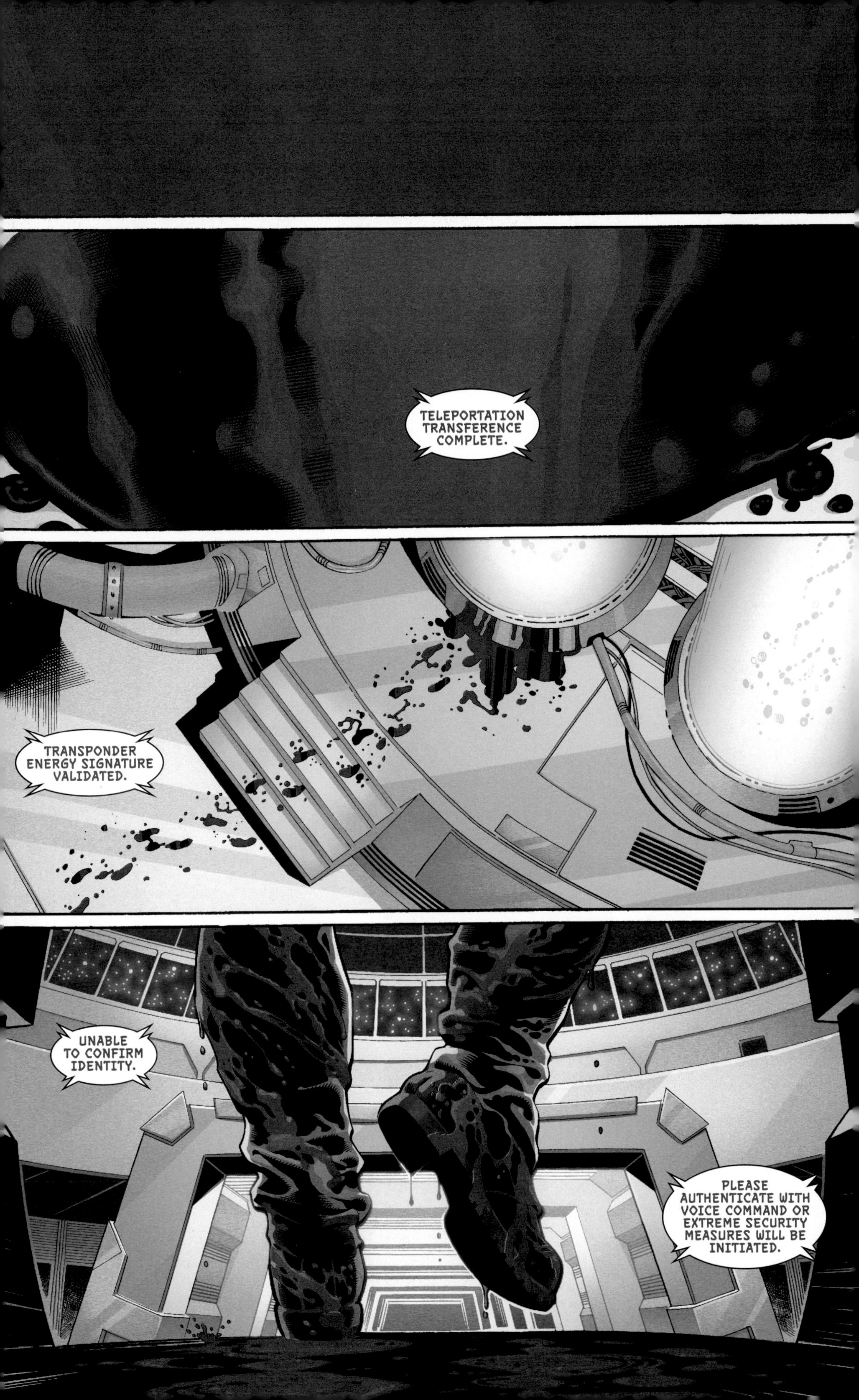
TELEPORTATION TRANSFERENCE COMPLETE.
TRANSPONDER ENERGY SIGNATURE VALIDATED.
UNABLE TO CONFIRM IDENTITY.
PLEASE AUTHENTICATE WITH VOICE COMMAND OR EXTREME SECURITY MEASURES WILL BE INITIATED.

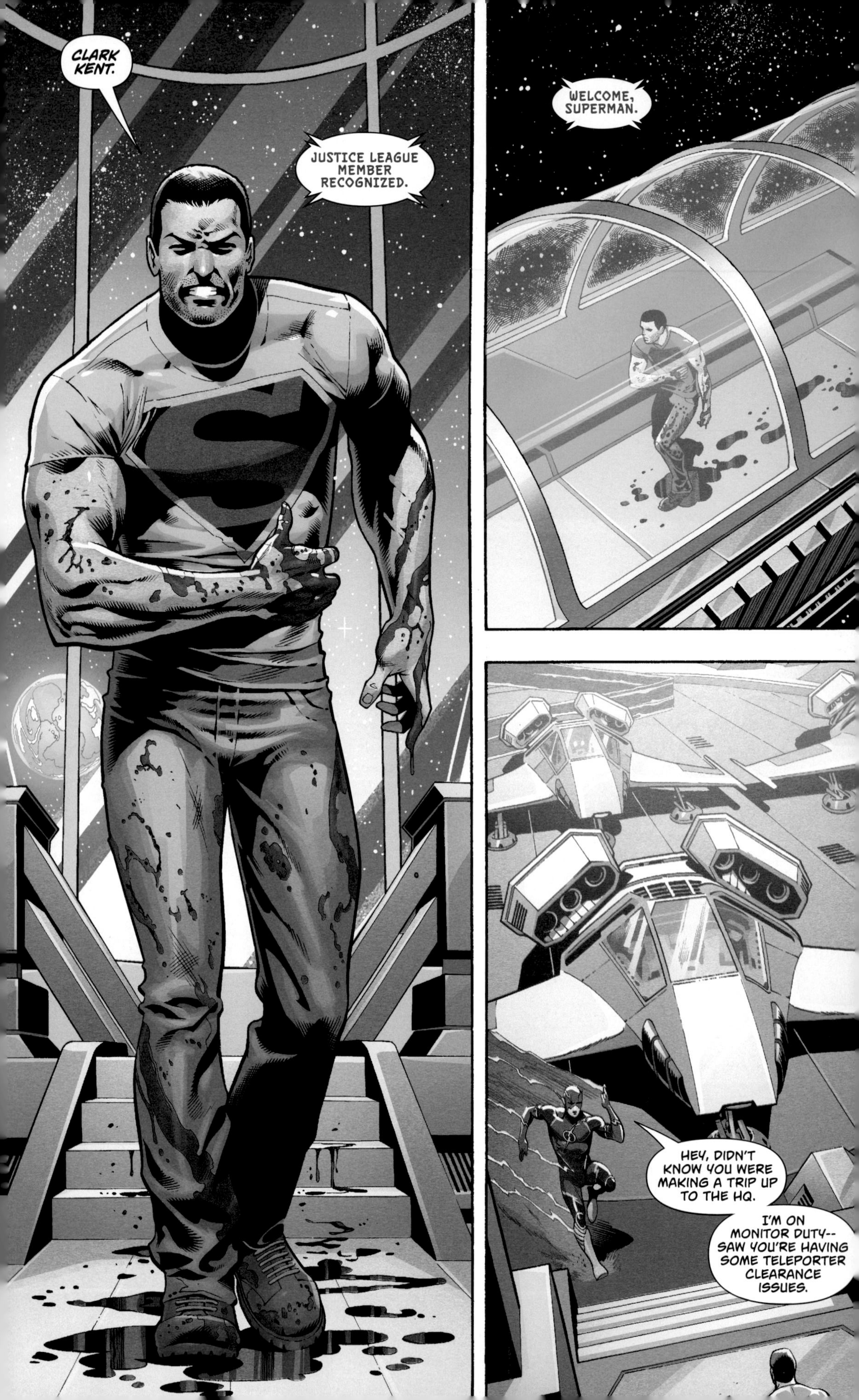
CLARK KENT.
JUSTICE LEAGUE MEMBER RECOGNIZED.
WELCOME, SUPERMAN.
HEY, DIDN'T KNOW YOU WERE MAKING A TRIP UP TO THE HQ.
I'M ON MONITOR DUTY-- SAW YOU'RE HAVING SOME TELEPORTER CLEARANCE ISSUES.

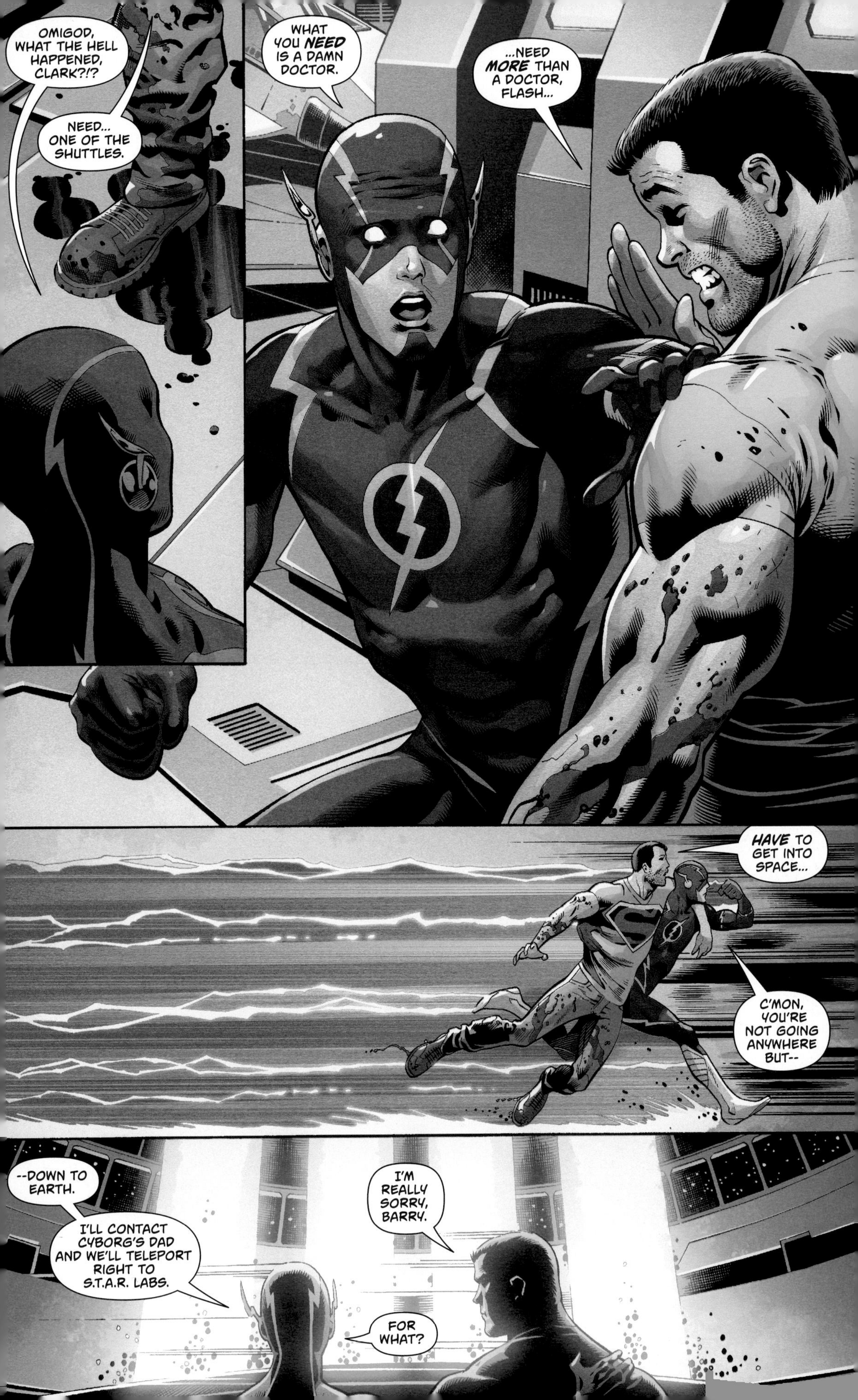
OMIGOD, WHAT THE HELL HAPPENED, CLARK?!?
NEED... ONE OF THE SHUTTLES.
WHAT YOU NEED IS A DAMN DOCTOR.
...NEED MORE THAN A DOCTOR, FLASH...
HAVE TO GET INTO SPACE...
C'MON, YOU'RE NOT GOING ANYWHERE BUT--
--DOWN TO EARTH.
I'LL CONTACT CYBORG'S DAD AND WE'LL TELEPORT RIGHT TO S.T.A.R. LABS.
I'M REALLY SORRY, BARRY.
FOR WHAT?

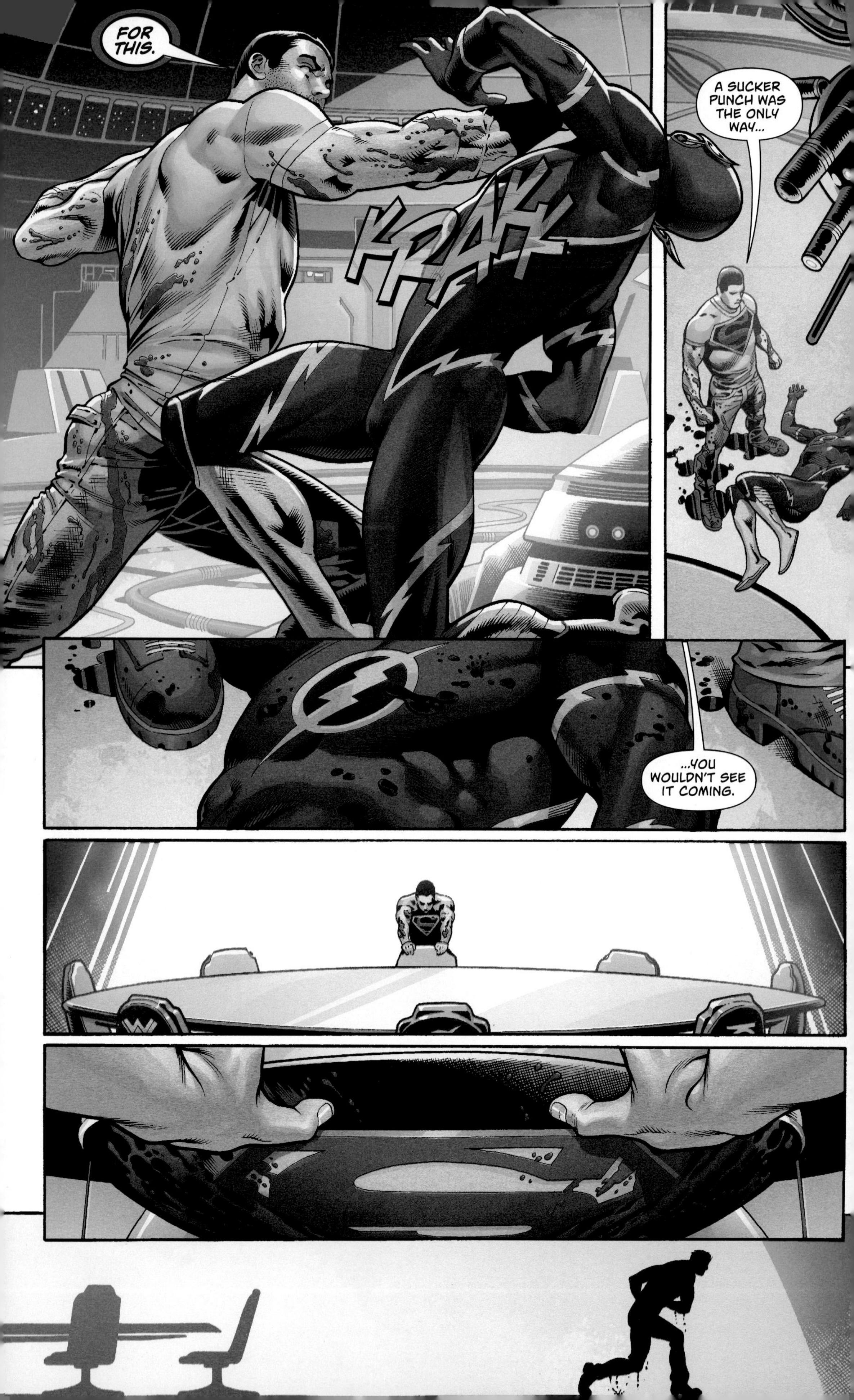
FOR THIS.
KRAK
A SUCKER PUNCH WAS THE ONLY WAY...
...YOU WOULDN'T SEE IT COMING.

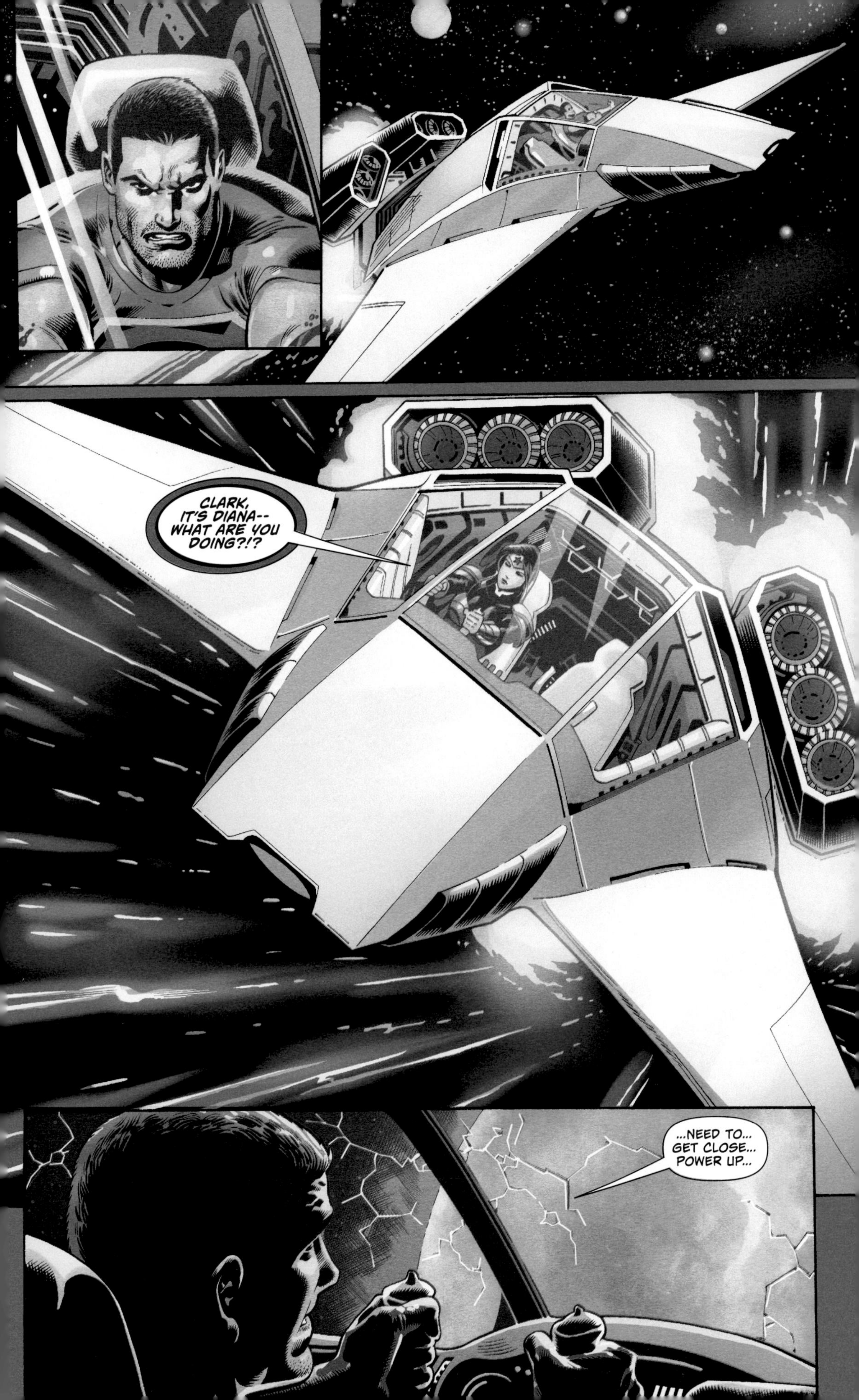
CLARK, IT'S DIANA-- WHAT ARE YOU DOING?!?
...NEED TO... GET CLOSE... POWER UP...

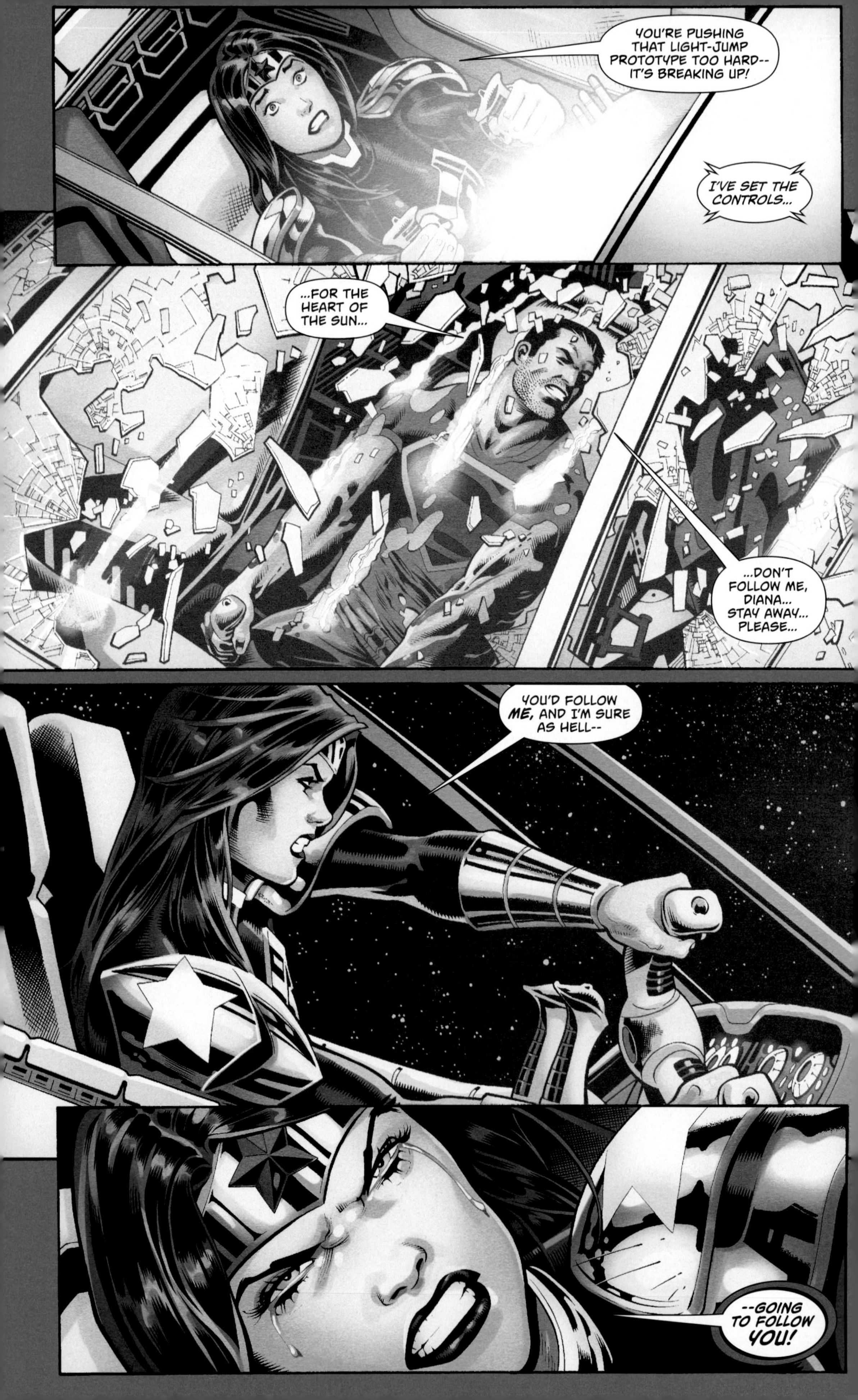
YOU'RE PUSHING THAT LIGHT-JUMP PROTOTYPE TOO HARD-- IT'S BREAKING UP!
I'VE SET THE CONTROLS...
...FOR THE HEART OF THE SUN...
...DON'T FOLLOW ME, DIANA... STAY AWAY... PLEASE...
YOU'D FOLLOW *ME,* AND I'M SURE AS HELL--
--GOING TO FOLLOW *YOU!*

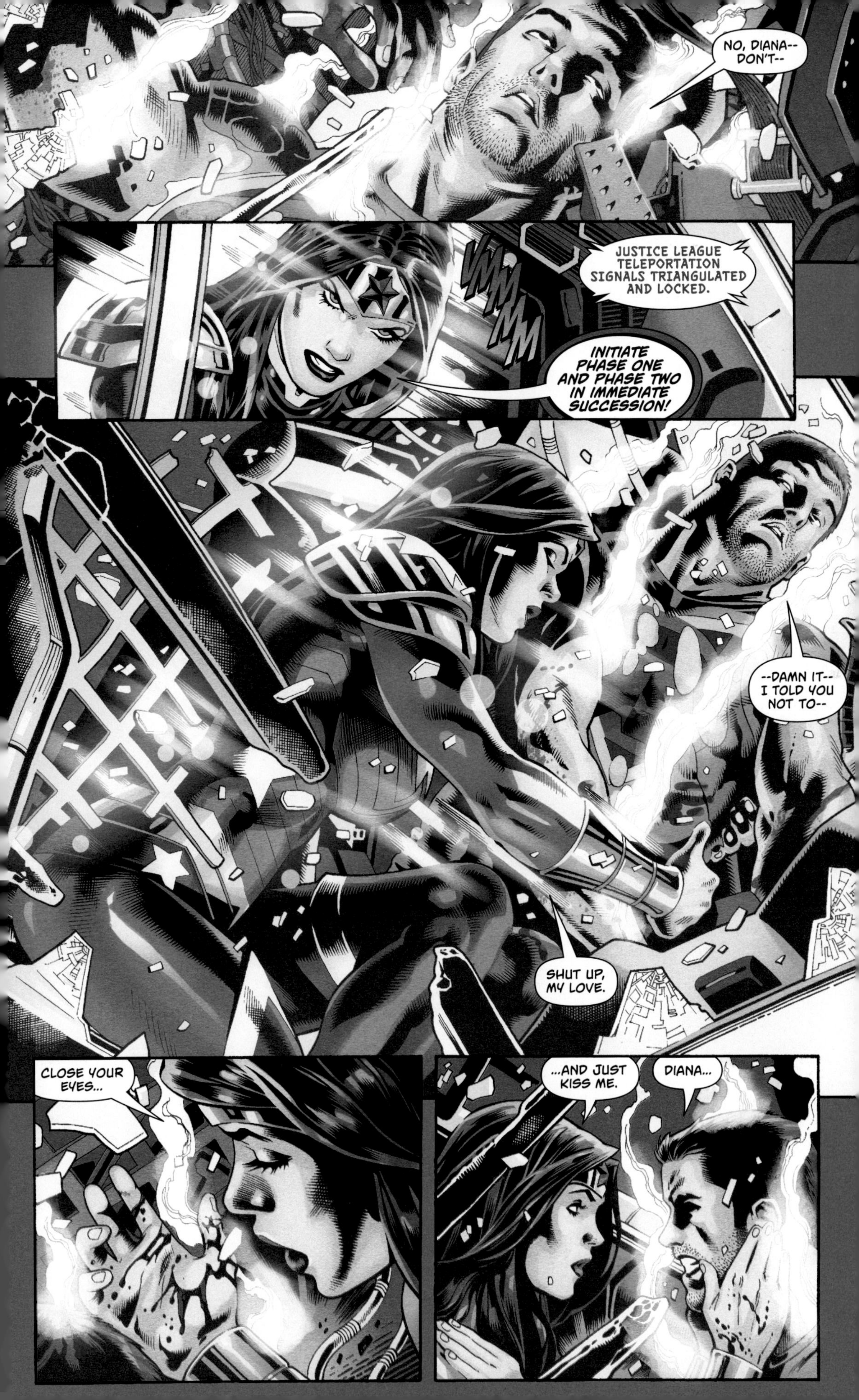
NO, DIANA-- DON'T--
JUSTICE LEAGUE TELEPORTATION SIGNALS TRIANGULATED AND LOCKED.
VMMMM
INITIATE PHASE ONE AND PHASE TWO IN IMMEDIATE SUCCESSION!
--DAMN IT-- I TOLD YOU NOT TO--
SHUT UP, MY LOVE.
CLOSE YOUR EYES...
...AND JUST KISS ME.
DIANA...

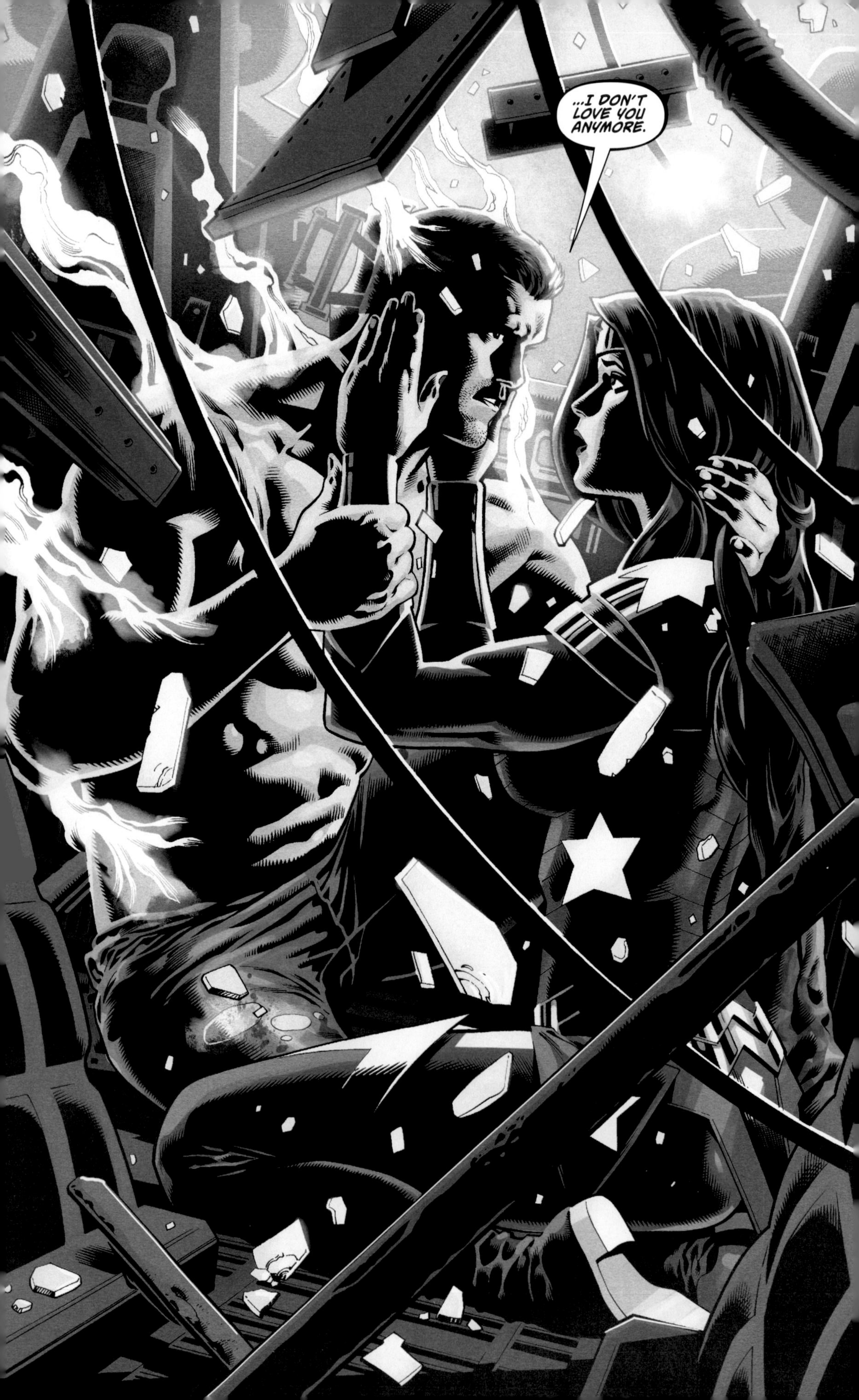
...I DON'T LOVE YOU ANYMORE.

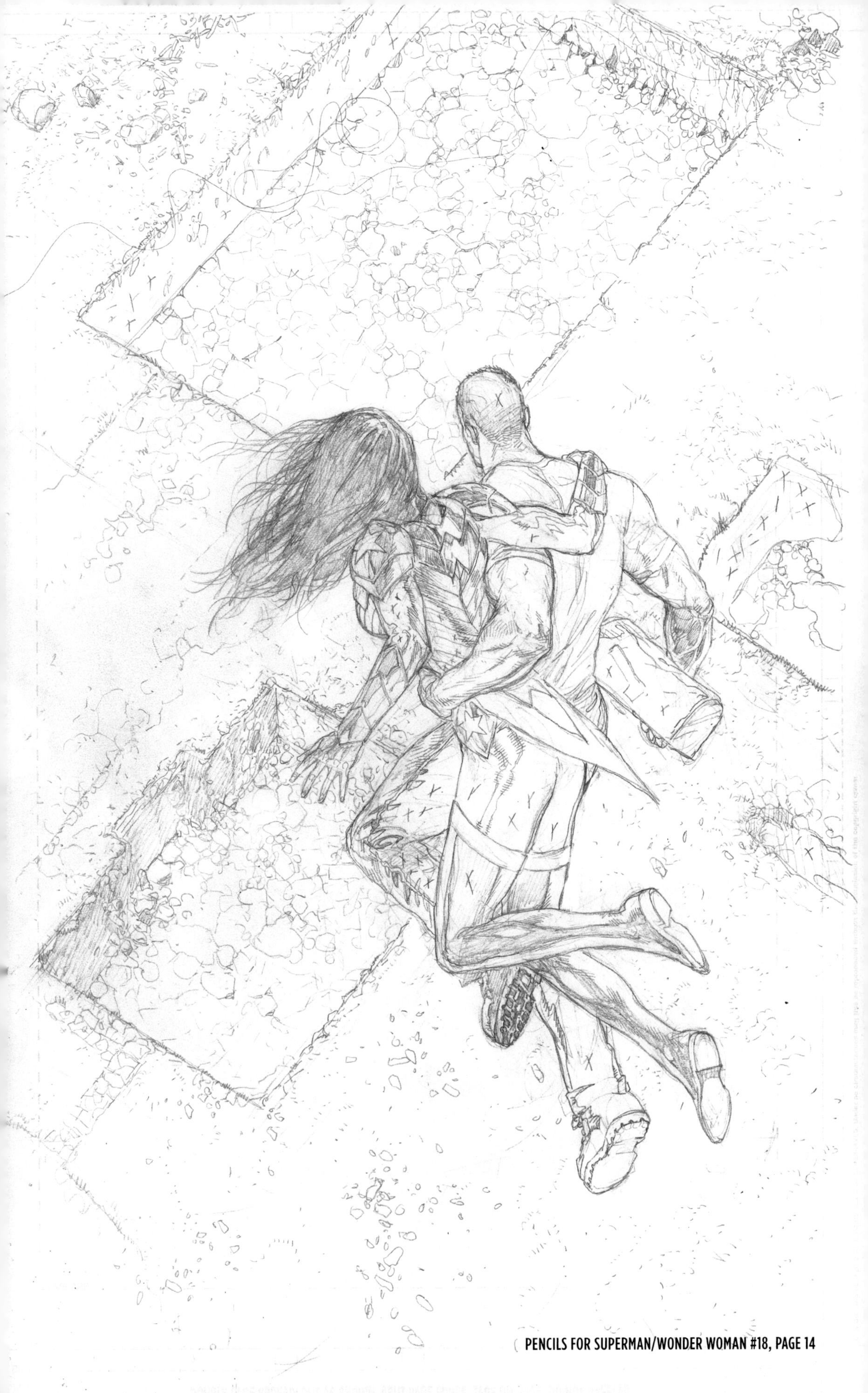

PENCILS FOR SUPERMAN/WONDER WOMAN #18, PAGE 14

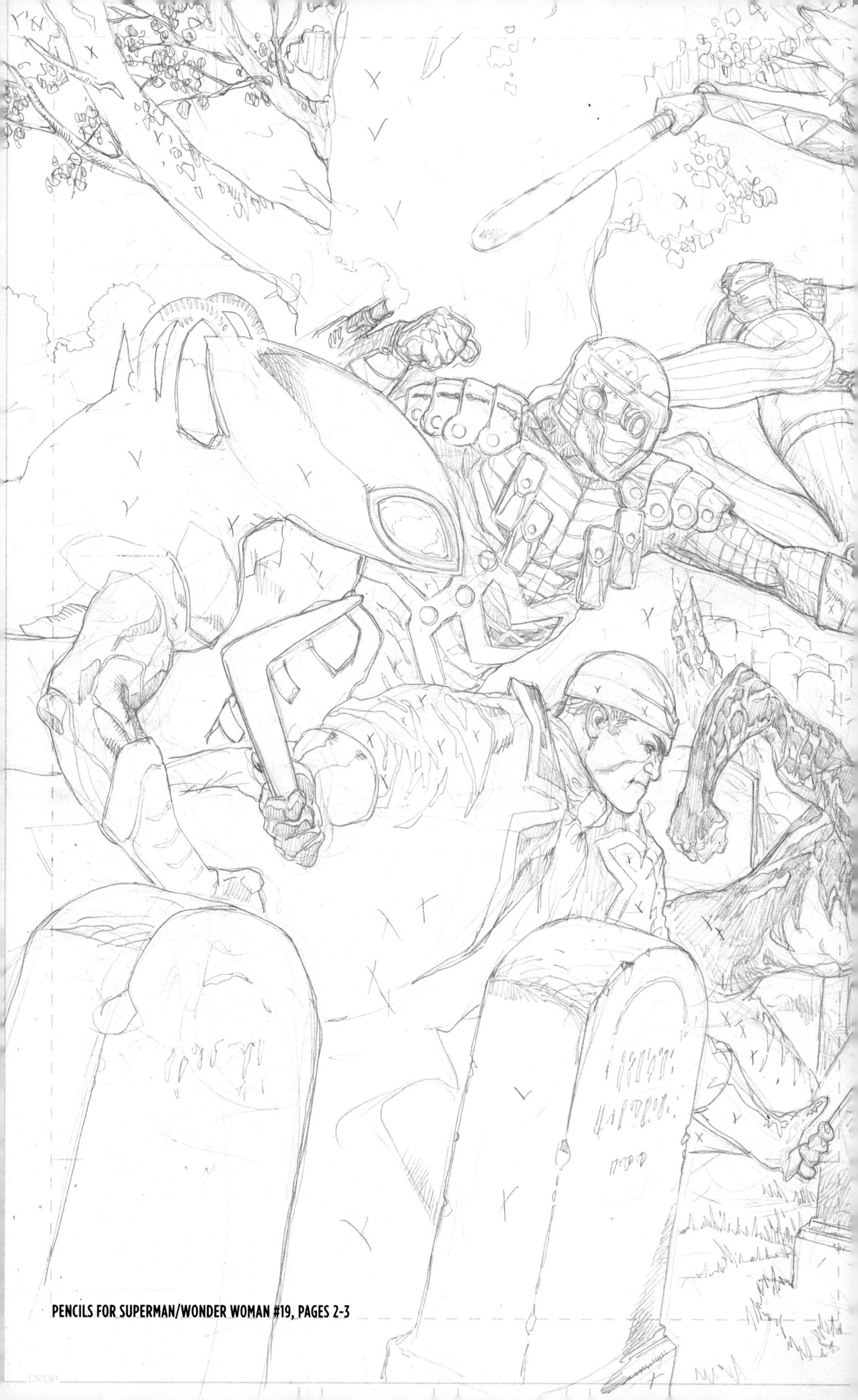

PENCILS FOR SUPERMAN/WONDER WOMAN #19, PAGES 2-3

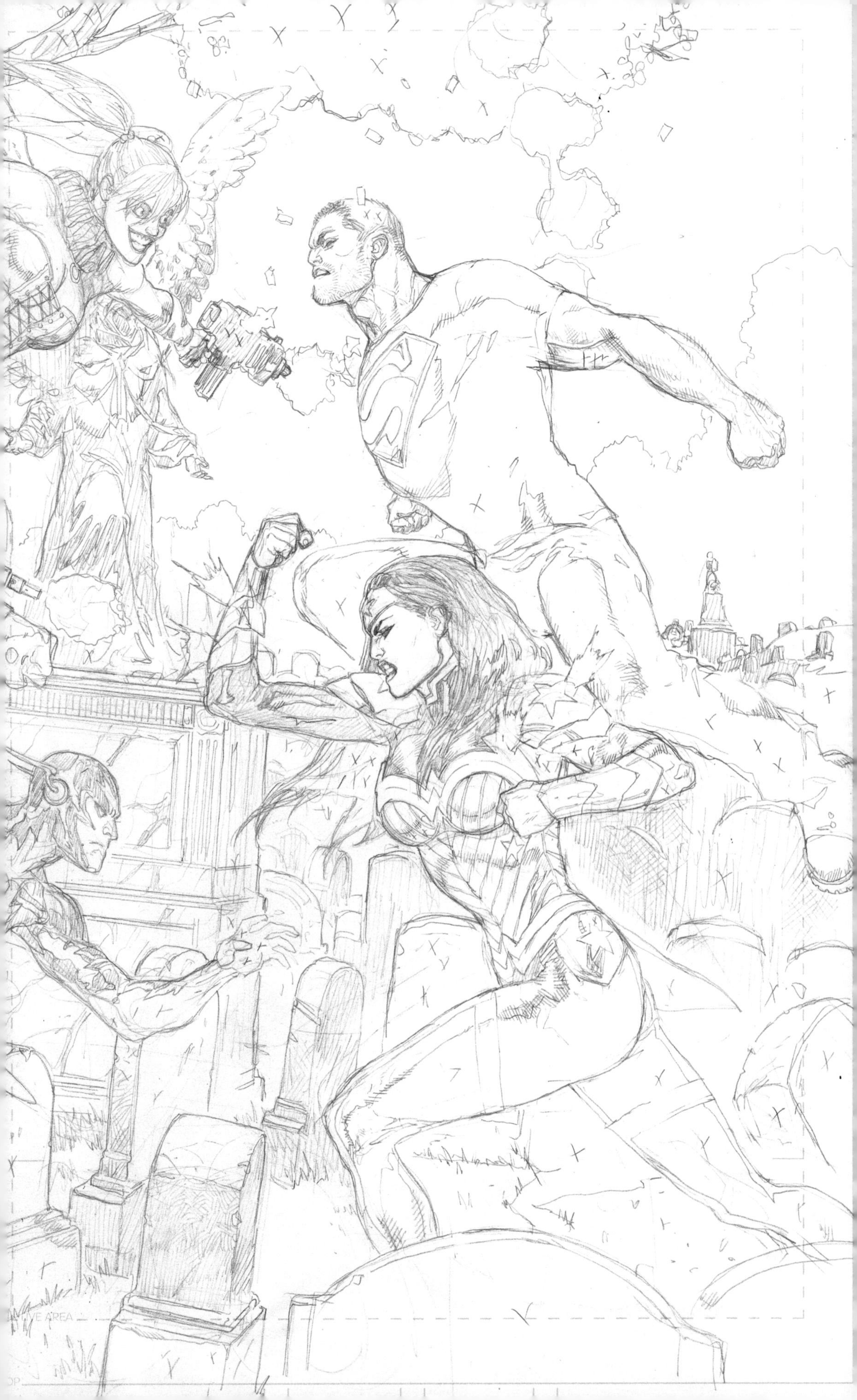

UNUSED LAYOUT FOR SUPERMAN/WONDER WOMAN #19, PAGE 6

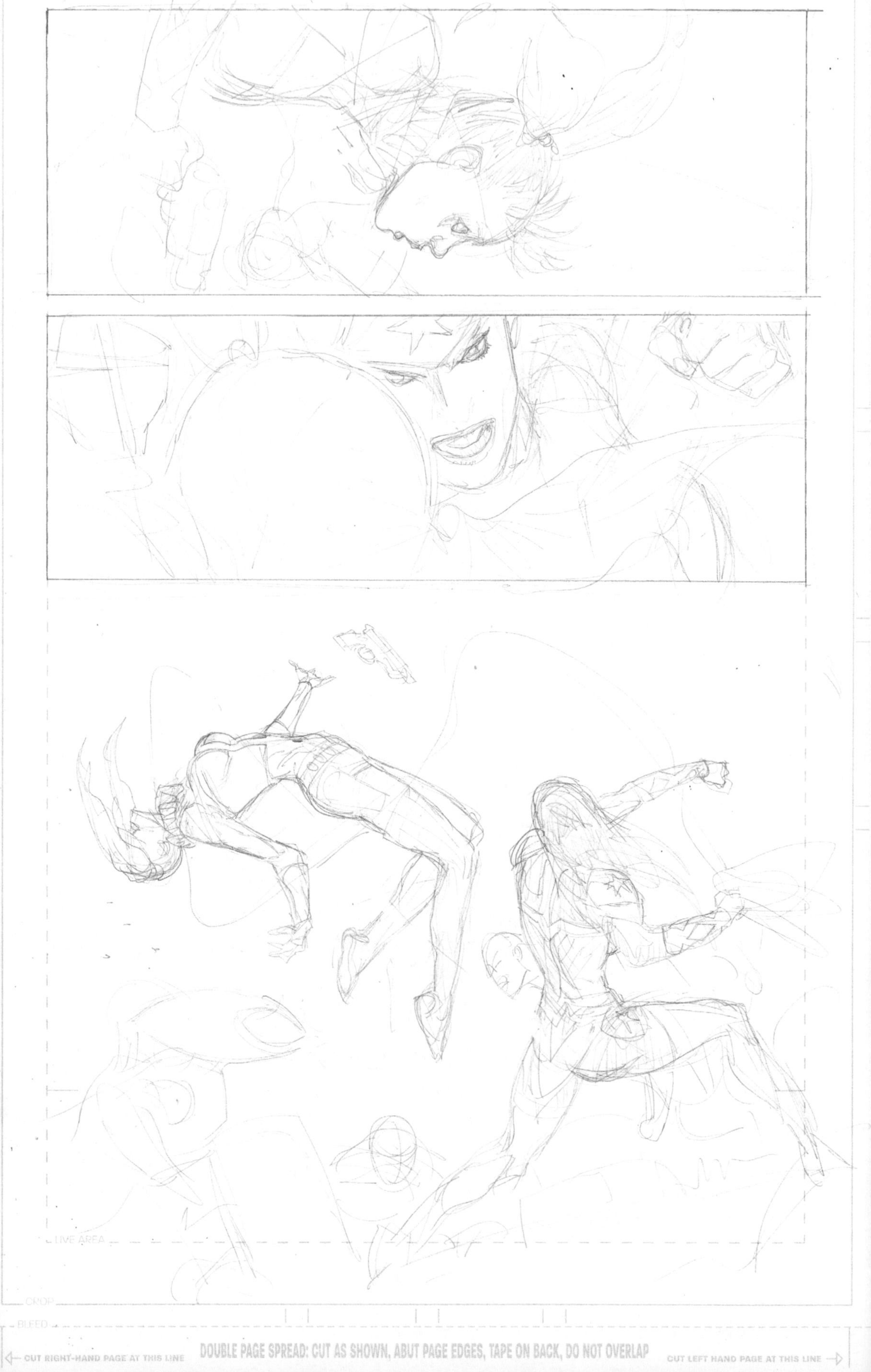
LIVE AREA
CROP
BLEED
CUT RIGHT-HAND PAGE AT THIS LINE
DOUBLE PAGE SPREAD: CUT AS SHOWN, ABUT PAGE EDGES, TAPE ON BACK, DO NOT OVERLAP
CUT LEFT HAND PAGE AT THIS LINE